AMERICA IN THE WORLD

AMERICA IN THE WORLD

UNITED STATES HISTORY
IN GLOBAL CONTEXT

CARL GUARNERI

Saint Mary's College of California

Boston   Burr Ridge, IL   Dubuque, IA   New York
San Francisco   St. Louis   Bangkok   Bogotá   Caracas   Kuala Lumpur
Lisbon   London   Madrid   Mexico City   Milan   Montreal   New Delhi
Santiago   Seoul   Singapore   Sydney   Taipei   Toronto

AMERICA IN THE WORLD: UNITED STATES HISTORY IN GLOBAL CONTEXT

Published by McGraw-Hill, a business unit of The McGraw-Hill Companies, Inc., 1221 Avenue of the Americas, New York, NY, 10020. Copyright © 2007 by The McGraw-Hill Companies, Inc. All rights reserved. No part of this publication may be reproduced or distributed in any form or by any means, or stored in a database or retrieval system, without the prior written consent of The McGraw-Hill Companies, Inc., including, but not limited to, in any network or other electronic storage or transmission, or broadcast for distance learning.

Some ancillaries, including electronic and print components, may not be available to customers outside the United States.

This book is printed on acid-free paper.

2 3 4 5 6 7 8 9 0 DOC/DOC 0 9

ISBN: 978-0-07-254115-1
MHID: 0-07-254115-6

Vice President and Editor-in-Chief: *Emily Barrosse*
Publisher: *Lisa Moore*
Sponsoring Editor: *Jon-David Hague*
Editorial Coordinator: *Sora Lisa Kim*
Marketing Manager: *Jennifer Reed*
Managing Editor: *Jean Dal Porto*
Senior Project Manager: *Rick Hecker*
Art Director: *Jeanne Schreiber*
Art Editor: *Ayelet Arbel*
Senior Designer: *Srdjan Savanovic*
Senior Production Supervisor: *Janean A. Utley*
Composition: *11/13 Palatino, by ICC Macmillan Inc.*
Printer: *45# New Era Matte, R. R. Donnelly*

Library of Congress Cataloging-in-Publication Data

Guarneri, Carl, 1950-
America in the world: United States history in global context / Carl J. Guarneri.
p. cm.
Includes index.
ISBN-13: 978-0-07-254115-1 (pbk. : alk. paper)
ISBN-10: 0-07-254115-6 (pbk. : alk. paper)
1. United States—History. 2. World history. I. Title.

E178.1.G9125 2007
973—dc22

2006047237

The Internet addresses listed in the text were accurate at the time of publication. The inclusion of a Web site does not indicate an endorsement by the authors or McGraw-Hill, and McGraw-Hill does not guarantee the accuracy of the information presented at these sites.

www.mhhe.com

For Julia and Anna

TABLE OF CONTENTS

❰ LIST OF MAPS AND ❱ ILLUSTRATIONS

MAPS

ILLUSTRATIONS

◀ NOTE FROM THE ▶ SERIES EDITORS

World History has come of age. No longer regarded as a task simply for amateurs or philosophers, it has become an integral part of the historical profession, and one of its most exciting and innovative fields of study. At the level of scholarship, a growing tide of books, articles, and conferences continues to enlarge our understanding of the many and intersecting journeys of humankind framed in global terms. At the level of teaching, more and more secondary schools as well as colleges and universities now offer, and sometimes require, World History of their students. One of the prominent features of the World History movement has been the unusually close association of its scholarly and its teaching wings. Teachers at all levels have participated with university-based scholars in the development of this new field.

The McGraw-Hill series—Explorations in World History—operates at this intersection of scholarship and teaching. It seeks to convey the results of recent research in world history in a form wholly accessible to beginning students. It also provides a pedagogical alternative to or supplement for the large and inclusive core textbooks which are features of so many World History courses. Each volume in the series focuses briefly on a particular theme, set in a global and comparative context. And each of them is "open-ended," raising questions and drawing students into the larger issues that animate world history.

This book by Carl Guarneri represents a coming together of two currents of historical thinking. One is a growing effort to "internationalize" the teaching of U.S. history, while the second seeks to find an appropriate place for the United States within the larger story of world history. The author addresses these twin concerns in two major ways. The first involves frequent comparisons, constantly juxtaposing aspects of U.S. history—colonial rule, slavery, immigration, imperial expansion, industrialization, and much more—with similar processes in other parts of the world. This kind of comparative history allows us to see more clearly the ways in which the United States was in fact a distinctive experiment and the ways in which its experience paralleled that of other societies.

Second, the author highlights the many and changing connections or intersections of the United States with the rest of the world. From the early frontier encounters of intruding Europeans with Native American societies to the emerging role of the United States as the sole global superpower, the impact of the world has decisively shaped American historical development. Increasingly in the twentieth century and beyond, the military actions, economic power, political influence, and cultural appeal of the United States have deeply affected the lives of people all around the world. In both approaches—comparison and connection—this book illustrates powerfully the unique ability of world history to illuminate our understanding of the past.

❰ PREFACE ❱

History textbooks traditionally describe the United States as a unique national experiment that split from Europe and developed apart from the main currents of global history. In recent years, historians impressed by mounting evidence of connections across oceans and borders have questioned this approach. *America in the World* builds upon this scholarship to offer a new view. It portrays an American history that from its origins to the present has been deeply enmeshed in events and processes beyond the nation's territorial limits. Its chapters consider the United States chronologically in global context as a frontier, a colony, a nation, and an empire. They show how at each stage of its development America was shaped by larger global processes, its experience was shared by peoples elsewhere, and its growing influence helped to change the world.

Tracking America's evolution from colonial frontier to global empire creates a framework that situates specific American events in world history and that gives sharper focus to questions of national uniqueness. Each chapter of this book recasts three or four aspects of U.S. history as international episodes by describing their larger contexts, then connecting or comparing them with developments elsewhere. For the most part, the narratives start with familiar topics in American history such as the Revolution or the Civil War, then work outward to their international dimensions. In some cases, however, they begin with topics central to world history, such as the African slave trade or the "rise of the West," and then look to the United States for evidence. Some issues have been the subject of much historical study or debate. Where this is true, I try to summarize previous scholarship and present additional information that is meant to clarify key questions. In other instances, I have ventured into new comparisons or internationalized narratives on my own. Whether original or indebted to others, my discussion of specific topics is meant to show how bridging the gap between U.S. and world history benefits both. World history is enriched, and today's global situation can be illuminated, by including the United States. At the same time, we can reach a deeper understanding of American history by situating it in the wider world to which it has always been connected.

HOW TO USE THIS BOOK.   Because this book joins U.S. and world history it can serve dual purposes: as a way to include the United States in introductory world history courses or as a way to reframe or supplement courses in American history. Either way, it is intended not as a comprehensive history of the United States, but as a selection of case studies that suggest how comparative and international approaches can produce a fresh and more accurate picture of America's place in the world. Each chapter begins with a Getting Started section that previews the major questions the chapter will address. Every chapter is also followed by an annotated list of a dozen or more Suggested Readings that I have drawn upon in writing this book, and from which readers can learn more about its topics.

A NOTE ON TERMINOLOGY.   Attempts to enlarge the framework of American history invariably run up against the limitations of language and the problem of cultural dominance. South America is part of America, too, and its peoples sometimes identify themselves by the term "American." Yet the United States long ago adopted "America" for its place and "Americans" for its people, and these terms have stuck. In this book I will frequently use "United States" (and "U.S." as its adjective) when referring specifically to the nation and its features. But "America," "American," and "Americans" appear throughout the text for variety and for lack of alternatives. There are no viable English-language replacements for "America" to describe the lands that became the United States, "Americans" to denote their inhabitants, and "American" to describe the sweep of their history, including the colonial era. I have most often used "the New World" or "the Americas" to refer to the entire Western Hemisphere. Note, too, that where unattributed words or phrases appear in quotation marks in the text, such as "civilized" or "manifest destiny," they reflect the usage of the time period and not my own.

ACKNOWLEDGMENTS

Works of historical synthesis such as this are built on a foundation laid by many scholars. I am indebted to numerous historians and other scholars who have explored the international dimensions of specific topics in American history or have provided a more globally informed glimpse of the whole. Some of these scholars are quoted and named in the text, and many others are credited in the list of readings that follows each chapter.

Certain historians deserve special thanks for their inspiration or assistance. Michael Adas, Thomas Bender, Charles Bright, Michel Cordillot, Ellen DuBois, George Fredrickson, Eliga Gould, Nancy Green, the late

John Higham, Bruce Mazlish, John McNeill, Thomas Osborne, Jacques Portes, Daniel Rodgers, Andrew Rotter, and Ian Tyrrell have suggested in their writings and in more personal contacts illuminating ways to incorporate the United States in world history's categories and narratives. Tom Bender also directed the La Pietra conferences on Internationalizing United States History that met in Florence, Italy from 1997 to 2000 under the joint auspices of New York University and the Organization of American Historians. There I joined several dozen scholars from around the world who shared ideas about reframing American history in global terms. Their insights have been reflected ever since in my writing. More recently I co-directed a National Endowment for the Humanities summer institute, co-sponsored by the American Historical Association and the Library of Congress, on "Rethinking America in Global Perspective." I owe a profound debt to the Endowment, to my friend and co-director John Gillis of Rutgers University (emeritus), and to our guest lecturers and 25 faculty participants from across the United States. Their unique perspectives on U.S. and world history and their deft critiques of this book's prospectus and one of its chapters were offered in time to guide my final revisions.

My colleagues in the Saint Mary's College history department read a draft chapter and offered helpful suggestions and much encouragement. Portions of other draft chapters or the book's introduction were presented to faculty and student audiences at the College of New Jersey, Colgate University, and UCLA, and in a series of lectures in Brazil sponsored by the now-defunct U.S. Information Agency. The ensuing discussions steered me to new sources and strengthened my interpretations.

Several people read the complete manuscript and improved it greatly with their comments and corrections. McGraw-Hill Series editor Robert Strayer read each chapter as it arrived in his email inbox and balanced praise with gentle and constructive criticism. Series co-editor Kevin Reilly added his voice at important moments to ease the publication process. Five outside reviewers, Alan Dawley of the College of New Jersey, Dane Kennedy of George Washington University, W. Bruce Leslie and Lynn Parsons (emeritus) of SUNY-Brockport, and Peter Stearns of George Mason University, gave the manuscript a close critical reading that tightened its organization, pointed out neglected topics, and saved me from errors of fact or judgment. My wife, Valerie Weller, read the near-final draft with an eye toward assuring its accessibility to the general reader. I am grateful for her many suggestions that enhanced its interpretive coherence as well as its clarity and tone.

At McGraw-Hill, Lyn Uhl enthusiastically supported this project when it was just an idea, and her successor, Jon-David Hague, helped me to carry the original plan through to completion. Beth Baugh, as developmental editor, Rick Hecker, as project editor, and Barbara Hacha, as copyeditor, guided the manuscript efficiently toward publication.

Finally, this book's dedication indicates my loving appreciation for my daughters, Anna and Julia Guarneri, and my high hopes for their generation. Their undergraduate studies and travels abroad have opened new national histories to me, inspired me to seek wider comparative reference points for U.S. history, and even reined in some of my errant generalizations. My fondest hope is that students who read this book will aspire to be good citizens of both the United States and the world.

C. G.

AMERICAN HISTORY AS IF THE WORLD MATTERED (AND VICE VERSA)

If you have grown up in the United States you have probably encountered it. In most schools the history curriculum is compartmentalized into two sections: the United States and all other places in the world, or "Us" and "Them." From the elementary grades onward, American and world history are often taught in alternate years and rigidly separated in content. This split makes little sense. The United States does not exist apart from events and trends in the larger world, and it never has. "No man is an island, entire in itself," the poet John Donne wrote, and this is also true of nations. American history is full of examples. As it developed from a frontier outpost of Europe, imported African slaves, received immigrants from around the world, and then began to flex its muscles as a world power, the United States has been enmeshed in ties of all kinds with the rest of the world.

Today we constantly talk about "globalization," the near-instant linkage of people around the planet through computers, multinational corporations, and mass entertainment. Yet it is crucial to realize that globalization has a long history. Today's global economy descends directly from the contacts across oceans originated by sailing ships five centuries ago. The colonies that became the United States were products of that "first globalization," born in the process of European expansion that mingled distant populations and ecosystems and created a global trade network in the 1500s. The United States and globalization share the same birthday. Ever since, whether as colony, nation, or empire, the fate of America has been joined to the world's.

Meanwhile, the world's fate has increasingly come to depend upon America. In the late nineteenth century the United States became the world's largest industrial producer, and in the next hundred years it developed into a superpower that owned colonies, operated overseas military

1

bases, intervened in two world wars, and influenced the lives of people everywhere. Just as it makes little sense to study American history in isolation from the world, it would be misleading to consider world history, especially in the twentieth century, without analyzing the impact of the United States.

Teaching nation-centered history, whether in the United States or elsewhere, tends to foster national cohesion and pride. This is a worthwhile and important mission, but it sometimes coexists uneasily with another aim of history: to determine the truth about the past. Building a nation, the French historian Ernest Renan declared, requires us to "get [our] history wrong." Renan was speaking about the power of national myths, inspiring stories—not always accurate—that tell a people who they are, where they came from, and where they should be going. One of the most powerful myths about the United States pronounces it a special place that developed fundamentally apart from the rest of the world and has been exempt from its problems. This idea, a variant of the belief that historians label "exceptionalism," is thoughtlessly reinforced rather than critically examined when we consider U.S. history in isolation.

Some scholars have suggested that the more powerful a nation becomes, the more it sets its history apart from others. Citizens of militarily weak or economically dependent countries automatically see themselves in terms of larger international forces, while those in imperial centers tend to stress their nation's unusual success or peculiar "genius." Lack of interest in the wider world is one of the dangers of the superpower mentality. As the United States exerts increasing influence around the world its citizens cannot afford to ignore its overseas connections and their impact. Informed citizenship requires a global vision, one that supplements local and national allegiances with awareness of nations' interdependence and concern for the global commons.

A different kind of myth than exceptionalism, one we can call "triumphalism," suggests that the United States was always destined to become the world's greatest power, exaggerates its influence, and often assumes that nations of the world will become, or want to become, "just like us." Like those world maps that place North and South America in the middle and cut Asia into two pieces located at opposite sides, Americans tend to have an inflated sense of their nation's centrality. No doubt, part of the growing appeal of courses in world history is the chance to question this "America-centric" view. The long histories of African, Asian, and European civilizations dwarf the United States' 200-year existence, and today's global array of societies demonstrates that the world remains a diverse mosaic of peoples rather than a cluster of American look-alikes or "wannabes."

Ultimately, the aim of bringing U.S. History and World History together is not to explode or confirm national myths like exceptionalism or triumphalism. Instead, its goal is twofold: to understand Americans' relation to other peoples—including connections and similarities as well as differences—and to trace their nation's evolving position on a globe dotted with other nations, a world that is shrinking dramatically today and has been for more than five centuries. In the context of global change, every nation's history is part of world history.

AMERICAN HISTORY IN GLOBAL PERSPECTIVE

In recent decades, scholars dissatisfied with the insularity of traditional American history have sought its larger contexts and connections. Opening a dialogue with world history, they are relating American events to global trends, tracking ideas and movements across national boundaries, and analyzing American history comparatively. This book incorporates their findings and adds some insights of my own. Examining selected American history topics in international context, it is meant to illustrate how this approach offers new perspectives on episodes like the slave trade, the Revolution, westward expansion, the Civil War, the Progressive movement, and the youth revolt of the 1960s.

How does an "internationalized" American history look different from traditional accounts? Dozens of specific examples will be given in the chapters that follow. Meanwhile, speaking more broadly, we can identify at least five ways that adopting a more globalized view has already begun to reframe the traditional narrative of American history.

NEW STARTING POINTS AND PLACES

Placing American history in a wider setting stretches its dimensions in space and time. The old-fashioned starting points, the Jamestown colony in Virginia (1607) and the Pilgrim settlement of Massachusetts (1620), open the story far too late, for Spanish and Portuguese colonization in the Americas preceded British efforts by more than a century and influenced them in crucial ways. To fix on the early 1600s is to shrink American history to mean only United States history, whereas its most revealing context in the early modern world was hemispheric rather than continental, "the Americas" rather than America. Thus, 1492 seems a more logical starting point, with its epochal encounter of two worlds that had previously been quite ignorant of each other. Yet even Columbus's journey must be examined as a product of European expansion in the 1400s and, earlier, the thriving European trade with Asia.

If we think of America as an extension of Western civilization we should also keep in mind the high points of that civilization from ancient times onward. As historian Paul Gagnon has written, "The plain fact is that American history is not intelligible . . . without a firm grasp of the life and ideas of the ancient world, of Judaism and Christianity, of Islam and Christendom in the Middle Ages, of feudalism, of the Renaissance and the Reformation, of the English Revolution and the Enlightenment."[1] Nor is Europe the only place to study, for we must also look across the south Atlantic for the origins of the slave trade that brought millions of Africans to the New World, and westward to Asia for the land crossing that brought the first humans—Native Americans—to the Western Hemisphere about 20,000 years ago. Whether we enter American history by analyzing American Indian civilizations or by digging deeply into the European past, a more global approach offers multiple places and earlier starting points for us to consider as we create its narratives.

DECENTERING EARLY AMERICA

Taking a more global approach means at times assigning America to the wings of the historical stage rather than the center. From early on, events elsewhere have directed American national life. From the opening of the Portuguese slave trade in 1444 and the reform of British colonial tax policy in 1763 to the assassination of Emperor Franz Ferdinand of Austria, which triggered World War I in 1914, life in America has been transformed at many times by outside influences. Shifting our focus to the places where these originated makes us recognize that before the mid-1800s the United States was a minor nation tucked in a corner of the world, a satellite orbiting on the edge of mighty Europe's gravitational field. Its survival depended upon developments beyond its borders, such as the Napoleonic Wars (1799–1815), which preoccupied the European powers during the first decades of the United States' fragile national existence, or the decision by Great Britain not to intervene on the side of the Confederacy during the American Civil War.

FOREIGN RELATIONS

Dependence on other peoples meant that from the outset the United States *had* to become involved in foreign affairs, contrary to a strong streak of isolationism that cautioned Americans against making alliances or commitments to other nations. Placing the United States in world history means paying special attention to the nation's involvement in the world beyond

[1]Paul Gagnon, "Why Study History?" *Atlantic Monthly*, November 1988, 46.

American borders. This can start with the struggle for independence, which Americans won largely because of help from France and Holland. In the following decades, leaders of the young United States tried to play off the European powers against one another to preserve America's neutrality and give it time to build viable institutions. Meanwhile, the saga of westward expansion in the 1800s, which is usually cast in national terms, should be reframed as a story of international conflict and negotiation, stretching from the Louisiana Purchase of 1803 to the Mexican War of 1846–48. As the United States grew in size and power, its actions on the world stage became less defensive and more aggressive. During the nineteenth and into the twentieth century, Americans crossed the Atlantic and Pacific Oceans in search of markets for their products and ideals, and they intervened frequently in the affairs of Latin America. By 1945 the United States' involvement in two world wars and its position as the dominant "superpower" made its international commitments impossible to miss.

Broadly considered, foreign relations entail more than contacts between governments. As historians now emphasize, transnational affairs encompass a wide spectrum of contacts between individuals and groups across national borders, including international trade, technology transfer, cultural exchange, missionary work, migration, and tourism. Each of these ties has played a part in shaping the lives of Americans, and many have influenced peoples around the world. All are fitting and important topics for a "globalized" American history.

COMPARISONS AND CONNECTIONS

The task of comparing and connecting the American experience to societies elsewhere adds a fourth feature to an internationalized American history: it pictures the United States as more enmeshed in worldwide trends and less exceptional than Americans like to believe. Many things we think of as uniquely American are not. Did the United States begin as a frontier outpost of European traders and settlers? So did many other nations. Did its colonists encounter native peoples, import African slaves, and eventually declare their independence from the mother country? So did many New World societies. Did it face political fragmentation, secession and civil war? The postcolonial "new nations" of nineteenth-century Latin America and twentieth-century Africa and Asia encountered similar problems. Did it receive millions of immigrants and become a multiethnic society? Nations such as Argentina, Australia, and Malaysia were also decisively shaped by immigration, and today (according to one estimate) there are fewer than 20 nations in the entire world whose population comes almost exclusively from one ethnic group.

REFINING NATIONAL COMPARISONS.   Topics like the frontier, slavery, and immigration invite us to compare U.S. history with that of other nations. The purpose of these comparisons is not to dismiss the notion of American uniqueness, but rather to test it against the facts and, where it remains valid, to define it in less absolute terms. Sophisticated comparisons help us to see the United States in the context of larger patterns and to develop a sense of the weave of similarities and differences that have created its national fabric. After we place the United States firmly in the world, we can break down simplistic dichotomies between America and a homogenized "other" that is the rest of the world. When this happens, we often discover that there remain subtle but important differences between American and many national histories. We learn, for example, that the United States has taken in newcomers from a wider variety of countries of origin than any other immigrant receiver, creating the foundation of its rich and sometimes conflicted "melting-pot" society.

TRACKING IMPORTS AND EXPORTS.   Connecting features of American history to larger global processes demonstrates how, contrary to isolationist mythology, the United States has always participated in international systems and trends. Throughout their history, Americans have taken in people, goods, and ideas from elsewhere and often transformed them in the process. Their importing of religious revivalism, an industrial revolution, and the "welfare state" are noteworthy examples. Looking outward, Americans have exported world-changing foods and manufactured products, from codfish and cotton to sewing machines and computers. They have broadcast innovative ideas abroad, such as democratic self-government and free-market capitalism, and they pioneered developments that surfaced later in other developed countries, such as assembly-line production and mass consumer culture.

Broadly speaking, the dominant flow has shifted over the centuries from a time when the United States was primarily an *importer* of money, goods, and ideas, to an era when it is a major *exporter*, able to project its economic and cultural power worldwide. American influence abroad has become a flashpoint of conflict as political and cultural controversies rage over worldwide changes that have been variously described as "American empire," "Americanization," or "cultural imperialism." We will discuss these controversies in Chapter 6.

RETHINKING PERIODIZATION

Finally, when we stand back to see how America fits into the big picture of world history, it becomes clear that we should arrange its periodization (its division into chronological segments) into fewer units covering more time. Because world history spans several millennia and surveys major changes across societies, it is usually divided into themes that stretch across centuries. By contrast, U.S. history, covering just a few hundred years, traditionally chronicles short-term changes in detail. It is typically divided into presidential administrations, which last only four to eight years; into decades, such as the "Roaring Twenties" or the turbulent 1960s; or at most into periods of two or three decades, such as the Jacksonian (1828–48) or the Progressive (1890–1920) eras. To relate American history meaningfully to developments in the wider world, it makes sense to adopt a "macro" not a "micro" approach, one that synchronizes with the longer time spans of world history and addresses its larger themes and processes.

FOUR STAGES OF AMERICAN HISTORY

This book divides American history into four overlapping stages that reflect the nation's global origins, its internal development, and its relation to other societies. During the **Age of Exploration and Contact, 1530s–1680s** (discussed in Chapter 1) North America was a "frontier" in a double sense. First, it was a remote extension of European colonization, a process that had begun earlier and developed more rapidly in the Caribbean islands, Mexico, and South America. Second, like those places it became a tense borderland between European and native societies. The contacts, collisions, and exchanges among peoples along this borderland transformed lives in the New and Old Worlds and set the pattern for European conquest, settlement, and rivalry in North America.

In the **Colonial Era, 1607–1783** (Chapter 2) Britain's North American possessions, like the New World colonies of Spain, Portugal, France, and Holland, took their place in an Atlantic commercial and capitalist system based mainly on crops and commodities produced by enslaved Africans. Plantation production and overseas trade transformed these colonies into complex societies featuring hierarchies of race and class at the same time it enriched European merchants and consumers. Beginning in the 1680s, a century-long global war between Britain and its imperial rivals shaped the conditions of the British and other European colonists' lives and ultimately ignited independence movements that erupted from Boston to Buenos Aires.

After independence, the United States, like other New World colonies that broke from European rule, embarked on the task of constructing viable national institutions. The American **Age of Nation-building, 1776–1930s** (covered in Chapters 3 and 4) stretched over a century and a half and divided into two overlapping phases. In the first stage the United States, like other New World nations, consolidated its national government against the threat of secession and moved inland to overtake native peoples and stretch its rule as far as possible. Second, by the mid-1800s, in tandem with other targets of British economic domination such as Germany and Japan, the United States began a program of modernization designed to ensure the nation's economic independence. Forging an American version of the Industrial Revolution, immigrant workers, business entrepreneurs, and political leaders transformed the nation into an economic giant. Although industrialization generated unprecedented wealth and underpinned the nation's rise to global power, it exposed problems of exploitation and inequality that turned Americans toward other industrialized nations in search of remedies such as labor unions, socialist movements, and welfare-state protections.

The United States' westward expansion in the 1800s was in many respects an imperial project, but in the **Age of Empire, 1880s–present** (the subject of Chapters 5 and 6) Americans took decisive steps to project their power overseas. As the nation's economic influence grew, its trade activities escalated into government intervention abroad. Beginning by joining Europe's race for trade privileges and colonies in Asia, American imperialism evolved into informal economic domination of developing nations, especially in Latin America. Meanwhile, involvement in two world wars propelled the United States to global leadership as American institutions and policies filled the void left by the collapse of European powers and their overseas empires. After World War II, the United States and an emerging rival with equally globalizing interests and ideas—the Soviet Union—engaged in a long and costly contest in which America's home front and foreign relations took on an imperial cast. At the Cold War's end, Americans and the world's other peoples faced the challenge of determining a stable new world order that avoided both the perils of American global domination and the chaotic free-for-all of capitalist globalization.

The four-part schema of frontier, colony, nation, and empire produces a bird's-eye view of America's place in the world, one that makes many of its major events and themes look different. Hovering above the nation rather than being bounded by its horizons from the ground, we can track events elsewhere that shared a common history and influenced one another. We can, for example, follow the African slave trade to several New World destinations whose plantation economies, population characteristics, and colonial or national policies shaped allied but somewhat different emancipation struggles and racial categories. We can locate the American Revolution in a series of colonial revolts that erupted when the overseas rivalries of Spain, France, and England escalated into external wars and internal disputes over taxes. We can place Americans' westward expansion in the context of the inland penetration by European settlers and descendants on imperial and national frontiers in Latin America, Asia, South Africa, and Australia. We can relate America's traumatic Civil War to struggles for national unification that were raging in contemporary Europe and Latin America. And so on, through the later themes of immigration, industrialization, war, and empire.

WORLD HISTORY WITH AMERICA INCLUDED

What about the other side of the question? What aspects of world history look different when an enlarged American history is taken into consideration? Although the primary focus of this book is on American history in world context, its analysis has implications for world history, too. There are at least five ways that incorporating U.S. history (and before it, North American history) changes the way historians describe key features of world history.

NORTH AMERICA'S IMPACT ON EUROPE

The impact of North America upon its Old World colonizers was far reaching. Adam Smith, the famous Scottish economist, declared in his *Wealth of Nations* (1776) that "the discovery of America" and the passage around Africa via the Cape of Good Hope were "the two greatest and most important events recorded in the history of mankind." Even allowing for hyperbole, it is clear that colonial America helped to transform the world beyond it. Its unexpected "discovery" by Europeans forced them to reexamine old ideas about geography, biology, and human history. More concretely, the "Columbian Exchange"—the global diffusion of plants, foods, animals, and diseases that took place after the voyages of exploration—altered the human geography and natural environment of all the world's inhabited continents. And the migration of tens of millions of people to the Americas (whether voluntary, in the case of most white settlers, or coerced, in the case of slaves) redistributed the world's population and often changed the society that migrants left behind as much as the one they entered.

It is not always possible to isolate single factors that produced huge transformations. Was exploitation of New World resources the reason Europe advanced beyond the great Asian civilizations in power and influence, or was the "great divergence" of East and West based on technological inventions like the steam engine? How much did the New World's precious metals contribute to the development of western capitalism? How indispensable were America's slaves and the cotton they raised to Britain's industrial revolution? Historians continue to debate these questions and may never agree on the answers. Yet few deny that during the era of colonization important influences crossed the oceans *from* the Western Hemisphere as well as *to* it.

VARIATIONS ON WORLD HISTORY THEMES

Including the North American colonies and the United States also enriches world history by considering their features as variants of important global processes. Generalizations about slavery or colonialism in the Western world would be useless if they did not take into account American experiences. Less obvious but equally true, world history topics that span oceans and continents, such as the rise of nationalism, the global industrial transformation, and the spread of socialism and the welfare state, ought to be framed with the United States in mind, either as an example or (in the case of socialism) a possible exception.

Many world historians are interested in large interpretive schemas borrowed from the social sciences. The United States can serve as an important case study verifying or questioning these broad hypotheses. How does the American experience fit into sociological generalizations about the nature of slavery, race relations, revolutions, or frontiers, for example? Does its history square with influential theories that nations, empires, or economies evolve in clear and predictable stages? Because many global developments had counterparts in the United States, American events can be used to test generalizations about trends in world history and demonstrate the range of particular cases they encompass. The tension between general patterns and particular cases is intrinsic to historical analysis, but it is especially important to world history. Analyzing global changes in their American context can help us understand it.

AN ATLANTIC SYSTEM OF TRADE AND MIGRATION

Incorporating the North American colonies and the United States into global history may not only modify old categories but also suggest new ones. For example, by tracing exchanges between America and other parts of the world, we can uncover a comprehensive "Atlantic system" of trade and migration. Originating with Caribbean and South American commerce and joined by the North American colonies in the 1600s, this elaborate network carried peoples and products across the Atlantic Ocean in both directions from four continents. Built initially on gold and silver, then drawing primarily upon slavery and staple-crop production, it forged economic and cultural ties that integrated Europe, Africa, and the Americas into its nexus and affected Asian societies as well. The Atlantic system supplemented and eventually superseded the Mediterranean and Indian

Ocean regional trading systems of earlier eras. It redirected wealth and power westward, underwrote the developing British Empire, and endured into the nineteenth century.

SHIFTS IN GLOBAL POLITICAL AND ECONOMIC POWER

Placing the Atlantic system into a larger historical trajectory illustrates a fourth feature of world history with America included: its analysis of the westward shift in world power toward the United States. America's ascent to global influence was given a crucial boost when the nation emerged victorious and virtually unscathed from World Wars I and II while its European rivals were devastated. How did American policies shape Europe's politics and economy between and after these wars? What impact did growing U.S. economic clout exert on the technological and consumer revolutions of the twentieth century and the globalized capitalism ascendant at its end? Answering such questions will highlight the extent of U.S. power beyond the nation's borders. It may also suggest its limits, for some of the twentieth century's most important developments, from the rise of communism and fascism to decolonization in Asia and Africa, derived from non-American sources and often played themselves out beyond American control.

THE UNITED STATES AS A DISTINCTIVE CIVILIZATION

Finally, coming to grips with the impact of the United States beyond its borders allows us to assess its special contributions to world history. Historian Gerald Early has famously quipped that "there are only three things America will be known for two thousand years from now: the Constitution, jazz music, and baseball."[2] It's worth noting that all three are descendants of mixed-continent marriages. The Constitution drew heavily on British legal precedents; jazz represents a blend of African and American idioms; and baseball derives from bat and ball games that have been traced as far back as medieval Europe. All demonstrate how an internationally aware American history complicates assertions of American uniqueness.

Does America represent a distinctive new civilization to compare with other major societies in world history? What is the relevance of America's experiments in representative government and multiracial diversity to the rest of the world? If, on the other hand, the United States has simply inherited leadership of the West from Great Britain or Europe generally, has it acted in distinctive ways? Do American ideals shape U.S. foreign

[2]Quoted in the film *Baseball*, directed by Ken Burns (PBS, 1994).

relations, or does America act the way great powers have traditionally acted? Does the spread of American-style capitalism herald a new stage in world economic development? These are big and difficult questions, but addressing them opens some of the widest vistas on American history and engages important controversies over the place of the United States in the great sweep of world history.

THE DEBATE OVER AMERICAN EXCEPTIONALISM

Whether we begin with American history and look outward to the rest of the world or start with world history and place the United States in it, a central problem facing us concerns the distinctiveness of American society. The issue of American exceptionalism looms over most attempts to place U.S. history in a wider context.

A CHOSEN PEOPLE.   Virtually every nation thinks of itself as unique, but the belief in their own nation's uniqueness—and superiority—is especially deeply rooted among Americans. The notion that Americans are a "chosen people" with a special destiny was voiced in so many ways by politicians, preachers, and patriotic orators that it became a ready assumption among Americans and only recently has been widely questioned. Of course, uniqueness is a comparative statement and a matter of degree. In its boldest and most powerful formulation, however, exceptionalism uses absolute language. It declares that the United States is unique, and singularly blessed, because it has been exempt from the forces and problems that have troubled societies in Europe and the rest of the world. Few persons familiar with the conflicts of American history and its engagement with other continents can accept this statement without reservations. But there are other, less sweeping, versions of exceptionalism that many thoughtful scholars support. Some refer to a particular trait or factor that has made American history unique. Others acknowledge contacts across borders and oceans but argue that on the whole the United States developed on a separate path from other countries.

EUROPEANS INVENT AMERICAN EXCEPTIONALISM.   Ironically, American exceptionalism was invented by Europeans. After Columbus's landing, the American continents served as blank canvases upon which early modern Europeans could paint their dreams, fantasies, and hopes (as well as their fears). Columbus himself thought that he had found in Venezuela the river that flowed from the Garden of Eden. Many European explorers and settlers embraced such utopian ideas, whether based on Biblical stories, popular legends about lost cities of gold, or the Enlightenment notion that a better civilization could be built from the ground up on "virgin land."

Most such dreams ignored the presence of native populations and the stubborn realities of the American landscape. All placed their hopes upon a fresh start in a place Europeans christened the "New World." "America," the great German writer Goethe rhapsodized, "you have it better than our continent, the old one."

AMERICANS ADOPT EXCEPTIONALISM.   Exceptionalist ideas arrived on the English settlers' first ships. John Winthrop, preaching in 1630 as the Puritans approached the Massachusetts coast, hoped that the Puritan colony could become "a city upon a hill," lighting the world with its example. After achieving nationhood, the people of the United States absorbed exceptionalist notions of themselves as eagerly as they took over the name "Americans" from the rest of the hemisphere. Declaring cultural as well as political independence from Britain, Americans built their national identity around the contrast between the United States and Europe rather than their common history and continuing ties. Americans' belief in their superior ways allowed many to brush aside their tainted record of racial conflict and the Civil War. Instead, they harped upon the nation's westward expansion, attraction to immigrants, economic success, and apparent military invincibility as evidence that theirs was a unique "promised land."

Wittingly or not, many American historians have taken part in this celebratory, nation-building enterprise. Most accounts of U.S. history have emphasized the fortunate distinctiveness of the American experience. Many writers simply assume America's uniqueness, but others have attempted to explain it. Why is it that America's history seems to diverge fundamentally from Europe's?

THE CASE FOR EXCEPTIONALISM

THE FRONTIER.   One enormously popular answer has been the frontier, which historian Frederick Jackson Turner eulogized in 1893 in a famous essay. On the westward-moving line where advancing settlers confronted the wilderness, Turner wrote, Old World ideas and habits were broken down and the democratic and individualistic traits that made Americans distinctive were formed. A rough equality of opportunity overcame distinctions of birth, and immigrants "melted" into a new people. Workers migrating to the frontier raised their condition as well as the demand for labor in the east, thus easing class pressures that in Europe erupted into violence. When looser frontier ways drifted eastward into more settled areas, Americans became purged of Old World influences and found their special national character.

Turner's ideas have not gone unopposed. Critics point out that relatively few urban workers or enslaved African newcomers reached the frontier. Others note that violence, race prejudice, and environmental plunder characterized life on the American frontier at least as much as Turner's virtues. Those who have compared the American frontier with similar environments in Canada, Latin America, and Russia—a task Turner never attempted—find common patterns of exploitation and inequality that fail to sustain Turner's claims about the frontier's democratic effects.

OTHER EXCEPTIONALIST THEORIES. Scholars who favor exceptionalist views have highlighted other factors that, they claim, developed a separate American way of life. One popular explanation is the absence of a feudal past. Although vestiges of European class privileges and vast landed estates appeared in a few British North American colonies, the availability of cheap land doomed hopes of duplicating the Old World system of titled nobles and bound peasants. America's rural white population—its founding majority—was made up of independent farmers or renters working toward ownership.

Other scholars have pointed out how America's independence struggle spawned democratic ideals and political institutions quite different from Europe's. Universal white male suffrage and mass political parties created a stable framework for resolving disputes and absorbed radical and third-party movements into the mainstream. Compared to Europe, the American political spectrum was narrow. (Some scholars argue that the labels "Right" for conservative views and "Left" for radical ones, which originated with the French Revolution, cannot be applied to the United States.) American politics excluded monarchists, marginalized socialists, and opened up ample middle ground for compromise.

Another cluster of exceptionalist theories centers on American abundance. Cheap land and vast natural resources encouraged entrepreneurship and attracted hardworking migrants. The possibility of becoming rich, or at least attaining middle-class status, motivated ordinary workers and dampened economic resentments. "Why is there no socialism in the United States?" a German sociologist asked, then answered it by pointing to the "roast beef and apple pie" on the tables of working families. Ironically, it was Karl Marx's followers who first coined the term "exceptionalism." In their usage it referred to the puzzle of why the United States had not followed the Marxist dictum that the most advanced capitalist nation ought to develop the most robust socialist movement.

Other candidates have been nominated to explain American exceptionalism. Many scholars have found America's uniqueness in its diverse population created by massive immigration and frequent intermixture—its "melting pot" or cultural "mosaic." Others assert the unusual importance of religion in American life, due in part to the absence of an established church or "state religion." Separation of church and state, they argue, stimulated a healthy competition for religious loyalties and saved religious life from decline or destruction when political winds shifted, as happened in many other nations.

WEIGHING SUCCESSES AND SHORTCOMINGS. Exceptionalist arguments harmonize with the mythology of America as a unique "experiment," and they usually pay compliments Americans like to hear. These include the notions that Americans are more religious than other societies, more pragmatic and less interested in socialism and other "isms," and more inclusive of diverse peoples. They are all middle-class, or at least potentially so since they live in the "land of opportunity." To be persuasive, however, the exceptionalist position must also encompass less flattering features of American uniqueness. Americans' unusually high per capita rates of violence and their strong opposition to "big government," for example, demonstrate that their rabid individualism can endanger the poor and unprotected. The treatment of native peoples by western settlers and their government—an issue not encountered inside modern Europe—led to their near extinction. Perhaps most obvious, the presence of slavery and the racist attitudes that outlived it bequeathed a legacy of racial conflict in the United States that had no parallel across the Atlantic. The problem of racial oppression in the land of the free became an iconic "American dilemma," in the words of one influential European observer.

AGAINST EXCEPTIONALISM

Viewed from the standpoint of world history, on the other hand, the United States emerges as an offshoot of European civilization. European influence was obvious in the colonial era. The dominant white settlers brought with them European ways of worshipping God, organizing families, and making a living that they practiced in their new environment. When the colonists declared independence from Britain, they justified it with natural rights theories developed in the European Enlightenment, and the new nation's Founders consulted the precedent of Greek confederacies and Roman republics while setting up their own.

THE U.S. AS EUROPE'S FRONTIER. As they moved westward, inhabitants of the young United States pushed the boundaries of European influence just as white explorers, missionaries, and traders had been doing for three centuries. "Frontier of What?" an historian of Europe asked when confronted with Turner's assertion that the frontier was the key to American experience. From the first fur traders onward, the American West became integrated into a global economic network that was dominated by the powerful nations of western Europe. Unlike the isolated, self-sufficient pioneers of legend, western settlers just this side of the wilderness furnished animal hides, crops, and minerals for areas of the world far across the Atlantic and Pacific Oceans. Turner's frontier was just the latest frontier of an expanding European capitalism.

TRANSATLANTIC TRENDS.   After independence, American history paralleled trends common in western Europe. The spread of democratic ideas and the rise of popular political movements revolutionized both places: America's Jacksonian era (1828–48), which brought universal white male suffrage and mass political parties, was paralleled by parliamentary reform in Britain and by continental revolutions that toppled monarchies. America's industrial revolution was a direct offshoot of Britain's and progressed through similar stages. As the Civil War raged between northern and southern states, Germany, Italy, and other European countries faced similar struggles over national unification. Labor movements arose from similar grievances in western Europe and the late nineteenth-century United States, and they drew from common ideological sources, Marxist and otherwise. When reformers of the Progressive Era (1890–1920) expanded government's responsibility for improving urban and industrial life, they looked to European programs of planning and "social insurance" for their models.

In some instances, the United States pioneered changes that occurred later in Europe. In others, Americans adopted or imitated changes that Europeans had begun. Both cases demonstrate how Americans and Europeans maintained close contacts and how the flow of ideas, money, goods, and people continued in the modern era.

The fact that the United States rose to world significance just as major western European nations, such as Britain, began to decline can also be used to underscore America's Old World "inheritance." When New York replaced London as the world's banking center in the 1930s and the United States assumed leadership in the Cold War alliance after World War II, America demonstrated its ability to succeed at the great-power game first developed in Europe.

AN ASSESSMENT

Which side is right, then: those who view the United States as exceptional, or those who interpret it as an extension of Europe? It should be clear that the evidence is mixed and that neither position can encompass all the facts of American history. Large-scale changes common to Western society were played out in both Europe and the United States. Yet in each place distinctive conditions led to different outcomes. Exceptionalists must acknowledge European inheritances and influences, but those who view the United States as part of the West must also factor in its unique environment, including its Native American and African populations. Only by analyzing specific features of American history carefully in internationally comparative terms can we measure the mix of outside forces and local conditions that created the nation's life.

BEYOND EXCEPTIONALISM: SETTLER SOCIETIES, GLOBAL ECONOMIC SYSTEMS, AND GEOPOLITICS

The binary terms of the exceptionalist debate, pitting the United States against Europe or even the rest of the world, are framed in categories that hide as much as they reveal. In its most popular guises, exceptionalism encourages simplistic comparisons between "us" and "them," dualisms that homogenize or stereotype "America" and "Europe" or exaggerate their differences by framing them in polarized terms. There are alternative strategies for placing American developments in world history, ones that avoid the pitfalls of exceptionalism and add benefits of their own. These have in common a multipolar view that sees the American experience as one variant among many in a larger common history. They also emphasize the nation's participation in networks of power and exchange beyond its borders. Such approaches include comparing the United States with several other "settler societies," analyzing America's transnational economic connections, and relating the United States to systems of global political order.

SETTLER SOCIETIES

One way to enrich comparative analysis of the United States is to consider a third reference group: other Western settler societies that, like the U.S., were established as overseas European colonies and gradually won their independence.

BRITISH SETTLER SOCIETIES.   Canada, Australia, and New Zealand shared important features with the United States. All four societies were built under frontier conditions on British foundations and were populated mainly by Europeans. Each combined British inheritances with the cultures of diverse peoples: native inhabitants, immigrants from Europe and Asia, and, in the case of the United States, African slaves. All eventually separated from the British Empire and developed their own democratic institutions, but they remained dependent upon Europe for investment capital, foreign trade, and cultural styles.

LATIN AMERICAN SETTLER NATIONS.   These British settler societies can in turn be compared with other settler sites on the worldwide European frontier of expansion from the seventeenth century onward. Latin America, often considered apart from Western civilization because of its high proportion of mixed-race and indigenous peoples, was also colonized by Europeans, primarily the Spanish and Portuguese. Its societies followed a trajectory from colonial status to national independence and industrialization that was broadly similar to the United States. Latin America's regional patterns corresponded with sectional divisions in the United States. African slavery profoundly shaped the plantation economies of the Caribbean and Brazil in ways recalling the U.S. South. Argentina, Chile, and Uruguay, by contrast, are temperate lands where European colonists and later immigrants created "neo-Europes" resembling the northern and western United States. Some historians have suggested that since North and South America followed parallel paths and featured similar divisions, U.S. history can be recast as part of a common history of the Americas.

On both continents the peoples of three worlds—Europe, Africa, and America—collided and forged a new, hybrid society through their conflict, cooperation, and mixing. In both places, too, that mixture was enriched in the twentieth century by large-scale Asian migration. The United States' twentieth-century experiment in "multiculturalism" had unique features, but in general terms it resembled similar projects undertaken simultaneously by other New World settler societies.

SOUTH AFRICA.   European settlers did not limit themselves to the Western Hemisphere. Casting an even wider net, we find instructive parallels to U.S. history in South Africa. There Dutch and then British settlers subjugated native peoples, pushed back the ranching and mining frontiers, and established a racially segregated society that has often been compared with the American South. The more we take a global view, the more clearly black-white relations in the United States, which are often considered an aspect of American uniqueness, turn out to be (in the words of the African American writer W.E.B. DuBois) "but a local phase of a world problem."

FROM EXCEPTION TO VARIATION.   When the United States takes its place among the many lands where European descendants spread their ways, sweeping claims for America's special uniqueness—from its frontier to its history of immigration—are recast in more modest terms. Instead of choosing one end of a bipolar comparison between the United States and Europe, we can locate American history along a spectrum of societies that were founded as frontier outposts of Europe and then experienced modern political and social transformations. Elements of American uniqueness remain, including the nation's sole emergence as a world power among the settler societies, but these can be seen as variations on international patterns rather than exceptions to them. Viewed as a settler society, the United States is distinctive but does not stand alone.

GLOBAL ECONOMIC SYSTEMS

Placing American history among the western settler societies encourages us to work outward toward transnational processes that shaped the nation's course. All the settler societies were the products of the expansion of European empires and trade networks after 1500, and each created its history in response to global transformations that were beyond its scope and power. To get a dynamic picture of how the United States has related to the rest of the world, we should supplement comparative analysis of its history with a "connective" description of its international contacts and moves.

"Where in the world is America?" ask two scholars analyzing the nature of today's globalization. Put in the past tense, it is an excellent historical question. Where has America stood in the world at various times in its history? What transnational forces, events, and movements have influenced it, and how did Americans influence them in turn? How, in other words, did the successive stages of America's development—as frontier, colony, nation, and empire—relate to evolving global political and economic processes?

ATLANTIC AND PACIFIC TRADING SYSTEMS.   The Atlantic system of trade and migration provides one useful framework for describing these relations. Charting its dynamics from Columbus's journeys to the twentieth century helps us understand many features of American society, including slavery and American race relations, American legal and constitutional ideas, evangelical Christianity (which is an Anglo-American phenomenon), America's industrial revolution, and its massive European immigration. The Atlantic basin, including its Caribbean inlet, is an international highway on which American travels and interventions have altered other nations' histories, especially during and after the twentieth century's two world wars.

This covers only part of the picture. Peering out the western side of the North American continent, we can chart a similar Pacific system with its own networks of colonialism, trade, migration, and international relations. To European explorers America was (in the words of historian Bernard De Voto) "an accident on the way to China." European demand for Asian spices and manufactures led to Columbus's search for a westerly route and his encounter with new peoples and continents. Spain's exploitation of New World gold and silver was driven by its need to balance its trade with China, and Spain's success spurred England's interest in exploring and colonizing North America. After independence, American trade with Asia grew in tandem with the young nation's wealth and naval power until it became by the late 1800s a significant factor in national policymaking. Interest and involvement in the Asian market cleared the way for the migration of Chinese, Japanese, and Filipino laborers, sparked America's annexation of Hawaii and the Philippines, and opened an imperial rivalry with Japan that culminated catastrophically in World War II.

WORLD-SYSTEM THEORY.   An even broader interpretive framework, introduced in the 1970s and still influential among world historians, encompasses both oceans and traces the development of an integrated world economy since the sixteenth century. According to this "world-system" approach, the increasingly wealthy and powerful "core" nations of western Europe came to dominate international finance and trade and established economic dependencies as they expanded to other continents. By conquering native peoples and organizing the shipment of raw materials and staple crops in return for industrial goods, these imperial centers brought distant regions on their "periphery" under the control of European merchants and rulers, from then on making them dependent upon the global capitalist market.

How does the United States fit into this schema? Applied in outline to America, a world-system approach begins with North America as an outpost on the world's periphery that becomes enmeshed in the web of colonization, mercantilism, and the slave trade. After independence, the United States achieved "semi-peripheral" status by consolidating national institutions, beginning to industrialize, and taking charge of its own internal peripheral zone, the western frontier. Elements of peripheral status lingered in the American South's "cotton kingdom" and in the nation's ongoing foreign debt (until 1914). Otherwise, the United States climbed rapidly out of dependence. After World War I it emerged as the prime inheritor of Europe's economic legacy and a major financial and military force around the globe. Thus in three centuries the United States moved from the periphery to the core of the world economy. Once the dependent of a European great power, it became a dominant international power itself.

GEOPOLITICAL SYSTEMS: ALLIANCES AND EMPIRES

The developing phases of the world economy have been paralleled by shifting systems of international relations. At various times in the modern world there have been different "geopolitical systems"; that is, international frameworks of alliance and competition by which the most powerful nations have waged war, kept peace, asserted their dominance, and created conditions for exchange. Placing America in world history involves examining its role in such systems as the great European rivalries for overseas empire during the 1700s, nineteenth-century Europe's precarious "balance of power" between competing nations, the "new" imperialism of the late 1800s targeted at Africa and east Asia, the international alliances that led to World War II, the global Cold War between communism and capitalism, and the controversial "New World Order" that features the United States as the lone superpower.

In both arenas—the world economy and the world political system—the United States gradually emerged from the margins of power and arrived at the center. This history raises questions that are directed outward from the nation's boundaries as well as inward. What domestic and international conditions enabled Americans to move from dependent to great power status? What justifications and debates accompanied the nation's increasing intervention abroad? What role did the United States play in the world wars and global political upheavals of the twentieth century? What effects have American economic initiatives and foreign policies had on other regions of the world?

EMPIRE. One of the oldest forms of organizing international relations, empire is also among the most elastic. It has been used to describe relations that range from territorial conquest and overseas rule to more subtle and consensual ways of controlling other peoples by means of international alliances, economic domination, or "cultural imperialism." As the United States grew in power, it practiced all these forms of control over nearby lands and distant peoples. In the nineteenth century, the nation expanded westward to the edge of the North American continent, then graduated to overseas colonization. In the twentieth century, it led a Cold War alliance against Soviet communism, moved to the center of the world's capitalist economy, and attempted to export its institutions and culture worldwide. America's imperial trajectory raises questions of world-historical importance. To what extent was the United States following the lead of Great Britain, which enforced a free-trade regime of globalization in the late 1800s and controlled a quarter of the world's peoples by World War I? Did imperial motives lurk behind America's idealistic leadership of the Cold War alliance? Is today's version of globalization just another word for American empire?

AGAINST TRIUMPHALISM. Charting the United States' rise to world power is not the same as saying that it was preordained or will last forever. If exceptionalists are prone to exaggerate American uniqueness, "triumphalists" tend to overestimate America's influence at every step toward its "rendezvous with destiny." Some scholars go so far as to assert that world history has "ended" with the victory of American-style democracy and capitalism and the demise of communist regimes in Russia and Eastern Europe.

Historians must remain skeptical about such claims. Despite John Winthrop's hope that the eyes of the world would be trained on New England's "city upon a hill," the fact is that the United States began its history as a tiny colony in a corner of the world obscure to Europeans. Far from being smoothed by "destiny," its path to world power was halting and unsteady, nearly cut off by a disastrous civil war and held back by isolationist fears. The degree to which America dominates today's world is hardly absolute, and the effects of America's actions for good and ill are hotly debated at home and abroad. How long "the American Century" that journalist Henry Luce proclaimed in 1941 will last remains unclear, for the histories of previous great powers chronicle their "decline and fall" as well as their rise. Whether we view current events as the product of an American empire or the result of a more diffuse globalization, we can be sure that the present world order is subject to change. Barring some unforeseen global catastrophe, human history does not end or even stand still.

The most accurate historical theories—indeed the only plausible ones—are those that depict societies and economies continuing to evolve into new relationships. Describing these changing international connections and determining the role of the United States in them is a crucial task for those who study American and world history.

SUGGESTED READINGS

Bender, Thomas. *A Nation Among Nations: America's Place in World History*. New York: Hill and Wang, 2006.
    —Calls for an enlarged national history by examining five episodes in American history: European exploration, the Revolution, the Civil War, late nineteenth-century imperialism, and twentieth-century social politics.

Bender, Thomas, ed. *Rethinking American History in a Global Age*. Berkeley: University of California Press, 2002.
    —A wide-ranging and sophisticated collection of essays in which scholars discuss multiple ways to internationalize the study of U.S. history.

Davies, Edward J. *The United States in World History*. London: Routledge, 2006.
    —A concise overview that concentrates on U.S. influence abroad in the modern period, especially American industrialism and mass culture.

Guarneri, Carl J., ed. *America Compared: American History in International Perspective,* 2nd edition, 2 vols. Boston: Houghton Mifflin, 2005.
—A collection of essays that place major topics in U.S. history in international context to demonstrate global connections and assess American uniqueness.

Hanke, Lewis, ed. *Do the Americas Have a Common History?* New York: Knopf, 1964.
—Brings classic and modern essays into a dialogue that examines the notion of a shared Western Hemispheric history.

Heffer, Jean. *The United States and the Pacific: History of a Frontier.* Notre Dame, IN: University of Notre Dame Press, 2002.
—Traces the long history of American exploration, trade, and colonization in the Pacific Basin.

Lipset, Seymour Martin. *American Exceptionalism: A Double-Edged Sword.* New York: W.W. Norton, 1996.
—A prominent political scientist affirms exceptionalism by analyzing Americans' ideas and values comparatively.

McNeill J. R., and William H. McNeill. *The Human Web: A Bird's-Eye View of World History.* New York: W.W. Norton, 2003.
—A concise world history that traces "webs" of cooperation and competition between societies over millennia, including an environmental perspective and incorporating the United States into the modern era.

Russo, David J. *American History from a Global Perspective: An Interpretation.* Westport, CT: Praeger, 2000.
—Relates selected features of U.S. history such as agriculture, religion, and social structure to larger world patterns.

Turner, Frederick Jackson. *Frontier and Section: Selected Essays.* Englewood Cliffs, NJ: Prentice-Hall, 1961.
—Includes Turner's classic essay on the significance of the frontier in American history.

Woodruff, William. *America's Impact on the World: A Study of the Role of the U.S. in the World Economy, 1750–1970.* New York, Wiley, 1975.
—Emphasizing technology, finance, and international trade, this study shows how the United States was initially shaped by global trends, then influenced them.

Woodward, C. Vann. *The Comparative Approach to American History.* New York: Basic Books, 1968.
—Includes classic essays by prominent scholars on aspects of U.S. history, such as the Revolution, immigration, and the Cold War, analyzed in internationally comparative terms.

CHAPTER ONE

THE NEW WORLD FRONTIER IN NORTH AMERICA

> **GETTING STARTED ON CHAPTER ONE:** How did differences between Native Americans' and Europeans' ways cause the collision of their worlds after 1492? Did England's penetration of the North American frontier follow Spain's example farther south, or did it take different forms? What foods, germs, and animals crossed the Atlantic in the three centuries after Columbus, and with what consequences?

After living for thousands of years in mutual ignorance, Old World and New World peoples met on Caribbean shores at the end of the fifteenth century. Two centuries of European exploration across borders and oceans culminated in this accidental encounter. Ever since the Crusades attempted to capture Jerusalem and the Venetian merchant Marco Polo undertook his celebrated journey to China, Europeans had been widening their horizons, searching for new trade routes to Asia and more territory to Christianize. By the late 1400s several European monarchs had consolidated their kingdoms and were competing for domination of the lucrative trade with Asia. Across the Atlantic, native peoples on two continents had built powerful empires and smaller societies that were engaged in complex trading networks, yet were unaware of lands beyond the seas. When Christopher Columbus landed on the Caribbean islands in 1492 he called the inhabitants "Indios" because he believed he had reached the East Indies (today's Indonesia). Soon others realized his mistake and its momentous implication: the people were Arawaks and their islands, as the Italian explorer Amerigo Vespucci pointed out, stood at the edge of a vast "New World."

Columbus never understood what had happened—mapmakers labeled the New World "America" in honor of the man who did. But Columbus's voyage began a process of European conquest and colonization that would continue for three centuries in the Americas. The land that eventually became the United States was one of many places in the New World where this expansion of European power collided with the ways of indigenous peoples. Influenced by prior imperial ventures in Ireland and on Atlantic islands, Europe's colonization of the New World in turn became a precedent for expansion into Africa, Asia, and Australia. Because it was the first, largest, and most unexpected of such transoceanic encounters, Europeans' "discovery" of the New World had an enormous impact, transforming the lives of the newcomers, the natives, and even those on other continents in ways no one had foreseen. Its effect was dramatic in its extremes, bringing catastrophe to Native Americans and a tremendous windfall to Europeans.

THE NEW WORLD AS FRONTIER.   American history has been closely tied to the concept of the frontier, but the word has a double meaning. In English it usually describes the edge of settlement, the farthest reach of a country, beyond which lies unexplored or uninhabited land. In most European languages, on the other hand, a "frontier" is a boundary or zone between two settled regions or nations—what Americans call a "border." After 1492, the New World was a frontier in both senses of the word. It was the frontier of European exploration and empire, the edge of settlement for those who sought new trade routes and realms to exploit and conquer. At the same time, it was a frontier between peoples, a borderland where the lives of millions of people from two continents—eventually three, once the African slave trade commenced—came into contact and often violent collision.

NORTH AMERICAN ENCOUNTERS.   Almost everywhere by the late 1600s, European conquerors and settlers gained the upper hand in this encounter. In North America, settlers were able to overrun Indian peoples in part because North American native societies were less populous, urban, and technologically advanced than those of Mesoamerica and Andean South America. For reasons that are still being debated, no great empires like the Aztecs of Mexico or the Incas of Peru controlled the vast territory north of Mexico. Spread out in villages over millions of square miles, North American Indians slowly and selectively adopted innovations of their southern counterparts like the cultivation of corn and the development of cities. The decentralization of native societies helped Europeans to gain a foothold, establish inland settlements at the Indians' expense, and eventually outnumber natives (as the Spanish never did in South America). Meanwhile, extensive Indian trading networks carried European diseases northward from the Gulf of Mexico, decimating some Indian societies before they saw white people.

NORTH AMERICA AS OUTLIER.   North America was penetrated by Europeans later than more southerly regions, and until the 1700s it was far less important than Latin America to world history. By the time the tiny English settlement at Jamestown, Virginia, survived its first difficult winter in 1607–08, Spain had ruled much of the Caribbean and most of Central and South America (except Brazil, declared by the Pope to be Portugal's) for a century and a half. The Spanish had built an imposing capital at Lima and a great cathedral and university in Mexico City. Gold and silver extracted from Spanish mines in Peru and Mexico were subsidizing European trade with Asia, and a flourishing Portuguese-controlled slave trade had brought Africans to the New World and established a staple-crop plantation system that became the dominant mode of agricultural production in the Americas. By contrast, North America had little to offer imperial powers intent on accumulating colonial wealth. Small numbers of French and British traders competed fiercely for the trade in animal furs with Indians, but this commerce could not sustain sizeable colonial settlements—in fact, it declined when they grew. Instead, lacking precious metals or valuable crops, North America's early colonists lived in rudimentary, wood-built villages and struggled to find a living. Until they adopted tobacco cultivation, their products amounted to a small fraction of the wealth of the Atlantic trade.

Only in hindsight can it be argued (as historian Walter McDougall does) that "North America was simply the greatest prize in the world *circa* 1600, and the fact that Britons won that prize rather than Spaniards, Frenchmen, Chinese, or Russians explains the shape of modern history more than anything else."[1] At the time, North America appeared even to its English colonizers as second-rate, leftover land, its settlements precarious backwaters. To be sure, the seeds of future prosperity and self-sufficiency were already being planted in the population patterns, ecological transfers, and regional economies of British "settler colonialism." But like seeds, these were embryonic possibilities buried from sight, dependent upon circumstance and competing with other organisms; it was by no means inevitable that they would sprout and flourish. It would take two centuries of complex social and political development for a prosperous, independent republic to emerge in British North America, and even longer for it to win a prominent position in the world.

---

[1]Walter A. McDougall, *Freedom Just Around the Corner: A New American History, 1585–1828* (New York: HarperCollins, 2004), xiii–xiv.

TIMELINE

25,000–15,000 B.C.E.	Asians begin migrating to North America across Bering Strait
c.1000 B.C.E.–650 C.E.	Cultivation of maize (corn) spreads from southwestern to northeastern North America
700–1200	Anasazi culture develops in Southwest
1050–1250	Cahokia attains its peak population and power
1300	Mississippian societies disperse in Southeast
c.1450	Iroquois Confederacy established
1450s	Portuguese use African slaves to establish plantation system on Madeira
1453	Ottoman Turks capture Constantinople
1492–1502	Columbus's four voyages open modern contact and exchange between Old and New Worlds
1494	Papal-sponsored treaty divides New World between Spain and Portugal
1497–1498	Portuguese sail around Africa to Asia
1517	Protestant Reformation begins with Martin Luther's challenge to Catholic Church
1519	First recorded voyage transporting slaves from Africa to the Americas
1524	Spain's Council of the Indies establishes imperial control over Mexico and the Caribbean
1534	Henry VIII cuts ties with Catholic Church, begins English Reformation
1535–1541	Cartier explores Canada for France
1539–1542	DeSoto and Coronado expeditions begin Spanish penetration of North America
1540–1850	Smallpox epidemics kill millions of North American natives
1566	England begins conquest of Ireland
1570s–1610	British explorers fail to find Northwest Passage
1588	English ships destroy Spanish Armada
1607	British found Jamestown, Virginia, their first permanent American settlement
1619	First African slaves brought to Virginia
1620	English colonists arrive at Plymouth, Massachusetts
1620s–1650s	England establishes sugar plantation colonies in Caribbean islands
1672	England enters slave trade by chartering Royal African Company

WORLDS COLLIDE: NATIVE AMERICAN AND EUROPEAN SOCIETIES IN THE AGE OF EXPLORATION

FIRST CONTACTS

Because Spanish ventures in the Caribbean, Central America, and Peru were so profitable, the North American mainland languished for decades on the outskirts of Spain's New World empire. Sustained Spanish exploration northward did not begin until nearly 50 years after Columbus landed in the Caribbean. In 1539, a band of 700 soldiers led by the explorer Hernán de Soto left Cuba, landed at Tampa Bay, Florida, and pushed their way inland in search of the native empire of Cibola, whose seven cities of gold had been described by the overheated imagination of an earlier Spanish scout. Marching hundreds of miles, de Soto demanded supplies and slaves from dozens of Indian villages in his path. Some native chiefs appeased the Spaniards with gifts of food and blankets—but no gold; others fought back, even with their villagers weakened by diseases caught from Gulf Coast traders. Harassed by warriors in present-day Alabama, de Soto drove his men westward to the Mississippi, on whose banks he died in 1542. The following year, 300 weary and desperate survivors of his expedition returned safely to Mexico by floating on homemade rafts.

In 1540 another Spanish expedition led by Francisco Vazquez de Coronado headed northward from Mexico through the scorching summer heat toward a complex of Zuni villages in present-day New Mexico. Also expecting to find splendid cities of gold, Coronado was disappointed to encounter the plain adobe walls of a modest apartment complex, or *pueblo*. Through a native interpreter Coronado read aloud the *requerimiento,* a notice demanding that natives accept the rule of the Spanish crown and embrace Christianity or else face enslavement or death. The Zunis responded by spreading sacred cornmeal on the ground to form a line that threatened supernatural harm if the Spanish crossed. When this failed, the natives shot arrows, and in the ensuing battle the Spanish, firing their guns and protected by armor, drove off the Zuni villagers and fed themselves on the pueblo's stores of corn, beans, and turkey. The Spanish continued north to the Great Plains, but they found no precious metals. Like de Soto's venture, their expedition returned to Mexico in failure.

While de Soto and Coronado pushed into the American South, the French sent Jacques Cartier to upper North America, a region beyond Spanish claims and control, to find gold mentioned by an earlier explorer and perhaps a passage through the continent's rivers to Asia. In three voyages between 1535 and 1541, Cartier found neither. Instead, he began trading with the Micmac Indians, who beckoned his men ashore by waving animal pelts on sticks. From them Cartier obtained furs to sell in Europe in exchange for metal fishhooks, arrowheads, and kettles. However, the small settlements that Cartier established on the St. Lawrence River in 1541 failed to survive, their inhabitants driven away by the bitter cold and the hostility of Indians who rebelled against increasingly desperate French demands.

Although they were fended off by indigenous peoples and ended in failure, the expeditions of de Soto, Coronado, and Cartier opened the era of European expansion into New World lands north of Mexico. Later settlements would become permanent, but these early encounters illustrated features that would characterize the collision between European and North American peoples over the next two centuries: the quest for riches, the exchange of goods, the power of legends about the New World, clashes of religious worldviews, the impact of disease, technological gaps in warfare and food production, and the violence of exploitation, enslavement, and resistance.

NORTH AMERICA'S NATIVE SOCIETIES

Coronado, de Soto, and Cartier learned the hard way that although cities of gold did not exist, North America was far from uninhabited. What European explorers and colonizers sometimes called the wilderness was home to between 7 and 10 million people north of Mexico. Their ancestors had begun crossing the Bering Strait from Asia 20,000 to 30,000 years earlier and gradually spread through the entire New World. Accommodating their ways of life to different geographic conditions, Indians in North America had evolved diverse cultures and spoke more than 300 languages by the time the Spanish arrived. Compared to the great Central American and Andean pre-Columbian civilizations, North American native societies were smaller and less advanced. This may have been due to the lack of plant species (before the arrival of corn) capable of sustaining dense settlements, or the shortage of tropical microclimates that allowed for rich biological diversity in a short radius. It also reflected the greater suitability of a hunter-gatherer existence to the North's wooded and subarctic regions. By the time European explorers arrived, major Indian centers in the Midwest and Southwest had dispersed due to overpopulation and ecological crises. As a result, North America on the eve of colonization was a continent of native villages. Its inhabitants clustered into six broad societal groupings.

THE ANASAZI.   In the arid American Southwest, the Anasazi and related peoples lived in stone and adobe towns and used elaborate systems of

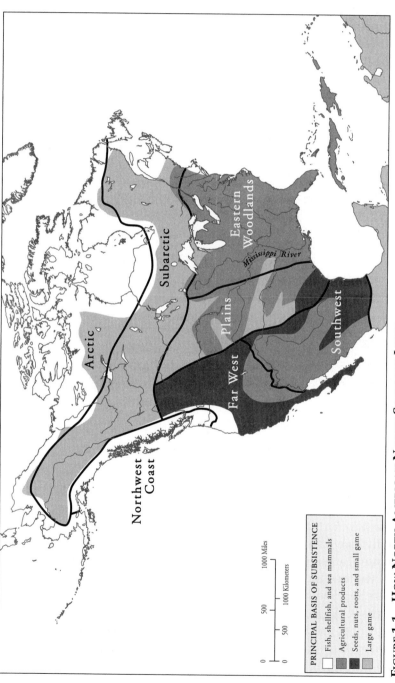

FIGURE 1-1 HOW NORTH AMERICAN NATIVE SOCIETIES LIVED

This map shows the diverse ways in which the native peoples of North America supported themselves before the arrival of Europeans. Living in different ecological niches, Native Americans survived largely on the resources available in their immediate surroundings, although trade networks connected them with other Indian peoples. Except in the Far West, Northwest, and colder northern regions, most native societies practiced farming but often combined it with other ways of producing food. (*Source: Used with permission from American History (11th ed.), by Alan Brinkley. Copyright 2003 by McGraw-Hill.*)

PRINCIPAL BASIS OF SUBSISTENCE

Fish, shellfish, and sea mammals
Agricultural products
Seeds, nuts, roots, and small game
Large game

irrigation to cultivate corn, beans, and squash—crops and techniques that had filtered northward from Mexico. After a prolonged drought that lasted most of the twelfth century, the Anasazi moved south and east to look for water and fertile soil. Eventually they resettled in today's Arizona and New Mexico, where they built the Acoma, Hopi, and Zuni pueblos. Their varied descendants were encountered by Coronado and collectively called the Pueblo Indians by the Spanish.

PEOPLE OF THE PLAINS.   As Coronado's men pushed northward to the Great Plains, they saw great herds of "shaggy cows," buffalo that were the main source of sustenance for bands of hunters. These seminomadic peoples included the Cheyenne, Arapaho, Pawnee, and Sioux. They raised corn or gathered berries where possible, but increasingly they relied upon their male warriors to kill deer and buffalo for hides and meat. Already fierce fighters, these tribes became even more formidable when they obtained horses and guns from Europeans.

MISSISSIPPIANS.   In the Mississippi and Ohio River valleys of the American Midwest and Southeast, more settled native societies thrived by raising corn, beans, and squash, which were gradually becoming the mainstays of North American natives' diet. The agricultural surplus of these Mississippian peoples resulted in a hierarchical social order and made possible dense settlements featuring plazas and earthen pyramids topped by wooden temples. The most impressive of these cities, Cahokia, was located across the Mississippi River from present-day St. Louis. Inhabited by as many as 30,000 people, it remained the largest Indian settlement north of Mexico until it was abandoned in the thirteenth century. Its influence survived in the tidy cornfields, temple mounds, and proud chiefdoms that de Soto encountered.

EASTERN WOODLAND PEOPLES.   A fourth group, the Woodland peoples of the Atlantic seaboard of present-day United States and southeastern Canada, included the Micmacs and Algonquians Cartier met along the St. Lawrence River. These tribes combined hunting, fishing, and agriculture according to their local climate and geography. Most lived in semipermanent villages, often farming and fishing in the summer, and then moving in smaller bands to hunt in winter. Divided into scores of tribes and balancing their main food-producing activities with the season and local habitat, these peoples clustered into small societies speaking different languages and rent by ancient rivalries. The major exception was the Iroquois, a league of six tribes whose territory covered what is now northern New York and Pennsylvania. Sometime before Europeans arrived—perhaps around 1450—the Iroquois formed a political confederacy that suppressed tribal feuds, enforced territorial claims against outsiders, and developed a more elaborate code of ritual and village life. Because of their unity and physical prowess, and because their territory was positioned between French and English zones of settlement, the Iroquois would figure prominently in colonial wars.

HUNTER-GATHERERS OF THE NORTH AND NORTHWEST.   On the periphery of these four groups were clusters of other native peoples that lived farther from the path of European settlement. The hunter-gatherer and fishing societies of California and the Pacific Northwest lived in relative ease and abundance in small villages comprising many language groups. They would remain quite undisturbed until the late eighteenth century, when Spanish missionaries and Russian traders penetrated the region. Finally, along the arctic and subarctic zones of the continent's northern third, societies of hunting and fishing peoples who had crossed from Asia as recently as 3,000 years ago introduced bow-and-arrow technology to North America. As the continent's animal population declined and the fur trade moved northward, these peoples would also be drawn into Europe's economic orbit.

VARIATIONS AND CONNECTIONS.   Contrary to later stereotypes about "typical" Indians, native societies of North America were enormously varied. Their practices ranged from hunting and gathering to farming and craft production, and their languages and religions were more varied than those of Europeans. In the centuries prior to European invasion, however, their ways of life were becoming somewhat more uniform. By examining the remains of settlements and grave sites, archaeologists have learned that native societies were linked in extensive trading systems by which disparate tribes shared goods and customs. Indian peoples not only exchanged foods, textiles, and pottery; they also adopted tribal rituals and new technologies such as the flint hoe and the bow and arrow. Perhaps most significant, they learned from one another how to cultivate corn, squash, and beans, the most important North American crops.

During the first millennium C.E. the cultivation of corn (or maize) spread northeastward from Mexico into the Southwest and eventually reached the Eastern Woodland peoples. Not all Indian peoples adopted agriculture readily. Some hunter-gatherers preferred migratory ways, perhaps sensing that reliance upon crops risked famine or that living in towns promoted infectious diseases. Other native peoples lived on land too dry to farm. Where the climate was favorable, most Native American peoples adopted cultivation as one way to bolster food production and ensure survival. Farming had important social consequences, reshaping native societies into larger and more complex units. It supported population growth and the emergence of large, permanent communities with an intricate division of labor, more elaborate religious and political hierarchies, and even the beginnings of social classes.

INDIAN SOCIETIES IN FLUX.   Native American history shows no straight-line progression from the adoption of agriculture to increasingly complex societies. Hunter-gatherer groups on the Atlantic and Pacific coasts developed stable, hierarchical settlements without farming. Meanwhile, in the mid-1200s the great settlements at Chaco Canyon in the Southwest and Cahokia on the Mississippi experienced ecological crises and their inhabitants dispersed into small villages and chiefdoms. By the time Coronado and de Soto pushed inland, these peoples had reconstituted themselves into new societies, such as the Southeastern Coosa (whose descendents the English called "Creeks"), who rebuilt regional trade networks and negotiated shifting political alliances.

THE FIRST AMERICANS: WAYS AND WORLDVIEWS

Partly due to spreading agriculture and stepped-up intertribal contacts, by the 1530s most North American native societies shared broad common characteristics, all of which set them apart from the Europeans they encountered. The contrasts in ideas and practices were especially dramatic in five areas: nature and religion, land and property, society and the individual, sex roles, and political organization.

RELIGION AND NATURE.   Native Americans believed that nature was infused with spiritual forces rather than separate from them. Animism, the idea that supernatural power resided in features of the natural world, taught them to appease the spirits of animals, plants, or the clouds by honoring them in religious rituals and by minimizing damage or waste. Shamans, skilled dreamers and visionaries, were called upon to heal sickness or promote good weather by communing with the proper spirits. The rest of the tribe cooperated by organizing appropriate sacrifices and by practicing restraint. Overfishing waters or exploiting the land risked facing the revenge of the spirits guarding these places, because according to Indian beliefs, humans must not violate the interdependence of all beings.

Due to this animistic worldview, most native peoples aimed for physical sustenance through a stable relationship with their environment rather than production of a large surplus that tested its limits. Contrary to romantic myths, all Indian peoples were not ecological angels. Some scholars believe that ancient horses and mammoths became extinct in North America thousands of years ago because they were overhunted. Much later, great Mississippian cities like Cahokia put so much pressure on the regional ecology that they disintegrated when their population reached its limit, diseases began to spread, and the soil of nearby farms wore out. Still, Native Americans' sensitivity to ecological limits and their relatively mobile and decentralized settlements permitted them to sustain their habitats over many generations. Their animistic perspective also discouraged mechanical invention, teaching Indians to rely instead upon intimate knowledge of the behavior of plants, animals, and weather for survival. At the very least, Indians' relatively low levels of population and technological development limited the damage they could inflict upon the natural environment, compared to the European invaders.

PROPERTY AND SOCIETY.   Indian beliefs about land and property followed from their ethic of interdependence. Although tribes marked out territorial boundaries, within these limits they held land in common and often worked it collectively. According to native beliefs, rivers, forests, and plains were given by the spirits of creation to all. To emphasize this point, tribal leaders oversaw the distribution of food during shortages, and many tribes developed elaborate rituals of sharing, hospitality, and gift giving.

Putting a premium upon harmony and survival, Indian social arrangements stressed the success of the group more than the individual. Individuals were identified by lineage or village more than their accomplishments. Personal ambitions like those of hunters or warriors were channeled into producing benefits for the group. Because land belonged to the tribe or village, its products were shared widely and society was more egalitarian than in Europe. Ideally, all North American Indians had a clear and fixed place in the tribal world. Most belonged to small economic units based on kinship rather than ideology. Families grouped into clans that took on different social or ritual tasks, and clans then gathered into tribes led by leaders or chiefs, often advised by councils of elders.

SEX ROLES.   Women played an important and at times central role in Indian public life. In many cases family membership was identified through the mother in what is called a "matrilineal" pattern. Iroquois women chose the men who represented clans at larger tribal meetings, and among southeastern tribes, political succession devolved upon the eldest child of the chief's eldest sister, leading to a number of female chiefs. Within the family, women also had considerable power. When sons married they often joined their wife's household. Divorce was simple, often initiated by the wife, and the children remained with her family. Most tribes practiced a strict sexual division of labor, but one that was somewhat different from Europeans. Except in areas requiring extensive irrigation, women cultivated the crops and men hunted.

TRIBAL GOVERNMENT.   Lastly, at the time of the Europeans' arrival, North American natives were organized in small political units, none of which came close in size to the Aztec Empire of Mexico, the Inca kingdom of Peru, or the increasingly powerful nation-states of Europe. In most cases native peoples organized into tribes and chiefdoms to facilitate cohesion and group defense. Tribal leaders were not autocrats. Their authority was limited and they wielded it only as long as they maintained the people's confidence. Although Indian peoples engaged in frequent trading with outsiders, only in unusual cases of crisis or continual warfare did they form larger alliances like the Iroquois confederacy. Internally, native tribes were held together by obligations of kinship, oral traditions of religion and myth, and frequent performance of rites and ceremonies. These unwritten codes, so unlike the printed records, legal systems, and government bureaucracies of Europeans, left the impression among some invaders that Indians lived by no rules or regulations at all.

TRANSPLANTED AMERICANS: EUROPEAN WAYS AND WORLDVIEWS

The Spanish and other European invaders brought with them a way of life that was in many ways diametrically opposite. Point for point, European beliefs and behaviors contrasted with those of Native Americans in ways that made conflict likely if not inevitable.

RELIGION.   Whereas Indians populated their world with numerous gods and spirits, the Christian invaders were "monotheists," worshippers of one supremely powerful God. Certain that theirs was the only true God, Europeans tended to interpret Indian invocations to spirits as idolatry or devil worship and to see shamans as witches. Whether members of religious orders or devout laymen, many Europeans were infused with a missionary spirit to spread Christianity to "infidels" in order to save others from eternal damnation and to spread God's kingdom. This applied not only to heretics and nonbelievers inside Europe, but also to any peoples encountered along the Europeans' trading routes.

NATURE.   Just as Christianity urged followers to enlarge its earthly domain, its Creator commanded believers to multiply their numbers and to dominate nature. Unlike Indians, Christians believed in a god who is outside of the physical world and who decreed that humanity "subdue the Earth and have dominion over everything that moves," according to the biblical Book of Genesis. Rather than being enmeshed in a complex web of interdependence with nature, humans lived atop a hierarchy of living things, all of which were created for their use. Thus while European religion revolved around a deity positioned in heaven, in earthly matters it tended increasingly to adopt a human-centered (or "anthropocentric") perspective.

It was true that humans could not predict earthquakes, prevent floods, or control other "acts of God," but a scientific revolution that was developing in the age of exploration—and that made it possible—increased the confidence of Europeans that they could understand and eventually harness natural forces for human gain. Armed with such views, European colonizers regarded as backward most North American Indians' way of living lightly on the land. To Europeans, by not constructing permanent farms and cities the natives were neglecting their divine duty and forfeiting their right to possess the land. The idea that "savage" hunters and gatherers held inferior claims on the land to "civilized" peoples, a concept codified into international law by the Swiss jurist Emmerich Vattel, provided legal justification for Europeans to take over Indian lands.

PROPERTY AND ECONOMY.   Because nature was a resource to be exploited, Europeans willingly allotted land to individuals in parcels to be bought, sold, cultivated, built upon, or otherwise "improved." Increasingly in the early modern period, private ownership of property became a fundamental part of Europeans' vision of progress, and its absence among peoples like the Indians became synonymous with backwardness. Much of European economic and political life rested upon land ownership. Those who owned land commanded the labor of the landless and oversaw the production of surpluses that enriched themselves and provided crops and manufactured goods for others. Property ownership was the primary gauge of individual wealth and in many countries the first requirement for a voice in political affairs. A huge apparatus of laws, courts, and banks arose to facilitate property transfers and to adjudicate disputes, increasing the value of literacy and accurate record keeping.

Such arrangements produced accumulations of wealth unheard of in pre-contact North America, but they also created a huge gap between the rich and poor that was alien to most Native American societies. When Europeans adopted profit-maximizing ways of land ownership and extended them to other means of production—labor and capital—they moved gradually toward a less regulated capitalist economy. Many European voyages of exploration and colonization were undertaken as capitalist ventures, organized by merchants or individual entrepreneurs who sold shares in their enterprise to hopeful investors. As European capitalism evolved from royally granted privileges to freer competition, it rested increasingly on the belief that unrestricted individual enterprise would automatically contribute to the betterment of all—Adam Smith's famous "invisible hand." Capitalism's encouragement of individual initiative corresponded to Christianity's growing emphasis upon self-discipline, temperate habits, and worldly success—norms that sociologist Max Weber labeled the "Protestant Ethic." This convergence of sacred and secular thinking points to the growing individualism of early modern European society. Europeans increasingly viewed the individual as the basic unit of society and personal advancement as its motor. This, too, contrasts with the prevailing communalism of Native American ways.

SEX ROLES.   One major exception to this wide field of action for individuals was the tightly confined position prescribed for women in the European world. According to prevailing European ideals, men dominated women, and fathers controlled households. Although women could reign as monarchs in the absence of a male heir, ordinary women had severely limited legal rights and no political voice. In contrast to the relaxed bonds of Indian marriage, divorce was forbidden to European Catholics, so controversial that it precipitated the dramatic schism between the Churches of England and Rome during the reign of Henry VIII.

GOVERNMENTS.   Finally, unlike the limited, small-scale governments of North American peoples, Europeans increasingly organized their political life around large and powerful nation-states ruled by ambitious monarchs. In the fifteenth century the kings and queens of western Europe emerged as new focal points of power by absorbing small dukedoms and city-states into their realms. Accumulating territory and claiming to rule by divine right, the monarchs of Spain, Portugal, France, England, and other European nations built loyal bureaucracies and mighty armies and navies. After securing their rule at home, they looked outward for new lands to conquer and resources to exploit.

EUROPEAN TRANSFORMATIONS

The ambitious, expansionist impulse of European society, so different from the inward, communal concentration of most Native American peoples, suggests why Europeans reached the New World and Indians did not cross the Atlantic. But contrasting cultural attitudes cannot by themselves explain the encounter. Instead, a specific series of changes built with the basic cultural "toolkit" that Europeans shared revolutionized early modern Europe and propelled Europeans across the seas.

GROWING CHRISTIAN MILITANCY.   During the Middle Ages, the Catholic Church consolidated its power in western Europe, unifying diverse peoples and urging them to spread the true faith worldwide. Its most formidable rival was Islam, an equally expansionist religion whose followers (called Muslims) had exported their faith and Arab civilization from its

Middle Eastern home to faraway regions in Africa, India, eastern Europe, and Spain. Between 1095 and 1272 European Christians organized a series of military crusades aimed primarily at wresting the biblical Holy Land of Palestine from Muslim control. Only partly successful as military ventures, the Crusades had important effects upon Europeans. One result was to strengthen their leaders' religious fervor, goading them to persecute outsiders in their midst such as Jews and to convert—by force, if necessary—any new peoples they encountered. Among the Spanish, this heightened religious zeal produced a church-sponsored Inquisition against Jews and false converts and culminated in the conquest of Grenada in 1492, ending the seven-century Muslim occupation of southern Spain and uniting the nation under the Catholic monarchy of Ferdinand and Isabella.

The Spanish brought the crusading fervor and brutal military tactics of this "reconquest" to America. The *requerimiento* by which Coronado offered the Zunis the options of conversion or death differed little from the ultimatums that had been issued to Muslims in Spain. Like Columbus, the Spanish conquerors believed that new lands had been opened to them by God as a reward for their religious zeal and a challenge to expand Christianity's domain. Later European colonists, including French Jesuit missionaries and English Puritans, shared the desire to establish godly realms in the New World. In their case religious expansionism received an additional push from the Protestant Reformation, which after the 1520s produced an all-out contest between Protestants and Catholics for minds, hearts, and territory in the Christian and "heathen" worlds.

TRADE WITH ASIA AND AFRICA.   Another effect of the Crusades was to stimulate trade with distant lands. Through contacts with Arab traders and the post-Crusade voyage of Marco Polo to the Far East in 1295, Europeans learned of the gold and ivory of sub-Saharan Africa and the treasures offered by Asia: spices from the East Indies, silks and porcelains from China, and cottons and gems from India. In the thirteenth century, the city-states of northern Italy attained great wealth by importing these luxury goods through Arab middlemen based in eastern Mediterranean ports, then selling them throughout Europe. In the 1400s, however, expansion of the Turkish Ottoman Empire disrupted the Mediterranean paths to the East and imposed heavy taxes on goods passing through. Then in 1453 the Ottoman Turks captured Constantinople and closed overland trade routes to Christians. With eastern passages blocked, European merchants and monarchs began looking westward for a sea route by which they could bypass areas under Muslim control to reach sub-Saharan Africa and Asia.

PORTUGUESE SUCCESS.   Portugal and Spain, facing the Atlantic Ocean at the western end of Europe, emerged as prime ports of departure. The Iberian (Spanish and Portuguese) monarchs, enlisting the aid of experienced Italian mariners like Columbus, seized the opportunity. Led by Prince Henry, called "the Navigator" for his promotion of maritime science, Portuguese explorers sailed down the African coast and by 1488 around it to the Indian Ocean. Seizing control of key ports on the African coast and in India and China, they dominated maritime trade in the Indian Ocean basin for the next century, although they had relatively little impact on Asia's great land-based empires. Immediately after this Portuguese success, the Spanish monarchs appointed Columbus to search for a westerly route across the Atlantic to Asia.

SCIENTIFIC PROGRESS.   Advances in seafaring technology made such expeditions possible. The Portuguese made improvements upon navigational instruments of Chinese and Arab origins such as the magnetic compass and the astrolabe. The latter enabled mariners to deduce their locations at sea from the angle of the sun above the horizon. Maps and sea charts based upon Arab knowledge and Portuguese measurements provided accurate guides to the African coast. At Prince Henry's maritime institute, the Portuguese developed the caravel, a compact and versatile ship that combined the square-rigged (side-to-side) sails of European ocean vessels with the Arabs' triangular lateen (front-to-back) sails for maximum efficiency in all winds. As they ventured westward into Atlantic waters, Iberian mariners learned about the clockwise, circular pattern of prevailing winds that would eventually propel them, and thousands of people later, to and from the New World. Ironically, in addition to these advances it was Columbus's gross miscalculation of the earth's expanse that inspired his voyage. Misinterpreting a ninth-century Arab source, Columbus was convinced that Japan beckoned only 3,500 miles across ocean waters from Spain, when the actual distance was nearly four times as far.

IMPERIAL AND CAPITALIST RIVALRIES.   That Columbus eventually won the backing of Ferdinand and Isabella testifies to his dogged persistence. It also demonstrates how much monarchs of the age were willing to gamble to win the race for empire. Seeking support among the rising commercial classes against feudal nobles, these monarchs found that their own expansionist ambitions meshed with the profit motive of merchants in Europe's emerging capitalist economy. In Portugal, Spain, and England, monarchs increasingly relied upon mercantile investors and adventurers to underwrite voyages of exploration in exchange for royal licenses that

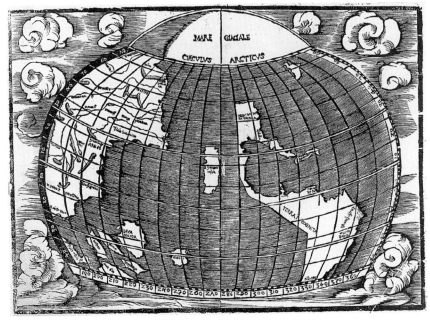

FIGURE 1-2   A EUROPEAN MAPS THE AMERICAS IN 1512
This map, prepared by the Polish cartographer Jan Stobnicza, shows that it took a long time
for geographers to realize the extent of the Americas and the Pacific Ocean. Note especially
the rudimentary state of knowledge about North America. Note also that "Cipangu"
(Japan) lies just west of Mexico, with the Asian mainland just beyond. (*Source: Used with
permission from* Traditions and Encounters *(2nd ed.), by Jerry H. Bentley and Herbert F. Ziegler.
Copyright 2002 by McGraw-Hill.*)

gave them territorial privileges and trade monopolies. In England, France,
and Holland, these royally chartered trading companies became powerful
players in national politics and international relations. Company agents
shared with their monarchs the "mercantilist" view that exploiting colonies
and reaping profits from foreign trade were the best way to build national
wealth (especially in gold and silver) as well as power.

Two consequences followed from this alliance of empire and capitalism, both of which boded ill for indigenous peoples in America and elsewhere. First, the fact that voyages of exploration and colonization were
intended to make profits increased the pressure on leaders to plunder
lands and exploit peoples they encountered. If gold and silver were not
available, explorers hoped to obtain marketable foods, furs, or other
crops and raw materials from natives and were willing to coerce their
labor to get them. From the Europeans' lust for colonial profits it was a
short step to the establishment of labor systems by which they exacted
tribute or enslaved native peoples. The desire to turn New World

colonies into sources of European profit and power ensured that what began as cultural clashes between natives and newcomers often ended in deadly combat.

A second result of the rise of mercantilist kingdoms was fierce competition among European nations for imperial supremacy. Begun as a race to corner the trade with Asia and Africa, European expansion developed into a contest over acquiring colonial territory, especially in the New World. Portugal and Spain, enjoying a head start over other western European powers, divided the New World between them through the Treaty of Tordesillas negotiated by the Pope in 1494. This arrangement confirmed Portuguese supremacy in the Indian Ocean but left all of the Americas to Spain—except Brazil, where Portuguese explorers had wandered from the African coast. Other European nations also looked westward. The French, as we have seen, sent Cartier to the St. Lawrence in the 1530s. More interested in trade than conquest, in 1564 they also established an outpost at Fort Caroline on the Florida coast. The French threat led Spain's King Philip II to renew colonization efforts in Florida, where a Spanish contingent established the port of St. Augustine in 1565, and to authorize an expedition to invade and destroy Fort Caroline.

CATHOLIC-PROTESTANT RIVALRY. Armed conflict between Spanish settlers and the Florida colony of Huguenots—French Protestants seeking refuge in the New World—demonstrated that as the Reformation spread, the imperial contest became entwined with the deadly enmity between Catholic and Protestant powers. England, Spain's chief rival in the Catholic-Protestant confrontation, countered Spanish claims to coastal North America by citing the voyage of John Cabot, a Genoese mariner who had mapped the Atlantic coast from Newfoundland to Massachusetts for the British king in 1497. However, for several decades the British did little to follow up on Cabot's explorations.

SPAIN'S DEFEAT. Nearly a century after Columbus, the English modestly entered the colonial race in the 1580s when a group of noblemen and adventurers established a short-lived settlement at Roanoke Island in Carolina. Angered by England's ambitions and determined to end its Protestant monarchy, Philip II sent a huge fleet to invade England directly. This Spanish Armada met a disastrous defeat off British shores in 1588, wrecked by a violent storm and outmaneuvered by swifter British ships. The Spanish monopoly in the New World was broken. Weakened by warfare and consoling themselves that North America had little to offer Europeans, the Spanish after 1600 grudgingly conceded settlement north of Florida and east of Texas to the French, British, and Dutch.

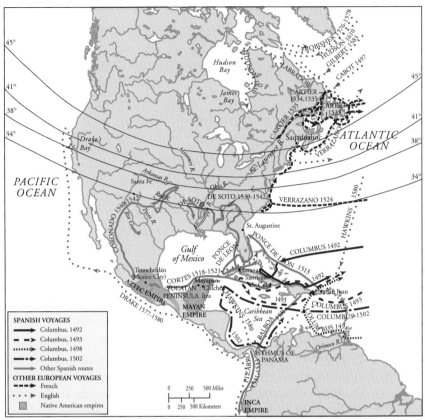

FIGURE 1-3   EUROPEAN EXPLORATION AND CONQUEST, 1492–1583
This maps shows the many voyages of exploration to and conquest of North America
launched by Europeans in the late fifteenth and sixteenth centuries. Note how Columbus
and the Spanish explorers who followed him tended to move quickly into the lands of
Mexico, the Caribbean, and Central and South America, while the English and French
explored the Atlantic coast of North America. Not until the 1530s did the Spanish and
French begin to penetrate the North American interior. (*Source: Used with permission from
American History (11th ed.), by Alan Brinkley. Copyright 2003 by McGraw-Hill.*)

COMPARATIVE PERSPECTIVES ON BRITISH COLONIALISM

Each of the European rivals developed different colonization plans, which
affected natives and newcomers in divergent ways. Historians often contrast the Spanish, French, and English New World frontiers as empires of
conquest, trade, and settlement, respectively. They portray the Spanish
forcing Indians onto mines and estates run by colonial elites, the French
exchanging furs with hunting tribes at trading posts, and the British pushing back Indians from the path of expanding white settlements. Of course,
each nation's imperial plans involved a combination of conquest, trade,

and settlement. Yet these activities had varying importance for each and were pursued in ways that were similar in some cases and unique in others. In North America, the British adopted the Spanish precedent of plantation slavery, but they also developed a distinctive variety of settler colonialism that supplanted the continent's native population and sowed the seeds of eventual self-rule.

ENGLAND'S LATE START

England was the last of the European powers facing the Atlantic to colonize the New World. Technological backwardness was one reason. The English lagged behind the Portuguese and Spanish in mastering the sea. The clockwise pattern of Atlantic winds sent ships effortlessly from the Iberian Peninsula to the Caribbean, but blew in the face of British seamen heading west to North America. It took decades for them to learn the safest transatlantic routes. English shipbuilders also gradually adopted Portuguese designs and modified them for guns, creating "galleons" that combined the firepower of Venetian galleys with the caravel's speed and maneuverability.

A BACKWARD BRITAIN.   There were deeper reasons for England's delayed entry into New World colonizing. Politically and economically, England of the early 1500s was too weak to marshal the required resources. England's population of 3 million in 1500 was far below that of Spain or France. The king had no standing army and a tiny navy, and his power was restricted by large landowners. The Tudor monarchs' alliance with Spain, cemented by Henry VIII's marriage to Catherine of Aragon, gave English merchants limited trading rights in the Spanish New World but inhibited English attempts to establish independent colonies.

By the late 1500s this situation changed, due in part to the Protestant Reformation, whose English outbreak Henry VIII triggered when he divorced Catherine without the Pope's consent, seized church properties, and had himself proclaimed head of the Church of England in 1534. England's conversion to Protestantism stimulated nationalist sentiments, broke the alliance with Spain, and set the nation on a collision course with that stronghold of Catholicism.

Ambitious and able, Henry and his daughter Elizabeth centralized the monarchy's bureaucracy, regularized the Crown's relationship with Parliament, and courted urban merchants as their allies against landed nobles. New laws reduced welfare assistance and set low wages, and bonuses were given to manufacturers who penetrated foreign markets. Elizabeth I granted exclusive trade privileges to merchant companies for exporting cloth to Russia and the Middle East or importing spices from the Far East.

This system of government-supported trade and manufacturing increased exports, enriched the merchant community, and filled the royal treasury with import revenues. Merchant capital and royal funds became available for overseas expansion. Finally, between 1530 and 1650, England's population doubled, in part because new crops from the New World were introduced at home. This population boom decreased opportunities for commoners at home, providing surplus laborers for overseas migration.

THE NORTHWEST PASSAGE.   By the last quarter of the sixteenth century the foundation was laid for England's entry into the colonial race. Still, the British had to give up two persistent delusions that Europeans imposed upon the New World. Like the French, the English initially viewed North America as little more than an obstacle on the way to the coveted spices and goods of the Far East. Both nations wasted decades searching for a "Northwest Passage" that would permit ships to sail through the continent to Asia. Although explorers continued to search for this imaginary waterway in the 1600s, after the failures of Martin Frobisher, John Davis, and Sir Humphrey Gilbert to discover it in the 1570s and 1580s, English merchants turned their attention to establishing settlements on the North American coast.

GOLD FEVER AND PRIVATEERING.   Even then, England's North American ports were intended less as permanent settlements than as bases to support British ambitions in the Caribbean, mostly raiding Spanish settlements and ships for gold. Like the Spanish before them, the English suffered from gold fever, believing in legends of "El Dorado," hidden troves of glittering ore, or New World cities of gold. Lust for gold sent Richard Grenville and Francis Drake on expeditions to South America in the 1570s. The patent granted to the Virginia proprietors anticipated the discovery of "Mynes of Goulde, Silver, and Copper," prompting the first arrivals to squander time on futile digs. While the Spanish found rich veins of gold and silver in Peru and Mexico, England's hopes failed to pan out.

In frustration, English seamen took to piracy. After Spain's Indian slaves extracted gold and silver from Andean and Mexican mines, English pirates stole the treasure from Spanish ships sailing homeward through the Caribbean. Elizabeth I legalized this practice as "privateering" (privatized naval warfare) in return for a share of the plunder and offered knighthoods to those who succeeded. During near-constant warfare with Spain from 1585 to 1604, the English sent scores of ships each year to harass Spanish vessels in the Caribbean and attack those using Iberian ports. Privateers such as Sir Francis Drake, Sir John Hawkins, and Sir Henry Morgan siphoned off as much as a third of the gold heading across the Atlantic from the New World. Once England suspended privateering in

1604, its proceeds helped to finance colonies. Permanent English colonization dates from this period, starting at Jamestown (1607), Plymouth (1620) and Massachusetts Bay (1630) in North America and Barbados (1627) in the Caribbean.

NORTH AMERICA AS LEFTOVER LAND.   One consequence of England's late start was its concentration on North America. By the time the English staked New World claims, the Spanish and Portuguese had taken the portions of the hemisphere most valuable for the precious minerals and exotic crops Europeans craved. Far from the great "prize" of 1600, North America was (in the words Columbus biographer Felipe Fernandez-Armesto) the "dregs" of European exploration. The English hoped that if the continent had no gold, it could at least replace imports from the Mediterranean and Asia. Colonization advocates like the elder Richard Hakluyt predicted that in Virginia the English would produce the olives, wines, and spices they ordinarily purchased from Spanish, Portuguese, and Dutch traders. Like the visions of golden cities, these promises vanished shortly after the colonists arrived.

It took decades to find valuable exports that could sustain permanent settlements. New England colonists relied upon furs, timber, and fish. Hampered by rocky soil and a harsh climate, they survived by becoming a seafaring people like their British forebears. Their shipbuilding, fishing, and carrying trade contributed little to the mother country, and in fact competed with it. English settlers in Virginia solved their export problem only when they discovered tobacco. Far and away the richest British colonies in the 1600s were tiny islands in the Caribbean, such as Barbados, which the Spanish had overlooked, and Jamaica, which the English wrested from Spain in 1655. English landowners who established sugar plantations on these islands reaped immense profits, and their crops became the most valuable export from British America for the next century and a half.

THE BRITISH EMPIRE AS IMITATOR

Another consequence of England's late start was its extensive borrowing. Trailing in the wake of Spanish conquests and Portuguese and Dutch trading successes, the British built their empire largely through imitation.

"INVENTING" THE NEW WORLD.   Their belief in American cities of gold demonstrates how the English inherited the Spanish habit of "inventing" the New World as much as "discovering" it. Since the Middle Ages, Europeans had fantasized about lost kingdoms and magnificent islands to the west. After Columbus the Americas became repositories for the hopeful

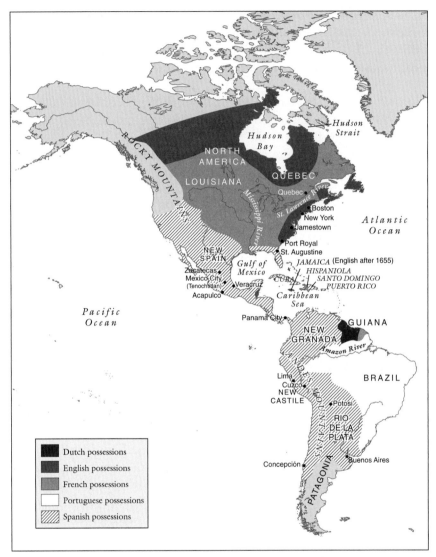

FIGURE 1-4   EUROPEAN EMPIRES AND COLONIES IN THE AMERICAS, C. 1700
Source: Used with permission from Traditions and Encounters *(2nd ed.), by Jerry H. Bentley and*
Herbert F. Ziegler. Copyright 2002 by McGraw-Hill.

dreams of European philosophers, theologians, and entrepreneurs.
Whether they embodied residual memories of the Garden of Eden, the
idea that the Americas had been providentially opened to Europeans (and
their native peoples destroyed) in order to propagate Christianity, or the
notion of the New World as a blank slate upon which the social contract
could be redrawn, such expectations were imposed upon the American
landscape by European newcomers. First the Spanish then the English

erased native place names and gave their settlements the names of Christian saints (San Francisco and Saint John), fresh starts (New Spain and New England), heavenly blessings (Providenciales and Providence), and mythical or projected arcadias (Valparaiso [Valley of Paradise] and Philadelphia [City of Brotherly Love]).

CONQUERING INDIGENOUS PEOPLES.   Visions of a new and improved version of Europe encouraged Europeans who drew up plans for godly towns and model governments to reject native peoples' claims to the land. The English learned from the Spanish experience that Native Americans could be subjugated and dispossessed.

The "Black Legend" promoted by Protestant historians well into the twentieth century proclaimed that the Spanish practiced deliberate and exceptional cruelty toward the New World's natives. In truth, English conquerors were often just as brutal. If the devastation they caused appeared less sweeping, this was mainly for lack of opportunity. Less developed and densely settled than lands farther south, North America lacked native empires and cities to sack. And by the time the English arrived, diseases that Spanish explorers and traders unwittingly introduced among North American natives had done much of their deadly work.

FRONTIER WARFARE.   Many English settlers professed a desire to get along with the natives. Especially during their tiny settlements' vulnerable first years, England's North American colonists learned to forge strategic agreements that assured peace with neighboring Indians. The colonists promised natives assistance against common foes, whether other native societies or European rivals like the Dutch or French. But when expanding English settlements intruded on native villages and hunting grounds, frontier skirmishing broke out and at times erupted into large-scale warfare. King Philip's War (1675–76), waged between Massachusetts settlers and a coalition of tribes led by the Wampanoag chief Metacom—labeled a king by the English—left a thousand New England colonists dead, more than six percent of their adult males. (The ratio of whites' deaths to their total population made this the deadliest conflict in American history.) Several thousand Indians died when the English settlers rallied to defeat them. For the next century, until the Indian population decreased in numbers and proximity, Britain's mainland colonists felt threatened. The first attempts to provide a unified government for the thirteen colonies in the 1750s were spurred by the need to cooperate against Indian attacks on the western frontier.

INDIANS AS COERCED LABORERS.   The combined impact of war and disease upon native peoples meant that the Europeans killed off potential laborers.

Spanish colonial authorities exacted tribute in the form of minerals or crops from conquered peoples, and colonial estate holders relied heavily on coerced natives to work their mines, ranches, and plantations. As Indians died off, the Spanish became more desperate. Coronado and de Soto conducted slave raids on the North American coast, Spanish missions on the North American frontier used Indian converts to raise cattle and corn, and captives in South American wars against native peoples were brought to the Caribbean to harvest sugar.

The first English colonizers hoped to duplicate Spain's economic success by exploiting native peoples for England's gain and their own. Britons who arrived at Roanoke Island in Carolina in 1585 tried to force local Indians to feed them and killed their chief when he refused. Twenty-five years later, Sir Thomas Gates was appointed governor of Virginia with instructions to conquer nearby Indians and render them English tributaries, compelled to make annual payments of corn and animal skins and to serve prescribed terms of labor. In both cases, the tiny settler population made such demands impossible to enforce. Not surprisingly, their attempts led to Indian reprisals.

In general, English colonists came to dislike the idea of using Indians as farm workers. Some believed that native peoples were physically inferior and unsuited to agricultural life. Others sought to avoid racial intermixture or pagan influence. Most important, English settlers feared that Indian workers would escape or invite retaliation from nearby tribal warriors. The solution applied in several mainland colonies, again borrowed from the Spanish, was to sell Indian captives into slavery elsewhere. Such was the fate of Metacom's wife and son, whom the victorious New Englanders sent to the West Indies. In Carolina and the southern colonies this practice became widespread. Intertribal warfare, growing Indian dependence upon European products, and the lure of profits from the sale of slaves encouraged its expansion. One study estimates that between 1670 and 1715, perhaps 40,000 southeastern Indians were captured, transferred to British colonists, then sold as slaves, mainly to West Indian sugar planters.

THE PLANTATION SYSTEM.   After they acquired Caribbean and mainland colonies, the British controlled agricultural lowlands where they could produce tropical staples for the European market. By the 1600s the Spanish, Portuguese, and Dutch had exploited similar lands in the Caribbean and South America, and the English learned from their precedent. The first British-run sugar business in Barbados was modeled on the Dutch enterprise in Pernambuco, Brazil. Dutch émigrés from Brazil taught the British how to grow sugar, supplied them with slaves, and controlled the marketing of their crop. Thanks to the sugar boom, Barbados and Jamaica became the richest of Britain's New World colonies.

What sugar did for the British Caribbean, tobacco—another crop transplanted from Latin America—accomplished for England's Chesapeake colonies. Since the native Virginia weed proved too harsh for Europeans, John Rolfe introduced "Spanish tobacco" from the West Indies in 1614. As tobacco production expanded in the second half of the seventeenth century, Virginia and Maryland began to resemble Caribbean plantation societies. Because their capital-intensive agriculture required large landholdings and heavy investment, both the British West Indies and the Chesapeake region produced huge disparities of wealth and became dominated by a powerful planter elite. The prevalence of large tracts owned by a hereditary class that benefited from unfree labor likened these plantation societies more to Brazil and the Spanish West Indies than to England or New England.

FROM INDENTURED SERVANTS TO AFRICAN SLAVES.   For a few decades, English planters relied upon white indentured servants to grow sugar and tobacco. Young men and women, forced to migrate by poverty and sometimes even kidnapped by procurers, were bound to a master for four to seven years in return for the cost of passage and a basic allowance of food, clothing, and shelter. Gradually, however, the indenture system declined in plantation zones. Harsh working conditions and the unhealthy lowland climate killed European workers in great numbers, prompted several rebellions, and discouraged additional white laborers from coming. Good local land became less available to servants who completed their terms in Virginia or on small tropical islands, while more generous terms and milder weather beckoned them to colonies further north, such as Pennsylvania.

As indentures plummeted, English planters turned to African slave laborers as their mainstay. The English knew that Latin American plantations had thrived using slaves, and once Dutch merchants broke Portugal's virtual monopoly on the African slave trade in the 1620s, English planters became their customers. A half-century later England formally joined the slave trade when the Royal African Company, chartered by Charles II, was given a monopoly on all English commerce with West Africa. Soon it built several forts and trading posts on the African coast where British manufactures were exchanged for slaves. By 1700 the Royal African Company and its independent British competitors became the largest carriers of slaves from Africa to the New World.

A detailed comparison between colonial British and Latin American slavery will be presented in later chapters. For now it is enough to note that the British slave system continued basic Spanish and Portuguese practices. As determined by Europeans, slaves' legal status as both persons and property lasted for their lifetimes and was passed on to children by their mothers. Slaves were bought, sold, punished, separated from family members, and even sexually assaulted within an accumulating framework of custom and law that gave enormous power to their masters. Most were put to work on large plantations growing staple crops such as sugar and tobacco, and later rice and cotton, for the world market.

In all these essentials, English colonial planters followed their predecessors. In fact, slaves brought from Africa to the Carolinas or Virginia had often been "seasoned," or introduced to plantation labor, in the West Indies. Stretching from Brazil northward to Virginia, slavery and the plantation system gave the warm coastal regions and tropical islands of the New World a broadly similar appearance. Economies of scale encouraged large landholdings where a few planters reaped fantastic profits and lived in luxurious "Big Houses" while slaves toiled long hours, and poor whites and free blacks sought a niche in the local economy. Especially in the Caribbean zone, a high proportion of African slaves to European settlers, the survival of African religions and customs, and the presence of mixed black and white offspring (called mulattoes in the British colonies) characterized the population of sugar islands, whether they were colonized by England or Spain.

BRITISH SETTLER COLONIALISM

At the same time, key differences between English and other European colonial arrangements were present at the outset, especially in the mainland colonies, and they became increasingly significant. Contrasts in population patterns and governance structures were most noticeable. Imperial policies and conditions in the European homelands combined to make most British New World holdings "settler colonies" dominated by a white European majority and most Iberian lands "exploitation colonies" where the large native and African population was ruled by small numbers of European settlers. In addition, England's heavy reliance upon private enterprise and its evolving tradition of parliamentary rule gave its North American settlers greater control over colonial resources and governance.

COLONIAL REHEARSALS: THE WINE ISLANDS AND IRELAND.   Before the Europeans settled lands across the Atlantic, they created the molds for their New World colonies by colonizing islands closer to their shores. Nearby imperial ventures became rehearsals for the conquest and settlement of distant territories.

The Iberian model was taken from the Portuguese occupation of uninhabited Madeira in the 1440s and the Spanish seizure of the Canaries from its native population in the 1490s. These Atlantic island groups lay within two weeks' sailing of Iberian ships that followed prevailing winds downward along the West African coast. On Madeira, Portuguese colonists owning huge estates began to grow sugar cane, transplanted from the Middle East, for export to the European mainland. In the 1450s and 1460s they replaced their Jewish and Muslim laborers (prisoners from Iberia's religious wars) with slaves brought from Africa, and Madeira became the Atlantic world's first full-fledged plantation colony. Following Portugal's example, Spain converted the Canaries to sugar cultivation, sending captured natives (called *Guanches*) to Madeira as slaves in exchange for African bondsmen. Together, Madeira and the Canaries became known as the Wine Islands because much of their sugar was used to make the popular sweet wine sold as "Madeira" around the world.

On the Wine Islands, the Iberian powers learned how a small force of invading colonists could become wealthy by conquering native peoples, transplanting tropical staple crops coveted by Europeans, and importing African slaves as workers. There the system of large-scale cultivation through plantation slavery was developed that would predominate in Brazil and the Caribbean for centuries. In all essentials—except for exploiting the native peoples' labor or mixing with them—the Wine Islands experience provided an influential template for the Spanish and Portuguese New World.

THE ENGLISH IN IRELAND.   England's alternative model derived from the colonization of Ireland in the late 1500s. Because Ireland was peopled by Catholics and located less than 60 miles west of England, English monarchs feared that it could become a beachhead for Spanish or French attacks and resolved to subjugate it. Beginning in the 1560s, Elizabeth I licensed a series of private expeditions that destroyed Irish villages and killed thousands of inhabitants. Sir Humphrey Gilbert and Sir Walter Raleigh, veterans of these brutal campaigns, used their Irish experience to shape their colonizing plans for North America.

Two important precedents were set in Ireland that would influence British colonization in North America. First, English prejudice against Irish "savages" was transferred to Native Americans. Since the rural Irish were poor, seminomadic Celts with a tribal form of social organization, the English regarded them as a wild, barbarous people to be subdued by any means necessary. Against resisters, the English conquerors used brutal techniques that would later be employed against American Indians, from the massacre of women and children to enslavement or consignment to special reservations. Little thought was given to converting the Irish to Protestant Christianity.

Second, in Ireland the English adopted the practice of colonizing through migration and settlement. Once the conquerors seized Irish lands, they recruited Protestant peasants from England and Scotland to replace the Irish, who were driven out wholesale from many of Ireland's counties. Besides securing Ireland for England and Protestantism, this migration brought other benefits. English merchants hoped to make profits from large tenant farms established in the colony, and peopling these lands provided an outlet for England's surplus population. The idea that the most desirable form of colonization involved establishing self-contained settlements of English migrants rather than mixing with or employing the local population was transferred directly to America, where the colonists at Jamestown and Massachusetts Bay built English-style farms and villages and separated themselves from native peoples.

BRITISH SETTLER COLONIALISM.   Except for large tenant farms, which were tried out and quickly abandoned, the practices of English colonialism in Ireland were replicated in North America. In contrast to Spanish and Portuguese lands, permanent European settlers predominated in the British colonies. Fewer than 250,000 Spaniards migrated during the first century of Latin American colonization. By comparison, more than 700,000 settlers came to the colonies from the British Isles in the 1600s, spurred by the movement to consolidate rural farms for commercial production (called "enclosure"), by religious persecution, and by the dislocations of civil war between royalists and parliament. Their numbers grew more rapidly than those of Europeans in Latin America because of a much lower death rate and the wider availability of land. By 1750, despite Britain's late start, there were five times more British than Spanish settlers in the New World.

English migrants came to stay and tried to re-create their former way of life as much as possible. In North America as in Ireland, British colonizing was a family affair. Colonists migrated in cohesive groups, sometimes with friends, relatives, or co-religionists from nearby English villages. British settlements featured a relatively even male-female sex ratio. Spanish and Portuguese migrants to New World colonies tended to be male soldiers or adventurers—only about a quarter were female—and the majority took marriage partners from the native or African slave population, creating a huge mixed-race element of the population. By contrast, British colonists found marriage partners inside the group and re-created family life and community life according to norms inherited from Europe. Even in North American colonies where plantation slavery took root, white settlers outnumbered African slaves, unlike most European colonies in the Caribbean. The exception was South Carolina, initially an offshoot of Barbados, where the population structure tilted toward the sugar islands' black-white ratios (1.5 to 1, compared to 3.7 to 1 in the British West Indies).

INDIAN REMOVAL AND REPLACEMENT

On the North American frontier, another feature distinguished British colonizing from that of the Catholic European powers: the settlers' relentless pushing aside of indigenous peoples.

INDIAN MISSIONS. On their northern frontier in New Mexico, Florida, and later in California, the Spanish used Franciscan missions as footholds in Indian territory and as buffers against other European powers. French Jesuits achieved some success spreading the Christian gospel among Hurons in the Great Lakes region. But missions to Indians were less common among the English. Their Protestant churches lacked inspiring rituals and Old World financial and institutional support. Bent upon doctrinal purity, the radical Protestants who settled much of British North America did not share Catholics' willingness to blend native religious practices into Christianity. For a brief time Puritan ministers in Massachusetts established more than a dozen "praying towns" where over 2,000 Indians were instructed in Protestant doctrine and British customs. But in New England and especially in colonies further south, the burgeoning British colonial population was more intent upon winning Indians' land than their souls.

THE "MIDDLE GROUND." On some colonial borderlands, greater parity in population and power between natives and newcomers, the desire to trade with Indians, and the presence of rival European powers created a situation in which Indian tribes exerted more autonomy and Europeans met them halfway. The best example of this "middle ground," as historian Richard White calls it, was the region around the Great Lakes in the upper Midwest and Canada. There, competition for the fur trade moved French agents, and to a lesser extent their English rivals, into alliances that recognized native peoples' territorial rights and practiced intercultural diplomacy in the form of reciprocal gift-giving and ethnic intermarriage. A similar borderland existed for a time in the lower Missouri Valley, where Spain, France, and England competed for Indian allies and goods.

INDIAN REPLACEMENT. When British military victories forced Spain and France to relinquish imperial claims east of the Mississippi during the 1700s, English settlers overran western lands and fluid colonial borderlands gave way to firm intergroup boundaries. The middle ground became divided ground. As their settlements grew through migration and natural increase, British colonists saw little need to use Indians as laborers or take them as marriage partners, unlike the Spanish in Mexico, the Portuguese in Brazil, or the French in Canada. By the late 1700s, British settlers had killed or cleared out the majority of Native Americans east of the Mississippi; by contrast, despite the fearful toll from disease, Indians still accounted for about 70 percent of Latin America's population. In the Spanish colonies, natives and slaves outnumbered Spanish and mixed-descent residents by more than five to one; the comparable ratio in British North America was three to one in white colonists' favor.

British settler colonialism reconstituted North America as a continent peopled by European whites to a degree not possible in lands south of the Rio Grande. (Only when large numbers of European migrants pushed into the sparsely populated temperate lands of Uruguay, Argentina, and Chile in the nineteenth century did Latin American "white settler societies" comparable to British North America emerge.) During the colonial era, historian Niall Ferguson has written, "New England really was a new England, far more than New Spain would ever be a new Spain."[2]

SETTLER LANDHOLDING AND SELF-GOVERNMENT

England's peopling—or more accurately, *re*peopling—of North America with settlers meant that migrants transplanted patterns of landholding and ideas of constitutional government from the home country. The colonies' dispersed landholding and representative government reflected trends toward greater individual freedom that were already at work in England. Both contrasted with Spain's New World practices, laying the groundwork for the divergent social and political careers of the British and Spanish colonies.

LEAVING FEUDALISM BEHIND.   Spain's colonists sought to construct New World societies based on familiar Old World feudal institutions. They envisioned society as a stable vertical hierarchy of classes governed by an aristocratic elite anointed by royal authority. Under the *encomienda* system, Spanish monarchs granted huge tracts of land to New World conquerors or court favorites whose privileges included ownership of Indian labor. This system broke down as the natives died off from disease, but a general pattern continued whereby leading families who owned vast plantations, estates, and mines controlled the colonial economy and reduced natives and mixed-race peoples to wage laborers or dependent tenants.

---

[2]Niall Ferguson, *Empire: The Rise and Decline of the British World Order and the Lessons for Global Power* (New York: Basic Books, 2004), 54.

Lacking the Spanish Crown's wealth and its feudal privileges, English monarchs turned to urban merchants, private investors, and loyal landowners to support New World colonizing. Private joint-stock groups such as the Massachusetts Bay and Virginia Companies and individual proprietors such as Lord Baltimore and William Penn (the founders of Maryland and Pennsylvania, respectively) were given the right to settle and develop New World lands. Although some proprietors tried to transplant feudal estates and rents, these arrangements did not last. Resistance from settlers, availability of land elsewhere, and proprietors' own hopes of attracting taxpaying workers doomed feudal experiments in Britain's seaboard colonies. Instead, family farms and businesses dominated the colonial economy, and nearly two-thirds of the colonies' white settlers were indentured servants, many of whom became small landowners after completing their terms. Britain's reliance upon large numbers of settlers and its departure from feudal landholding practices diffused property ownership widely among white colonists, creating broad opportunities for economic advancement as well as laying the foundation for representative government.

SEEDS OF SELF-GOVERNMENT.   In the *conquistadors'* wake, the Spanish Crown moved quickly to assert royal authority over native peoples and the settler minority. Spain established a huge imperial bureaucracy that reached into all aspects of colonial governance. Established in 1524, the royal Council of the Indies supervised government, church, and commercial activity in the Spanish New World. Its regulations determined colonial matters from large trade questions down to the appointment of local officials and the layout of new towns. In the next two decades the viceroyalties of New Spain, with its capital in Mexico City, and Peru, with its capital in Lima, were formed and then subdivided into judicial and administrative districts ruled by appointed officials sent from the home country. Taxes from colonial gold and silver production funded an elaborate and intrusive network of overseers that subjected colonies to the decrees of Spanish rulers and discouraged local initiative.

British colonial governance was less uniform and centralized. Distracted by religious strife and civil war between king and Parliament at home, English monarchs of the early 1600s paid little attention to New World colonizing. Even if they had, lack of resources and limits on their power meant that they could not duplicate Spain's expensive overseas bureaucracy. Colonial governance varied widely in North America, depending on the colony's origins as a corporate, proprietary, or royal venture. In most places, however, British settlers took advantage of their isolation to establish local assemblies elected by landowners. After England's domestic wars ended with the "Glorious Revolution" of 1688, when Protestant rulers William and Mary were seated firmly on the throne, the majority of North American colonies were placed directly under the Crown. Yet the prerogatives of royally appointed governors and officials were fiercely contested by settlers. Britain's ongoing struggle between king and parliament had its counterpart in North America: just as Parliament compelled England's kings to concede it supremacy, the colonists pressured British authorities to recognize their elected local assemblies. These deliberative bodies, ironically expanding simultaneously with slavery, distinguished Britain's North American colonies from those of other European powers. Thanks to widespread land ownership, lax imperial supervision, and evolving constitutional ideas, white males in the thirteen seaboard colonies enjoyed a greater degree of political power than colonists in New Spain or even Englishmen at home. The consequences of their relative political and economic freedom would become apparent only in the 1700s, when imperial wars and economic plans pushed Britain to tighten control over its transatlantic possessions.

ECOLOGICAL IMPERIALISM AND THE POST-COLUMBIAN EXCHANGE

From the moment Old World explorers set foot in the New World, there began a mutual transfer of diseases, plants, and animals that historians have labeled "The Columbian Exchange." Since it continued for centuries after 1492 we might more accurately call it the Post-Columbian Exchange. The people of the eastern and western hemispheres had lived in biological as well as cultural isolation from one another for thousands of years. Evolving separately, their ecosystems developed widely different forms of plant, animal, and germ life. Full-scale European exploration changed everything rapidly. Whether by accident or deliberately, the exchange of life forms between Old and New Worlds transformed human existence in both places, bringing benefits but also disasters. In ways no one could foresee, this contact became a matter of life and death for millions of humans on both sides of the Atlantic.

COMPARING THE AMERICAS

In this transfer of plants, animals, and germs, North America and its colonists played a secondary role compared to the Caribbean and South America. Because southerly regions were the first landfall for European sailors, Spain and Portugal's explorers became the first Europeans to taste New World foods and to offload their animals and diseases. Columbus himself took such an active part in this exchange that it deserves to include his name. On his second expedition to the Caribbean (1493), his men brought along horses, cattle, sheep, dogs, pigs, chickens, and goats and such plants as sugar cane, onions, and banana trees. Here was a transcontinental ecological invasion so swift and sweeping that it may never be matched.

Other factors besides timing made the North American theater of exchange less dramatic. Because its native population was smaller and more scattered than that of Central and South America, the lethal impact of Eurasian germs was less swift and obvious, linked to the gradual process of settlement rather than the sudden conquest of cities and civilizations. Tropical and semitropical areas surrounding the Caribbean produced a greater variety of foods that were unavailable in Europe. Mesoamerican and Andean Indians were the world's best breeders of food plants: over the course of centuries they had domesticated corn, potatoes, beans, and squashes, crops that proved useful to Europeans and were widely adopted abroad. North American Indians, lacking native food plants suitable for breeding, tended to follow southern agricultural innovations. Finally, the tropical regions of America had ideal conditions for growing valuable non-native foods that Europeans formerly obtained by trade with Asia and Africa. Citrus fruits, bananas, sugar cane, and coffee could be raised on Caribbean plantations where Europeans controlled production and reaped the profits themselves.

NORTH AMERICA'S ROLE.   By comparison, North America seemed to have little new or important to offer Europeans. When traders and settlers came to the mainland, they sent back fish, furs, and timber to the Old World. The fur trade fueled the Anglo-French rivalry, and New World timber built Europeans' oceangoing ships, but only fish had a significant impact on lifestyles or life expectancies abroad. In general, North America's similarity to Europe in climate and geography made it a less useful source than southerly regions for marketable products. Only when tobacco was cultivated there in the 1600s, and cotton a century later, did North America's value as an exporter of new crops become clear.

In the long run, however, the North American sector of exchange became crucially important. As in regions further south, Eurasian germs weakened natives' resistance to white invaders, even though some tribes used animals and technology borrowed from Europe—horses and guns— to defend themselves. But unlike the tropics, where small numbers of Europeans relied on imported slaves to do the work, European settlers found North America's temperate climate congenial and they came in droves. Heavy reliance upon white immigrants allowed Europeans eventually to make over much of North America in the image of their homeland. In the United States and southern Canada, as in other "neo-Europes" such as Australia and Argentina, Europeans accomplished a massive transplanting of their biological forms and ways of life. More than in the tropics, indigenous plants and animals were overwhelmed by imported species just as Indians were moved aside for white settlements. By the 1800s, Europeans in temperate zones were growing familiar protein foods like wheat and beef, and the neo-Europes had become the richest New World societies. Their success helped to extend the domination of the global economy by Europeans and their descendants into the twenty-first century.

THE IMPACT OF DISEASE

The first contacts between Old and New World inhabitants were the most catastrophic because Europeans carried a host of silent and invisible microbes that set about ravaging Native American communities immediately. European germs became epidemic killers in the New World, accidental allies of the conquest. Europeans had been exposed to epidemic diseases over thousands of years and developed the antibodies to withstand or survive them, but Native Americans, isolated in an environment that lacked lethal infectious diseases (except tuberculosis), had little or no resistance to new germs. When smallpox, measles, influenza, typhus, and diphtheria traveled in the earliest crossings, they killed natives in appalling numbers. Fifty years after Columbus landed on Hispaniola (later the Dominican Republic) in 1492, fewer than 2,000 native inhabitants remained out of a total population of half a million that Columbus had estimated. Smallpox killed nearly half the Aztecs within a few years of Cortes's landing. All told, between 50 and 90 percent of the native people of Mexico and the Caribbean died from disease within a century of contact with Europeans. (By comparison, the toll taken by the Black Death in mid-fourteenth-century Europe was around 30 percent.) Later arrivals of cholera, malaria, and yellow fever, the latter two diseases byproducts of the slave trade, continued the slaughter.

NORTH AMERICA'S HIDDEN HOLOCAUST.   The death rate in North America was similarly high, but the destruction was less obvious because Indian settlements were smaller and more mobile and because epidemics spread in the interval between exploring and colonizing. The first brief encounters sowed seeds of death. In 1585 Sir Frances Drake's marauders, who had caught typhus in the Cape Verde Islands, brought it when they raided Spain's outposts in Florida. Around St. Augustine, Drake reported, "the wilde people . . . died very fast" and blamed the English God for their fate. All European explorers in North America—Spanish, French, British, Dutch, and Russian—told similar stories. Often they expressed disappointment over losing Indians as potential trading partners, religious converts, or coerced laborers; it was mostly the British colonists, with their plans to settle permanently, who exulted over the good fortune of having potential enemies removed.

Disease moved inland ahead of such settlers, destroying whole tribes long before colonists arrived. When de Soto trudged from Florida to the Mississippi in the early 1540s, he saw vast cultivated fields and villages with temples shaped like earthen pyramids, remnants of the great native Mississippian societies. Yet when the French came to settle this region around 1700, these Indians were gone, their temples and farms replaced by sparse Chickasaw or Choctaw villages whose inhabitants little resembled the advanced Indian people who preceded them. Diseases contracted from coastal tribes who had been infected by Spanish sailors began to kill the Mississippian Indians by the time de Soto passed through, and his exploration completed the grim reckoning.

In Canada, New England, and the upper Mississippi Valley, indigenous peoples had contact with British and Basque fishermen or French fur traders years before other Europeans came to stay. The ensuing outbreaks of influenza or typhus cleared the path for colonial settlement. In the early 1600s, for example, a major flu epidemic broke out among the Pennacook Indians in coastal Massachusetts, initiated by contact with shipwrecked French sailors. As many as 80 percent of the Pennacooks died before the first British colonists arrived at Plymouth in 1620. When the colonists landed they found abandoned villages, caches of stored food, and cleared farmland ready for them to seed and fertilize—it is not surprising that they believed God was on their side. From coastal European settlements the devastation penetrated inland. In the 1630s, epidemics of smallpox, probably transmitted by New England colonists, reduced the Iroquois and Huron populations of the Great Lakes region by as much as 50 percent.

The pattern was repeated as British colonists, and after them Americans, pushed west only to find that indigenous societies had been weakened or even extinguished by diseases. As the American explorers Lewis and Clark followed the Missouri River in 1804, local Indians recounted the damage that smallpox, probably caught from French fur traders, had done to tribes in the Dakota region a few years before. Scholars estimate that in the nineteenth century, smallpox destroyed perhaps half the Indian population between the Mississippi River and the Rocky Mountains. The grim inland march of disease facilitated European conquest and reinforced white settlers' inclination to view western tracts as vacant lands that were theirs for the taking. Many settlers were unaware that vast stretches of North America's frontier were not virgin land, but widowed land, recently depopulated by their own deadly germs.

At the same time that British and American traders pushed westward to the Rockies, other Europeans and Americans were inadvertently infecting native peoples of the Pacific coast. Establishing a string of missions northward from San Diego to San Francisco between the 1760s and the 1790s, Spanish friars introduced smallpox among Indians of central and southern California. By the latter decade a handful of Russian, British, Spanish, and American trading ships began converging each year on the Pacific Northwest. In 1804, while Lewis and Clark were trekking through present-day South Dakota, the American brig *Lelia Byrd* stopped along the Oregon and California coasts to acquire sea otter pelts from natives for the China trade. The boat's captain reported that one California Indian settlement was recently reduced by shipborne disease from 7,000 to 50 "souls." As on the Atlantic and Gulf coasts, smallpox, tuberculosis, and measles caught from Europeans ravaged Pacific Coast Indian communities and spread inland through intertribal trade. There was one difference, however: on the Pacific Rim it was whites who transmitted syphilis to previously unexposed natives, rather than vice versa.

DISEASE AND THE SLAVE TRADE.   Disease promoted the slave trade by removing Indians as potential plantation laborers. To solve this shortage, Spanish and Portuguese colonists stepped up transport of slaves from West Africa to Brazil and the West Indies in the 1500s. Less susceptible to disease and increasingly available as the trade expanded, enslaved Africans quickly outnumbered Native Americans in the Caribbean. When tobacco and rice cultivation took over North America's southern colonies, black slaves surpassed the Indian population there by 1750.

COMPARISON WITH AFRICA.   One way to put the impact of germs in the Post-Columbian Exchange into perspective is to compare it to European encounters with central Africa. Whereas diseases brought by Europeans permitted rapid conquest of the Americas, in tropical Africa the tables were turned. Local exposure to outside germs, begun by trade with Muslims before 1200, allowed sub-Saharan peoples to adapt gradually to foreign disease. Because few perished from pathogens brought by Europeans, African peoples greatly outnumbered those who tried to conquer or colonize them. In contrast, African-bred diseases like malaria and yellow fever presented huge obstacles to European penetration of the continent's interior. European traders and missionaries died in large numbers from these scourges and the horses they relied upon were weakened by local parasites. The disease barrier of central Africa helps explain why Europeans failed to establish colonial rule in the region until 400 years after their traders first explored the Ivory Coast, which was about the same time that Columbus landed in the Caribbean.

African germs added a new dimension to the Post-Columbian Exchange by determining areas of white settlement. Malaria and other diseases brought by slave ships were an important reason why English settlers gravitated to colonies on the temperate North American mainland. The Pilgrims, for example, first considered settling in Guiana on the South American coast but chose North America because they feared tropical diseases. The path of disease from Africa ensured that the Americas' temperate zones would attract more white settlers, while tropical and semi-tropical lands became more racially diverse.

NEW WORLD GERMS AND MEDICINES. Did any New World germs kill Europeans? The exchange was remarkably one-sided. Without large domestic animals like pigs or sheep, Indians had avoided the main hosts of infectious diseases transmitted to humans, and they had no major lethal contagions to pass to Europeans. The one exception was syphilis, a venereal disease that Columbus's men contracted and bequeathed to Europeans in 1493. Yet syphilis quickly evolved into an endemic malady that led to death only if victims remained untreated for years.

Compounding this unequal transfer of disease was a lopsided exchange of remedies. By the late 1700s, when Europeans and their descendants began to develop vaccinations against smallpox, measles, and typhus, it was too late to save Native Americans who had perished from these scourges. Meanwhile, the health of Old World peoples was enhanced by New World plants and herbs used as medicines. Quinine, for centuries the only effective treatment for malaria, is made from the bark of the South American cinchona tree. About half of today's European list of approved medicines (called a *pharmacopoeia*) is derived from Native American remedies.

NEW WORLD FOODS

CORN AND POTATOES. The exchange of plants and foods between Old and New Worlds also benefited Europeans disproportionately. Among crops the Americas contributed to the Old World, corn and potatoes were especially important. In an early and amazing feat of genetic engineering, corn (or maize) was bred by Indians from dissimilar ancestor species by the second millennium B.C.E., probably in central Mexico. Hardy, fast-growing, and easily stored, corn offered more nutrients and higher yields per acre than European grains such as wheat, rye, and barley. Introduced by native peoples to the colonists, corn became an important dietary staple among settlers from Mexico to Massachusetts. When brought back to

Europe, Africa, and Asia, it became a key food for peasants and livestock in many regions.

A second influential New World food, potatoes were first cultivated in Peru. Potatoes provided more balanced nutrition than other starches; they could thrive in wet northern climates with short growing seasons; and they were protected against theft by being stored underground, where they lasted up to a year. North American colonists adopted them eagerly, especially where the soil and climate did not support traditional European grains. Potato cultivation reached Pennsylvania in the 1680s, probably on a return trip from Britain, then spread rapidly northward. For a time, Europeans viewed potatoes with contempt, labeling them poor people's food or complaining that they were difficult to digest. Eventually the potato's advantages were recognized, and in the nineteenth century it became a staple food in Ireland and an important part of the common diet eastward across northern Europe into Russia.

COD. While corn and potatoes originated south of the Rio Grande, the most important food that North America provided was neither a crop nor unique to the New World. Codfish thrived in the North Sea and North Atlantic; the Norsemen, who learned to preserve cod by drying it outdoors, consumed it on voyages to Greenland and Labrador around the year 1000. The Basques of northern Spain salted cod before drying it, making it palatable for years. In the 1400s these seafaring people stretched their fishing grounds westward to the edge of North America, where they probably discovered two shallow ocean shelves, the Grand Banks off Newfoundland and the Georges Bank off Massachusetts, which hosted the world's largest codfish population. In 1497, John Cabot, exploring for England, reported that the waters off Newfoundland were teeming with cod. Within decades, thousands of fishermen from France, Spain, Portugal, and England were conducting annual expeditions to the Banks. England's New England colonists, who learned their skills from Europeans, entered the business in the 1630s and became key suppliers for the West Indies and the mother country. Salt-dried cod was preserved and portable protein; it sustained crews on ocean voyages, fed slaves on Caribbean plantations, and became a mainstay of Mediterranean diets. As early as 1550, 60 percent of all fish eaten in Europe was salt cod, a percentage that remained stable for the next 200 years due to the bountiful North American supply. (Bountiful but not inexhaustible: when overharvested by huge trawling ships in the second half of the twentieth century, the New World's cod fisheries gave out.)

NEW WORLD FOODS AND OLD WORLD POPULATION. The Americas also gave beans, squash, and peppers to the rest of the world. Italian cuisine

was transformed by the introduction of New World tomatoes. Sweet potatoes, peanuts, and Brazilian manioc (also called cassava or tapioca root)
became essentials of the common diet in central Africa and parts of Asia.

All these foods proved beneficial by increasing the variety and supply
of nutrients in areas outside the Americas. Potatoes, along with corn and
manioc, played an especially important part in increasing human survival. Where these crops were adopted they raised nutritional levels, reduced crop failures, and boosted population growth, contributing to the
great surge in world population that began in the 1700s. Potatoes helped
Ireland triple its population in less than 100 years after 1750. Rapid population growth in Europe and Africa in turn benefited Europe's colonies: it
produced millions of overseas migrants, whether free or enslaved, to
work on New World farms and plantations.

NON-AMERICAN CROPS TRANSPLANTED

Dozens of crops were also transferred from the Old World to the New.
Wherever possible, European settlers tried to grow familiar foods from
home to approximate their traditional table fare. In the British colonies of
Massachusetts and Virginia, these included apples, pears, plums, cherries,
spinach, peas, carrots, cucumbers, lettuce, beets, onions, and cabbages.

WHEAT.   Europeans especially valued wheat for bread, and they searched
for New World climates and soils favorable to it. By the late 1700s and early
1800s, New York, Pennsylvania, and the Ohio Valley emerged as important
producers of wheat for southern Europe. Eventually farmers found the
best conditions on the broad grasslands of Argentina and the northern
plains of North America, where wheat grew better than any native foods.
When Indians were forced off the prairies in the mid-nineteenth century
these lands were fully opened for wheat production and export.

RICE, SUGAR, AND COFFEE.   Before 1750, however, sugar and rice were
much more valuable export crops, providing exotic foods in great demand
abroad. Rice, whose cultivation was probably introduced by African slaves,
became South Carolina's primary staple commodity and the British
colonies' third largest plantation crop after sugar and tobacco. Sugar, a fla-
vor enhancer as well as a stimulant, was first domesticated in the East
Indies and grown in the Middle East before being introduced to the
Atlantic and Caribbean islands. Its sweet taste pleased European palates,
made tea and coffee less bitter, and disguised rotting food—an important
task in an age before refrigeration. Columbus took sugar cane plants
to Hispaniola on his voyage of 1493, and later it was produced on vast
plantations in sixteenth-century Brazil. Sugar became the chief reason

the English colonized islands in the Caribbean. Britain's enormous home consumption, its far-flung empire, and its trade in Asian tea played key roles in spreading sugar globally. On the North American mainland, only Louisiana emerged as a major producer. More than any crop, sugar brought European planters and African slaves to the New World.

Another stimulative and mildly addictive food, coffee came later than sugar to the New World. Coffee drinking began in Arabia in the fifteenth century and reached Europe by the mid-1600s, where coffee-houses sprang up to stimulate business and social life. The Dutch grew coffee beans in their East Indies colonies, but much of the world's crop today derives from a single plant taken by the French to the Caribbean island of Martinique in 1723. From Martinique and Haiti, coffee cultivation spread to Colombia, Central America, and especially Brazil, which became the world's largest producer in the nineteenth century. In the North American colonies, drinking coffee became a patriotic duty in the 1770s when colonists boycotted British tea as a tax protest, and the habit became cheaper after independence voided British restrictions on trade with the French Caribbean. Americans eventually preferred the stronger drink. Like cotton, coffee was a second-stage Atlantic staple, introduced long after Columbus and still booming in the nineteenth century after sugar prices had dropped due to overproduction.

TOBACCO AND LIQUOR

Unlike sugar and coffee, tobacco is a plant native to America. A drug rather than a food, it was first domesticated in South America and was grown by Indians in Mesoamerica and southeastern North America by the time Europeans arrived. Many colonists encountered it as they met natives, for pipe smoking was a common tribal greeting for visitors. The strong tobaccos in use at the time had a soothing, even euphoric effect on smokers, and by the late 1500s the "Indian weed" was beginning to spread beyond Iberia to England and the European continent, despite being branded as immoral and unhealthy by critics. Smoking and chewing tobacco became a popular fad that gave rise to a huge transatlantic trade. Introduced in Jamestown, "Spanish tobacco" from the West Indies emerged as Virginia and Maryland's staple crop and became the British mainland colonies' most valuable export. Not until the twentieth century were its health dangers widely recognized.

The drug Europeans introduced in return, hard liquor, had more obvious unhealthy consequences. In the pre-contact era, some Indian peoples made wine and beer, and the Iroquois fermented maple sap to produce mead. But these beverages had low alcoholic content and were generally restricted to ritual use. In contrast, Europeans, especially northerners, were heavy drinkers who had learned to distill beverages into liquors such as rum, gin, and brandy that had high alcohol content. At times colonists introduced Indians to hard liquors without malice, but often they sought to weaken their wills in negotiations over trade or land. The impact was disastrous, for Native Americans had no experience with hard alcohol, no rules to regulate its use, and perhaps an unusually strong physical reaction to it. (The degree to which genes affect alcohol abuse is still debated by scientists.) Alcohol became the bane of many Indian communities' existence, promoting disorganization and violence that left native societies more susceptible to conquest and further disrupted them afterward.

HORSES AND CATTLE

Old World animals had more beneficial effects upon native peoples. Because the Americas had no domesticated animals larger than llamas and dogs, the horses, pigs, sheep, goats, and cattle the Spanish brought with them had a profound impact in changing native diets and ways of life. Bothered by few natural predators, these animals multiplied rapidly in the New World's open spaces and rewarded small farmers with their milk, hides, or meat. In the Andes, Mexico, and the present-day southwestern United States, herding of sheep and goats became a central occupation, providing native peoples with a ready source of protein and wool. Throughout the Americas, pigs proved hardy and prolific animals. They accompanied explorers as a portable meat supply, flourished without tending in captivity or the wild, and became a central dish in the meals of colonists and indigenous peoples. Before long, pigs became as destructive as they were useful, stripping whole regions bare of root vegetables and grasses.

Horses and cattle had the most dramatic impact. First brought to America by Columbus, horses helped the Spanish conquistadors to overpower native peoples. As their use spread through Spanish outposts, Native Americans acquired them by trading, raiding, or rounding up runaways. By the 1700s, the peoples of the Great Plains were using horses to revolutionize their way of life. Formerly, tribes like the Sioux and Pawnee were settled farmers who lived in sod houses, relied upon women to raise corn and squash, and sent men out on foot to hunt buffalo and other animals. After they obtained horses, the Plains Indians concentrated upon hunting buffalo and wild cattle from horseback. Permanent houses were replaced with light tepees that could be packed on horses to follow the buffaloes' seasonal movements. Crop cultivation was abandoned and women's status declined accordingly. Horses focused the Plains tribes' way of life around hunting by male warriors, who were spurred by competition for buffalo grounds to engage in frequent intertribal raids. The Plains Indians' skill in mounted warfare helped them resist white encroachment more effectively than eastern tribes, although they eventually met defeat after advancing settlers destroyed their buffalo herds.

Carried to the eastern seaboard of North America on the earliest British ships, horses were also indispensable for clearing forests and plowing fields. Together with oxen, they provided the muscle that allowed British settlers to practice subsistence farming and, where possible, to raise staple crops for the world market. Some British colonists used horses to raise livestock on their western frontier, especially in Carolina, where African slaves may have been the first to be called "cowboys." But the Spanish, some of whom had practiced ranching on the dry Iberian plains, took the lead in large-scale cattle ranching. They introduced separate breeds of cattle into Florida as early as the 1560s and New Mexico in the 1590s. Both breeds found their way northward, and the famous Texas longhorns descended from the latter. Wild cattle roaming the southern plains of the present-day United States provisioned native peoples with ample supplies of meat and hides. In the nineteenth century, after white settlers pushed back Indian settlements, the enormous herds of livestock that fed on the Great Plains stretching from northern Mexico to Canada sustained a hugely successful meatpacking industry.

SUMMING UP: AN ECOLOGICAL IMPERIALISM

As befit North America's late "discovery" by Europeans and its less exotic flora and fauna, its native plants and foods had less effect upon the Old World than those from the rest of the hemisphere. On the other hand, transplanted Old World organisms had a tremendous impact north of Mexico. The Post-Columbian Exchange was far more important to North America than North America was to it. The similarity of North America's temperate zones to Europe and heavy reliance upon European immigrants as settlers meant that in time the continent was made over biologically in the image of the Old World. Settler colonialism transferred Europe's vegetable gardens to North America and eventually its granaries and slaughterhouses, too. Rather than "exchange," historians increasingly use the term "ecological imperialism" to describe the colonization of the "neo-Europes," temperate New World areas like most of North America where Europeans not only replaced the native population but also successfully transplanted their ecosystems and ways of life. Where European animals, germs, trees, and crops flourished, European settlements prevailed to the near-exclusion of other peoples.

There were at least four sets of consequences. For Native Americans, this transplantation was devastating. Epidemic disease ravaged their populations and sapped their resistance to white incursion, while the expansion of settler farms and ranches forced them off ancestral lands. To native peoples, the calamity of physical and cultural destruction far outweighed the benefits of horses and new foods. For Africans, too, the positive impact of New World manioc and peanuts cannot be compared to the horror of the slave trade, which will be discussed in detail in the next chapter. For Europeans, on the other hand, biological expansion into North America brought tremendous benefits. Rather than the gold, silver, and tropical foods of South America and the Caribbean, North America offered more prosaic but enduring advantages: enormous supplies of wheat, corn, and beef to feed Europe's masses, cotton to assist its Industrial Revolution, and colonies to absorb Europe's surplus population and extend its rule. For North America's white settlers, disease did much of the dirty work of clearing the frontier of Indians, while the continent's temperate climate created a healthful environment and its fertile soils made farmers rich. Profits from trade with Europe were used to build cities and industries that eventually competed with imperial centers. Ironically, the British proved so successful at transplanting their way of life to North American colonies that before long, they faced movements to declare these settlements independent of the imperial homeland.

SUGGESTED READINGS

Crosby, Alfred. *The Columbian Exchange: Biological and Cultural Consequences of 1492.* Westport, CT: Greenwood, 2003.

_____. *Ecological Imperialism: The Biological Expansion of Europe, 900–1900.* Westport, CT: Greenwood, 2004.
   —New editions of pioneering studies of the transfers of plants, animals, and disease.

Elliott, John H. *Empires of the Atlantic World: Britain and Spain in America, 1492–1830.* New Haven: Yale University Press, 2006.
   —This grand synthesis stretches from exploration to colonial independence and compares the empires built by Spain and England in the Americas.

Ferguson, Niall. *Empire: The Rise and Decline of the British World Order and the Lessons for Global Power.* New York: Basic Books, 2004.
   —Describes the course of British colonialism crisply, colorfully, and favorably.

Fernandez-Armesto, Felipe. *The Americas: A Hemispheric History.* New York: Modern Library, 2003.
—Succinctly contrasts North and South America in the pre-contact and colonial eras, stressing southern "superiority."

Josephy, Alvin M. Jr., ed., *America in 1492: The World of the Indian Peoples Before the Arrival of Columbus.* New York: Knopf, 1992.
—Excellent essays on a wide variety of native societies and themes.

Mann, Charles. *1491: New Revelations of the Americas Before Columbus.* New York: Knopf, 2005.
—Brings together recent archaeological and anthropological evidence to portray Native Americans as more numerous and scientifically advanced than previously thought.

Nash, Gary B. *Red, White, and Black: The Peoples of Early North America*, 5th ed. Upper Saddle River, NJ: Prentice-Hall, 2005.
—A well-written synthesis that is particularly strong on Indian-white interactions.

Parry, J. H. *The Age of Reconnaissance: Discovery, Exploration, and Settlement, 1450–1650.* New York: Praeger, 1969.
—A classic account of the background, events, and processes of European exploration and settlement.

Taylor, Alan. *American Colonies.* New York: Viking Penguin, 2001.
—A panoramic history that includes the full range of North America's native peoples, European colonizers, and African slaves, along with environmental considerations.

Weber, David J. *The Spanish Frontier in North America.* New Haven: Yale University Press, 1992.
—Expertly examines Spanish explorations, missions, and policies in the American Southwest.

White, Richard. *The Middle Ground: Indians, Empires, and Republics in the Great Lakes Region, 1650–1815.* Cambridge: Cambridge University Press, 1991.
—Describes borderlands where European rivals and Indian nations coexisted and negotiated territorial rights before American independence altered the equation.

CHAPTER TWO

THE BRITISH COLONIES IN THE ATLANTIC WORLD

GETTING STARTED ON CHAPTER TWO: What role did Britain's North American colonies play in the Atlantic system of trade, including the African slave trade? How did the massive transfer of goods, ideas, and people transform colonial society? What impact did the Atlantic trade have on Europe's development and its competition with Asia for world wealth and power? How did the American Revolution, the French Revolution, and Latin American independence movements relate to Europe's imperial wars and compare with one another?

In the centuries after Columbus's landfall, a steady flow of people, goods, money, and ideas to and from the Americas demonstrated that the Atlantic Ocean was not a formidable barrier but a waterway that connected the islands and continents on its shores. An integrated Atlantic system of trade and migration began forming in the era of European exploration, and in the 1700s it evolved to become a complex network of exchanges. Constructed by people from four continents, this transoceanic system replaced the Mediterranean Sea as western Europe's main thoroughfare, rivaled the Indian Ocean trade route between Europeans and other peoples, and helped to boost Europe to global preeminence. Across the Atlantic's broad highway, Americans, Europeans, and Africans traveled, exchanged products, sought freedom or promoted slavery, negotiated their identities, and competed for power.

Britain's North American colonies, established on this system's margins, were gradually absorbed into its flows. In the 1700s the Caribbean Sea remained the hub of transatlantic trade, but contacts across the North Atlantic increased dramatically. Northern Europe's exploding population spilled overseas as migrants from Scotland, Ireland, and Germany sought refuge or opportunity on North America's shores. The growth of the African slave trade extended market-crop cultivation to mainland colonies such as South Carolina and Virginia, much as it had already flourished in the West Indies. Colonists on the northern half of the continent, unable to produce crops valuable to Europeans, found ways to profit by provisioning plantations and carrying goods along the Atlantic's complex web of circuits. By 1750, Britain's North American colonies boasted almost 2 million inhabitants, nearly 10 times the number in 1700, and their economies grew faster than England's. By finding a niche in the Atlantic world, their settlers joined its network of producers, traders, and consumers.

The colonists became increasingly vital to British industry as consumers. American colonists' demand for British goods helped sustain the world's first Industrial Revolution in the parent country, and cotton production, which boomed shortly after American independence, assured Britain's industrial preeminence. In these ways, and later by serving as Europe's breadbasket, North America contributed to European nations' surge in power and wealth past their ancient Asian rivals, China and India.

British colonial society, in turn, was changed by its transatlantic connections. The arrival of hundreds of thousands of black and white migrants transformed the fluid early settlements of the North American seaboard into established societies dominated by large landowners and merchants and clearly divided by color and class. Shaped by its commercial ties to the British Empire, society in the North American colonies increasingly mirrored that of the imperial center.

That resemblance included the shared language of liberty and common institutions of constitutional government. From England the colonists inherited a system of limited representative government that they practiced in their own elected assemblies, and access to New World land stimulated political participation among white male property owners. Accustomed to a wide sphere of self-government and lax imperial oversight of their economy, North American colonists viewed themselves as equal partners in the British Empire. Imperial officials disagreed. After England defeated France in 1763 and established primacy among European powers in North America, the British government abandoned its traditional "benign neglect" by tightening control over the thirteen colonies' land, money, and governance. The colonists responded with outcries in defense of their "British liberties." When countered by the imperial government, these protests escalated into an epochal rebellion against British rule. In the 1770s, conflicting interests in the Atlantic system burst into an anticolonial war that opened a world-transforming Age of Revolution.

TIMELINE

1519–1867	European slave traders transport 11 million Africans to the Americas
1650	Sugar surpasses gold and silver as New World export
	English Navigation Acts begin regulation of colonial trade
1689	England, France, Spain, and Holland begin wars over empire fought until 1815
1700	West Indies surpasses Brazil in sugar production; Britain becomes largest slave carrier
1700–1800	Approx. 300,000 African slaves brought to North America
1710–1776	Influx of 300,000 Scots-Irish and German immigrants to thirteen colonies
1730–1765	Evangelical Great Awakening spreads in Great Britain and the thirteen colonies
1756–1763	Seven Years' War fought in North America, Europe, the Caribbean, and Asia; Britain wins control over eastern half of North America
1763–1774	British Parliament and George III enact stricter laws controlling colonial trade, taxation, governance
1776	Britain's thirteen colonies declare independence
1778	France, later joined by Spain and Holland, allies with North American colonists against Britain
1781	Americans and French force British surrender at Yorktown
	Spain suppresses colonial revolts in New Granada and Peru
1783	Treaty of Paris officially ends Revolutionary War, recognizes U.S. independence
1789–1799	French Revolution overthrows monarchy for republic, ends with Napoleon in power
1791–1804	Revolution and independence in Haiti (Saint-Domingue)
1807	Napoleon opens invasion of Spain and Portugal, deposing their monarchs
1808	U.S., following British lead, outlaws importation of African slaves
1811–1828	Spain's Central and South American colonies declare and win independence
1820s	Cotton surpasses sugar as leading export crop of the Americas

THE ATLANTIC SYSTEM, THE SLAVE TRADE, AND COLONIAL SOCIETY

Like their imperial competitors in Spain, France, and Holland, British officials believed colonies essential to the nation's prosperity. Overseas settlements were meant to supply food and raw materials to the imperial center, while the colonies' European settlers, African slaves, and Indian traders provided a growing market for English manufactures. This simple two-way relationship was woven into more complicated patterns by specific regional economies in the colonies, by the African slave trade, and by Parliament's regulation of trade. At its center, the system used the labor of unfree immigrants to benefit European peoples on both sides of the Atlantic.

THE THIRTEEN COLONIES AND THE ATLANTIC SYSTEM

MERCANTILIST POLICIES.   Mercantilism, the prevailing economic wisdom in eighteenth-century Europe, decreed that nations should amass more wealth than their rivals by exploiting colonies and dominating foreign trade. To the English, this meant that most goods flowing to and from its colonies should pass through their ports. The Navigation Acts and other regulations passed by Parliament between 1650 and 1733 were meant to benefit British shipping and manufacturing. Commerce in the empire had to be conducted in English or colonial ships. Certain valuable colonial exports such as tobacco, sugar, and indigo were designated to be transported only to England or its colonies, from which they could be re-exported elsewhere, bringing a tidy profit to British merchants. Similarly, European goods had to pass through England, where they were heavily taxed, before being shipped to the colonies. This often made these goods so expensive that colonists bought English-made products instead. Finally, to reward producers who served the colonial market, Parliament subsidized the production of textiles, gunpowder, and other items and prohibited colonists from manufacturing wool, hats, and iron in quantities large enough to export.

MERCANTILISM'S BENEFITS.   These regulations sound harsh, and they especially penalized tobacco planters, who could not sell directly in the lucrative European market. Yet on the whole, mercantilist policies succeeded in enriching British and colonial elites and in stimulating economic growth in both places. British manufacturers enjoyed an expanding market for their products, and English merchants and shippers profited from the "carrying trade." Between 1700 and 1770, the number of British merchant ships nearly tripled, and reshipments of colonial sugar and tobacco accounted for half of all British exports. Britain's New World colonists, meanwhile, found a ready market for their staple crops and could purchase English manufactured goods at low prices and on easy credit.

Because colonial merchants competed in many areas on the same terms with English traders, they discovered their own commercial opportunities in imperial trade. Philadelphia and Boston merchants moved into West Indies routes, traders in Newport, Rhode Island, transported slaves from Africa, and those in Boston and Charleston shipped codfish and rice (once the latter was permitted in 1730) to southern Europe. Colonial merchants added to their profits by trading illegally with French or Dutch Caribbean islands. Most of the molasses that fed New England's rum distilleries, for example, arrived illegally from the French West Indies. When suspicious cargoes were unloaded at North American ports, British officials often accepted bribes to look the other way. From time to time, Parliament passed tough new measures aimed at smugglers, but by tempering London's threats with lenient enforcement, British colonial authorities shrewdly preserved a trading system that rewarded most of its operators.

SUGAR IS KING.   At the center of the Atlantic system was a thriving commerce in staple crops, the majority produced by slave labor. From the 1640s onward, sugar from the West Indian colonies was by far the most valuable product of Britain's New World possessions. Europeans craved sugar as a sweetener for tea and coffee and a convenient source of caloric energy, and their seemingly insatiable demand kept prices high. By 1770, the annual worth of West Indian sugar and molasses shipped abroad reached one and a half times the value of exports from all other British American colonies. Prominent West Indian planters, many of them absentee owners living in England, amassed huge fortunes and influenced Parliament to pass legislation enlarging their markets and profits.

NORTH AMERICAN NICHES.   Initially overshadowed by the West Indies, Britain's mainland North American colonies eventually found their place in the Atlantic trading system. The southern colonies sought to duplicate West Indian success by adopting plantation agriculture. Tobacco, grown first by white indentured servants and then by enslaved Africans in the Chesapeake region of Virginia and Maryland, became the mainland colonies' most valuable staple, reaching an annual export value of about one fifth that of West Indian sugar by the 1770s. Rice and indigo, grown by African slaves who provided both labor and expertise in cultivating these demanding crops, were South Carolina's main contributions to imperial trade. Together, their market value reached approximately half the value of tobacco exports by 1770.

Because plantation products dominated the Atlantic trade system, the role of Britain's northern colonies was auxiliary but still significant. First,

FIGURE 2-1   SUGAR AND SLAVES

This engraving of 1667 depicts operations on a sugar plantation in the British Caribbean colony of Barbados. A European supervisor (lower right) directs African slaves as they haul cane, crush it to extract its juice, and boil it to produce molasses. Slave-produced sugar remained the most valuable crop in the Atlantic trading system into the early 1800s. *(Source:* Arents Collection, New York Public Library, Astor, Lenox and Tilden Foundations. *Used with permission from* Traditions and Encounters *(2nd ed.), by Jerry H. Bentley and Herbert F. Ziegler. Copyright 2002 by McGraw-Hill.)*

they provided West Indian plantations with basic foodstuffs. By the mid-1700s more than half of the nonslave colonies' trade went back and forth to the West Indies, never touching European shores. New England sent timber and livestock to expand sugar plantations and salted fish to feed West Indian slaves. Wheat from Pennsylvania and the middle colonies furnished flour to Caribbean planters (and after 1750 to southern Europeans). In return, North American merchants and farmers received sugar, molasses, and fruit from the West Indies as well as bills of exchange that could be swapped for British goods.

A second opportunity seized by the nonslave colonies was to engage in shipping within the imperial system. Enterprising New England merchants built thousands of vessels whose captains competed with the English merchant marine and eventually surpassed them in tonnage. By 1770, New England's earnings from the carrying trade exceeded the value of its export products. Half the ships leaving its ports were bound to other mainland colonies to distribute British manufactures or to gather crops for export to England. Colonial vessels returning from the Caribbean brought molasses, which was distilled into cheap rum and brought to Africa to exchange for slaves. New England ships carried a small fraction—less than a tenth—of the Africans transported in the British slave trade, and in the 1700s less than 10 percent of New England's residents were slaves, most employed in urban households. In less direct ways, however, the region relied upon plantation slavery for its commercial prosperity.

Finally, settlers in Britain's temperate mainland colonies played an important economic role in the imperial system as consumers. Using bills of exchange from intercolonial trade and profits from shipping, New England merchants and middle colony farmers purchased British manufactures. Their growing appetite for consumer goods, combined with southern planters' need to clothe slaves and their desire to build luxurious houses, completed the transatlantic trade cycle by providing a market for British-made products such as textiles, glass and pottery, metal goods, and furniture.

TRIANGULAR AND OTHER TRADE ROUTES.   All these exchanges combined with imperial regulations and the African slave trade to open dozens of shipping lanes crossing the Atlantic and coursing up and down its sides. Sometimes shaped by two-way trade, at other times formed into triangles or even rectangles, the English sector of the Atlantic system traced a cat's cradle of routes that tied together Europe, Africa, the Caribbean, and North America. Its influence reached inland to tobacco plantations in Maryland, sawmills in New Hampshire, manufacturing towns in England, and farm villages in Gambia, joining the fates of people who lived thousands of miles apart on three continents.

THE AFRICAN SLAVE TRADE

The majority of voyages across the Atlantic and along its shores involved slavery, from buying and selling slaves to the exchange of slave-grown crops and acquisition of supplies for plantations. The Atlantic system was fueled by the largest forced migration in human history. When white settlers proved insufficient or native peoples were weakened by germs, Europeans turned to Africans for exploitable labor. Their backbreaking work extracted from the New World's soil a more lasting form of wealth than precious metals. African slaves turned colonial regions with the largest slave populations into the wealthiest European settlements.

THE POPULATION PARADOX.   The numbers are staggering. Between 1519 (the first recorded shipment of slaves from Africa to the New World) and 1867 (the last verified voyage from Africa to Cuba), nearly 10 million slaves landed in the Americas. This was more than five times the number of Europeans who migrated to the Americas in the 370 years after Columbus's landing. Paradoxically, this black numerical superiority mutated into

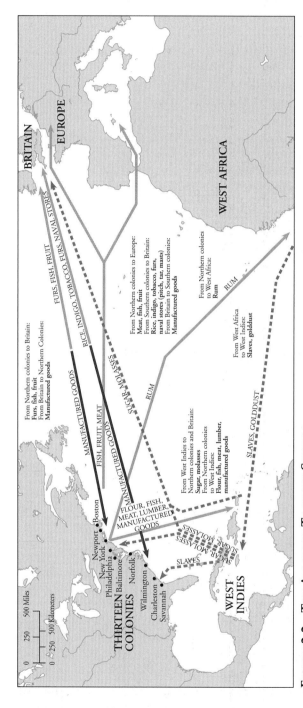

FIGURE 2-2 THE ATLANTIC TRADING SYSTEM

This map illustrates the complex pattern of trade that fueled the colonial American economy in the late seventeenth and eighteenth centuries. A simple explanation of this trade is that the American colonies exported raw material (agricultural products, furs, and others) to Britain and Europe and imported manufactured goods in return. Although that explanation is accurate, it is not complete because the Atlantic trade was not a simple exchange between America and Europe, but a complex network of exchanges involving the Caribbean, Africa, and the Mediterranean. Note the exchanges between the North American mainland and the Caribbean islands, the trade between the American colonies and Africa, and the wide range of European and Mediterranean markets in which Americans were active. Not shown on this map, but also very important to colonial commerce, was a large coastal trade among the various regions of British North America. (*Source: Used with permission from American History (11th ed.), by Alan Brinkley. Copyright 2003 by McGraw-Hill.*)

white settler preponderance. By 1820 there were more than 12 million Europeans and their descendants in the New World and only about 7 million people of African origin. The cause of this reversal was a vast difference in birth rates, mortality, and environment. Whereas white settlers enjoyed a comparatively healthful existence, conditions on most New World plantations killed off laborers and placed the traffic from Africa on a treadmill, transporting more and more slaves just to keep their New World numbers steady.

ROOTS OF THE SLAVE TRADE.   Slavery was not a new social practice for Europeans or Africans. Imposed upon outsiders, the indebted or desperately poor, and especially upon captives taken in war, slavery flourished in ancient Greece and Rome and persisted in Europe into the Middle Ages. Although slaveholding faded from existence in western Europe by the 1300s, it continued at the eastern end of the Mediterranean when Christians and Muslims enslaved each other during religious wars and when Arab overlords used African slaves as household servants or agricultural workers. Most West African societies took slaves from neighboring kingdoms, and by 700 C.E., African traders began transporting slaves northward in caravans across the Sahara Desert for sale to Arabs. During the next millennium, several million enslaved Africans were taken through this trans-Sahara route to the Mediterranean or across the Indian Ocean from East Africa to the Middle East. The status of these slaves was not fixed or automatically passed on to children. In Europe as well as Africa and the Middle East, slaves occasionally accumulated wealth and power or were adopted into their owners' families.

THE ATLANTIC TRADE.   After 1500, the demand for slave labor on New World plantations swelled the annual stream from Africa into a torrent and threw its victims and their children into perpetual servitude. In scale, consequences, and brutality, the Atlantic slave trade far surpassed its predecessors. Recent studies based on exhaustive analysis of ships' records give us the most accurate count yet of the transatlantic slave trade. Slave ships from European nations (and some from the Americas) made approximately 40,000 voyages to the West African coast, taking just over 11 million slaves, 9.6 million of whom survived the journey. Thus, on average, 15 percent of the Africans perished, mostly victims of disease, during the notorious two-month Middle Passage to the West Indies. Millions more died while being marched together in ropes or chains to the African coast and held in gathering pens before transport.

The slave trade built upon established practice, having the cooperation of African as well as European profiteers. Armed warriors from West Africa's coastal regions penetrated inland to take captives from settled agricultural villages and weaker political states. The majority of slaves came from the curving 3,000-mile-long region of West Africa that stretched southeastward from Senegambia around the Bight of Biafra to the Congo River, then south to Angola. After taking captives to the coast, African agents exchanged them with European ship captains for guns, alcohol, textiles, or iron goods. Except for the direct connection between Angola and Brazil, slaves were transported along varied routes that produced a mixture of African peoples at most New World destinations.

ONE SLAVE'S TESTIMONY.   The narrative of Venture Smith, one of the few Africans who left a written account of his capture and transport, personalizes the trauma of the slave trade. Born in 1729 as Broteer Furro, the son of a local prince in Guinea, Smith was captured six years later in a raid by an enemy tribe that was "instigated by some white nation." After witnessing his father tortured and killed by the raiders, the child was forced to march 400 miles to the Gold Coast. There he was canoed out to a slave ship from Rhode Island, whose steward purchased him for four gallons of rum and a piece of calico (cotton), renaming the boy Venture because he was a business investment. The New England traders took on 260 slaves and sailed for Barbados, a voyage that Venture remembered as "ordinary" except for an outbreak of smallpox that killed 60 Africans. Nearly all the survivors were sold to West Indies planters, but Venture was brought to Connecticut. After several decades he earned enough money by hiring himself out to purchase his freedom and that of his slave family. Despite its atypical ending, Smith's journey typified the violent disruption that the slave trade inflicted on its captives.

CONSEQUENCES FOR AFRICA AND EUROPE.   For people who remained in West Africa, the slave trade also brought negative changes. Recent historians argue against exaggerated claims that the slave trade destroyed West Africa's economy and stunted its population growth. Yet profits from the traffic in human beings did promote centralized African states and encourage regional warfare. The rulers of coastal Dahomey and Asante became powerful despots who monopolized the sale of slaves, used warrior slaves wielding European guns to raid the African interior for captives, and controlled their peoples' access to European goods. The slave trade also shifted gender relations, creating a shortage of men that raised work demands upon African women. Through its influence, hereditary forms of slavery began to appear among African peoples.

In contrast, the benefits of slave labor to Europeans and American colonists were obvious. By forcibly redistributing population around the Atlantic rim, the slave trade increased the prosperity of European peoples at the expense of Africans. Historians estimate that the manufactured goods exchanged for slaves were worth less than a third as much as the goods slaves produced in the Americas for sale in Europe. As middlemen in this trade cycle, slave traders and plantation owners profited handsomely. With such riches at stake, European nations competed fiercely to control the traffic in African lives.

THE BRITISH SLAVE TRADE AND NORTH AMERICA.   As with New World colonizing, the British were latecomers to the slave trade. By the time England made the transition to slave labor in Barbados in the 1640s, Portuguese ships had spent a century importing nearly half a million Africans to Iberian New World colonies. Initially the British relied on Dutch traders to furnish African laborers, but in the 1690s, when West Indian sugar production boomed and merchants began competing with the Royal African Company, British involvement surged. In the 1700s England surpassed Portugal as the largest transatlantic carrier of slaves, and by 1807, when the British outlawed the trade, nearly 3.5 million Africans had been transported on British ships. This was more than a third of the total number of slaves who arrived in the Americas.

Relatively few Africans were carried to North America, which existed on the margins of the Caribbean vortex of the slave trade. Of the 9.6 million New World arrivals from Africa, only 361,000 came directly to British North American colonies and the young United States. If we adjust the figure upward to account for arrivals from the West Indies, then add the 28,000 slaves taken into French (and Spanish) Louisiana, the total number of slaves brought to regions north of the Rio Grande comes to just over 414,000, or less than five percent of the entire slave migration. Two-thirds, or 281,000, came between 1700 and 1776, and another 98,000 enslaved Africans arrived between 1776 and the end of the U.S. trade in 1808.

The thirteen colonies and the early United States were also comparatively minor participants in the business of transporting slaves. Slaving ships from North America, based primarily in Rhode Island, took about 220,000 slaves from Africa between 1714 and 1807. Most were brought to the West Indies. This trade in human captives was dwarfed by the 2.5 million slaves transported by British ships in the same period, yet it enriched prominent merchants in New York and New England.

SLAVERY AND RACE IN THE COLONIAL AMERICAS

Although the thirteen colonies were bit players in the Atlantic slave trade, and their fields of tobacco and rice sprouted as offshoots of Caribbean operations, by the late 1760s the American South emerged as a major plantation society employing nearly half a million slaves. A century later, southern whites in the United States held nearly 4 million slaves, the highest number of any nation in the New World. The South was a dramatic exception to the pattern of slave population decline elsewhere in the Americas.

UNIQUE DEMOGRAPHICS OF NORTH AMERICAN SLAVERY. Comparison between the American South and the British West Indies highlights this striking contrast. Britain's Caribbean colonies imported about five times the North American number of slaves. Yet census counts in the two places show dramatically different survival patterns. In 1780, the mainland colonists supported a slave population of 576,000 while the British West Indies housed only 350,000. By the 1830s, the number of African Americans (free and slave) reached five times the number imported to U.S. territory, while the black and free colored population of the British Caribbean had shrunk to less than half the number of slaves brought to the islands.

Alarmingly high death rates in the West Indies and unusually low ones on the North American mainland made most of the difference, and a higher proportion of childbearing female slaves in North America also helped. Epidemic diseases and a brutal work regimen made Caribbean plantations graveyards for Africans. More than a third of the slaves on Barbados died within three years of their arrival, and the island suffered an annual population decrease of 4 percent in the 1700s despite the continuous influx of slaves. Meanwhile, North America's slave population not only survived but became self-reproducing. Slaves in Virginia and Maryland were given a rudimentary but generally sufficient diet, and they avoided tropical diseases. Their survival rates, although lower than those of North American whites, were much higher than those in the Caribbean and better than those in England. Longer life expectancies for female slaves meant more slave children. Comparison with Spanish or Portuguese New World colonies shows the same contrast. Less than 5 percent of all slaves shipped to the New World landed north of Mexico, yet by 1825 this region was home to over 35 percent of African descendants in the Americas. The long-term natural growth of the black population made North America's slave society unique among African enclaves in the New World.

VARIATIONS IN SLAVE SOCIETIES. Population growth was not the only difference among New World slave societies. Scholars studying slavery have uncovered other factors that shaped these societies and explain their differences. Instead of stressing religious or ideological distinctions between British or Latin American colonies, these findings emphasize economic and structural variables that were independent of white settlers' backgrounds.

PLANTATION VS. URBAN SLAVERY.   The most basic factor that shaped slave societies was the presence of the plantation system. Where slaves worked on plantations to produce crops for export, they endured the most brutal form of servitude, regardless of which European nation controlled the colony. Whenever cash crops were enjoying boom times, such as in eighteenth-century rice-growing South Carolina, plantation life devolved into unabashed brutality. The lure of profits induced planters to go to extremes in driving and punishing slaves. By contrast, where slaves were used as domestic servants or artisans, and especially in cities, where public scrutiny and a more tolerant climate of opinion tempered slave owners' behavior, the conditions of slave life were somewhat better.

VARIATIONS IN SUPPLY.   A second factor determining the character of slave societies was whether the African slave trade was open or closed. Wherever slaves were cheap and plentiful, as in the Caribbean in the late 1700s, masters felt free to work them to death and replace them with newcomers. By comparison, when the slave trade was closed, as in the United States after 1808, planters were given an incentive to protect their investment by providing slaves with basic sustenance. A continuous flow of slaves also created artificially high male-female sex ratios because planters considered male workers stronger and more reliable than women. Overall, two male slaves were brought across the Atlantic for every female, an imbalance that inhibited slaves from establishing family life and kept down their birth rate. In the United States, legal slave imports were halted relatively early and planters encouraged slave women to mate with other slaves, although systematic forced mating was infrequent. North America's faster transition to a balanced sex ratio allowed blacks to construct family networks that helped them survive the ordeal of bondage. One result was that by legal emancipation in 1865, black women slightly outnumbered men in the United States, a pattern that was rare in other slave societies.

RACE RATIOS AND THEIR IMPACT.   Another kind of ratio, the simple proportion of blacks to whites, was the third and perhaps most significant factor differentiating slave societies. This had far-reaching and sometimes paradoxical effects. In the whitest settler colonies, such as Pennsylvania or Massachusetts, where slaves composed a small fraction of the total population, they posed little perceived threat to social order and were allowed basic access to education, religion, and even some legal rights. In plantation zones such as Virginia, however, where slaves' numbers nearly equaled whites, and especially in coastal South Carolina and the British West Indies, where they outnumbered them, slave owners lived in fear of revolts and took elaborate measures to control the black majority. Repressive slave codes enforced legal subjugation and decreed fierce punishments for rebellious or runway slaves.

Especially in Latin American plantation colonies, high black-white ratios may have benefited slaves by making possible greater access to freedom. Slave societies with a majority black population featured greater numbers of free blacks. In 1820, for example, the proportion of free blacks to slaves was one to two in Cuba and one to three in Brazil, but only one to six in the United States. In general, the need for skilled black labor prompted masters to free slaves. In the British mainland colonies, white settlers were numerous enough to fill most jobs, and laws discouraged or forbade manumission (the freeing of one's slaves). But smaller white migration to Spanish and Portuguese colonies left landowners desperate for wage-earning carpenters, cattle tenders, or overseers, or even for militiamen to defend against foreign intruders. Where ex-slaves became numerous and took on important roles in the colonial economy, whites were less inclined to identify blackness itself with perpetual servitude.

High black-white ratios also promoted racial intermixture. White minority colonizers, spurred by a shortage of white women, took African women as mistresses, concubines, or wives. Due to such liaisons and others with native peoples, eighteenth-century Latin American societies became the most racially mixed in the world. To some extent this followed Iberian precedents, because the Spanish and Portuguese had been mingling with Muslims and North Africans through centuries of trade and regime changes. But New World circumstances accentuated Iberians' relatively inclusive racial and sexual attitudes.

English colonists were more rigid—when they could afford to be. In the northern mainland colonies the migration of European families established a rough equality of the sexes and allowed settlers to maintain racial boundaries. In the American South, following a brief early period that featured some racial mixing between poor whites and blacks, the numbers of African and white women grew in tandem, offering no special incentive for white men to put aside racial misgivings. Yet where British women were harder to find, Englishmen were "not . . . restrained by ethnocentrism in finding release for their sexual urges," as historian Gary Nash puts it.[1] On Jamaica, Barbados and other Caribbean islands, British men imitated the Iberians by consorting with and sometimes marrying their slaves. No laws prohibited interracial sex and marriage, and the mixed-race children of black-white relationships, labeled mulattoes, were given a unique legal status (in Jamaica) and found their own social niche between whites and blacks.

---

[1] Gary B. Nash, *Red, White, and Black: The Peoples of Early North America,* 5th ed. (Upper Saddle River, NJ: Prentice-Hall, 2006), 160.

That such contrasts existed within England's colonial domains suggests that distinctions between "exclusive" British and "inclusive" Iberian attitudes about race, although real, were less important in determining the character of New World slave societies than more impersonal variables. Colonial slave societies ranged along a spectrum of types according to their dominant crops, access to the slave trade, and racial composition. In the case of British North America, however, these variables and exclusionist racial attitudes tended to reinforce each other.

COLONIAL SOCIETIES IN BLACK AND WHITE

Over time, the particular combination of North America's demographic and cultural conditions produced a distinctive, racially bifurcated social pattern. Rapid population growth, low black-white ratios (on average), and limited importation of slaves enabled African Americans to create a unique community blending their diverse African heritages with European settler influences. At the same time, English and other European colonial settlers began merging into a hybrid white society whose dominant cultural influence was British. Increasingly, black and white colonists developed into two homogeneous and separate colonial peoples.

EMERGENCE OF AFRICAN AMERICANS.   Compared to places like Brazil and Cuba, where the slave trade remained open to the 1850s, North America experienced a faster and more complete fusing of African peoples into a new racial and cultural identity as African Americans. Colonial slaves came from diverse African regions and groups: they were Ibos, Yorubas, Wolofs, Ashantis, Mandingos, and others, each with their own language, rituals, and family practices. Yet the process of finding cultural common ground began in African slave pens and continued aboard vessels bound for the New World. This mixing accelerated dramatically as diverse African peoples encountered one another and lived together on colonial plantations.

Slaves forged African American ways of kinship, recreation, and worship that blended African memories with European influences. Perhaps the most vivid example was Black Christianity, which inflected white Christian beliefs and practices with emotional shouting and singing and lent liberationist meanings to the biblical "promised land." Due to the comparatively early end to the slave trade and frequent interaction with whites, African American society featured less obvious and less intact cultural survivals from Africa than those that endured among black Cubans or Brazilians. Nevertheless, clear evidence of African heritage could be found in colonial slaves' food, funeral rites, songs, and music as well as their reliance upon herbal cures and conjurors. Not surprisingly, specific

"Africanisms" survived longest where West Indian slaves brought to the mainland maintained them or where slave majorities persisted. In the isolated Sea Islands of South Carolina, West African names and handicrafts and an African-English mixed language called "Gullah" flourished into the nineteenth century. Still, by the late 1700s, most North American slaves were second- or third-generation residents who adopted Christian names and beliefs and who shared a culture of blended and diluted African and American ways.

COLONIAL IMMIGRATION AND THE WHITE MELTING POT.   A similar story of blending unfolded among British North America's white colonists. Unlike the Spanish, who forbade the immigration of foreigners to their New World colonies, British authorities encouraged it, offering cheap land and religious toleration to foreign Protestants. Atlantic trading ships provided convenient and inexpensive transportation. As a result, perhaps 300,000 non-English immigrants arrived in the thirteen colonies during the eighteenth century.

Pushed by high rents, poor harvests, and restrictive English laws, more than 150,000 farm laborers and artisans left Ireland and Scotland between 1730 and 1776, the majority Scotch-Irish Protestants from northern Ireland. Many moved to the colonial backcountry, where they settled on open land or wrested it from Indians, developing habits of fierce independence that sparked skirmishes with natives and occasionally local uprisings against colonial authorities. Another 100,000 migrants came from the German Rhineland to the middle colonies, especially Pennsylvania, where tidy farm settlements dominated by the misnamed "Pennsylvania Dutch" caused Benjamin Franklin to fear that German newcomers would "never adopt our Language or Customs." They will "shortly be so numerous as to Germanize us instead of our Anglifying them," Franklin predicted.

Franklin's fears proved ungrounded. Eventually, whether on the frontier or in more densely settled areas, most non-English immigrants blended with English settlers and their descendants in daily life, work, and marriage. "I could point out to you a family whose grandfather was an Englishman, whose wife was Dutch, whose son married a French woman, and whose present four sons now have four wives of different nations," one French colonist in New York boasted. By 1776 the colonial white population was more diverse than ever—only 60 percent were English (rather than Irish, Scotch, German, or other European) in background—yet white settlers were well on their way to coalescing into a British-dominated white society.

THE RACIAL DIVIDE.   This process had ominous racial consequences. White colonists increasingly replaced ethnic with racial identity, and the more fluid interactions of early settlements gave way to a hardening of racial lines and ideologies. Lumping all Africans together as black allowed British settlers to develop a full-fledged racial justification for slavery. Racial ties were used to mitigate class tensions among whites and to affirm a caste difference from blacks. Increasingly, to be black meant to be a slave. Colonists in Virginia and South Carolina used these terms interchangeably and codified this practice by restricting manumission (voluntary freeing of slaves by owners). Historians have spent a great deal of ink arguing whether slavery or race prejudice arose first among early Americans. It seems clear that the two mutually reinforced one another. English prejudice against "heathenism" and blackness, dating from the first contacts with Africans in the 1500s, smoothed the way for their enslavement, while slavery itself crystallized and hardened racial discrimination into a deeply ingrained social practice.

A related consequence was enforcement of an unusually rigid color line between blacks and whites. Some New World slave receivers, such as Brazil, developed a large number of mixed-race categories between black and white, with intermediate steps marked by gradations of color and economic status. By contrast, the North American colonies created a system—later called the "one-drop rule"—that lumped together persons with any degree of black ancestry and called them black. Colonial laws prohibited racial intermarriage, and when mixture occurred anyway, they offered no special legal or social status to mulattoes. The demographics of settler colonialism reinforced the color line because the predominance of white settlers created few needs for freed slaves as skilled workers or sexual partners. As white settlers' backgrounds grew more diverse, they built their identity on the negative basis of a caste system defined by color. Instead of a thorough blending of newcomers, the transatlantic migration of diverse peoples led to rigid sorting by race.

THE CONSUMER REVOLUTION, THE GREAT AWAKENING, AND COLONIAL "ANGLICIZATION"

By increasing economic and cultural ties between England and the North American seaboard, the Atlantic trade constructed another, more positive foundation for white colonists' collective identity. In the 1700s those who aspired to middle-class status avidly adopted English customs and trends, hastening the creation of a common Anglo-American culture and encouraging colonists to think of themselves not as diverse settlers but as provincial Britons.

THE CONSUMER REVOLUTION.   In the 1700s the combined forces of urbanization, rapid population growth, and increased workshop production sparked a "consumer revolution" in Britain that made more and more goods available to families above the poverty line. The Atlantic trade exported the consumer revolution by showcasing an "empire of goods" to colonists. As the price of British manufactures fell and colonial incomes rose, white American families began acquiring more household amenities. Carpets covered wooden floors, comfortable chairs replaced homemade benches, English teapots appeared in the kitchen, and wooden spoons were upgraded to silverware—the last a change that Benjamin Franklin noted in his own household. North American colonists became consumers in a double sense: first, more and more of their goods were bought from merchants rather than made at home or traded with neighbors, and second, they began to purchase items that went beyond meeting survival needs but were desired for convenience, aesthetic effect, or social status. As consumer choices expanded, shopping emerged as a routine and pleasurable activity in colonial towns. Social occasions such as tea drinking and card playing became consumption rituals as well as opportunities to use special accessories or show off new possessions.

The transatlantic consumer revolution was an important step on the path to a full-blown market economy in the developing sector of the Atlantic world. It signaled the strengthening of commercial links between Britain and its American colonies. Already tied to England by lines of export, the colonists became hooked on British imports. The consumer trade improved living conditions among whites and remodeled their villages from crude settlements to "civilized" towns resembling those that dotted the parent country. But it also left colonists increasingly dependent upon goods and credit supplied by English merchants. This relationship produced conflict in hard economic times.

THE GREAT AWAKENING.   The Atlantic system transmitted religious ideas as well as material goods. On board the same ships as English manufactures were Protestant ministers who exported the Great Awakening to America. This was an outburst of religious fervor that coursed through the American colonies in waves of excitement from the 1720s to the 1760s. At "revival" meetings, often held outdoors, itinerant preachers delivered fiery sermons to enormous crowds. Adopting theatrical techniques, these evangelists entertained audiences with dramatic gestures and personal testimonies. Subtly modifying old Calvinist strictures, they assured listeners that confessing their sins and accepting the Gospel would bring a "new birth" that could transform them and society into models of Christian behavior.

Historians usually portray the Great Awakening as a purely American phenomenon in which homebred ministers like Massachusetts's Jonathan Edwards recalled sinners to the stern discipline of Puritanism.

But revivalism was a transatlantic, Anglo-American movement. Its most successful practitioner was George Whitefield, a charismatic English minister who made seven whirlwind tours of the American colonies between 1739 and 1765 and became an international celebrity. Whitefield and others like him used the growing transatlantic ties of transportation and communication to spread the "awakenings" through the British Empire from its core to peripheries in Scotland and North America and back again. Although Whitefield and other evangelists preached against the rule of Mammon, their methods imitated the marketplace. Faced with the decline of established churches in Britain and its colonies, revivalists borrowed the techniques of commercial entrepreneurs to attract believers and to induce them to support Protestant organizations voluntarily, whether these were traditional churches or the numerous new sects that sprouted in fields that the revivals had plowed.

Through the Great Awakening, the British colonists experienced their first transatlantic and intercolonial cultural movement. Just as Whitefield's tours knitted scattered local revivals into a religious campaign, the Awakening forged new links between Britain and the colonies, leading to further exchanges of religious and political ideas. Without intending to, the Great Awakening aligned religion with the consumer revolution and colonial "Anglicization." While repackaging Protestantism for the consumer marketplace (in the process prefiguring today's TV evangelists), it also stamped colonists along England's North Atlantic periphery as eager provincial participants in a benevolent Protestant empire that was headquartered in the imperial center.

In these and in a host of other ways, from the Virginia planters' mimicking of the British gentry to the widening gap between the rich and poor in colonial cities, North American colonial society increasingly resembled the model of Great Britain. From their constant exchanges on the Atlantic highway, white settlers on the continental seaboard were becoming more rather than less British over time. Dependent upon foreign trade, the thirteen colonies were integrated into the Atlantic world through contacts with the British Empire more than by relations with each other. Only after Britain began reorganizing imperial relations in 1763 were they driven apart from the parent country and into each other's arms.

THE GREAT FRONTIER AND THE GREAT DIVERGENCE: AMERICA'S IMPACT ON EUROPE

The Atlantic trading system transformed colonial society and had damaging effects in Africa, but what was its impact upon Europe? How significant was the New World's bounty beyond the nutritious new foods introduced to Europe through the Post-Columbian Exchange?

DEBATING THE NEW WORLD'S ECONOMIC IMPACT.   In 1792, exactly 300 years after Columbus's first voyage, the Académie Française sponsored an essay competition on the question: "What influence has America had on the politics, commerce, and customs of Europe?" The question remains vital as historians weigh the moral and material effects of transatlantic contact. The Columbian sesquicentennial (500th anniversary) in 1992 inspired soul-searching books that highlighted the disastrous consequences of European overseas expansion for indigenous peoples. It also renewed a lively debate among economists and historians over the impact of the Atlantic system upon Europe and the world economy. We have already noted that Adam Smith, a founder of modern economics, called Europeans' discovery of America and their passage around Africa to Asia "the two greatest and most important events in the history of mankind." Highlighting the economic effects Smith had in mind, German statesman Friedrich von Gentz contended in 1795 that these new sea routes "opened the greatest market, the greatest inducement to human industry, that had ever existed since the human race emerged from barbarism."

THE "RISE OF THE WEST."   In hindsight it is clear that sometime between 1500 and 1800, Europe's economic and military power surged ahead of Asia's and began to control the world's resources, a process that continued into the twentieth century. When did Europeans create and dominate an integrated capitalist world economy, and what role did the New World play in this process?

Historians differ on the crucial dates and developments involved. Those who believe that a Europe-based world economy took shape in the 1500s emphasize the impact of European exploration, conquest, and trade. By contrast, those who argue that the Industrial Revolution and modern imperialism were the crucial factors in the rise of the West begin the break around 1750. Whichever turning point they champion, some historians look for the clue to Europe's rise in features that are internal to Europe itself, such as the Protestant Reformation, the rise of commercial capitalism, the emergence of the modern state, or technological innovation. Others suggest an alternative possibility: that some external factor triggered Europe's success and kept it going in crucial ways. The Americas are a leading candidate.

THE AMERICAS AS EUROPE'S TRANSATLANTIC FRONTIER

The idea that the Americas played a crucial economic role for Europe was refocused over a half-century ago when historian Walter Prescott Webb connected the New World directly to the rise of the West. Expanding Frederick Jackson Turner's claim that the western frontier had conferred important benefits upon the United States, Webb argued that from 1500 to 1900 the Western Hemisphere itself functioned as Europe's "Great Frontier," returning similar benefits across the Atlantic.[2] Without denying that preconditions in Europe favored the rise of capitalism and industry, this view made the opening and exploitation of the New World crucial to Europe's 400 year era of sustained prosperity.

Those who see the Americas as Europe's "Great Frontier" contend that Europe's opening of the Americas dramatically improved the ratios between population, land, and capital for Europeans. By exploiting and settling the Americas, Europeans expanded the land available to them by a multiple of six, acquired an outlet for their surplus workers, and accrued unprecedented capital in the form of gold, silver, and profits from trade. This shift to a surplus of land and capital launched the European economy on four centuries of boom, which waned only when the New World frontier closed around 1900. Webb and his supporters argue that easily extracted products, especially precious metals, were the "primary windfalls" that spurred European capitalism in the 1600s and 1700s. The longer-term cultivation of plantation crops (and later free-labor farm products like wheat and beef) created "secondary windfalls" that sustained capitalism (and aided the Industrial Revolution) in the later 1700s and the 1800s.

How accurate is this view? What generalizations can historical evidence support concerning the impact of the New World's, and particularly North America's, precious metals, trade, and land upon Europe's development?

NEW WORLD GOLD AND SILVER

THE PRICE REVOLUTION AND ITS IMPACT.   From 1500 to 1650, Spanish mines in Mexico and Peru produced more than 180 tons of gold and 16,000 tons of silver. Nearly one fifth was siphoned off directly by the Spanish monarchy, but the rest found its way through German, Dutch, and Italian bankers—and English privateers—into the European and world economy. New World diggings multiplied the amount of silver coin circulating in Europe during the 1500s by a factor of nine. The influx of gold and silver, together with increasing population, led to a dramatic rise in prices, initially in Spain and then throughout Europe. This "price revolution" raised the cost of living faster than wages, worsening the already harsh existence of Europe's common people. For nations, the inflationary surge had varied effects. The influx of bullion boomeranged upon Spaniards. By

[2]Walter Prescott Webb, *The Great Frontier* (Boston: Houghton Mifflin, 1952).

filling the Spanish kings' coffers it encouraged them to enter debilitating wars in the Netherlands, North Africa, and Italy, and even to invade England in 1588. Because it raised the price of Spanish-made goods, the surplus of gold encouraged imports from other European nations. In an ironic twist, Spanish consumption of luxury goods underwrote the expansion of manufacturing in Holland and England and enabled Spain's competitors to surpass its economic development. In the end, Spain's treasure trove of gold proved a curse, not a godsend. As a German historian of the 1600s remarked, "Spain kept the cow and the rest of Europe drank the milk."

SILVER AND THE ASIAN TRADE.   Few of Europe's manufactured goods could be used to trade with Asia because they were inferior in quality, so currency was required. Much of Spain's New World silver passed through European hands to China via the Mexico-Manila trade route begun in the 1560s, or through more indirect channels. New World metals allowed Europeans to purchase increased quantities of Asian spices, cloth, and porcelain, easing if not erasing their chronic trade deficit with the Far East. Some historians believe that the demand for silver in China, the world's largest national economy, drove New World mineral production just as much as Europe's need for currency. Given the importance of trade with Asia, the two were closely related. Even their effects were parallel: China's absorption of silver, which became the sole basis of its currency, may have led to an inflationary crisis similar to Spain's, with the comparable effect of weakening the Ming Dynasty, leading to its collapse in 1644.

SILVER AND EUROPEAN DEVELOPMENT.   Historians who date the emergence of a Europe-dominated world economy from 1500 emphasize the role that gold and silver played in financing military campaigns, colonial ventures, and global trade. Yet although Latin American silver helped fuel the Atlantic and Pacific trades, its wider impact on European development is still disputed. Was New World bullion used to build armies, underwrite colonies, and industrialize Europe, or simply to pay for foreign luxuries such as spices and fabrics that contributed little to Europe's economic growth? Did the influx of precious metals give Europe a crucial advantage over Asian economies?

Whatever impact the New World's gold and silver had on the Old World, its effect peaked before the effective colonization of North America. The Spanish found no cities of gold (or silver) above the Rio Grande, nor did the French above the Ohio and St. Lawrence Rivers. The bulk of the British take from the privateers' looting of Spanish treasure was used to raise armies and pay for trade with Asia, not to establish home industries or American colonies. Apart from their role in sheltering Caribbean pirates, Britain's North American holdings were nearly irrelevant to Europe's circulation of gold and silver. Until the California Gold Rush of 1849 and the Nevada silver boom of the 1860s, America north of Mexico added insignificant amounts to the world's supply of bullion.

THE ATLANTIC TRADE AND THE INDUSTRIAL REVOLUTION

Besides accumulating gold and silver, another practice of European mercantilism was the establishment of trade monopolies with overseas colonies that furnished crops and served as markets for the home country's products. How much did the Atlantic trade in foods and fibers contribute to the Europe's developing economy? More specifically, did American slave-produced products make possible the world's first Industrial Revolution, which occurred in England in the second half of the eighteenth century?

BRITAIN'S GLOBAL TRADE.   Trade statistics offer a comparative perspective that diminishes the likely effect of transatlantic exchanges. Trade *within* Europe played by far the largest role in integrating and modernizing Europe's economy. For Great Britain, the world's first industrial power, the value of trade with the rest of Europe in 1750 was greater than that with North America, the West Indies, and Asia combined. The British imported flax, grain, timber, and wine from the European continent, and the domestic European market provided the largest and most reliable consumer base for British manufactured goods, especially woolens.

Britain's other exchange partners—Asia, the West Indies, and North America—had a roughly equal trade volume with England in 1750. There were important differences, however. British trade with Asia and the West Indies was heavily skewed toward imported foods and raw materials: Indian cotton, Chinese tea, and Caribbean sugar. Because trade with Asia involved mostly the exchange of bullion for fabrics and tea, it had only an indirect impact on the Industrial Revolution, acting as a spur for Britons to tax cotton imports or to cut the cost of manufacturing cloth by replacing workers with machines.

SUGAR AND THE INDUSTRIAL REVOLUTION.   Historians have long debated the significance of West Indian sugar for the Atlantic economy and the industrialization of Europe. No doubt, sugar gave a metabolic lift to the Industrial Revolution. Especially when used in tea and coffee, it boosted the human energy that helped to power industrial production. More directly, some historians have argued that profits from the slave trade and slave labor—both devoted overwhelmingly to sugar production—gave a crucial push to European capitalism. Others counter that profit margins in the slave trade were no better than other commercial ventures, and that dozens of domestic British industries generated comparable earnings. Sugar and slavery were too small a sector of the British economy to create more than a marginal addition to industrial capital. Caribbean planters preferred to buy more slaves or luxury items, absentee owners put their fortunes into landed estates in Britain, and most slave-trade merchants did not invest in industry. Britain's new industries were financed mainly through the personal savings and family connections of small entrepreneurs.

Viewed more broadly, however, trade in sugar and slaves was part of the larger Atlantic system that sustained population growth in the West and encouraged specialized production—both preconditions for industrial development. Adam Smith claimed that the Atlantic trade generated a more elaborate division of labor, which he saw as the key feature of industrial production. Because New World planters grew only stimulants like sugar and tobacco, they purchased food from elsewhere. Planters used stimulant crops and the northern colonies used earnings from the West Indies trade—an indirect benefit of sugar production—to pay for British manufactures. Britain also used industrial goods, especially cloth, to trade for slaves in Africa. Thus England's trade in sugar and slaves created an intercontinental network involving four regions—England, Africa, the West Indies, and North America. Its exchanges stimulated agriculture and industry, promoted the division of labor among these regions, increased purchasing power at all stops, and encouraged cheaper manufacturing through machinery.

NORTH AMERICA AS AN INDUSTRIAL MARKET.   This systemic view places special emphasis on the North American colonies as markets for England's manufactured goods. Although Britain's imports from North America came in a distant third behind those from the West Indies and Asia, the value of manufactures it exported to North America exceeded those sent to Asia or the Caribbean throughout the 1700s, and in the second half of the century it grew rapidly. North America's free settlers created a larger market for finished goods than Caribbean slaveowners. With demand stimulated by rising incomes and easy credit, mainland colonists enjoyed a growing share of Britain's "consumer revolution." They bought cloth, furniture, and kitchenware, and they ordered metal goods that British laws discouraged them from making themselves: half the nails produced in England, for example, were sent to its American colonies. By the 1770s, American colonists imported almost half of England's manufactured exports, surpassing continental Europe as a market for British goods. To be sure, when compared to Britain's large domestic market, these New World orders gave British manufacturing a small push, but it was a significant and growing one.

AN ASSESSMENT.   No doubt England would have undergone an Industrial Revolution without the slave-produced sugar of its New World colonies or the growing North American market. The Industrial Revolution was the product of long-term improvements in Europe's agricultural, financial, and technological capabilities, capped by crucial additions in the mid-1700s to its energy sources (coal and steam), metal production (improved iron) and mechanical inventions (textile spinning and weaving). These changes occurred largely independent of the Atlantic system. Yet the benefits of the Atlantic trade, especially its spur to specialized production and its creation of colonial demand for manufactures, gave them a significant boost. American purchases helped British industrialism develop more rapidly than it would have otherwise.

AMERICAN LAND AND THE "GREAT DIVERGENCE"

COTTON AS A "SECONDARY WINDFALL."   After the Industrial Revolution got underway, American food and fiber products played a crucial role in sustaining it. Cotton from the American South fed Britain's textile mills, making cloth manufacturing England's most important export industry. The key breakthroughs in mechanized spinning that jump-started Britain's Industrial Revolution occurred in the 1760s. At the time, most of England's raw cotton came from the West Indies and the Middle East, but machine production dramatically increased the demand, leading to sharp price rises that would have stunted the industry's growth without the entry of American cotton onto the market. Beginning in 1793, when Eli Whitney's cotton gin enabled workers to separate fibers and seeds easily, southern planters filled Britain's growing needs. By the 1820s, cotton surpassed sugar as the leading crop shipped from the Americas to England. Americans supplied British mills with the cheap cotton they needed to cut costs and out-compete India on the world market. The South's cotton did not spark the textile revolution, but it kept Britain's machines humming and gave England its competitive edge. It qualifies as a "secondary windfall" that sustained Europe's prosperity and influence during the second stage of industrialism.

EXPLAINING THE "GREAT DIVERGENCE."   Cotton and other New World crops figure prominently in recent studies of the "rise of the West." Impressed that China's and India's manufacturing output equaled Europe's in 1750, many world historians now look for explanations of the "great divergence" between East and West in the eighteenth century. Why did the modern industrial order originate in northwestern Europe and not east Asia, despite comparable levels of productivity and living standards in the two regions? One answer looks at these regions' resources and ecological limits and sees the New World as a crucial difference.

THE NEW WORLD COMES TO EUROPE'S RESCUE.   In the 1700s, both east Asia and Europe were heading toward an ecological limit to their development that was imposed by overcrowding, deforestation, and soil depletion. But while China's expanding hinterlands only copied its problems, Europe was able to draw upon its New World periphery (and its own reserves of coal, which replaced timber for fuel) for crucial relief. Help from the New World took three forms. First, the adoption of potatoes, corn, and other New World crops by European farmers multiplied the calories they produced per acre, allowing them to feed Europe's growing population. Second, Europeans used the New World as a distant agricultural province, exploiting slave and emigrant labor to grow sugar, cotton, and wheat that fueled industrial transformation back home. Third, and most important, the mass migration of laborers to the New World made possible continuous and self-sustaining industrial growth. Slaves from Africa and migrants from Europe furnished the cheap labor to produce food and fiber staples. These migrants then created an expanding consumer market for British manufactures and (in the case of European immigrants) a receiving community for Europe's surplus population. In relation to the European core, America became a special kind of periphery, one that could expand geographically and populationwise indefinitely and whose crop exports and manufacturing imports stimulated each other in a continuous circular pattern.

IMPLICATIONS.   The idea that American land allowed Europe to burst its constraints and to enter a prolonged economic boom connects the "Great Frontier" to the "Great Divergence." Whether the exploitation of the New World's "secondary windfalls" explains the economic divide between East and West after 1800 will no doubt be vigorously debated by world historians. Whatever they conclude, their studies suggest that North America of the 1700s deserves to be included in the world-historical picture. As historians shift Europe's decisive split with Asia forward from 1500 toward 1800, more may move from emphasizing Mexican silver or Caribbean sugar to stressing the impact of North American cotton and wheat. Any modern response to the French Academy's question of 1792 must now assess the impact of North America's farms, plantations, and markets.

By anyone's reckoning, however, North America's most powerful economic effect upon Europe began not in the 1700s but the 1800s. In the century after independence, the continent's interior was forcibly opened and American cotton, wheat, and beef came to dominate the world market. Before that, North America's most important export was not a crop but an idea: its example of a republican revolution.

THE SHOT HEARD ROUND THE (ATLANTIC) WORLD: THE AMERICAN REVOLUTION

Seventy years after the fact, Ralph Waldo Emerson wrote that the colonists who took a stand against British soldiers beside his grandfather's house in Concord, Massachusetts in April 1775 fired a "shot heard round the world." The American Revolution began as a quarrel within the British Empire and escalated into an anticolonial war for independence. It ended by creating a new nation and inspiring similar revolts elsewhere in the Atlantic world.

THE GLOBAL IMPERIAL CONTEXT OF REVOLUTION

Viewed from across the Atlantic, the American Revolution was an unforeseen by-product of the long, escalating rivalry between European imperial powers. After 1689, England, France, Spain, and Holland entered a century-long series of wars by which they contended for dominance in western Europe and for territory and trade in Asia and the Americas. The War of the League of Augsburg (1689–1697), the War of the Spanish Succession (1701–1714), the War of the Austrian Succession (1740–48), and the Seven Years' War (1756–1763) had counterparts in North American conflicts that British settlers named after the reigning monarchs or, in the case of 1756, after their local enemies, the French and Indians. Waged on an increasingly global scale, these costly wars prompted the monarchs of Spain, France, and England to reorganize imperial finances and colonial governance to refurbish royal treasuries and bolster colonial defenses. New taxes and regulations met growing resistance from aggrieved settlers in the New World and, in some cases, from disfranchised classes at home. Both groups were armed with potent Enlightenment ideas about natural rights and popular (rather than royal) sovereignty that justified their dissent and, where compromise proved impossible, spurred them to revolt.

EMPIRE IN THEORY AND PRACTICE.   Tensions between colonists and imperial capitals in Europe were heightened by gaps between imperial theory and practice. In theory, the authority of European monarchs over their colonies was absolute. High colonial officials appointed by the king transmitted royal decisions and oversaw their enforcement. In Spain's case, a vast and complex bureaucracy centrally directed from Madrid sought to control colonists' religious, economic, and political lives. Yet there were few places where imperial control was truly absolute. Infrequent transatlantic communications, varied local conditions, and popular resistance meant that royal decrees were often modified and sometimes ignored. "I obey, but I do not execute" became the formula invoked by colonial administrators in Mexico, Colombia, and Argentina. Exploiting their distance from Spain, Latin American settlers learned how to exert indirect or hidden influence over colonial rule.

In British North America, popular control was more overt and the divide between imperial theory and practice especially large. On the one hand, the colonists were British subjects, their trade was subject to mercantilist restrictions, and parliamentary laws and royal decrees announced by colonial governors set their policies. On the other, imperial power was so dispersed as to be ineffective and at times invisible. The early British Empire was a loose association of locally self-governing colonies over which Britain's rule was limited and often contested. The thirteen coastal colonies had vague boundaries and diverse systems of landholding. Many boasted local assemblies that imitated and increasingly claimed to replace Britain's House of Commons. Power in this patchwork empire was not concentrated in London, but was a matter of negotiation between the colonies and the imperial center. Because Britain did not have the means to enforce its will unilaterally, its authority rested on the consent of provincial governments that were controlled by property-owning settlers.

The relationship between colonists and imperial officials at times grew tense, but two factors made it workable for Britons on both sides of the Atlantic. First, colonial elites willingly acknowledged a degree of British authority over their lives. Belonging to the empire protected them in wartime, gave them wide access to markets and manufactures, and confirmed their identity as English men and women, with the legal and political privileges that this implied. Second, for their part, British officials were generally content to practice "benign neglect." Because they were preoccupied by wars on the European continent and lacked the men and money to coerce obedience from colonists, British policymakers left them alone as long as colonial products and tax revenues flowed in and outright rebellions against British rule remained rare. Finally, because the West Indies were far more important sources of wealth than North America, Parliament scrutinized their trade and governance more closely. Thus due to their special circumstances, the North Americans were ceded a considerable measure of autonomy within the empire. Over the course of 150 years they came to regard these "liberties" as their birthright.

THE SEVEN YEARS' WAR. This customary arrangement between the colonists and Britain was shattered when George III and his ministers decided to turn the theory of imperial control into reality. The catalyst was the Seven Years' War (1756–63), a European struggle for geopolitical advantage that, unlike previous imperial wars, started in the New World and spread to the Old. The spark was ignited in the Ohio Valley, where the French and English pursued rival claims to land, river routes, and the fur trade. When a contingent of Virginia militiamen led by young George Washington blundered into attacking a detachment of French troops near present-day Pittsburgh, they opened a culminating conflict between England and France that coursed through Europe, aligned its nations on either side, and stretched to the outer reaches of European expansion. This "Great War for Empire" escalated into a worldwide conflict. Major battles were fought in Europe, North America, the Caribbean, West Africa, India, and the Philippines. The war's global reach demonstrated the value Europeans placed upon their overseas empires. Its origins in the trans-Appalachian West heralded the emergence of North America as a prime arena of imperial competition.

In the North American phase of the war, which officially opened after British General Edward Braddock's defeat on the Pennsylvania frontier in 1755, the French, English, and various Indian peoples jockeyed for control of lands just west of the Appalachians. Some southeastern and Ohio tribes fought British incursions before making peace, but the most powerful native alliance, the Iroquois Confederacy, attempted to maintain the policy of neutrality that had allowed it to trade with both French and British colonists and to play them off against one another for 50 years. When British forces captured the city of Quebec in 1759, the Iroquois, hoping to hold their position by siding with the winners, allied with England. The next year the British took Montreal, ending hostilities on the mainland. Still, the war raged on for two years in the West Indies and elsewhere before the dual treaties of Hubertusburg and Paris in 1763 settled the parties' claims.

THE WAR'S IMPACT. The Seven Years' War produced a new balance of power in Europe and North America. The defeat of France and its ally Austria consolidated Prussia's dominance in central Europe. Britain, which won stirring victories on land and at sea, secured the great colonial prizes: most of France's holdings in India and all of French Canada. Spain, which had joined France near the end of the war, ceded Florida to England and received Louisiana west of the Mississippi from France to compensate for its losses elsewhere. By winning the war, Britain removed France from contention in North America and extended its imperial holdings westward to the Mississippi and northward to all of Canada east of the Continental Divide.

WANING OF THE "MIDDLE GROUND."   The war also weakened the position of Indian peoples on the Great Lakes and southeastern frontiers. With France and Spain now out of the picture, native tribes lost much of the diplomatic leverage they had wielded as intermediaries on the West's "Middle Ground." In 1761 the Cherokee were forced to open lands to British settlers, and at the war's end, British officials banned the practice of giving western tribes gifts and ammunition. Alarmed by the flood of settlers in the Ohio Valley, the Ottawa chief Pontiac formed an intertribal alliance that captured important British forts in the region before being repulsed by the British. Pontiac's uprising (1763–65) ended in a truce that replaced the restrained diplomacy of the "Middle Ground" with constant tensions between Indians and Britain's westward-moving colonists.

REORGANIZING EMPIRE.   Imperial rivalries were disastrously expensive. By the end of the Seven Years' War, winners and losers alike faced financial crises caused by their extensive borrowing. The responses of the British, Spanish, and French monarchs were broadly similar: to raise taxes and assert greater political control over their subjects. They spurred analogous protests, too: colonial revolts in Britain's and Spain's American colonies, and rising agitation for representative government in France. The debts of empire set the stage for an Atlantic Age of Revolutions.

England emerged from the Seven Years' War grandly victorious but saddled with new burdens. Britain had doubled not only its holdings in North America but also its national debt. Interest payments alone threatened to consume the majority of the government's annual expenditures. The problem of paying the debt and raising additional money to secure the newly acquired colonial lands preoccupied George III, the ambitious young monarch who had inherited the throne during the war. Because taxes in Britain were much heavier than in its colonies, the king's ministers, beginning with George Grenville, looked to North Americans to pay a larger share of the empire's costs.

The king and his advisers had in mind additional, more strategic, objectives. Taxes could be used to pay the salaries of Crown-appointed governors and other officials, thus outflanking resistant colonial legislatures. Keeping the North American colonists near the eastern seaboard would prevent costly wars with Indians, discourage contacts with Spanish officials on the Mississippi, collar the inland fur trade for British companies, and reserve western lands for the king's disposal. Finally, stricter enforcement of antismuggling laws and other mercantilist regulations would ensure that New World markets remained the preserve of England's merchants and West Indian planters. Overall, the intent behind George III's program was to replace Britain's traditional "benign neglect" with focused plans for economic exploitation and centralized control of colonial finance and administration. Having secured its New World empire, England was now determined to act like an imperial power.

"A LONG TRAIN OF ABUSES AND USURPATIONS."   The new program was implemented by a series of measures that affirmed Parliament's right to tax the colonies and control their lands. Although few in England doubted this authority, rebellious Americans later declared these laws "a long train of abuses and usurpations." The Sugar Act (1764) tightened enforcement of the navigation laws by creating special courts for smugglers and allotting cargo prizes to sailors and customs officials who caught them. The Stamp Act (1765) required that virtually all documents printed in the colonies display a stamp purchased with British coins. The Proclamation of 1763 restricted colonists' movement west across the Appalachians. In 1774 it was followed by the Quebec Act, which gave the territory between the Ohio and Mississippi Rivers to the recently acquired French Canadian province and recognized the rights of Catholics there—thus angering land-hungry British colonists and offending their anti-Catholic prejudices. The Townshend duties enacted in 1767 imposed taxes on several essential items imported to the colonies.

The final measure, the Tea Act of 1773, demonstrated both the wider context of the imperial crisis and the subordinate place the Americans occupied in British policymakers' minds. To bolster the sagging fortunes of the East India Company, which the king had chartered to control trade with India, Parliament allowed the company to bypass merchants in the New World colonies and sell tea at reduced prices directly to the Americans. By this act's provisions, Britain's main colonial agent in India would be rescued, its British investors would be rewarded, and the royal treasury would collect more tea duties from America. Meanwhile, the Americans would be enticed by lower tea prices to accept a parliamentary tax, and their merchants would be dealt a crushing blow.

THE LOGIC OF IMPERIAL CONTROL.   As historian Edward Countryman has noted, the Tea Act showed that George III's reforms were designed to reduce the North American colonies to dependent partners in the British imperial system, much like India itself. Southern plantations already fit well into Britain's Atlantic trade, and northern farmers could be left alone because they raised crops not needed in Britain. But Boston and New York, with their growing manufacturing workshops, coastal trading networks, and wealthy merchants, competed directly with England and represented a potential threat. Through the taxes and restrictions of the 1760s and

1770s, Britain moved to curtail development in these seaports and skim off its profits. This was the same strategy that England pursued simultaneously in India and Ireland. As these lands came under British rule, the king and Parliament pushed aside local merchants, stifled local industry, and enforced an economic "underdevelopment" that allowed the imperial center's manufacturers and merchants to prosper. When Britain shook off "benign neglect" and tightened its imperial grip after 1763, it was attempting to force its North American colonies down the same path.

SEPARATING FROM THE EMPIRE

RESISTANCE AND REVOLUTION. The Americans, however, were too far along the road to self-rule to turn back. Drawing upon the transatlantic language of representative government and British rhetoric about "liberty," colonial spokesmen encouraged popular protests against the new laws. Outspoken colonists evolved from grudgingly accepting mercantile duties to repudiating all "taxation without representation" in Parliament. Faced with tax resistance and consumer boycotts, Parliament repealed the Stamp Act and most of the Townshend duties. But after well-organized "Tea Parties" dumped the East India Company's cargo into Boston and New York's harbors, the British cracked down. Parliament suspended the operation of colonial governments and closed seaports. Colonial rebels, now denying the right of Parliament to legislate for them on any matter, organized shadow governments and stocked ammunition for their militias. In April 1775, when a contingent of British soldiers intending to destroy the rebels' stockpiles exchanged deadly volleys with a colonial militia at a bridge in Concord next to the house of William Emerson, Ralph Waldo Emerson's grandfather, colonial resistance erupted into an anticolonial war.

COMMON SENSE AND INDEPENDENCE. Setting out to integrate North America's colonies into a uniform empire, Britain succeeded instead in uniting them against imperial rule. The passionate writings of a transatlantic radical pushed Americans to the final break. Thomas Paine, a disgruntled British customs officer who followed Benjamin Franklin's advice to migrate to Philadelphia, penned the best-selling pamphlet *Common Sense* in January 1776. While Thomas Jefferson and John Adams spoke for colonial planters and merchants aggrieved by Britain's policies, Paine mobilized the colonies' artisans and small farmers. In no-nonsense prose that invoked the "rights of man," not "British liberties," Paine mocked the colonists' lingering allegiance to the king and their pride in British identity. Monarchy, Paine explained, was a "ridiculous" form of government that exalted the will of a "crowned ruffian" over the sovereignty of the people. Colonists who clung to British rule ignored the absurdity of "supposing a continent to be perpetually governed by an island." Rejecting talk of reconciliation, Paine told colonists that their destiny was to build a republic; he sketched a preliminary blueprint and suggested that they announce their independence immediately. Six months later—more than two years after armed hostilities had broken out—the Continental Congress approved a declaration to "a candid world" that the "United Colonies" had become "free and independent states."

THE REVOLUTION AS A GLOBAL WAR.   Winning independence took seven more years, constant diplomatic maneuvering, and decisive foreign assistance. On the frontier, both Britain and the colonists urged Indian peoples to remain neutral. Trusting neither side and lacking a French alternative at hand, tribal communities split. In the northeast, for example, most Iroquois sided with the British, but the Oneidans backed the Americans. The dislocations of war dispersed Indian communities, and their divisions and dwindling numbers diluted their impact on the war's outcome.

African Americans also split over the Revolution, largely because the British promised slaves freedom whereas the Americans refused. Five thousand blacks fought for the colonists, but more than 80,000 southern slaves fled plantations to the British lines, enticed by Britain's Dunsmore Proclamation of 1775 that offered emancipation to those willing to assist the redcoats. When defeat loomed, the British evacuated nearly 10,000 African Americans by ship. Some were sold into slavery in the West Indies and others taken to London, but the largest contingent was resettled in Nova Scotia as indentured servants.

Along the American seacoast, the British army proved unable to hold colonial cities without popular support, and General George Washington's ragtag Continental Army developed effective tactics of retreat and counterattack. But the Americans might not have defeated the British without European help. The French, hoping to weaken Britain and reverse the humiliation of the Seven Years' War, immediately sympathized with the rebels. Although neutral at the war's outset, they supplied most of the weapons and ammunition used by the rebels as well as many volunteer soldiers. In 1778, following the colonists' surprising capture of a large British army at Saratoga, France offered the Americans a formal alliance. In 1779 and 1780, the Spanish and Dutch also declared war on Britain. A League of Armed Neutrality led by Catherine the Great of Russia demanded an end to England's blockade of French ports. Thus by 1780, the American Revolution had evolved into a global imperial war that pitted Britain against most of Europe.

The decisive victory in North America was engineered by the Franco-American alliance. In October 1781, Washington's army, supplemented by

FIGURE 2-3   THE BRITISH SURRENDER
This contemporary drawing depicts the formal surrender of British troops at Yorktown on October 19, 1781. Columns of American troops and a large French fleet flank the surrender ceremony, suggesting part of the reason for the British defeat. General Cornwallis, the commander of the British forces in Virginia, did not himself attend the surrender, but sent a deputy in his place. *(Hulton/Archive/Getty Images) (Source: Used with permission from* American History *(11th ed.), by Alan Brinkley. Copyright 2003 by McGraw-Hill.)*

French forces under General Rochambeau, pinned Lord Cornwallis's British troops on the Yorktown peninsula in Virginia while French Admiral De Grasse's fleet prevented their reinforcement or retreat by sea. Cornwallis surrendered. British officials considered sending additional forces to subdue the Americans, but with the French fleet threatening the British sugar islands, the Spanish besieging Gibraltar, Holland capturing British markets in the East Indies, and additional fighting looming in India and South Africa, the British decided to cut their losses. In the Treaty of Paris (1783), scheduled to take effect once Britain reached terms with the colonists' European allies, Britain recognized the thirteen colonies' independence and bequeathed them the additional British territory between the Appalachian Mountains and the Mississippi River.

BRITISH EXPANSION REDIRECTED.   Some historians have called the American Revolution "England's Vietnam." Faced with a popular revolt in a distant land where unfamiliar terrain and irregular warfare made conquest impossible, the British, like Americans 200 years later in southeast Asia, were forced to withdraw. But if the analogy is meant to imply imperial decline, it is off the mark. The British were galled by the colonists' victory, but prompt settlement of new territories compensated for their loss.

The American Revolution indirectly helped to develop three British colonies that eventually became new nations. Thousands of loyalist families fled the thirteen colonies for Canada, where the provinces of New Brunswick and Upper Canada (later Ontario) were organized to accommodate the influx, and which their descendants transformed into a thriving British colony. Britain's West African colony of Sierra Leone was another indirect product of the American revolt. Four hundred African American refugees who had been freed and sent to London were resettled there in 1787 by a group of charitable London merchants, and they were joined by 1,200 black loyalists from the Nova Scotia settlement. Finally, when Georgia and other American colonies no longer accepted prisoners sentenced to exile for crimes committed in England, British officials turned to Australia, which Captain James Cook had claimed for the Crown in 1770, as their new dumping ground. Far from dampening British ambitions, the American Revolution stimulated British expansion elsewhere. Casting about for additional trade and territory in Africa, Asia, the Pacific, and the Middle East, Britain continued to build its empire. Its heyday was still a century ahead.

SISTER REVOLUTIONS: AMERICA AND FRANCE

By breaking away from the British Empire, the American colonists triggered an Age of Revolution in the Atlantic world. The American Revolution was the first act in a long revolutionary drama extending from the 1770s through the European Revolutions of 1848. The Americans' success helped inspire colonists in Latin America to separate from Spanish rule. It also emboldened French citizens to proclaim their rights and discard their monarchy for a republic. How was the American Revolution connected to these popular struggles against kings? What features did they share, and how were they different in aims or outcome? In what sense was the American war for independence a "revolution"? Where does it stand in the spectrum marked by radical social revolution at one end and the simple transfer of political power between elites at the other? Addressing these questions clarifies the nature of the American struggle and helps us to gauge its place in world history.

To many historians, the French Revolution of 1789 was the greater upheaval, an earthquake that shook Europe's foundations and changed the course of world history more fundamentally than the colonists' republican experiment on Europe's periphery. The French Revolution destroyed feudalism and invented socialism; it toppled kings and spurred nationalist uprisings in Europe; and it shifted the worldwide balance of power. By comparison, the American Revolution had fewer immediate effects and influenced other peoples more by example than conquest. True enough in the short run, this contrast became open to question as the United States grew into a regional and world power in the next century. In any case, the fact that American revolutionaries encouraged the French in 1789 gave them a part in its drama.

THE AMERICAN IMPACT IN FRANCE.   The most basic way the American Revolution led to the French upheaval was by bankrupting the French monarchy. Both revolutions burst from the strain that imperial rivalries placed on royal budgets. Just as George III revamped colonial taxation to pay for the Seven Years' War, Louis XVI's ministers tried to fix the crippling budget deficit that resulted from France's defeat in 1763 and its support for the American patriots of 1776 by proposing a general tax on landed property. The American Revolution originated in a dispute over Parliament's right to tax; the French Revolution began with debates over what might constitute a legitimate "parliament" to vote on taxes. The Estates General, the elected convention that the French king had reluctantly convened to approve his tax reforms, opened its proceedings by considering plans for a representative national assembly that could limit or perhaps abolish the monarchy.

This move suggests that the American Revolution hastened the French upheaval in another way: by showing that "subjects" could become "citizens." The Americans provided a contagious example of how a sovereign people could remove kings and embed new ideas of individual liberty and equality in representative governments. Thousands of French soldiers served in the American war for independence and returned with fervent republican convictions. One of them, the Marquis de Lafayette, a liberal nobleman who had fought beside Washington at Yorktown, came to symbolize ties between the two revolutions. After the Parisian mob attacked the Bastille on July 14, 1789, Lafayette sent Washington the key to the infamous prison, declaring that the French had followed the Americans' lead in destroying the "fortress of despotism."

In the early, constitution-making days of the French Revolution the American experience took center stage. During the 1780s, the Declaration of Independence and the new American state constitutions had been publicized by America's popular envoy in Paris, Benjamin Franklin. After the Revolution broke out, their influence became apparent. The French Declaration of the Rights of Man and of Citizen (1789) adapted language from the Declaration of Independence as well as Virginia's Declaration of Rights to French conditions. America's example helped inspire the famous Tennis Court Oath, in which the Third Estate, encompassing all Frenchmen who were not nobles or clergy, vowed to continue meeting until the king accepted a constitution. As members of the French National Assembly debated that constitution, they analyzed the American experience of balancing the representation of aristocrats and commoners in legislatures with upper and lower houses.

FROM THE FRENCH REPUBLIC TO NAPOLEON.   In short order, however, domestic conflicts and opposition from foreign monarchs spun the French Revolution into a dizzying spiral that left its American prototype far behind. France's constitutional monarchy ended in 1792 after Louis XVI was captured while fleeing the country. Lafayette, who had accepted a leadership post in the king's army, fled for his own life and endured imprisonment in Austria for five years before American appeals helped obtain his release. In 1792 the newly elected National Convention established a republic and the following year executed Louis XVI. Soon war began to derail the revolution as royalist uprisings in the provinces threatened the new regime and the French faced an invasion by Germans and Austrians. Internally, there was continued strife. During the Reign of Terror, the ruthless Jacobin leader Maximilian Robespierre took control of the republic, confiscated the estates of emigres, and sent thousands who opposed his actions to the guillotine. In 1794 the Convention intervened to overthrow Robespierre and set up rule by a five-person Directory, which governed shakily until 1799. At that point, the military hero Napoleon Bonaparte, recently returned from victories in Italy and Egypt, began his relentless drive toward political power by coopting the electoral process, centralizing government bureaucracy, and channeling revolutionary fervor into wars of imperial conquest. By 1804, when Napoleon declared himself emperor, the French had come full circle, pledging allegiance to a vision of French empire even grander than the old royal regime's, but now imposed in the name of "liberty, equality, and fraternity."

COMPARING "SISTER REVOLUTIONS."   Because the French overthrew a domestic monarch rather than an overseas one, and because they aimed to tear down medieval social structures that did not exist in the thirteen colonies, their revolution became a more profound social upheaval. French revolutionaries waged war on the Catholic Church, abolished hereditary titles and class privileges, totally reorganized government (several times), and gave birth to modern socialist ideas. In its Napoleonic phase, the Revolution imposed new rulers and a secular legal code on conquered nations. This sweeping agenda made the French Revolution a more frightening specter to nineteenth-century European rulers than the American Revolution, and a more attractive model to twentieth-century Marxist revolutionaries.

It is revealing that Thomas Paine, the fiery author of *Common Sense*, became hated for opposite reasons in the two sister republics. Increasingly criticized as too radical by many Americans for his attacks on unequal rights and organized religion, Paine left the Anglo-American world for Paris, where he barely escaped Robespierre's guillotine for his bourgeois, small-government sympathies. Paine's problems demonstrate that the American revolutionaries prized individual liberty, whereas the French were more intent upon imposing social equality. The French sought to remake the political and social order; the Americans wanted to return to the freedoms they had enjoyed before the British king and Parliament withdrew them.

In the thirteen colonies there were few feudal privileges to abolish, no closed craft or occupational guilds to pry open, and no powerful churches that buttressed the monarchy. The social character of the American Revolution was incidental to its origin as a struggle for political independence. Although the war with England did kill 25,000 colonists and uproot a Loyalist minority, many of whom emigrated and lost their property, the Revolution did not fundamentally reorder American society.

REVOLUTION OR REFORM?   There were some significant changes, however. Slavery, which the French temporarily abolished in their colonies, came under attack from Quakers and free blacks during the American independence movement. Through laws or court decisions it was gradually eliminated in several northern states where it had been a marginal institution, although it remained protected in the southern states where the plantation economy dominated. Property requirements for voting were reduced in several states, and governors' powers were curtailed. A heightened democratic ethos meant that the new state legislatures had a larger proportion of men of "moderate" means than their colonial predecessors. Schools were opened to train women as mothers and teachers of republican citizens. And in New England, legislators eventually withdrew tax support for the Congregational Church, which had been funded by government under the Puritans.

All these were incremental steps toward a more democratic society, not the drastic overnight changes of a social revolution. Recent historians who argue that the American Revolution was socially radical make their case by stretching its effects over eight decades, from the 1760s to the 1830s, and by labeling "revolutionary" the gradual and (with the crucial exception of slavery) quite peaceful working out of egalitarian implications latent in the Declaration of Independence. This pattern fits the British notion of "reform" better than the French experience of revolution—with the proviso that unlike in Britain, where political elites offered concessions to vocal nonvoters, in the United States the power to elect or even to become public officials rested with average white males.

REVOLUTIONS AND CONSTITUTIONS.   The features that most qualify as radical, especially in world-historical terms, were the American Revolution's political ideas and institutions. The Americans' grievances arose from colonial experience but their language transcended it by invoking natural rights and popular sovereignty, concepts that extended the impact of the transatlantic Enlightenment. The Declaration of Independence announced that "all men are created equal," endowed with the same right to "life, liberty, and the pursuit of happiness." Its second and final paragraphs asserted that when governments fail to protect these rights, their overthrow warrants the creation of new independent states. This was the "right of revolution" that would later be cited by anticolonial leaders and nationalist heroes from Venezuela's Francisco de Miranda to Vietnam's Ho Chi Minh. For the Americans, and for the French after them, revolution became a mandate to "begin the world anew" and set an example for humanity.

The most influential precedent was the Americans' model of constitutional government. The institutions the Americans devised to protect their rights—constituent conventions, declarations of rights, written constitutions, representative legislatures, a federal system, separate branches of government, and the separation of church and state—made a profound impression on the French in 1791, despite the very different social and political contexts in the two nations. These constitutional ideas permeated the European Age of Revolution that the French started, surfacing in specific features of new republican regimes in Holland, Switzerland, and Italy, in the French Constitutional Assembly of 1848, and in the German Frankfurt Assembly of 1848. Ignaz Paul Vital Troxler, the Swiss philosopher responsible for that nation's federal system, believed that the U.S. constitution was "a great work of art which the human mind created according to the eternal laws of its divine nature," and "a model . . . for . . . republics in general."

REVOLUTION AND INDEPENDENCE IN THE AMERICAS

Similar sentiments were voiced in the southern half of the New World in the 1820s. When independent Latin American nations emerged from Spanish and Portuguese rule, many latched onto federalism as a way to form stable regimes out of societies run by regional strongmen and torn by economic and racial divisions. As settler movements aimed at ending imperial control, the North American and Latin American campaigns for independence shared common features and faced similar problems. But American federalism proved no panacea during Latin Americans' chaotic process of state formation. In most new southern republics, social divisions and political inexperience resulted in a history of military takeovers and fragile democracy, a saga that highlighted by contrast the advantages bequeathed to the North Americans by their colonial past.

Between 1790s and 1828, nearly all the colonies of Central and South America broke away from their rulers in Spain and Portugal and confirmed their independence through military victories. Although each new nation's revolutionary history was distinctive, there were important broad similarities between these revolutions and that of Britain's thirteen colonies; but there were also telling differences.

ORIGINS OF LATIN AMERICAN REVOLUTIONS.   Both the British and Spanish colonial rebellions grew out of protests against imperial reforms. Tighter imperial governance and tax increases sparked a revolt in 1781 against Spanish rule by wealthy colonists in New Grenada (present-day Colombia, Venezuela, and Ecuador) and a native rebellion in Peru led by the Incan chief Tupac Amaru. Both outbreaks were suppressed by Spanish authorities. Meanwhile, the American Revolution inspired Latin American liberals (those who favored representative government and a secular state) to continue plotting independence. Translations of *Common Sense* and the Declaration of Independence circulated in revolutionary Argentina. The South American liberator Simón Bolívar idolized George Washington and praised the U.S. constitution, although he believed its central government too weak to ensure stability in revolutionary Venezuela and Colombia. Venezuelan agitator Francisco de Miranda forged plans for Latin American independence during a visit to the United States in 1783. After defeating Spanish forces, his countrymen planned to issue their declaration of independence on July 4, 1811, but legislative approval delayed it. "Two great examples lie before our eyes, the American and the French Revolutions," Miranda wrote. "Let us discreetly imitate the first; let us carefully avoid the disastrous effects of the second."

FIGURE 2-4   INDEPENDENCE IN LATIN AMERICA BY 1830

Source: Used with permission from Traditions and Encounters *(2nd ed.), by Jerry H. Bentley and Herbert F. Ziegler. Copyright 2002 by McGraw-Hill.*

THE HAITIAN EXCEPTION.   Despite Miranda's advice, it was France's actions, not the North Americans', that helped trigger most of the Latin American independence movements. The first blow was the most stunning and the most radical. Inspired by the French Revolution, the free "colored" (mixed-race) population of Saint Domingue (later known as Haiti) obtained the vote. Their success in turn inspired a rebellion by Haiti's slaves that erupted even before French revolutionaries outlawed slavery in their colonies in 1794 and continued after the French revoked the law. Over the course of a dozen years, the Haitian Revolution developed from a revolt of ex-slaves and radical whites into a slave rebellion, and then a war against foreign intervention. Great Britain, sensing that Haiti was up for grabs and worried that the Haitian uprising might spread to its West Indian plantations, sent more troops to Haiti than it dispatched after 1776 to suppress the thirteen colonies' rebellion, but to no avail. More than half of Britain's soldiers died on the island, most the victims of disease.

In its culminating phase, the uprising in Haiti became an independence struggle against the French, which finally succeeded in 1804. Led not by white elites but those they oppressed, the Haitian Revolution was uniquely radical among the New World colonial rebellions. Eventually it became an inspiration for twentieth-century anticolonial revolutionaries in the third world. In 1800, however, it served as a cautionary example to colonial elites of the likely consequences if independence movements were allowed to develop into social convulsions. Subsequent Latin American revolutions broke from European rule but stopped short of advocating political and social equality between white settlers and indigenous or African people of color. They were political independence movements, not social revolutions.

CONSERVATIVE "CREOLE REVOLUTIONS." In 1807 and 1808, Napoleon ignited these more conservative independence movements when his armies invaded the Iberian Peninsula, exiling the Portuguese royal family to Brazil and deposing Ferdinand VII of Spain. Homegrown colonial elites throughout Spanish America seized this chance to push aside the *Peninsulares*, or ruling class from the Iberian homeland, and institute new governments run by creoles (colonial-born whites). These juntas, or governing councils, at first proclaimed their loyalty to the king, but when they were opposed by colonial officials and were denied autonomy after Ferdinand was restored to the throne, they pushed for independence. One by one, beginning with Mexico in 1810, Venezuela, Colombia, Argentina, Central America, Peru, Bolivia, and Chile declared their separation from the Spanish empire. After a long military struggle led by Bolívar in the north and by José de San Martín in Argentina and Chile, Spanish forces in South America were finally defeated in 1824. Only Cuba and Puerto Rico remained Spanish colonies.

Unlike the revolution in Haiti, these "Creole revolutions" were settler revolts led by colonial-born descendants of the European conquerors seeking to separate from the parent country but not to extend rights to African slaves or indigenous and mixed-race peoples. In policies and temperament they ranged from relatively liberal movements in Chile and Argentina, settler colonies where slavery had little influence, to strongly conservative ones in Brazil and Mexico, which were badly divided by race and class. In Mexico, Spain's richest New World colony, independence was the work of wealthy elites and church officials who had defended Spanish rule against peasant rebellions in 1810 and 1813. Seizing power when news of a liberal military coup in Spain reached the colony in 1821, these Creole traditionalists cut off popular protests by establishing a monarchy and crowning Colonel Agustín de Iturbide its emperor.

COMPARING "CREOLE REVOLUTIONS."   How did the American Revolution compare with the Latin American "Creole revolutions"? In both movements, settlers of European descent separated from their parent country, a process quite different from twentieth-century revolutions in which colonized African or Asian native peoples fought against Western imperialist control. Like Latin American colonists, North American rebels were intent on establishing colonial "home rule," but not extending "rule at home" to indigenous peoples or imported Africans. New World independence movements had strict racial limits. The United States outlawed the overseas slave trade in 1808 and most Spanish American republics followed suit shortly after independence. But new American nations that relied heavily on plantation crops, such as Brazil (which adopted a constitutional monarchy in 1822) and the United States, resisted revolutionaries' calls to end slavery. Virtually all the new nations imposed property requirements that prevented most ex-slaves from voting. Similar restrictions excluded native peoples from full citizenship, although population patterns dictated different kinds of settler domination. In much of Central and South America, native and mixed-race majority populations continued to be used as dependent farm and ranch laborers, while in British North America, as Argentina and Chile, whites increasingly outnumbered the native population and pushed them off desirable lands in wars of "removal" during post-independence decades.

DIFFERENT REVOLUTIONS, DIFFERENT OUTCOMES.   In other ways, North American and Latin American independence movements diverged dramatically in their dynamics and outcome. By proclaiming equal rights among whites and defending traditional liberties, the North Americans successfully incorporated free settlers of different social classes into their revolution and the new governments it formed. Latin American societies, more committed to class hierarchies and privileges, found little basis for united opposition to Spanish rule or unanimous allegiance to new governments after the revolution. In North America, white merchants, artisans, laborers, and farmers had aired their grievances and compromised differences in colonial assemblies. By contrast, neither Spain nor Portugal had permitted elected legislatures and municipal councils in their New

World colonies, leaving their former colonists without political experience or inherited frameworks for governing. While Latin American nations debated the merits of monarchies versus republics and tinkered endlessly with federal constitutional models—many imported from the United States—North Americans benefited from their long apprenticeship in self-government. Their colonial assemblies were converted into state legislatures and their charters into state constitutions, ensuring a relatively smooth transfer of authority.

Other factors contributed to political turmoil in Latin America and comparative stability in the North. Although all new republics in the Americas limited voting rights to free men of property, their landholding patterns differed radically. Enormous colonial-era land grants entrusted power to planter and rancher minorities in Latin America, but widespread land ownership enabled the vast majority of white male settlers in the new United States to vote, and gradual elimination of property requirements widened popular access to power. The long Latin American wars for independence created powerful military commanders who resisted control by civilian authorities, and to whom frustrated citizens sometimes turned for efficient government. As a result, democratic institutions were often ignored or swept aside by regional warlords (called *caudillos*) or military dictators. In the United States, civilian control of the military was ensured by General Washington's deference to the Continental Congress and, after the Revolution, by the disbanding of the national army. Finally, relations between church and state proved more contentious in Latin America. The Catholic Church's colonial-era alliance with the Crown and its monopoly over education led to perennial conflict, and sometimes civil wars, in newly independent Mexico, Colombia, and Argentina between liberals who sought to reduce its powers and traditionalists who aimed to preserve them. In the young United States, the variety of Christian groups made church monopolies impossible, and although constitutional separation of church and state did not eliminate churches' political power, it made it less formal and direct.

Due to such differences, the road to effective constitutional government proved rockier in the post-revolutionary years in Latin America than in the United States. North Americans profited from a colonial legacy of constitutional government, relative political autonomy, and widespread economic opportunity when they embarked upon nationhood. Still, it must be noted that this did not free them from other serious problems they shared with Latin America's new nations: frequent threats of foreign intervention, persisting regional divisions, and fierce conflict over slavery. As the next chapter will show, these issues proved so intractable that they threatened the existence of the new United States.

Suggested Readings

Bailyn, Bernard. *Atlantic History: Concepts and Contours.* Cambridge, MA: Harvard University Press, 2005.
  —An elegant sketch of the main features of Atlantic history by a scholar who pioneered a transatlantic approach to colonial history.

Benjamin, Thomas, Timothy Hall, and David Rutherford, eds. *The Atlantic World in the Age of Empire.* Boston: Houghton Mifflin, 2001.
  —Gathers readings from important recent historical works on the Atlantic economy, its flow of peoples, and the Atlantic revolutions.

Countryman, Edward. *The American Revolution,* revised ed. New York: Hill and Wang, 2003.
  —An excellent, readable synthesis of modern scholarship on the Revolution.

Dubois, Laurent. *Avengers of the New World: The Story of the Haitian Revolution.* Cambridge, MA: Harvard University Press, 2004.
  —A vivid narrative history that unravels the complexity of the first and only successful slave revolution in the Americas.

Dunn, Susan. *Sister Revolutions: French Lightning, American Light.* New York: Faber and Faber, 1999.
  —An engaging comparative analysis of the two revolutions, with provocative final chapters on their legacies.

Elliott, J. H. *The Old World and the New, 1492–1650.* Cambridge: Cambridge University Press, 1970.
  —Suggests how the early Americas influenced Old World theology, history, and anthropology as well as the European economy.

Langley, Lester D. *The Americas in the Age of Revolution, 1750–1850.* New Haven: Yale University Press, 1996.
  —Compares the North American and Latin American independence movements and their resulting societies.

Marks, Robert B. *The Origins of the Modern World: A Global and Ecological Narrative.* Lanham, MD: Rowman & Littlefield, 2002.
  —A succinct synthesis that incorporates recent scholarship on the economic importance of Asia and moves the "rise of the West" forward to 1750–1800.

Meinig, D. W. *Atlantic America, 1492–1800,* Vol. 1 of *The Shaping of America.* New Haven: Yale University Press, 1986.
  —An innovative historical geographer's view of colonial North America in Atlantic context, featuring excellent maps and diagrams.

Nash, Gary B. *Red, White, and Black: The Peoples of Early North America,* 5th ed. Upper Saddle River, NJ: Prentice-Hall, 2006.
  —A thoroughly multicultural narrative that summarizes recent work on the African slave trade and colonial society.

Palmer, R. R. *The Age of the Democratic Revolution: A Political History of Europe and America, 1760–1800.* 2 vols. Princeton: Princeton University Press, 1959.
   —The classic study that links and compares the French and American Revolutions, placing both in an Atlantic Age of Revolution.

Pomeranz, Kenneth. *The Great Divergence: China, Europe, and the Making of the Modern World Economy.* Princeton: Princeton University Press, 2000.
   —An influential study of factors that led to the "rise of the West" after 1750, stressing England's access to coal and the Americas' contribution.

Schama, Simon. *Rough Crossings: Britain, the Slaves and the American Revolution.* New York: HarperCollins, 2006.
   —Traces the impact of the Revolution on African Americans and black loyalists' fate in Nova Scotia and Sierra Leone.

Sparks, Randy J. *Two Princes of Calabar: An Eighteenth-Century Atlantic Odyssey.* Cambridge, Mass.: Harvard University Press, 2004.
   —Based on the recently discovered letters of two African captives, this narrative portrays the human side and the inner workings of the slave trade.

CHAPTER THREE

MAKING A NATION

GETTING STARTED ON CHAPTER THREE: What problems did the young United States have in common with other new nations, and how did it address them? How did international developments influence the new nation's democratic politics and foreign policy? How did the American westward movement compare to frontier expansion in other settler societies? In what ways were the American antislavery movement, the Civil War, and Reconstruction distinctive variants of global trends in the nineteenth century?

The nineteenth century ushered in a global age of nation building. Nationalist agitation was encouraged by the Age of Revolution's ideal of self-government and promoted by liberals' equation of "peoplehood" with nationality. It spread by example and through competition in the increasingly interconnected world economy. Nationalism was put to work in many ways, some of them opposed: it was used to justify nation-based empires, to resist them or break them up, to merge small states into bigger ones, to incite democratic revolutions, or to cement authoritarian rule. After nationalists achieved victory and determined the territorial homeland, the task of nation building remained. This involved constructing efficient national governments and other public institutions as well as forging agreement on national identity and citizenship. In some cases, such as France and Japan, the nation's boundaries and cultural identity were already set, and the focus turned to building a centralized state. In others the process was reversed. "We have made Italy," the philosopher Massimo d'Azeglio reportedly declared in 1861 after several Italian provinces were joined under one government, "now we have to make Italians."

In the United States, as in other New World nations that emerged from anticolonial revolts, the development of national institutions, territory, and identity occurred simultaneously and sustained one another.

115

Making a nation, in Americans' particular circumstances and ambitions, meant creating a viable republic; that is, a government resting on popular sovereignty and elected representatives. It also meant building a strong sense of national identity, securing the nation's borders, expanding inland, and—a problem mostly unforeseen at independence—resolving a growing internal division over slavery. This was a daunting agenda, one that speeded up stages of national development that were proceeding more slowly in most European settler societies or, in France after 1789, moving so fast that they doomed its republican experiment within a decade. Americans accomplished the job with such success that they astonished skeptics at home and abroad. During their first century they constructed a republican government—the most advanced in the Western world—spread its territory westward to the Pacific Ocean, and developed their economic and military prowess to the verge of becoming a world power.

This achievement did not come without conflict. Westward expansion brought violence against Native Americans, and national unity emerged only after a ghastly civil war. Nor did it occur in isolation from the rest of the world, despite Americans' conviction that they were a people set apart. Independence did not extricate Americans from global systems of economic exchange and national rivalry that were still dominated by Europe. Their quest for security took place during the continuing war between France and England, a struggle that threatened to drown the infant republic in its vortex. Westward expansion meant incursion into lands claimed by other nations, involving the young United States in negotiations with France and England and war with Mexico. And even as frontiersmen penetrated North America's interior they remained tied, like Americans on the eastern seaboard, to an economic system governed by Europe's rules.

Slavery, the young nation's most important link to the Atlantic economy, increasingly divided Americans into opposing sectional camps. Like Latin American slave societies, the American South prospered by furnishing slave-grown raw materials to industrial Britain—in its case, mainly cotton. Meanwhile, the movement to restrict or abolish slavery—itself an outgrowth of transatlantic contacts—gained ground in the nonslave Northern states, which were committed to strengthening the national government and modernizing the nation's capitalist economy. Abolitionism threatened the livelihood of slave societies throughout the New World, and secession movements plagued many of the new republics in Latin America. In the United States the two forces collided to imperil the nation's very existence. The struggle over slavery's westward expansion opened two decades of political conflict that culminated in the secession of eleven southern slave states. Only after the North won a long and bloody civil war could the states declare themselves "united" under the central government, and could the initial phase of American nation building be considered completed.

TIMELINE

1787	United States federal constitution drafted
1793	Imperial wars between France and England reopen; United States declares neutrality
1800	Thomas Jefferson elected U.S. president, transferring power peacefully to Democratic-Republicans
1803	United States purchases Louisiana Territory from France
1807–1815	Great Britain bans African slave trade, followed by the United States, Netherlands, and France
1812–1815	War of 1812 between United States and Great Britain
1815	Napoleon's final defeat at Waterloo; European monarchies restored
1823	Monroe Doctrine proclaimed
1828	Andrew Jackson elected president, opening U.S. "Age of the Common Man"
1830–1831	Second wave of European revolutions and new constitutions
1831	Slave revolts led by Nat Turner in Virginia and Sam Sharpe in Jamaica
1832–1838	Indian Removal in the United States coincides with "Campaign of the Desert" against Argentina's Indians
1833	Britain declares end to slavery in West Indian colonies
1835–1840	Tocqueville publishes *Democracy in America*
1846–1848	United States-Mexican War results in acquisition of California and Southwest
1848	Third wave of revolutions in Europe; U.S. women's rights movement organized
1850–1860	Unsuccessful compromises over slavery in U.S. western territories
1852–1853	Secession of Buenos Aires from Argentina
1859–1871	National unification of Italy and Germany

1861	Lincoln becomes U.S. president; southern states complete secession from Union
	Civil War opens between United States and Confederate states
	Czar Alexander II frees serfs in Russia
1862	U.S. Homestead Act provides free land to western settlers
1865	Confederate armies surrender, ending U.S. Civil War
	Thirteenth Amendment ends slavery in United States
1865–1877	Post-Civil War Reconstruction in U.S. South
1867	Collapse of Napoleon III's colonial empire in Mexico
	United States purchases Alaska from Russia
	Canadian confederation organized
1876–1890	Last phase of U.S reservation wars
1879–1880	Final "Campaign of the Desert" against Argentina's Indians
1888	Slavery abolished in Brazil

THE UNITED STATES AS A NEW NATION

"The Government of the United States, since its institution, has scarcely evinced any thing else but proofs of weakness," Felix de Beaujour, Napoleon's Counsel General, wrote in 1810. "So extended an empire as theirs can never be kept together by so feeble a bond as a federative government." The United States "will dissolve before they have been formed into a great body of a nation."

From today's superpower vantage point, it is hard to realize how fragile the young nation was shortly after independence. Like Beaujour, many foreign observers expected America's national experiment to be brief. True, the American revolutionaries (with crucial assistance from France and Holland) had defeated the British at Yorktown in 1781. They had also negotiated a generous peace. The Treaty of Paris (1783) not only recognized American independence but also extended the republic's boundaries north to the Great Lakes and west to the Mississippi River. Yet winning national independence was simpler than securing it. Across this vast territory Americans had to establish a government that would command popular allegiance and survive a turbulent infancy.

THE "FIRST NEW NATION."   As the first major European colony to mount a successful revolt and a global pioneer in popular government, the United States became, in sociologist Seymour Martin Lipset's phrase, "the first new nation." The fate of other nations that emerged from anti-colonial revolts or political revolutions in later decades suggests that the odds are stacked against establishing a lasting political system, especially a democratic one. Their story, from the French republics that followed the Revolutions of 1789 and 1848, to newly independent Latin American nations in the nineteenth century, to many European colonies in Africa and Asia that won their independence after World War II, has been marred in many cases by descent into chaos and division, and in others by reversion to authoritarian rule. In contrast, the Americans adopted a constitution that has endured to this day. They developed a political party system that settled most policy differences through legislative debates and decisions, maintained orderly transitions from one presidential administration to another, incorporated new western states, and extended democratic rights through peaceful reforms. No other new nation could boast such a record. Why did the young United States survive with representative government intact while so many others failed?

To start with, the new nation benefited from a favorable colonial legacy. As noted in Chapter 2, Great Britain allowed North American colonists to manage their own production and much of their trade, so that by independence they were well positioned to develop the nation's economy. Immigrants to the colonies formed a property-owning settler population committed to stable government. Most important, through their elected assemblies North American colonists enjoyed a 150-year apprenticeship in self-rule not granted to settlers in the Spanish, Portuguese, French, or Dutch empires. Experience in financial and political affairs helped smooth the transition from colonial rule to national self-government. For more than two centuries after independence, Americans watched other new nations struggle to establish democratic institutions and wondered why they could not "be like us." They forgot that at its birth the United States enjoyed unusually favorable conditions for representative government.

Even so, the nation's success was not guaranteed, nor was it total. Difficult choices by national leaders, crucial constitutional compromises, innovations on European political practices, and ambitious efforts to construct a national identity shaped American public life in the decades after independence. All contributed to building the nation, but none were enough to prevent its descent into civil war.

THE PRESIDENCY AND THE CONSTITUTION

WASHINGTON AS A NATIONALIST LEADER. One danger was avoided at the outset. All new nations face the problem of preventing autocratic rule by their founding elites. Revolutions often produce charismatic leaders who command patriot troops and embody popular aspirations, but after independence is won, these men can easily become dictators who destroy representative government. George Washington, hailed as a hero for leading the Revolutionary army to victory over great odds and chosen by acclaim as the nation's first president, might have taken this path, but did not. Instead, Washington used his enormous popularity and prestige to ease his fellow Americans' transition to stable republican government.

As commander of the Continental army, Washington deferred to the principle of civilian control. This prevented the army from becoming a political force that interfered with or took over government operations, as happened in many later new nations. As president, Washington renounced grand titles and autocratic ways. He brought contending political factions into his cabinet, refused to serve more than two terms of office, and presided over a peaceful transition of power. When he retired from public life in 1797, Washington became the first head of a modern state to turn over office to a duly elected successor. His restrained and judicious approach gained precious time for the new nation and set the mold for its political life. More than any other achievement, Washington's worldwide historical reputation rests on his example as a nationalist military hero who became the modest leader of a republic. His career became the model for Simón Bolívar when he returned to Colombia after the Latin American wars for independence and refused to become monarch. Washington and Bolívar's actions form a striking contrast to the increasingly authoritarian careers of nineteenth-century nation-builders such as Napoleon and Otto von Bismarck or twentieth-century postcolonial leaders like Kwame Nkrumah of Ghana or Sukarno of Indonesia.

THE CONSTITUTION OF 1787.   A second crucial problem faced by all new nations is the construction of an enduring constitutional framework for representative government. In the United States the federal Constitution of 1787 played a decisive formative role. It is important to remember, however, that the constitution Americans now revere was actually the *second* constitution of the new nation's government. The first was a failure.

Conventional wisdom in the eighteenth century warned that republics could not extend over large geographic areas and confederations would descend into anarchy in the absence of centralized authority. In its first decade, the American republic threatened to confirm these maxims. Free of the British king, the former colonists, still wary of centralized power, set up a loose union of states under the Articles of Confederation (1781–1789), each with one vote in a national legislature whose scope was strictly limited. This government proved indecisive and powerless, unable to raise taxes, police the Indian frontier, or control regional outbreaks by disgruntled dissenters. When delegates to a constitutional convention met in Philadelphia in 1787, they decided to scrap it and begin anew.

The Constitution these Founders hammered out strengthened the national government but controlled its powers through a series of compromises and innovations. The powers of Congress were broadened to include taxation, interstate commerce, and the general welfare. Members of its lower house were elected directly by the people for brief terms, but those in the upper house, the Senate, were chosen by the states for longer terms—a compromise between democratic and aristocratic approaches. Large states held more places in the House of Representatives, where seats were based on population, while small states were appeased by granting every state two senators. A potentially powerful president and cabinet were established to enforce the laws and direct public policy. Meanwhile, Congress's and the President's actions could be tested against the Constitution by a Supreme Court composed of judges with lifetime tenure. By dividing the national government into executive, legislative, and judicial branches, the Founders provided a series of checks against accumulation of power. A similar dispersion of authority took place among the federal, state, and local governments, which gave the new nation the innovative and sometimes unwieldy structure of a federal republic. Shortly after the constitution's ratification, these protections against centralized power were supplemented by a Bill of Rights, which was incorporated through an amendment process that helped to assure that the Constitution could be updated when necessary.

RELATIONS BETWEEN CHURCH AND STATE.   Determining the relationship between church and state is a third formidable task faced by new nations. The Bill of Rights guaranteed freedom of worship and forbade laws establishing an official national religion. Committed to freedom of conscience but also steeped in Protestant Christianity, the American Founders looked for a middle ground. By giving no religion a favored place, they repudiated the practices of European monarchs, who used national churches to suppress dissent and bolster their rule. No church would be supported by national funds, while the states, under pressure from religious minorities, gradually cut their ties with specific Protestant dominations. On the other hand, unlike later republican revolutionaries in France or Mexico, Americans did not set up an aggressively secular state. The Declaration of Independence invoked "nature's God"; presidents declared national days of prayer and thanksgiving; chaplains served Congress and the armed forces; and the government exempted religious organizations from taxation.

The "wall of separation" Thomas Jefferson envisioned between church and state proved to be somewhat porous, often to the benefit of both. Treated on equal terms, American Protestant churches adopted democratic ideas and marketing techniques to reach the widest possible public, while the new nation gained support from millions of believers who pledged allegiance to its implied commitment to godly ways. Still, when religious differences spilled over into politics they proved difficult to resolve. Conflicting religious opinions about slavery fed passions that led to the Civil War. An upsurge of evangelical Protestantism and an influx of Catholic immigrants in the mid-nineteenth century opened a struggle over the role of religion in government that continues in various forms to the present.

SLAVERY AND FEDERAL-STATE RELATIONS. The new constitution was designed to form "a more perfect Union," but the document was not perfect, nor was it complete. Securing its adoption required important evasions, two of which returned to haunt the new nation. The first concerned slavery, whose existence contradicted democratic ideals but was considered an economic necessity in cotton and tobacco-growing regions. Several Northern states, where slavery was limited and not economically vital, had already taken steps to end the institution, but Southern slaveholders would support no union that threatened the cornerstone of their society. The new constitution embodied compromises that recognized slaveowners' prerogatives without using the word "slavery" itself. Fugitive slaves had to be returned to their owners; the international slave trade would continue for 20 years before Congress could restrict it; and slaves counted as three-fifths of a person when the government levied taxes upon states and apportioned their representatives in Congress. The Founders had not made the nation "half slave and half free," as critics later charged, but finding it divided, they left it that way as the price of union. The full bill would come due 75 years later in a bloody sectional war.

Another evasion concerned relations between the states and the new federal government. The federal constitution declared itself the "supreme law of the land," but it left unanswered key questions about states' rights. Could sovereign states legally refuse to enforce federal laws within their borders? Could they choose to secede from the Union? The Constitution did not say and the Founders themselves left ambiguous pronouncements. The nation's first century was clouded by frequent controversies over foreign policy, war, the tariff, and slavery in which various dissenters, in the North as well as the South, sought to nullify federal laws within their states or threatened to take those states out of the Union.

THE CONSTITUTION'S IMPACT ABROAD.   Despite its flaws, the Constitution quickly took its place as one of the main exhibits of Americans' nationalistic pride. It illustrated a paradox fundamental to American nationalism. The product of unique circumstances and particular controversies, it was nevertheless expected, like democracy itself, to be applicable anywhere. Promoted by admirers abroad and certified by the nation's prosperity, the Constitution exerted a powerful attraction for new antimonarchical governments in the nineteenth and twentieth centuries. Specific features, such as its presidency, bicameral legislature, separation of powers, and Bill of Rights, were adopted by Norway (1814), Belgium (1830), Switzerland (1848), the Chinese Provisional Constitution of 1912, and Mexico (1917). Many new Latin American republics latched onto U.S.-style federalism, hoping to form stable regimes out of colonial societies torn by regional conflicts or racial divisions. Argentina appropriated the U.S. model nearly wholesale in 1853, and its judges sometimes cited American Supreme Court precedents in deciding cases. Not surprisingly, the constitution drawn up by Americans for Liberia in 1847 and that imposed by the U.S. forces occupying postwar Japan a century later echoed its language and provisions.

Yet the U.S. model did not work everywhere. The American constitution "arrived in the mail like a magic lock, without instructions or a key," Chile's Isabel Allende complained. In Mexico, Brazil, and elsewhere, federalism entrenched veto power in state or provincial governments and allowed contradictory local and national policies to coexist. In other cases it encouraged secession movements. In Liberia, Venezuela, and Belarus, adopting the U.S. presidential system rather than Britain's parliamentary government created an opening for authoritarian rulers. Experience would show that America's Constitution could be beneficial to other nations only when it fit with local democratic aspirations, traditions, and practices. In many cases its provisions simply dressed authoritarian rule in an elaborate republican costume.

DEMOCRACY AS A TRANSATLANTIC MOVEMENT

EMERGENCE OF POLITICAL PARTIES.   A fourth and final problem of new republics, the channeling of political divisions into orderly political parties, was handled less deliberately than the creation of a constitution, but with surprising success. The Founders feared political parties as instruments of private interests rather than the public good. Their constitution contained no provisions for them; in fact, it was explicitly designed to prevent what James Madison called "factions" from gaining power. Nevertheless, the alliances that sprouted to ratify or oppose the new Constitution gradually developed, once crystallized by Alexander Hamilton's proposals to strengthen federal power, into a two-party system that organized public opinion and contested elections. By 1800 its outlines emerged as the division between followers of Hamilton and Thomas Jefferson. The Jeffersonians, who were called Democratic-Republicans and later simply Democrats, favored decentralized government, agrarian interests, and white supremacy. The Hamiltonians, labeled Federalists and then Whigs, leaned toward a strong national government, commercial interests, and moral reforms such as temperance and Sunday observance. For the next half-century this developing party system absorbed almost every shade of political opinion into an orderly democratic process.

EUROPEAN PRECEDENTS AND CONNECTIONS.   Few American constitutional and political innovations were completely novel. The United States was a new nation in age but not in lineage. The idea that Americans "invented" their constitution ignores the rich heritage of European ideas and practices that the Founders drew upon. The framers of the Constitution of 1787 borrowed its rationale and many of its arrangements from Enlightenment philosophers such as John Locke, David Hume, and the Marquis de Montesquieu. They studied ancient Greek confederacies and the modern Dutch republic, citing Roman precedents for a "mixed" form of government that combined elements of monarchy, aristocracy, and democracy. Their Bill of Rights promised Americans traditional British legal protections such as a notice of criminal accusation, trial by jury, and no "cruel or unusual" punishments—some taken directly from the English Bill of Rights of 1689.

American political parties also took cues from abroad. Arguments over foreign policy were defining issues for the emergence of a two-party system. While the Federalists were friendly toward Great Britain, and their idol, George Washington, adopted the cabinet from England's ministerial system, Jefferson's Democratic-Republicans tilted toward a pro-French foreign policy and followed French precedents when they formed the first "grass-roots" American party. Local Democratic-Republican societies, formed by Americans sympathetic to the French Revolution, were organized in imitation of French Jacobin clubs as political pressure groups and watchdogs of the people's liberties. Eventually more than 40 of them coalesced into statewide groups and a Congressional caucus that backed Jeffersonian measures and men.

As the Democratic-Republicans and Federalists evolved into the Democrats and Whigs, they in turn learned lessons from Britain's parliamentary parties. British ties were especially important to the Whigs, who took their name directly from one of Parliament's two major parties. The party of "progress" in Britain in the early nineteenth century, the Whigs represented non-Anglican Protestants and opposed royal power in the interests of the industrial and commercial classes as well as social reform. The American Whigs felt religious, class, and ideological ties to their British counterparts, seeing themselves not only as the opponents of "King Andrew" (their label for President Jackson), but also the champions of economic modernization and moral reform. Their shared name demonstrates that American political parties were not simply grounded in local issues but orbited in the wider transatlantic political world. They developed by adopting rhetoric and methods of publicity from British parliamentary precedents, and then applied them to conditions in the new republic.

JACKSONIAN DEMOCRACY IN INTERNATIONAL PERSPECTIVE.   This was not mere copying, however. In the early nineteenth century, the staid, hierarchical world of the Founders evolved into a boisterous democratic society, and the Americans moved far beyond their British predecessors. Americans of the 1820s and 1830s pioneered modern electoral politics. Sweeping out the old gentlemanly style of "standing" for office and "running" for it instead, they ushered in a new era of mass parties and popular democracy. President Andrew Jackson, a rough-hewn Western lawyer and military hero, became the charismatic symbol of this "Age of the Common Man" (1828–1848).

Jacksonian Democrats were genuine innovators. They surpassed British-style parliamentary parties of the propertied classes by eliminating property requirements for white male voters. They held raucous nominating conventions and established cheap newspapers that preached the party line. Jackson's supporters distributed the "spoils" of office—a British word first used in the plural by Americans in 1830—and with these appointments they hatched America's first generation of professional politicians. Building the world's first mass political party, Jackson's Democrats transformed the way Americans voted and governed.

Yet dramatic as it was, America's Age of the Common Man had parallels elsewhere. While Jackson was in office, Irish Catholics rallied around the fiery orator Daniel O'Connell and won the right to sit in the British Parliament (1829), middle-class Englishmen got the vote through the Reform Act of 1832, the French again overthrew their monarchy in the July Revolution (1830), the Belgians broke off from Dutch rule (1830), and the Poles rose up against the Russian Czar (1830–31). In Latin America, Venezuela and Chile adopted republican constitutions (1831). These movements developed in separate contexts but were aware of each other, and all aimed at the expansion of representative government. In some cases they were also nourished by transatlantic exchanges of people and ideas. Especially noteworthy were exiled British radicals who joined the left wing of Jackson's Democratic Party and led its push for public education, trade unions, and free land. Across the Atlantic, a call for the vote issued by American women's rights advocates in the revolutionary year of 1848 inspired feminist agitation in England, France, and Sweden. Viewed in tandem, Jacksonian democracy and its counterparts abroad can be seen as the second stage of the Age of Revolutions that crisscrossed the Atlantic until the mid-nineteenth century. Less implicated in anticolonial wars than the first, this stage centered on nationalist movements and constitutional demands that extended democratic rights.

DEMOCRACY AND THE MARKET REVOLUTION.   This common transatlantic democratic surge calls into question the notion that uniquely American factors such as the frontier created Jacksonian democracy. Instead, it points toward shared underlying forces that were transforming Atlantic societies in the 1820s and 1830s. As the spreading capitalist market touched people's lives as wage earners and consumers, its uncertainties led them to demand a political voice and made banks and tariffs hot-button issues. In the advanced capitalist economies of Northern Europe and North America, a commercial middle-class sector emerged. In Europe it positioned itself between the old landed elites and the laboring classes; in the United States it dominated the civic sphere because it also included farmers. Dramatic advances in transportation and communication, such as steamships, railroads, and telegraphs, diffused democratic ideas and carried the immigrants and exiles who promoted them. The popular press, built upon improved printing processes and rising literacy, mobilized a force first given a name by the British: "public opinion." Arising simultaneously and reinforcing one another, these forces helped create the ideas and movements that gave birth to modern democratic societies.

The causes were similar, but the results differed. American democrats kept a step or more ahead of their European counterparts. The political aim of most European liberals was a constitutional monarchy with a representative legislature and restrictive property qualifications for voting. In Britain this was achieved peacefully through "reforms" conceded by Parliament; elsewhere in Europe, liberals lacked even such indirect channels to political power and resorted to revolution. Meanwhile, the Jacksonians enjoyed a republican government and they democratized male suffrage by defeating the kind of commercial and professional elites who were *leading* many European revolts. According to the American historian Henry Adams, if American and European liberals of the early 1800s agreed that "the next necessity of human progress was to lift the average man upon an intellectual and social level with the most favored," the Americans "stood at least three generations nearer than Europe to their common goal."[1] Adams should have said "average *white* man," because while Jackson's supporters liberalized suffrage for whites, they opposed doing so for free blacks and defended slaveowners' privileges. This glaring contradiction aside, for half a century after the French Revolution of 1789 descended into dictatorship and empire, the United States was the most advanced example of the transatlantic march into the democratic age.

FOREIGN COMMENTARY. This vanguard position suggested to many European and Latin American thinkers that their political destiny could be foretold, for better or worse, by the United States. Early nineteenth-century America became a magnet for politically minded tourists. Hordes of visitors came by ship to take the measure of America's political system and its way of life. If the young United States was the first mass democracy and if democracy was the wave of the future, should the rest of the world be pleased or troubled? Did political democracy work, or would it only create havoc, as conservatives predicted? Could a society dominated by common people accomplish great goals or aspire to excellence in the arts?

Hundreds of these instant experts published their impressions for curious readers back home and Americans eager for foreign approval. These travelogues tended to reflect the ideological positions visitors had brought with them. Thus, liberals like Argentina's Domingo Sarmiento and Britain's Harriet Martineau generally reacted favorably to what they saw, whereas monarchists like Felix de Beaujour and the Duke of Saxe-Weimar were critical. Out of this flurry of foreign commentary came one acknowledged masterpiece, the French aristocrat Alexis de Tocqueville's two-volume *Democracy in America* (1835–1840), an elegant and penetrating treatise on the implications of democracy for politics and society. Some of Tocqueville's most perceptive insights concerned specifically American phenomena, such as his warning that the presence of slavery and racial prejudice foreshadowed a violent internal war, or his famous prediction that the United States and Russia would become great power rivals in the twentieth century. But Tocqueville also pointed out to fellow Europeans two key paradoxes of the coming democratic wave. Although it brought freedom to many people, Tocqueville wrote, democracy fostered a "tyranny

---

[1]Henry Adams, *History of the United States During the Administrations of Thomas Jefferson* (1891; repr. New York: Library of America, 1986), 108.

of the majority" that enforced middlebrow tastes and social conformity. Its mobile society channeled citizens into a private "individualism"—a new word Tocqueville borrowed from French socialists—that focused on moneymaking and induced political apathy. To counter these problems, Tocqueville expressed the hope that Americans' habit of forming voluntary societies such as clubs and church groups would sustain their civic life.

AMERICAN NATIONALISM AND NATIONAL IDENTITY

Only when he encountered Americans' strident nationalism did Tocqueville abandon his customary detachment. "Nothing is more annoying in the ordinary intercourse of life than this irritable patriotism of the Americans," he wrote. Their "national pride has recourse to every artifice and descends to every childishness of personal vanity."

There was indeed an artificial and insistent quality to American nationalism as it emerged in the first half of the nineteenth century, but this did not diminish its strength. At the time, most statesmen and philosophers, having European examples in mind, agreed that blood, land, and history were a nation's essential ingredients; ardent nationalists claimed allegiance to a common ethnic or linguistic heritage, an ancestral territory, and (in French writer Ernest Renan's words) "a long past spent in toil, sacrifice, and devotion." The United States, only a generation old in the 1820s, had none of these. Except for Indians, its population had recently come from elsewhere; it had evolved from diverse colonial settlements; and it had no long past to celebrate.

CONSTRUCTING NATIONAL IDENTITY.   Renan declared that nationalism "cannot be improvised," but Americans proved him mistaken. In just a few decades, early nineteenth-century writers and artists conjured up a past for the United States, stocking it with memorable characters, places, and events: heroes like Patrick Henry, George Washington, and Daniel Boone; sacred shrines such as Plymouth Rock, Valley Forge, and Independence Hall; and a string of stirring scenes from the landing of the *Mayflower* to the last stand at the Alamo.

Despite the nineteenth-century emphasis on ancestral roots, it is clear that nations are built, not born; they are "imagined communities" whose leaders try to attract people's allegiance by winning their hearts and minds. Like the United States, many nineteenth-century European and settler nations diligently invented traditions for their people, symbolized them with anthems and flags, and taught them in history lessons to schoolchildren. Until World War I the United States, unlike Germany, Japan, and others, left this job to private individuals and businesses rather than the government. And it faced a somewhat different task. In Europe, governments had to detach existing legends and loyalties from church and village and affix them to the nation. In the United States and other newly independent settler societies, the task was to create national identity out of essentially new materials. Like Latin America's new republican citizens, Americans built a constitutional structure at the same time they developed a common peoplehood, and they acquired much of their national territory only after they became independent. Americans addressed this problem by incorporating the constitution and missionary expansion into their national self-definition.

The Revolutionary War gave Americans a rich source of national mythology and an emotionally charged reference point that was lacking in Canada, Brazil, and other settler nations that did not separate violently from the mother country. The struggle for independence also bridged Americans' past to their future, which they considered more important. More than ancestral ties, Americans were joined by shared adherence to the political principles embodied in their founding documents, the Declaration of Independence and the Constitution. Their first national motto, *E pluribus unum* (Out of many, one), expressed this consensual version of peoplehood that melded together different states and ethnic groups. Their second motto, *Novus ordo seclorum* (A new order for the ages), pointed Americans decisively toward the future, suggesting that their break with history would change the world.

AMERICAN EXCEPTIONALISM. As voiced by patriotic writers and statesmen, American nationalism embodied a strong "exceptionalist" sense of being a people set apart from others, standing outside the stream of history and even exempt from its burden. Attempting to declare cultural as well as political independence from Britain, Americans ignored transatlantic ties and instead built their national identity upon a dramatic contrast between the Old World and the New. The former symbolized aristocracy, monarchy, corruption, superstitious religion, and the dead weight of the past; the latter stood for democracy, republicanism, innocence, enlightened Christianity, and an unbounded future. Much of the exceptionalist vocabulary had existed for centuries; Americans simply absorbed into their nation-building agenda the utopian promises many Europeans had projected onto the New World in the era of discovery. By adopting the shorthand name "America," they took those visions from the rest of the hemisphere and gave their nation a metaphoric tag that conjured up dreams of a promised land.

Most of the key phrases of nineteenth-century American nationalism faced toward the future and invested the young nation with a providential mission. Ministers portrayed Americans as a "chosen people" like the Hebrews of the Bible, destined for greatness if they kept to God's plan. Expansionists expressed through "Manifest Destiny" the belief that the Almighty ordained the extension of the nation's territory and influence throughout North America. Presidents Jefferson and Lincoln proclaimed America's republican experiment the "last, best hope" for humanity. Although the United States refrained from sending military aid to nationalist revolutionaries in Europe or South America, many Americans saw their nation as a shining example of republican government for the rest of the world. American nationalism thus revolved around twin ideas—an exceptionalist assertion of uniqueness and an expansionist sense of mission—that at first appear contradictory but turn out to be opposite sides of the same coin.

Many new nations have infused their emergence with a sense of destiny, but Americans developed an especially passionate conviction of their world-historical importance. "Within two generations of independence," historian Daniel Rodgers has written, "the margin dwellers of the seventeenth century and provincials of the eighteenth century had reimagined themselves as vaulted into history's very forefront—model nation to the world, thorn in the side of Europe's old and decadent monarchies, torchbearer of progress itself."[2]

NATIONAL FAILURES. Americans' optimism and self-importance fed upon an early career of political innovation, geographic expansion, and economic growth. But the new nation was not an unblemished success, morally or institutionally. It housed a slave society that endured despite the Founders' assertion that all men were created equal. Its notion of citizenship was implicitly and often explicitly racial, centered on whites and not extended to Indians, African slaves, and nonwhite immigrants. Its emerging democracy was led by white men who expanded their voting rights while increasing restrictions on free blacks. Above all, it failed to prevent the Civil War, which developed in part out of these contradictions. The war signaled a massive systemic breakdown that later Americans passed over when they celebrated their new nation's success and touted its example to others. America's constitutional innovations, its two-party system, and its shared national identity were not enough to prevent an internal cataclysm that finally secured nationhood, at the cost of 620,000 lives. American nationalism would be based on blood after all.

---

[2]Daniel T. Rodgers, "An Age of Social Politics," in *Rethinking American History in a Global Age,* ed. Thomas Bender (Berkeley: University of California Press, 2002), 251.

NATIONAL SURVIVAL ON EUROPE'S PERIPHERY

In the early years of the republic, patriotic orators never tired of depicting "the rising glory of America" against the "fading gleam of Europe's setting ray." Edmund Burke, a British champion of American independence, claimed that the founding of the United States "made as great a change in all relations, and balances, and gravitations of power, as the appearance of a new planet would in the system of the solar world."

Burke and the American patriots were getting far ahead of themselves, for the new nation's position was much humbler. Political independence did not cut the United States loose from existing international systems of politics and trade, which were still controlled by Europe. After the American Revolution, Europe remained the hub of the world's economic and military power and would be for another century. England, France, and Spain were the great powers in wealth, population, and military strength. Spain had declined but still owned a vast overseas empire, which France and others coveted. In the 1780s, Britain, France, and Spain still controlled the Western Hemisphere, encircling the Americans and threatening access to the oceans. As long as the United States remained a military nonentity heavily dependent on trade with the West Indies and Europe, its fate hinged on the oscillations of European war and diplomacy. The infant nation's most pressing problem was how to survive the conflicts among European powers.

NEGOTIATING NEUTRALITY

This realization was brought home to Americans by the continuing wars between Britain and France. The last, and longest, broke out in 1793 and raged off and on for two decades in Europe and on the world's oceans, transforming the world's political map and presenting the United States with a life-threatening crisis. Like many weak countries throughout history that found themselves caught between competing powers—from Greek city-states confronted by Athens and Sparta to third world nations pressured to side with the Americans or Soviets during the Cold War—the young United States sought safety in neutrality. President Washington was intent upon separating American politics from Europe and avoiding foreign controversies, which might deform or even destroy the nation in its vulnerable early years. In 1793 Washington issued a proclamation of neutrality whose general course was followed by later presidents.

Maintaining American neutrality was complicated by domestic political divisions between Federalists, who favored England, and Democratic-Republicans, who leaned toward France. Still, the young United States enjoyed advantages over small European countries like the Netherlands, which tried to stay neutral but got caught in the crossfire between Britain and France. Stripped of its overseas colonies and occupied by France for two decades after 1795, Holland ceased to be a republic or a world power. Unlike Holland, the United States was an ocean's distance away from the main arena of conflict. Its extensive terrain made it difficult to conquer, and it had no possessions the European powers considered particularly valuable.

Much hinged upon American leaders' ability to balance between France and England and to play them off against one another. Because Americans had little clout, this in turn depended largely upon the Europeans' demands. The United States was implicated in the conflict by its revolutionary past and its continuing trade, and neither side was inclined to respect its neutrality. Technically, France and the United States were still allies, bound by the Treaty of 1778 by which France aided the Revolution. England, on other hand, put pressure on the United States by maintaining its frontier forts and confiscating American goods being shipped to the European mainland. Provoked by European intrigues and predations on the high seas, the United States lurched from crisis to crisis, narrowly avoiding war with England in 1793, then with France in 1798. In Jay's Treaty (1795) the United States got England to withdraw from the northwest forts but did not break Britain's monopoly of the seas. The treaty outraged Democratic-Republicans, who saw it as a *de facto* alliance with England, and it launched the French into a "quasi-war" against American shipping. Meanwhile, without the naval protection that a formal alliance with Britain could provide, Americans were forced to sign humiliating treaties with the Barbary states of North Africa, in effect paying bribes to prevent pirates from preying on American ships in the Mediterranean.

Gradually, however, some of the advantages of neutrality became apparent. In negotiating Pinckney's Treaty (1795), the Americans used Spain's fear that the new republic might join forces with France to gain important concessions. Spain agreed to recognize America's southern boundary with Spanish Florida and granted American boatmen free navigation of the Mississippi River, the west's commercial lifeline to the Gulf of Mexico and beyond. Similarly, the Americans' pledge not to join with England helped obtain France's assent to United States withdrawal from the 1778 alliance. Most spectacularly, the Louisiana Purchase enabled the infant United States to reap the benefit of its unique situation, turning a potential disaster into a windfall.

THE LOUISIANA PURCHASE. When the brilliant and power-hungry French general Napoleon Bonaparte seized power in 1799, he launched a career of imperial conquest eastward through Europe and into Egypt.

Looking toward the west, he expected to suppress the continuing slave revolt in Haiti, then to use that island as a base to rebuild the French empire in North America. In 1800 Napoleon persuaded the Spanish king to return the vast territory, then called Louisiana, between the Mississippi and the Rocky Mountains to France by a secret treaty. When word of this transfer reached Americans they were alarmed. Some feared that Napoleon's boundless ambition would lead France to reconquer Quebec or even wrest the trans-Appalachian west from Americans' shaky hold. President Jefferson, convinced that any nation controlling the mouth of the Mississippi must be "our natural and habitual enemy," in 1803 dispatched an envoy to Paris to offer to purchase New Orleans. By this time, the march of events had played into America's hands. Napoleon's troops, bogged down in a brutal guerrilla war in Haiti and devastated by yellow fever, proved unable to suppress the island's slave revolt, which had developed into an independence movement. Tired of this peripheral conflict and needing cash to renew the war in Europe, Napoleon abruptly gave up the idea of a New World empire. He offered the whole of Louisiana to American officials for $15 million. Rather than have Britain seize the territory, he preferred that it fall into American hands. His advisers, including Felix de Beaujour, assured him that the young republic would pose no serious threat to European powers for a long time to come.

The Louisiana Purchase was a stunning stroke of good fortune made possible by young America's neutrality but also by its remoteness and lack of significance to Europe. On Europe's far western periphery the menace of Napoleonic conquest was suddenly gone, and the United States was able to double its size for the bargain price of four cents an acre— money gladly lent to America by British bankers. Jefferson saw the purchase as an insurance policy guaranteeing the nation room to expand for centuries without generating large cities, which he detested, or internal wars (time proved him wrong on both counts). Swallowing his constitutional scruples, he presented the treaty to the Senate for approval after it was already signed.

NAPOLEON AS A FOUNDING FATHER.   In retrospect, the fearsome Napoleon looms as one of America's unacknowledged Founding Fathers, less benign than Washington or Jefferson but nearly as important. The Spanish colonies of Latin America owed their nationhood to his invasion of Iberia in 1807–08, which lopped off their king and triggered New World independence struggles. The young United States not only benefited from his hasty decision to sell Louisiana; it also profited from his army's march across Europe. For sixteen crucial years of the early Republic's life (1799–1815), the French emperor gave the weak, distant nation the time to grow by preoccupying Britain and preventing its European rivals from exercising imperial ambitions of their own.

THE WAR OF 1812 AS A TURNING POINT

At the time it did not look that way. America's crisis of neutrality continued when France's war with Britain resumed in 1803. Napoleon's conquest of all Europe was checked only by Britain's control of the seas. To maintain that grip, Britain resorted to seizing American merchant ships that were trading with France and the West Indies and "impressing" (drafting by force into the British navy) any men on them thought to be British. American presidents tried drastic measures to avoid war—first an embargo (1807) that stopped almost all trade between the United States and Europe, then "non-intercourse" (1809), which reopened trade except to Britain and France. Neither worked, and both generated fierce resentment, even secession threats, in New England and New York, whose commercial economies were devastated. Napoleon appeared to moderate his blockade of England, but the British continued their seizures and impressments. These harassments, along with western-state "war hawks" who wanted to remove British influence on the Indian frontier, caused Americans to risk going to war in 1812.

The War of 1812 demonstrated how vulnerable the young nation's tiny army and navy left it. American expeditions to Canada failed miserably, while the British effectively blockaded the coast. In August 1814 the British sailed up the Potomac River and set fire to the Capitol and the White House. The only decisive American victory on land, at New Orleans, happened after the peace treaty had been signed. On the other side, Great Britain, its treasury depleted and its forces stretched thin by fighting simultaneously against Napoleon and the Americans, proved unable to secure the Great Lakes or to occupy the vast new republic. The war ended in stalemate in 1815 with a treaty that simply looked toward settling the two nations' differences through future negotiations.

IMPORTANCE OF 1815.   The year 1815 was a critical turning point in the young United States' international position. Though hardly a clear-cut victory, the war with Britain ensured the nation's survival by discouraging Britain or other European powers from challenging the United States militarily again. Afterward, America would conduct small wars on its frontier, but this would be its last war against a European nation until 1898. Britain's conclusive defeat of Napoleon, also in 1815, cleared the way for its leaders to settle future disputes over boundaries peacefully with their former American colonies. The young United States could not match

Britain's naval and economic power, but British leaders began to see America as a useful counterweight to the post-Napoleonic coalition of conservative monarchs in Russia, Austria, Spain, and France, who threatened peace and progress in both hemispheres. Britain's adroit manipulation of the balance of power among competing European monarchs maintained peace in the Atlantic world for the next 40 years. For the United States, this amounted to "free security," as one historian has called it. Following Washington's policy of avoiding foreign entanglements, the United States refused to be a formal member of the European alliance system. Yet it enjoyed its benefits without incurring its risks, as the Monroe Doctrine demonstrated.

THE MONROE DOCTRINE.   The United States, eager to spread republican principles and to rid the hemisphere of colonial powers, became the first to recognize the new Latin American republics that broke away from Spain between 1808 and 1822. But Spain was anxious to recover these lands and was pledged support by Tsar Alexander of Russia, who had forged a "Holy Alliance" linking his nation with the reactionary thrones of France, Austria, and Prussia. Among major European nations only Britain opposed their intervention, fearing French resurgence and intent on protecting its own close commercial ties with Latin America. The British foreign secretary, George Canning, proposed that Britain and the United States make a joint declaration against European intervention. But American policymakers, led by Secretary of State John Quincy Adams, decided to go it alone. In his annual message to Congress in December 1823, President James Monroe declared that from now on the Americas were no longer open to colonization or political interference from European powers.

Critics later interpreted the Monroe Doctrine (as it came to be called) as an early assertion of America's international prowess or a charter for its own imperialist intervention in Latin American affairs, which happened frequently after the 1890s. At the time it was neither. Prompted by sympathy for the Latin American republics and concern over Russian outposts in California, the Monroe Doctrine affirmed the principle of hemispheric independence from Europe. Its announcement by the United States carried no force across the Atlantic; it was respected only because it was backed by secret British negotiations with France and Britain's pledge to combine its navy with American armies to enforce it. Again the pendulum of European power had swung to America's favor. Canning's boast that he had "called the New World into existence, to redress the balance of the Old" overstated the case, but his claim that Britain orchestrated a halt to Spanish or French resurgence in the New World came closer to the truth than the fantasy that the young United States scared European monarchs away from Latin America.

Thanks to crucial assistance from France (in the Louisiana Purchase) and Britain (in the Monroe Doctrine and peaceful negotiations over the Canadian border and the Oregon territory), as well as its own policy of neutrality and its stubborn defense in the War of 1812, by the 1820s the young United States had vindicated its nationhood and secured its borders. Now it could stretch its dominion westward without any European enemy standing in the way. And without help from the British or French, Native American peoples were unable to stop the advance of white settlement.

FRONTIER EXPANSION IN A SETTLER SOCIETY

In a famous essay published in 1893, historian Frederick Jackson Turner claimed that the western frontier had played a crucial role in shaping America's unique history. Free land on the edge of settlement fulfilled America's promise of opportunity for millions of pioneers and immigrants. Facing the struggle to survive against the wilderness, these frontier settlers, according to Turner, developed habits of practicality, individualism, and democracy that indelibly marked American national character.

HOW UNIQUE WAS THE AMERICAN FRONTIER? Whatever the merits of Turner's claims for the frontier's effects on Americans—and they have been hotly disputed—two other implications of his theory must be questioned: the idea that the American frontier was unique and the notion that it was unpopulated. When we step back to view it in a larger context than national history, the American frontier becomes part of a worldwide movement, its thrust simultaneous with and broadly comparable to other nineteenth-century frontiers where the settler societies of temperate North and South America, Australia, and South Africa expanded their territorial limits. The rapid expansion of these "neo-Europes" was the latest chapter in the long history of European expansion that began with Columbus and was continued for four centuries by colonists and their descendants. In the nineteenth century this expansion, fueled by massive immigration and new developments in transportation such as railroads, accelerated until Europeans and their descendants controlled most of the globe.

The frontier was also not "free land." Turner's image of it as the boundary between "civilization" and "wilderness" reflected the myths promoted by eager expansionists, not the eye of an unbiased historian. Like nineteenth-century frontiers elsewhere, the American West was a borderland where settlers of European origin confronted other settlers, such as Mexicans, who held conflicting territorial claims. As they pushed into the continent's interior, settler groups in the United States, like those in South America, Africa, and Australia, also encountered indigenous peoples and eventually dispossessed them of their land. In this and other ways, the drama of Americans' westward movement in the nineteenth century shared basic features with the inland expansion of other neo-Europes.

ADVANCING FRONTIERS IN WESTERN SETTLER SOCIETIES

There were several broad similarities. On most neo-European frontiers, the pressures to expand came from white settlers with varied agendas. Traders, missionaries, miners, ranchers, farmers, and real estate speculators all sought at various times to control the pace and character of frontier expansion. Many held divergent ideas about land use, property rights, and relations with native peoples. Traders and missionaries, for example, counted upon peaceful exchanges with productive native communities, while farmers and speculators denied native peoples' land rights and wanted to take ownership for themselves. Would-be farmers fought with ranchers over the right to parcel lands and enclose them, using the law in Australia and sometimes extra-legal violence in the United States. Perhaps the most aggressive white settlers were miners lured by rumors of new "strikes" and farmers seeking new lands for booming crops like cotton and coffee. The young nations' central governments, like imperial governments before them, at times tried to slow down white incursion, fearing costly wars with natives. In the United States, for example, the Supreme Court tried to assert Indians' status as tribal nations in 1832 when state laws in Georgia stripped the Cherokees of their property. But when confronted with frontier skirmishes or Indian reprisals, governments almost always used armed force to back settlers' claims and expand their rule. And national leaders eagerly joined the push when frontier resources were especially desirable, like gold or silver, or when they feared that another nation would outrace them to new territories.

MINING, CATTLE, AND FARMING FRONTIERS.   Each of the different kinds of frontiers—mining, cattle, and farming—had its own way of life that depended more on geographic and population patterns than national borders. Ranching practices and horsemen's lives varied little from the *gauchos* of Argentina and *vaqueros* of Mexico to the cowboys of Texas. Much of the distinctive dress and lore of the western cowboy was derived from Latin American predecessors, who supplied him with his tools and vocabulary: the mustang, bronco, chaps, lasso, and rodeo. Gold rushes in California, Australia, Peru, and Canada brought comparable waves of male immigrants from Europe and China, created raucous mining camps overnight, and followed the same boom-and-bust pattern. Almost everywhere, permanent settlers on interior farms and plantations built the churches, schools, and courthouses that enabled frontier conditions gradually to resemble settled coastal districts. Turner, like many evolutionist thinkers of his time, saw frontier development as an orderly sequence that compressed the 6,000-year progression of civilization from hunting and gathering to pastoral and agrarian and then to urban life into less than a century. The actual pattern was a disordered and uneasy coexistence of different types of white settlements that periodically erupted into conflict over political influence and land rights.

NEW STATES AND PROVINCES.   In most cases, settler nations expanded by creating states or provinces that eventually attained equal status to other regions in a confederation-style national government. The United States set the pattern with its land cessions and western ordinances of 1786–87, which rejected the colonial model of establishing subordinate new settlements that had been employed by Britain and other European powers. Instead, Congress divided lands west of the Appalachian Mountains into new states that joined the Union as equal partners after passing through a stage of territorial governance. Similar arrangements incorporated frontier lands in Canada, Mexico, Brazil, and Australia into national governments.

SETTLER EXPANSION AND INDIAN REMOVAL.   Almost everywhere, indigenous peoples were the casualties of frontier expansion. Independence for New World nations shattered the old borderland diplomacy of the "middle ground." The social mixing and respectful negotiation between European agents and Indians that occurred when native groups exerted diplomatic leverage between rival European empires disappeared when they faced a single nation pushing inland. International pacts gave way to one-sided policies decreed by expansionist nation-states, and fluid borderlands became fixed boundaries.

On their frontiers the new nations extended the practices of "settler colonialism" by which they were initially peopled, replacing native peoples with white newcomers. Prompted by hunger for land and aided by diseases and superior weapons, white settlers pushed native peoples out of the way, often destroying their communal landholding and traditional patterns of life. Some nations, like the United States and Canada, signed treaties with demoralized tribes or their purported representatives, who formally ceded lands to national governments. In many cases, including Tasmania and mainland Australia, white herders and settlers simply overran tribal settlements, outnumbering natives and killing them at will. Native people resisted, sometimes inspired by charismatic prophets like the Shawnee Tenskwatawa, the Sioux Wovoka, or Squsachtun, whose Indian Shaker religion crossed from the United States into Canada. These shamans merged Christian and indigenous religious influences and promised to restore tribes to pre-contact conditions. When fighting broke out, armed troops in the United States, Chile, Argentina, and New Zealand conquered native warriors and opened tribal lands to white newcomers. To provide for Native Americans after conquest, the United States and Canada adopted a system of Indian reservations, remote lands where uprooted tribes could resettle, often far from their ancestral grounds. In Latin America the most common pattern was not to establish reservations (or *colonias*, as they were called in Argentina), but for Indians to blend with settlers or to retreat to inland villages beyond the line of white settlement.

ENVIRONMENTAL PLUNDER. One native custom swept away by white expansion was the Indians' practice of living in relative balance with nature. Wherever settler societies pushed toward the frontier, environmental plunder ensued. Spurred by growing demand on the world market, traders compelled native peoples to harvest fish and animal furs to the brink of extinction. Miners dug indiscriminately for gold or silver, leaving blasted landscapes and toxic dumps as their residue. North American timber was "clear cut" rather than selectively harvested, while in South America huge tracts of the Amazon rainforest were felled for rubber plantations. In the United States, commercial farmers of wheat or cotton disdained crop rotation and other conservationist methods, certain that they could move westward to new land when theirs gave out. More than 20 million American buffalo were slaughtered in the second half of the nineteenth century—some for hides, but many simply to clear the path for railroads and white settlement. Not until the frontiers began to fill up in the early twentieth century did New World governments start to rein in their settlers' wasteful ways.

AMERICAN VARIATIONS ON FRONTIER THEMES

Within the bounds of these broad similarities, five features especially characterized frontier expansion in the United States. The first was its amazingly rapid pace. The American "West" was a quickly receding destination, referring to land just across the Appalachian mountains in the 1810s, the trans-Mississippi plains in the 1840s, and the Pacific Coast by the next decade. The cattle frontier lasted only three decades in the United States, from the 1860s to the 1890s, while in Latin America it spanned three centuries. During the Oklahoma land rush of 1889, towns of 10,000 people sprang up overnight. The speed with which Americans settled western lands and acquired others through treaties, purchase, or conquest was virtually unprecedented among the settler societies. Only in Australia, with its much smaller and less-organized Aboriginal population, was the neo-European takeover of vast lands as rapid and successful, but there the vast majority of whites clung to the coastline and frontier settlements were lonely outposts.

There were many reasons for America's swift expansion. The settler population increased rapidly through natural growth and (after 1840) massive immigration from Europe. Growing demand for cotton and wheat on the world market spurred farmers to pressure the government to open up more western lands. Political leaders responded with generous land policies and subsidies to railroads, whose construction then pushed the frontier farther west. Beginning with California in 1848, rushes for gold, silver, lead, and copper erupted one after another until the 1880s, accelerating settlement beyond the measured pace of agricultural expansion. Mining booms caused white adventurers to leapfrog over the Rocky Mountain basin to California, then set off a series of mad dashes in every direction—Nevada, South Dakota, Colorado, and the Southwest—to fill in the intermountain West.

All this was possible because of a second notable feature of American expansion: its lack of powerful enemies. The young United States was a minor player in world politics but a major power on its own continent. Native Americans, weakened by centuries of disease and bereft of European allies, were pushed westward in a series of forced agreements and brief wars. And after white Americans had purchased Louisiana and acquired Florida by treaty from Spain (1819), there was little foreign resistance to their westward thrust. Only a thinly populated British Canada to the north and a weak, newly independent Mexico to the southwest stood in the way.

THE MEXICAN WAR AND MANIFEST DESTINY.   The United States' annexation of Texas (1845) and its war with Mexico (1846–48) illustrated how quickly the latter nation was overcome. It also showed how the nation's restless, wealth-seeking population was encouraged by a national government committed to "Manifest Destiny." Mexico had allowed American settlers to enter its northern province of Texas in the 1820s. Several thousand settlers, mostly Southerners, had done so, but they defied the law by retaining their slaves and refusing to convert to Catholicism. In 1836 the American settlers rebelled against Mexican rule and despite an unsuccessful stand at the Alamo won their independence. Annexation of Texas to the United States was complicated by war threats from Mexico and the slavery question, but the election of Democratic President James Polk, an

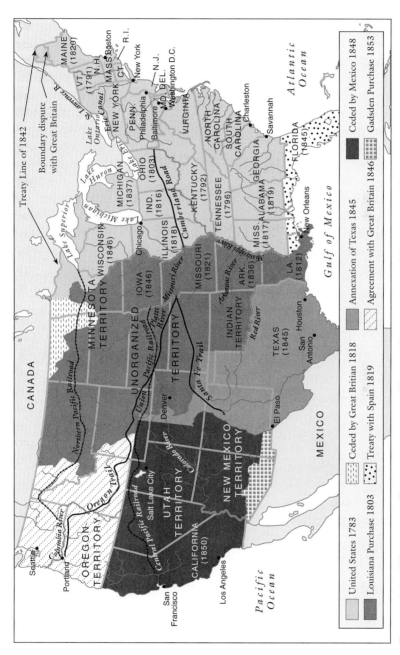

FIGURE 3-1 **WESTWARD EXPANSION OF THE UNITED STATES IN THE NINETEENTH CENTURY**

Source: *Used with permission from Traditions and Encounters (2nd ed.), by Jerry H. Bentley and Herbert F. Ziegler. Copyright 2002 by McGraw-Hill.*

141

ardent expansionist, in 1844 smoothed the way. After Texas had been acquired, Polk was determined to establish the Rio Grande as its southern border despite the fact that American settlers had not penetrated that far. A champion of Manifest Destiny, he also wanted the United States to take hold of California before England or another European power wrested it from vulnerable Mexican authorities. When Polk's offer to settle the boundary dispute and purchase California and New Mexico was snubbed by the Mexican government, he provoked a war by sending American troops into the disputed Texas territory. After American troops overwhelmed the disorganized Mexican army in the brief conflict, Mexico recognized the Rio Grande boundary and ceded California and New Mexico to the United States for $15 million. These cessions and the Texas annexation added a tract to the United States that was even larger than the Louisiana Purchase. Together with Polk's negotiation of the Oregon territory's northern border with British Canada in 1846, they transformed Americans' continent-spanning ambitions into reality.

FRONTIER MYTHOLOGY.   The influence of frontier images and ideologies like pioneering and "Manifest Destiny" was a third key feature of America's westward expansion. Frontier mythology was not unique to the United States. Other neo-European nations developed a popular image of pioneers as settlers who brought civilization to the wilderness in their covered wagons. In many cases settler expansionism was tinged with racist beliefs that white settlers could develop the land more effectively than native peoples, who were seen as seminomadic inferiors. Perhaps the descendants of Dutch settlers in South Africa—fervent Protestants like many nineteenth-century Americans—came closest to sharing American frontier myths. These "Boers" trekking into South Africa's interior to flee British rule (and preserve slavery) saw themselves, like Americans, as a chosen people destined to build a godly republic in the wilderness. But nowhere else did images of frontiersmen, cowboys, and homesteaders become so central to national identity, and to foreign perceptions of it, as in the United States. Unlike the outlaw "bushrangers" of Australia or the defiant gauchos of Argentina, American pioneers were hailed as the spearhead of the westward march of an entire people. In popular mythology as well as the writings of many historians, these figures were the "true Americans" who embodied national traits of individualism, initiative, and democracy.

THE U.S. AND RUSSIAN LAND EMPIRES.   The continental mission of Manifest Destiny also set the United States apart. American expansion involved not simply filling in existing national borders but extending them from ocean to ocean. No South American nation stretched from the Atlantic to the Pacific, and Britain's joining of Canada's western territories to Ontario in the 1860s was spurred by internal trade concerns and fear of the United States more than by nationalist ideology. Perhaps the nearest contemporary parallel to the Americans' continental ambition was the Russian empire's relentless eastward expansion into Siberia, which czarist spokesmen interpreted as integral to that nation's mission to become a world power. Americans claimed to have inherited a similar destiny. On their Pacific shore the "westward course of empire" through the ages—from Egypt to Greece to Rome to modern Europe and its American offspring—would reach its grand climax. Expansionist spokesmen did not hesitate to envision the United States as an empire—as long as one had in mind contiguous land rather than overseas possessions, and with the proviso that theirs was, in Jefferson's words, an "Empire of Liberty" rather than colonial rule.

FEDERAL INDIAN POLICY. The fourth prominent aspect of westward expansion in the United States, the conquest and subjugation of Native Americans, was the most massive and systematic displacement of native peoples among nineteenth-century settler nations. It extended and formalized the pattern of racial separation that began among the British seaboard colonies. The process occurred in two stages. During the 1830s, Indian tribes in eastern states were "removed" westward across the Mississippi. President Jackson backed southern state officials by insisting that the "Five Civilized Tribes" be relocated to Indian Territory (later Oklahoma) by force if necessary. By terms of the Indian Removal Act (1830), more than 40,000 Cherokees, Choctaws, Chickasaws, Creeks, and Seminoles exchanged their villages and farms under duress for western lands. As many as 5,000 died as federal soldiers herded them across the Mississippi along the infamous "Trail of Tears."

Within a few decades, millions of Americans headed west across the Mississippi River, negating Jackson's pledge that Indians could roam there forever. Inevitably, white pioneers encroached upon Indian hunting grounds and conflicts erupted. To reduce the bloodshed and make way for economic development, the federal government decided in 1851 to confine the Indians to small reservations in remote areas that white settlers had bypassed. Many of the Plains Indians, seminomadic hunters skilled with horses and guns, defied the army regiments sent to round them up. From 1851 to 1890, when the massacre of a Sioux encampment at Wounded Knee closed the era of Indian warfare, armed conflicts between the U.S. army and tribal warriors caused thousands of deaths. Occasionally the Indians prevailed, as when General George Custer's 256 men were overwhelmed by Sioux warriors at Little Big Horn in 1876. But eventually, the government's larger, better armed forces won out.

EXCLUSIONIST AND INCLUSIONIST FRONTIERS.   Historians and sociologists have made the distinction between racially "exclusionist" and "inclusionist" frontiers. On the first, white settlers sought to subjugate or exterminate, but not to integrate, native peoples; on the second, a *mestizo* (mixed white and Indian) population blended racial and cultural elements of both conqueror and conquered. Some scholars relate the difference to contrasting cultural biases between settlers of British descent, on one hand, who favored racial purity, and descendants of Iberians on the other, darker-skinned settlers with a long history of intermixture with Muslims and other Mediterranean peoples. Other scholars attribute patterns of exclusion or inclusion to different population ratios between settlers and natives. Generally speaking, when white settlers greatly outnumbered native peoples their social lives were separate; when native people outnumbered white settlers, the two groups tended to mix and intermarry more.

The American West was a frontier of exclusion, although not entirely or uniquely so. Its white settlers overwhelmed the Indians in numbers and force, and the custom of segregation was encoded by the reservation system. American history was paralleled in Argentina, whose two bloody offensives against the Pampas and Patagonia Indians, the Campaigns of the Desert (1833–36 and 1879–1880) coincided almost exactly with the two U.S. drives and imitated their tactics. (The Indian wars in Argentina and Chile refute the theory that all Iberian settlers established inclusive frontiers.) The American reservation system was adopted with modifications in Canada, where a more scattered native population and slower white expansion resulted in less violence. It is true that in Canada a distinct population of Métis, or French-Indian mixed-race people, emerged to resist government encroachment in Manitoba and demanded separate recognition and territory. Even so, there and on the primarily exclusionist nineteenth-century frontiers of Argentina, Australia, New Zealand, and the United States, white settlers normally maintained social distance from natives and did not readily exploit them as cheap labor, as the Brazilians did with Indian rubber tappers or the British with Zulu miners in South Africa.

Yet American Indian policy was not consistent, for strong assimilationist pressures coexisted with exclusion. Beginning in 1887, the United States offered Indian heads of household citizenship and the option of acquiring individual farmlands, although severe restrictions were attached. Native American youths were placed in government-sponsored boarding schools that taught vocational skills and attempted to erase Indian cultural identity. Similar land allotment schemes and government schools were set up in Canada. In both cases these policies had contradictory effects. While land allotment shrank reservation holdings, the framework of treaties and cessions that whites used to take over native lands eventually gave American Indians, like the First Peoples of Canada and the Maoris of New Zealand, the chance to use Western legal systems to defend themselves and preserve what remained of their ancestral lands.

LAND OWNERSHIP. A fifth defining feature of America's westward expansion was the ease of land ownership for white settlers of modest means. Much of the West was government land, and federal surveys sectioned it into checkerboard grids that facilitated sales in progressively smaller and more affordable portions. The Homestead Act of 1862 offered land to settlers for a nominal registration fee and a promise to stay and improve it for five years. Under its provisions, more than 400,000 claimants, including many immigrants from Britain, Germany, and Scandinavia, gained title to farms in the American West. Thousands of additional tracts were bought from railroad companies and speculators. Although homesteading and land purchase did not guarantee success, they helped sustain the American dream among westward migrants and they made the American frontier a symbol of economic opportunity. A similar law, the Dominion Lands Policy, was adopted by Canada in 1872 and made the Canadian West the preferred destination of land-seeking immigrants after prime U.S. homestead acreage became scarce. By contrast, despite passage of Australian "selection" laws in the 1860s modeled on the American Homestead Act, most frontier freeholds there were taken by large pastoralists. Vast backwoods sheep or cattle stations set up by these proprietors were worked by hundreds of itinerant hands who had little chance to become independent landowners. In much of Latin America the story was even less egalitarian: the richest interior lands were given to holders of enormous estates that produced crops for export, such as sugar, beef, or coffee. Immigrants and other workers who migrated to South American frontiers became wage laborers or tenants far more often than ranchers or small farmers.

EXPANSION, DEVELOPMENT, AND THE WORLD ECONOMY

FRONTIERS OF EUROPEAN CAPITALISM. Like other New World frontiers, the American West was connected to the world market. Lonesome cowboys, luckless gold diggers, and isolated homesteaders dominate the popular mythology of western settlement, but these images reflect the myth of American individualism more than economic reality. Rather than maverick loners turning their backs upon civilization, frontiersmen were the advance guard of Euro-American capitalism. Whether individual ranchers and farmers in North America or farm laborers in South America, westward migrants furnished raw materials and foodstuffs for the hemisphere's coastal regions and for Europe. The nineteenth-century American

West was rapidly integrated into the "periphery" of the capitalist world economy, providing hides, crops, and minerals for metropolitan centers on the East Coast and especially in Europe. From Rocky Mountain trading posts where American entrepreneurs captured the fur trade from Britain in the 1820s to furnish beaver hats for men strolling Parisian boulevards, to railroad depots in 1880s Kansas where the cattle drives ended and the long trip to Chicago slaughterhouses and European markets began, successive American frontiers were connected to the Atlantic economy and the export market as their lifeline.

What was true of the West was accurate for the young nation as a whole. After independence, the United States remained largely an economic satellite of England. Nearly half of its exports—raw materials and crops—were sent to England and most of its imports—manufactured goods and tropical foods—arrived from Britain and its colonies. Cotton was the pre-eminent export, accounting for more than half the value of American shipments before the Civil War. The cotton gin and the expanding system of plantation slavery made possible large-scale production in the South to satisfy the British textile mills' seemingly insatiable demand. By 1860 the South provided about 80 percent of England's raw cotton, and British textile production reached the point where more than 20 percent of English workers owed their living to cotton. Through the cotton trade, the largest of the New World's slave societies fueled its first industrial giant, and both grew rich in the process.

Cotton was not the only crop sent abroad. Exports of American beef, pork, wheat, and corn grew exponentially during the nineteenth century. New England entrepreneurs, lacking good soil, had to be especially ingenious. Henry David Thoreau, who in 1846 retreated to rural Walden Pond in Massachusetts, watched workers cut its frozen surface into huge ice cubes that were put on insulated ships. Some New England ice was transported as far away as British India. That same year, New England ships made up more than three-quarters of the world's whaling fleet, supplying oil for lamps around the world. British and European cities remained the central market of the Western world's economic system, providing the customers and much of the capital for America's expansion. Writing at the time of the Civil War, economist Henry Carey reminded his fellow Americans that "all our great [rail]roads are merely spokes of a wheel whose hub is found in Liverpool."

FROM ECONOMIC COLONIALISM TO INDUSTRIAL DEVELOPMENT. This "neocolonial" relationship of economic dependence persisted in the American South, where cotton was declared "king" but in reality was subservient to British lords, just like wool in Australia or beef in

Argentina. In the American North, however, economic relations were changing by the 1860s in ways that separated the northern states from southern ones and also distinguished the nineteenth-century United States from Argentina, Australia, and other settler societies that remained dependent on British capital. A global trend was at work: wherever British industrial might threatened to overwhelm local economies in the mid-nineteenth century, from China and Japan to the New World, nations undertook "self-strengthening" initiatives in response. The American program, reflected in private investments as well as public promotion of transportation and industry, was an early and outstanding success.

Britain's domination of the U.S. economy was reduced over time by two factors. First, rising production meant that Americans began to rely less on European imports and become more self-sufficient. By the 1870s the United States developed a favorable balance of trade, exporting more than it imported. Agricultural production, still three-fourths of total exports in 1870, was multiplied by mechanical inventions such as the McCormick reaper for harvesting wheat. Increased output led Americans to expand their markets beyond England and the European continent to Canada, Latin America, and Asia. Thus Commodore Matthew Perry steamed an American gunboat flotilla into Tokyo harbor in 1853 and forced a commercial treaty upon Japan. Americans opened mercantile and insurance offices in most of the world's major ports, where they competed with European traders. By boosting production, diversifying their exports, and finding markets around the world (as well as at home), nineteenth-century Americans not only became less dependent upon Britain and other European powers, they made the nation a major economic force.

A second change was that rivalry for the inland trade lifted urban areas of the Northeast to a more advanced stage of economic development. Merchants in Boston, New York, Philadelphia, and Baltimore competed with New Orleans for trade with western hinterlands. Between 1820 and 1860 their entrepreneurship, assisted by government promotion of economic growth, built thousands of miles of canals and railroads that linked the continent in a transportation network that outdid any in the world over a comparable distance. Gathering in western products and brokering their transportation to Europe in exchange for manufactured goods, these merchants became powerful agents of economic change. The "transportation revolution" they initiated built the distribution network for a more self-sufficient American economy, and the profits they invested in manufacturing (which the national government protected from British competition by a tariff that raised the price of imported manufactures) helped spur an American industrial revolution. Over time, through this process of "import substitution," East Coast cities began to compete with

Europe as financier and manufacturer to the American South and West. In terms of the world economy, the dynamic commercial capitalism of the North and the beginnings of industrialization moved much of the nineteenth-century United States, unlike its South American counterparts, to "semi-peripheral" status, preparing it to rival and eventually surpass European economic powers.

WESTWARD EXPANSION AND SLAVERY.   Inside the United States, the South was the great exception to this change. While northerners mechanized farm production and increasingly invested their resources in transportation, finance, and industry, the southern states remained committed to slave production of staple crops like cotton, tobacco, and sugar. This pattern moved west with Americans as southerners replicated the slave plantations of the Southeast's "Cotton Kingdom" and northerners built efficient farms and bustling commercial centers tied to the Northeast. By extending the two sections' differences westward, expansion heated up their competition. Sectional tensions mounted as the North appeared to be winning the race to occupy western lands and profit from their trade. When the North's canals and railroads penetrated inland, western states increasingly sent their crops eastward rather than down the Mississippi, cutting the South out of the economic loop. The northeastern and western states were drawing closer together economically and socially at the same time that the North and South's economies were diverging.

A final feature that distinguished America's westward expansion from others was thus its entanglement with the growing controversy over slavery. Expansion intensified the rivalry between free and slave states for control of the nation's economy and politics. To many Americans it seemed that the moral and economic fate of the republic depended upon whether freedom or slavery would prevail, and this hinged upon which side could gain the most western lands and votes. Step by step, the contest between northern and southern ways of life in the western territories led to war.

COMPARATIVE VIEWS OF SLAVERY, CIVIL WAR, AND EMANCIPATION

The struggle over territorial slavery in the United States was the most violent collision between two forces that clashed elsewhere in the Atlantic world. On one side, the modernizing societies of the North Atlantic—Great Britain, Holland, France, Denmark, and the American North—developed democratic ideas and capitalist practices to the point where slavery became discredited, even though these societies had profited from connections to slavery and the slave trade. On the other, middle and south Atlantic slave societies—the Southern states, Caribbean islands, and Brazil—which had prospered by concentrating production on export crops grown by slaves, defended slavery as the key to social order and economic success. Plantation slavery and the movement to abolish it—both products of Europe's centuries-long expansion—reached their peak simultaneously in the nineteenth century, with momentous consequences.

NORTH AMERICAN SLAVERY IN COMPARATIVE PERSPECTIVE

As described by travelers from the modernizing nineteenth-century North, the South's "peculiar institution" seemed a remnant from earlier, less enlightened times. Yet southern slavery was not unique in its heyday. It shared essential similarities with the slave system still active on plantations in Brazil and Cuba. In all three places, slaves were held for life, inheriting their status from mothers and passing it on through the generations. And unlike slavery in the ancient world, bondage was imposed only upon people of color, whether Indians or Africans.

There were also important differences among Atlantic slave societies. The earliest historians who compared slavery in the United States with its counterpart in Latin America portrayed U.S. slavery as uniquely harsh, comparable to Nazi concentration camps in its brutality and effect. By contrast, it was said, slavery in the Spanish and Portuguese New World was less oppressive. Untainted by the Anglo-Americans' extreme racism and removed from the pressures of an expansive capitalist economy, planters in Brazil and Cuba gave greater autonomy to their slaves. The burden of bondage was also lightened by protections against excessive abuse that Latin American governments and the Catholic Church extended to slaves.

SLAVERY IN THE UNITED STATES AND BRAZIL.   Careful comparison between slavery in the United States and Brazil in the nineteenth century questions this contrast, producing a more mixed picture. In both places the law recognized that slaves were persons as well as property, but in neither were protections against inhumane treatment consistently enforced. In Brazil as well as the United States, religion was used by masters to support slavery, not to mitigate it. Brazilian slaves, like those in the Caribbean, were somewhat freer to own personal property and develop their own exchange economy than North American slaves. But they were also more likely to commit suicide or to be abandoned by owners when disabled, ill, or aged.

On balance, it appears that slavery in the United States was less physically harsh than slavery in Brazil, but more difficult for its victims to escape, especially by being granted freedom. Hundreds of southern slaves ran away each year, but most returned or were captured before reaching the free states. Southern slave rebellions broke out sporadically, most notably that led by Nat Turner in Virginia in 1831. By comparison, however, Brazilian slaves engaged in larger and more frequent insurrections, and runaway slaves established sizeable hideaways (called maroons or *quilombos*) in Brazil's thinly settled interior. Slaves in Brazil rebelled more often because they were detached from their families, recently arrived, and often treated brutally. As noted in Chapter 2, Brazil and other sugar plantation societies relied heavily on a steady flow of slaves taken from Africa. Brazilian masters preferred young unattached men and worked them relentlessly, inflicting types of punishment unknown in North America and producing a high death rate. In the southern United States, slavery became more "normalized." The international trade ended in 1808, more than 40 years prior to Brazil's curtailing of it, and slaves were increasingly assimilated into a generalized African American culture. Their natural population growth was a sign that American planters fed, clothed, and housed laborers at subsistence levels. A more balanced sex ratio allowed slaves in the United States to construct family networks that helped them to cope with the ordeal of bondage, although family members were often cruelly separated.

The worst feature of North American slavery, comparatively speaking, was the southern states' restriction of manumission, the legal freeing of slaves by owners. Because whites in Brazil were outnumbered, blacks and mulattoes (black-white mixed-race persons) were often freed to perform skilled and semiskilled labor outside the plantation's walls. In the American South, such work was reserved for white men, who were in plentiful supply. The fact that there were 16 times as many slaves as free blacks in the South (in Brazil, the ratio was three to one) was symptomatic of a society that indelibly labeled blacks inferior and refused them a meaningful role in free society.

Instead of softening, this attitude hardened in the second quarter of the nineteenth century, when slaveholders, although a minority among southern whites, strengthened their political hold on southern states. The cotton boom and Indian removal gave a huge stimulus to southern slavery. During the antebellum years (1830–1860) the largest American plantations attained the classic form of the Old South legend, with a magnolia-lined road leading to a stately, columned "Big House" that hid the squalid slave quarters behind. Planters argued that slavery, formerly tolerated as a "necessary evil," was really a "positive good" that sustained the economy and "civilized" an inferior race. Due to its rising slave population and soaring cotton prices, the American South had become the world's most extensive and robust slave economy.

AMERICAN SLAVERY AND RUSSIAN SERFDOM. In the Western world of the 1830s, only Russia, with approximately 11 million serfs, was a larger stronghold of unfree labor than the American South. Russian serfdom provides intriguing parallels with American slavery as well as important contrasts. Both systems of coerced labor grew on Europe's periphery in the 1600s and endured into the 1800s. Both combined profit-minded production for the wider market (although in Russia this was mainly domestic) with a precapitalist mode of organization based on ownership of labor rather than wages. Yet differences in the distribution of power among landowners, laborers, and government created opposite paths to emancipation in these two expanding land empires.

Serfdom, which refers to the obligation of servile (unfree) peasants to their landlords, existed in various forms in Europe for more than a thousand years, from the ninth century to the nineteenth. The practice declined in western Europe after the thirteenth century, but in eastern Europe and Russia an opposite trend prevailed. A shortage of labor, increased demand for grain, and vast land grants to nobles led landlords and governments to expand serfholding and tighten their control over it. By the early 1800s, more than half of Russia's peasants were serfs, with lives so similar to slaves that the labels were used interchangeably. Like New World slaves, Russian serfs inherited their status, were bought and sold, and were employed primarily as farm laborers.

Nevertheless, two features of Russian serfdom highlighted its differences from southern slavery. First, serfs enjoyed a greater degree of independence than American slaves, whose owners constantly intruded into their daily lives. Unlike southern slaves, Russian serfs lived on vast estates with numerous fellow laborers and had little contact with owners, who were often absentees. By tradition, serfs worked three days a week for owners and three for themselves. Most were given small parcels of land to grow food for their families and for sale at market, a practice that was rare among slaves in the South. Russian peasants also regularly elected officials of the *mir*, or village commune, which assigned labor obligations and apportioned lands among serfs. Through the *mir*, serfs collectively petitioned Russian officials for redress, called strikes against landowners, and under extreme circumstances organized rebellions. The existence of large estates and peasant communes explains why serfs resorted to collective forms of resistance more than the individual rebels and runaways among southern slaves. And peasant life, which gave Russian serfs experience in family farming, market relations, and group decision-making, prepared them for a smoother transition to freedom than American slaves.

Serf holders had little power to prevent this transition. A second difference between Russian and American arrangements was the slaveowners' greater control over their political environment. Southern slaveholders dominated local governments and enjoyed a tradition of immunity from federal interference with state-sanctioned slavery. This political independence, combined with a strong sense of racial privilege, enabled American planters to mount a formidable defense of slavery. By contrast, Russian nobles depended heavily upon the tsar and the central government for their privileges and the armies that kept serfs under control. When the tsar issued decrees concerning serfs, Russian landowners had little choice but to obey them.

In the 1850s American slavery and Russian serfdom underwent a crisis. In Russia, the serf population began to decrease after 1833 when poor harvests raised mortality rates and many serfs escaped by joining the army or running away. Stung by Russia's defeat in the Crimean War against the British, French, and Ottoman Turks (1853–1856), Tsar Alexander II became determined to modernize its economy, including transforming serfs into free farmers and wage earners. After the emancipation plan was announced, Russian landowners grudgingly acceded and even helped to draft its provisions. By terms of the 1861 decree, freed serfs were given small plots of farmland and landowners received "redemption payments" from them as compensation.

The American South's crisis was a matter of outside opposition, not internal decline. Despite claims that southern slavery had reached its natural limits in the 1850s, evidence indicates that it was flourishing. High prices for cotton on the world market generated record-breaking profits. Employment of southern slaves in mining and manufacturing suggested that slavery could endure in an industrialized economy. Instead, events outside the South caused a crisis. As opposition to slavery mounted in the northern states and Great Britain, white Southerners increasingly rowed against the current of public opinion. Demographic trends accelerated this moral shift. At odds with northern politicians over the expansion of slavery, slave-state representatives began to lose clout in Washington when the South's population growth fell behind the North's. Gradually, but unmistakably, federal power was shifting from protecting slaveholder interests to threatening them. In the United States, as in Russia, emancipation would come by decree from the central government, but only against planters' fierce resistance and in the course of a bloody sectional war.

ANTISLAVERY AND THE ORIGINS OF THE CIVIL WAR

The rise of antislavery opinion in the United States was part of a momentous change in Western culture. Just as the system of slave labor was reaching its crest in the early nineteenth century, the tide of history turned against it. Slavery, which had been practiced and justified since Biblical times, began to be seen as immoral and intolerable. As intellectual and spiritual opposition to slavery mounted and the changes brought by industrialization seemed to outmode it, slavery increasingly lost its economic logic and political support.

TRANSATLANTIC ABOLITIONISM.   Moral opposition to slavery arose in the North Atlantic world among both religious and secular thinkers. British and American members of the Society of Friends (called Quakers), who concluded that slavery was unchristian, created the first antislavery organizations in the 1770s. Within a generation this network was supplemented by abolitionist societies that grew out of the religious revivals of British and American Protestant churches. Evangelical Protestants preached immediate conversion to Gospel truth, the equality of all God's children, and the need for social improvement—all of which could support antislavery organizing. Antislavery agitators, like revivalist preachers before them, followed a northern transatlantic circuit, shuttling frequently between Britain and the United States to whip up popular support. British abolitionists Charles Stuart and George Thompson gave hundreds of speeches in the United States while Americans William Lloyd Garrison and Frederick Douglass conducted extensive tours of Britain. Antislavery agitators included eloquent ex-slaves like Douglass and William Wells Brown as well as white middle-class women, such as Elizabeth Cady Stanton, who linked abolition to the campaign for women's rights.

Like Stanton, many abolitionists were secular opponents of slavery inspired by concepts of human rights and democratic equality that circulated in the Age of Revolution. The notion that all men were created equal questioned not just kingship and nobility but the justice of owning humans as slaves. After these convictions took hold, they spread through the same advances in transportation and communication that diffused democratic ideas on both sides of the Atlantic.

Antislavery sentiment grew strongest where moral opposition merged with economic considerations. Abolitionist ideas found a hearing in the northern states, as in Britain, in part because slavery was only indirectly important to the economy. More than this, these dynamic capitalist economies seemed to prove that work for wages was more productive and efficient than coerced labor. Antislavery publicists contrasted the tidy farms, humming factories, and chugging railroads of competitive free-labor societies with the unkempt, backward ways of slave regions. Their propaganda appealed to a general belief in progress and reflected the confidence instilled by North Atlantic industrial capitalism. Of course, slave-based production, particularly of cotton, had helped fuel the Industrial Revolution, but now it seemed that population growth and immigration could provide plantations with plenty of cheap wage labor.

The British succeeded first in making antislavery a popular crusade. Hundreds of thousands signed petitions calling for abolition of the slave trade, and their parliamentary allies pushed through a ban in 1807. Under moral and economic pressure from Britain, the United States outlawed the importation of slaves the next year, as the Constitution permitted. The Netherlands and France soon followed suit. The British took an even more momentous step in 1833 when their newly enlarged electorate permitted passage of an Act of Emancipation. By its provisions, some 750,000 slaves in British colonies acquired their freedom after a transitional period of six years. The French Revolution of 1848, which installed a Second Republic, also freed the roughly 330,000 slaves in France's overseas colonies.

COMPARING BRITISH AND AMERICAN CONTEXTS.   American abolitionists were inspired by these successes, but ending slavery proved to be much harder in the United States. Slavery in British and French colonies was distant from the homeland, and by the 1830s it had an important but not dominant economic impact there. In the United States, abolition threatened the livelihood of nearly half of the country's states, and it questioned enforcement of white supremacy over 4 million blacks. White Southerners could accept termination of the foreign slave trade because natural population growth assured them a steady supply of slaves. But they vehemently opposed abolition and threatened to break up the Union if it won support. Huge political and legal obstacles also blocked the American abolitionist movement's progress. Whereas British colonial interests had diminished clout in Parliament by the 1830s, the South, through the Democratic Party, had controlled the Presidency, the Senate, and the Supreme Court for a generation. And whereas Parliament's undisputed power made unilateral abolition possible, the American federal government had no legal authority over slavery in the states.

These differences in contexts and attitudes were highlighted by contrasting responses to two slave rebellions that broke out almost simultaneously in 1831. In Virginia, Nat Turner led a rampage in which he and dozens of fellow slaves raided local plantations, killing nearly 60 whites. Four months later, a sit-down strike among Jamaica's slaves led by Sam Sharpe escalated into a bloody 10-day war with British colonial authorities involving more than 50,000 slaves. Both Turner's revolt and the Jamaican "Christmas Rising" were suppressed and their leaders were killed, but they had opposite consequences. Pressured by a horrified British public, Parliament voted for emancipation just over a year after

Sharpe's execution. Meanwhile, although Turner's revolt prompted a brief legislative debate in Virginia over ending slavery, its long-term effect was to shore up support for slavery in the state and to justify a campaign against "interference" by northern abolitionists.

TERRITORIAL SLAVERY AND THE CIVIL WAR.   Because of obstacles posed by widespread white support for slavery and the limits of federal power, the American abolitionist crusade evolved into a more indirect and moderate attack: a movement to stop slavery's expansion beyond existing state lines. The Louisiana Purchase (1803), Indian Removal in the 1830s, and the annexation of Texas in 1845 opened southwestern lands to young men from Virginia and the Carolinas eager to become wealthy planters. White Southerners swarmed to the western frontier where land was plentiful, and slaves were purchased from traders who brought them "down river" from the upper South. As long as cotton was valuable, Southerners insisted on the right to extend plantation slavery to new lands. They warned that restricting its spread would choke off economic opportunity and eventually kill slavery itself.

Southerners' eagerness to extend slavery took on an international dimension through "filibusters," private adventurers, often Mexican War veterans, who invaded foreign countries in Central America and the Caribbean in hopes of accruing personal wealth and adding territory to America's Manifest Destiny. The most notorious of these filibusters, William Walker of Tennessee, led two failed expeditions to Mexico before sailing to Nicaragua in 1855, proclaiming himself president, and legalizing slavery. Walker's regime survived only until 1857, but it was supported by proslavery Southerners who had been clamoring for the United States to purchase Cuba from Spain and acquire other Caribbean plantation lands.

Most whites in the northern states cared little about slaves, and their states discriminated against free blacks. Several midwestern states even banned their entry. Still, many white northerners feared that extending the plantation system would block the mobility of free workers and strengthen slaveowners' hold on national politics, preventing homestead laws, protective tariffs, railroad subsidies, and other modernizing measures. Political pressure from northerners prevented President Franklin Pierce from going to war with Spain over Cuba, but keeping slavery out of western lands proved more difficult. Legal precedent for banning territorial slavery existed in early federal ordinances and the Missouri Compromise of 1820, a congressional deal that had established a line dividing slave and free areas in the Louisiana Purchase lands. There were also precedents for permitting territorial slavery, however.

The question of slavery in the West was reopened by the American acquisition of California and New Mexico following the Mexican War. After four years of acrimonious debate, another elaborate congressional bargain, the Compromise of 1850, settled this issue, but only temporarily. Its admission of California as a free state broke the tradition of "pairing" the entry of new slave and free states, and as the latter began to outnumber the former, Southern whites asserted their right to establish slavery in the remaining territories. Kansas became the struggle's focal point. In 1856 guerrilla warfare broke out between proslavery and antislavery settlers there, and the Supreme Court's Dred Scott Decision (1857), which denied that Congress had the power to ban slavery from the territories, did little to quell the violence. In 1860 the slaveholders' demand for federal guarantees of territorial slavery split the Democratic Party, in effect giving the presidency to the Republican candidate, Abraham Lincoln. The election of a president who condemned slavery as a "moral evil" and was committed to preventing its expansion prompted South Carolina, and eventually 10 other southern slave states, to secede from the Union and form the Confederate States of America in 1861. Thus the dispute over territorial slavery, emblematic of a larger divergence between North and South, shattered America's political party system and broke the Union as well.

THE CIVIL WAR IN INTERNATIONAL CONTEXT

Like the war over American slavery, the end of American slaveholding came indirectly. The North fought the Civil War to restore the Union. Only after a year and a half of costly battles—mostly Union defeats—did Lincoln, using his authority as military commander-in-chief, proclaim slaves free in rebel areas. The Emancipation Proclamation (1863) was a war measure primarily and an act of justice secondarily. Designed to demoralize Confederates, to encourage slaves to run away and enlist in the Union army, and to win favor abroad, it was carefully crafted to exclude the four slave states that remained loyal to the Union. Lincoln delayed issuing it out of fear that at least one of those states, Kentucky, would jump to the Confederacy. Earlier he had failed to persuade congressmen from the loyal slave states to accept gradual, compensated emancipation, even when coupled with funds to colonize freed slaves abroad. Only with Northern victory in the war and passage of the Thirteenth Amendment in 1865 did all slaves in the United States gain freedom.

The Union's indirect path to emancipation and persistent slaveholder opposition to it suggest that without the Civil War, slavery would have lasted for several decades in the United States. That would have made the United States the last Western nation to abolish slavery. The Dutch

Empire ended slavery in 1867, Spanish Cuba and Puerto Rico in 1886, and Brazil two years later. Except for the Haitian revolution of the 1790s, all New World slave societies but the United States achieved emancipation peacefully.

WHY CIVIL WAR?   Why did it take a civil war to end slavery in the United States but not elsewhere? In contrast to slaveowners in the British West Indies or serf holders in Russia, white Southerners rejected government offers of compensation for releasing their human property. And unlike Caribbean planters and Russian nobles, southern elites wielded enough political power to forestall abolition and enough economic clout on the world market to believe that their region could prove viable as an independent nation.

It is instructive to return to a comparison with Brazil to help explain slavery's tenacious hold in the American South and why it came to a violent end. Brazil's gradual abandonment of slavery was spurred by British moves against the slave trade, which caused a steep decline in the slave population. Sugar prices had peaked on the world market, decreasing the need for slave labor. Emancipation began in 1871 with a law freeing slave children when they reached adulthood, and voluntary abolition was encouraged by the government's policy of importing immigrant workers to replace slaves on coffee plantations. When the national legislature finally declared emancipation in 1888 there was no strong opposition. Freeing slaves did little to disturb race relations in Brazil because large existing free-black and mulatto populations prevented rigid racial barriers from forming between ex-slaves and others.

By contrast, slavery in the United States in the 1850s was self-reproducing and thus independent of the foreign slave trade. The plantation system remained profitable because of the demand for cotton, and instead of declining, it was expanding into western lands in competition with Northern farmers and workers. The South was avoided by immigrant workers who might replace slaves, and white Southerners enforced a rigid line of color and status between the races that would be threatened by emancipation. A final crucial factor can be added: because slavery was concentrated in one region in the United States (unlike Brazil), this helped to unify slaveholders, promoted sectional feeling, and gave the South enhanced political power in the American federal-style political system. This distinctive combination of features shaped the South's slave society and underpinned slaveowners' all-out defense of their customs and privileges. The eventual result was civil war.

WARS OF NATIONAL UNIFICATION.   If we put aside for a moment the roots of the conflict in slavery, it becomes clear that the Civil War was also a nation-building struggle. Its combatants were the rival agendas of the modernizing, centralizing North and the traditional, states-rights South, and its trigger was southern secession from the federal Union. The Northerners' plan to unite the states under a strong central government and the southern states' dogged resistance aligned the American struggle with wars of national unification that were occurring in Europe and the Americas in the same decades. Throughout the Western world in the mid-nineteenth century, centralized nation-states emerged as the most powerful contenders to assure the autonomy of new nations, to guide their economic growth, and to fend off international threats. National governments in Italy and Germany were formed by merging independent dukedoms or city-states; in New World nations, strong central governments developed by tightening the loose bonds that federal-style national constitutions had established. In many cases national unity was cemented by armed defeat of local dissent or outside interference.

Italy's jigsaw puzzle of republics, duchies, and kingdoms was pieced together in a series of political maneuvers, foreign interventions, and military campaigns that lasted from 1859 to 1870. The process was so prolonged, complex, and bloodless that it defies comparison with the United States, although President Lincoln saw enough similarities that he asked the Italian nationalist hero Giuseppe Garibaldi to lead a contingent of Union troops.

Some historians have likened Lincoln to Otto von Bismarck, the brilliant, ruthless Prussian prime minister who masterminded the unification of Germany between 1864 and 1871 by ignoring Parliament and provoking a series of advantageous foreign wars. Lincoln's determination to preserve the Union at all costs and his willingness to suspend civil liberties during the war may recall Bismarck's ruthless tactics. But Lincoln was no Bismarck. The American president insisted that democratic elections proceed during wartime; he agonized over mounting war casualties; and he resisted calls—even from his own secretary of state—to start foreign wars for political advantage. Although the goal was the same—national unification under a strong central government—the struggle in the United States was to tighten federal control and prevent a sectional split rather than to combine existing duchies and republics into a new political unit, as in Italy and Germany. In fact, the Civil War was so fierce precisely because it pitted against each other two kinds of passionate nationalism at work in the nineteenth century—*consolidating* nationalism, as in Germany and Italy, and *breakaway* nationalism, as in Hungary and Poland.

LATIN AMERICAN PARALLELS.   The same forces faced off in Latin America. Perhaps the closest parallels to the American case were the secession movements and civil wars that plagued the new republics of South

America. Rooted in conflicts between centralist and localist factions and involving such issues as tariffs and representation, these schisms illustrate the ongoing tensions between consolidation and secession that typified New World nation-building.

Two examples come from Brazil and Argentina. In 1834, the province of Rio Grande do Sul attempted to secede from the Brazilian empire and form a republic. The dispute involved taxes on the cattle trade and aligned the region's ranchers against the central government, whose policies favored the industrializing sector. The link to Europe's nationalist struggles was affirmed when the Italian revolutionary Garibaldi became involved. In 1839 Garibaldi organized a small naval force that invaded Santa Catarina, a neighboring province, and upon their victory proclaimed it a republic also. With two Brazilian provinces in revolt, the conflict threatened to escalate into a major war. But the Brazilian government's concessions, including a tariff on imported beef, together with the failure of rebellions to spread, caused the rebels to sign an armistice and return to the Brazilian fold in 1845.

The Argentine rebels were more successful. In 1853, following the overthrow of dictator Juan Manuel de Rosas, a new constitution was drafted by a national convention. Before it became operative, the province of Buenos Aires, jealous of its autonomy and its monopoly on customs revenues, seceded from the Argentine republic. In this case, unlike the United States, it was the most populous and modernized province that left the Union. A tense period of coexistence erupted into war in 1859, and two years later the troops from Buenos Aires forced their foes to retreat. When the smoke cleared, the nation was reunited on terms favorable to Buenos Aires: the rebel governor, Bartolomé Mitre, became Argentina's president and Buenos Aires became the national capital. Unlike American slaveowners, Argentina's rebels won their struggle to retain control of the national government.

Neither of these Latin American wars corresponded perfectly to the American Civil War. Neither came close to that war's ferocity, and their alignment of centralists and decentralists with urban vs. rural and tariff vs. free-trade divisions was not always parallel. Still, they demonstrate that nation-building remained incomplete in the New World's federative nations for decades after independence. Throughout the Americas in the 1800s, new republics faced secession movements or tried to contain fierce struggles between localist and centralist factions, which were called "federal" and "unitarian," respectively, in much of Latin America. Beleaguered liberal presidents like Abraham Lincoln, Argentina's Mitre, or Mexico's Benito Juárez, who were committed simultaneously to representative rule and national unity, had to resort to force to consolidate control by the central government.

CIVIL WAR DIPLOMACY.   Although it was a domestic rebellion, the Civil War had important international effects. It introduced weapons of modern warfare—breech-loading and repeating rifles, ironclad ships, even submarines—that were adopted elsewhere and transformed subsequent wars into even deadlier encounters. The combination of nationalist fervor and modern technology reaped an appalling harvest of death in the United States and found counterparts abroad in the Taiping Rebellion in China (1851–1862), the Indian Mutiny against British rule (1857–1859), and the War of the Triple Alliance that pitted Brazil, Argentina, and Uruguay against Paraguay (1864–1870). In terms of the world economy, the Union's blockage of Confederate cotton shipments led to a reorganization of global cotton production as Britain, France, and other imperial powers established new supply sources among farmers and tenants in Egypt, India, and Africa.

The Civil War also registered a crucial diplomatic victory for the Union, which managed to prevent recognition of the Confederacy by Great Britain and France, each eager to see a disunited States and to dominate the new Confederate nation. Napoleon III of France, nephew of the great emperor, took advantage of the American Civil War (and Mexico's disarray after its own civil war of 1858–1860) to set up a puppet monarchy in Mexico headed by Archduke Ferdinand Maximilian of Austria. The French then proposed to join England in recognizing the South. Everything depended upon Britain, whose threatened intervention was difficult to forestall. Nevertheless, U.S. leaders managed this through a deft combination of reserve and decisiveness. Successful Union diplomacy required timely concession by Lincoln in the Trent Affair (1861), when the Union navy interfered with Britain's neutral shipping rights (just as Britain had done to the United States prior to the War of 1812). It was aided by the North's provision of wheat during Britain's bad harvests, which offset English factories' need for southern cotton. It was also helped by Lincoln's Emancipation Proclamation, which aligned the Union squarely with antislavery Britain. But the Union's cause in Britain was assured only when its victories at Gettysburg and Vicksburg in July 1863 demonstrated that the North would win the war.

AMERICAN POWER ON THE RISE.   The ultimate Union triumph in 1865 marked the emergence of the United States as a military power to be reckoned with. Before the war, the young nation played a minor role as Europeans calculated the balance of power; now it became an equal factor in their equations. Britain hesitated to back the Confederacy in part because it feared risking a general European war, with England and France having to defeat an alliance between rising powers Russia and the United States.

After the war was over, the United States enforced the Monroe Doctrine, helping to restore the liberal government of President Juárez in Mexico. Secretary of State William Seward pressured France to withdraw its troops from Mexico, and a large federal army was sent to the Rio Grande. When France pulled out, its puppet government fell, Mexican patriots executed Maximilian, and Juárez returned to power. In 1867, Russia abandoned its expansionist plans for North America by selling Alaska to the United States for $7,200,000. The Russians' retreat and the collapse of Maximilian's regime ended European territorial ambitions in North America. At last in position to police the continent, the United States was becoming a world power comparable to Britain, France, and Germany.

CANADIAN CONFEDERATION. The Civil War had another effect on the North American continent: the creation of modern Canada. Fearing that the Alaska Purchase was the victorious Union's first step toward conquering Canada, Britain took steps to unite all its Canadian possessions under one government. The Canadian federation of 1867 was designed to fortify Canada against American annexation. It also incorporated the lesson learned from the Civil War that only a more powerful federal government could prevent internal secessions. Spearheading the age of nationalism in North America, the Civil War indirectly helped to consolidate America's neighboring nations.

EMANCIPATION AND RECONSTRUCTION IN WIDER FOCUS

At home, the most dramatic consequence of the Civil War was the emancipation of nearly 4 million slaves. Such a drastic and unforeseen change raised controversial questions. With slavery gone, what new systems of economic organization and social relations would emerge? Would political rights be granted to freedmen?

EMANCIPATION IN PLANTATION SOCIETIES. Every plantation society in the Americas that underwent emancipation saw bitter conflict over the role of freed slaves. Ex-slaves wanted to control their lives and own land, but planters expected them to continue as an exploitable labor force harvesting crops for export. In most cases, local white elites controlled the process by which slaves were freed and, as voters, employers, and landlords, played the dominant role in defining the new order. On Caribbean islands where slavery ended peacefully, emancipation was gradual, and former masters were compensated for their loss of human property. In Jamaica and Barbados, for example, the British government paid owners large indemnities and the ex-slaves had to work three-quarters time without pay for their former masters for six years. Even where former slaves managed to become landowning peasants, as happened on larger islands where land was available, the great majority were prevented from voting by outright exclusion or, in British dominions, prohibitive property requirements.

AMERICAN SUCCESSES AND FAILURES.   Was the situation similar in the United States? Paradoxically, white Southerners' fierce resistance to abolition created conditions that favored more drastic social change. The fact that it took a civil war to end slavery in the United States gave the South the character of a conquered province and the North greater authority to dictate the terms of emancipation. As made official in the Thirteenth Amendment, emancipation was immediate and uncompensated. When congressional Republicans took control of Reconstruction in 1867, they legislated a dramatic break with the southern past. Former slaveowners were largely excluded from drawing up new southern state constitutions and former Confederate officials were banned from holding office. Most remarkably, the Fourteenth and Fifteenth Amendments extended basic civil rights and male suffrage to the former slaves.

The United States was the only post-emancipation society in the Americas to grant freed slaves equal political rights, at least temporarily. The antislavery movement laid the basis for this extension of democracy, and by serving courageously in the Union army, African Americans had earned the respect due to full citizens. It is important to note, however, that Reconstruction legislation had as much to do with Republicans' ambitious plans for the South as with any abstract belief in racial equality. According to northern Republicans, the ex-slaves would form the mass of southern voters who would keep the region loyal to the Union. Their support would enable new state governments to establish public-school systems, build railroads and factories, and in other ways make over the South in the image of the modernizing North. This proposed "reconstruction" of southern economic and social life, made necessary by wartime devastation and desirable by the northern Republicans' progressive worldview, was the second unique feature of the post-emancipation United States. No such program of social development accompanied other New World emancipations. This aspect of American Reconstruction was paralleled at the time only by the "Great Reforms" modernizing the army and government that accompanied Tsar Alexander II's program for emancipating Russian serfs in 1861.

Unfortunately for the ex-slaves, the Republican program construed freedom according to the limited guidelines of America's competitive, individualistic society. The federal government set up a Freedmen's

Bureau to supervise labor contracts and adjudicate disputes, but this and other protective measures were only temporary. Proposals to confiscate disloyal planters' estates or in other ways distribute land to ex-slaves were considered too radical and were defeated in Congress. As a result, most freedmen became tenant farmers or sharecroppers, often on the same land where they had been slaves, and their goal of land ownership remained a distant dream. As Reconstruction wound down in the 1870s, the federal government backed away from protecting freed people's civil rights and left them to fend for themselves. Gradually, white Southerners rallied around the Democratic Party under the banner of white supremacy and regained control of their state legislatures. These reactionary governments reversed important gains blacks had won and found ways to exclude them, legally and otherwise, from exercising their right to vote. To replace the clear racial boundaries of slavery, southern whites devised an elaborate system of social segregation—the so-called Jim Crow laws—that reasserted a rigid status hierarchy between whites and blacks. Tragically, this third distinctive feature of the post-emancipation United States, which was consistent with the rigid color line established under colonial slavery, proved to be the longest lasting.

RECONSTRUCTION'S LEGACY. When the struggle over Reconstruction ended, there remained a pattern of white control and black dependency that resembled the inequalities of slavery. Despite a promising start, the outcome of emancipation in the United States seemed disappointingly similar to the Caribbean story. As in other post-emancipation societies, slaves had won "nothing but freedom," as one freedman complained. Nevertheless, the short-lived American experiment in racial equality brought significant advances in southern blacks' condition, some of which, like increased literacy, continued in the era of reactionary rule. Even more important, it put on the books federal laws and constitutional amendments that guaranteed legal equality. These would support the struggle for racial justice in the next century. The "Second Reconstruction" during the civil rights era of the 1960s was made possible by the limited successes of the first Reconstruction but also made necessary by its substantial failures.

Divided into slave and free states and torn by divergent sectional histories in the early nineteenth century, the United States had been a patchwork nation. It took the crisis of secession and civil war to unify the country under its national government. Americans emerged from the end of Reconstruction as citizens of a consolidated nation-state, but they left an unfinished agenda of racial equality to later generations.

Suggested Readings

Berger, Thomas R. *A Long and Terrible Shadow: White Values, Native Rights in the Americas*. Seattle: University of Washington Press, 1992.
   —A Native American rights advocate parallels the experience of Indians dealing with governments in North and South America.

Cunliffe, Marcus. *The Nation Takes Shape, 1789–1837*. Chicago: University of Chicago Press, 1959.
   —A British historian places early U.S. history and especially foreign policy in an Atlantic frame.

Davis, David Brion. *Inhuman Bondage: The Rise and Fall of Slavery in the New World*. New York: Oxford University Press, 2006.
   —The leading historian of slavery and abolition situates their New World histories in global context and illuminates important historical issues and controversies.

Degler, Carl N. *Neither Black nor White: Slavery and Race Relations in Brazil and the U.S.* Madison: University of Wisconsin Press, 1986.
   —Carefully compares life in and after slavery in the two largest New World slave societies.

Foner, Eric. *Nothing but Freedom: Emancipation and Its Legacy*. Baton Rouge: Louisiana State University Press, 1983.
   —Compares Southern Reconstruction to Caribbean experiences in emancipation.

Fredrickson, George M. *White Supremacy: A Comparative Study of American and South African History*. New York: Oxford University Press, 1981.
   —A superb comparative history of two settler societies, with many insights about race, frontiers, and nation-building.

Johnson, Paul. *The Birth of the Modern: World Society, 1815–1830*. New York: HarperCollins, 1991.
   —This lively narrative locates the origins of democracy and industrialism in international, especially Anglo-American, innovations of the early nineteenth century.

Kolchin, Peter. *Unfree Labor: American Slavery and Russian Serfdom*. Cambridge, Mass.: Harvard University Press, 1987.
   —This detailed comparison of coerced agricultural labor systems in distant lands reveals surprising similarities and differences.

Lipset, Seymour Martin. *The First New Nation; The United States in Historical and Comparative Perspective*. New York: W.W. Norton, 1979.
   —A sociologist considers the young United States a new nation comparable to emerging twentieth-century nations in Africa or Asia.

Nichols, Roger L. *Indians in the United States and Canada: A Comparative History*. Lincoln, Neb.: University of Nebraska Press, 1998.
>—Especially strong on the nineteenth and early twentieth centuries, this study integrates the history of the two nations and the Indian peoples within their borders.

Slatta, Richard N. *Cowboys in the Americas*. New Haven: Yale University Press, 1990.
>—A colorful survey of common cowboy practice and lore on North and South American frontiers.

Tocqueville, Alexis de. *Democracy in America* (1835–1840), translated by Arthur Goldhammer. New York: Modern Library, 2004.
>—Classic and still-relevant treatise by a brilliant French aristocrat on the nature of American democracy and its implications for Europe's future.

Weaver, John C. *The Great Land Rush and the Making of the Modern World, 1650–1900*. Montreal: McGill-Queen's University Press, 2003.
>—Describes and compares the ways Europeans and their descendants appropriated and distributed frontier lands in North America, Australia, New Zealand, and South Africa.

CHAPTER FOUR

INDUSTRIALIZING THE NATION

GETTING STARTED ON CHAPTER FOUR: Which features of the U.S industrial revolution were borrowed from abroad, and which were American innovations that were copied elsewhere? How do global patterns of migration help us understand America's immigration history and its "melting pot" society? What can we learn about transatlantic similarities and differences from historical debates over the "problem" of socialism in the United States? What forces led to the development of "welfare states" in the industrialized West, and how did the United States become one?

For two centuries after 1800, much of the world was reshaped by the growth of cities and industries and the accompanying migration of millions of people. From western Europe and Japan in the nineteenth century to Russia, China, India, and Latin America in the twentieth, these forces transformed developing nations in modern times. The United States was one among many countries that built railroads and factories, took in migrants from faraway lands, and spawned huge cities. In fact, scholars use general terms like "industrialization," "immigration," and "urbanization" expressly to give a common label to social processes that occurred in different times and places around the world, yet were fundamentally similar.

Workers and citizens in major industrial nations also adopted common strategies to control these forces and to cushion their worst effects. Throughout the industrialized world, farmers, factory workers, and middle-class professionals formed associations to protect their interests and to promote programs for reforming or even overturning industrial capitalism. The most direct challenge came from workers who organized unions to strike for better working conditions and a fairer distribution of wealth. Eventually, labor unions and reform associations turned to government to redress their grievances or ameliorate social conditions. In the United States and elsewhere, citizen activists injected their agendas into existing political parties or created new ones to press demands for universal suffrage (including votes for women), greater government planning, and labor and welfare legislation. Working within government and often outside it, such groups promoted ideologies like socialism and welfare-state liberalism that had originated in Europe, and they modified them to fit their nation's circumstances and cultural traditions.

How do we square these common features of western industrialism with the persisting belief that American society is unique and its history has been exceptional? Did social and economic trends of the nineteenth and twentieth centuries "Europeanize" the United States, as many Americans feared? Or were there political, economic, or cultural factors that made Americans' approach to industrialism unique?

This chapter places four aspects of America's industrial transformation in the context of global trends in the same era. It uncovers basic similarities between America's experience of the industrial revolution, immigration, socialism, and the welfare state and that of other nations. It also notes important differences, such as Americans' unusually strong preference for individualist values and private initiative rather than government controls. Yet even as we keep such differences in mind, a broad-gauged analysis makes clear that America's transformation of the late nineteenth and early twentieth century is more accurately described as a distinctive variant of global changes rather than a unique exception to them.

TIMELINE

1800–1900	Europe's population doubles, spurring migration
1830	First U.S. railroad line is built, based on British prototype
1848	Marx and Engels publish *Communist Manifesto*
1868	Meiji Restoration sparks Japanese industrialization
1870–1930	Great wave of European immigration to the Americas
1880–1940	Western Europe, Australia, and New Zealand construct welfare states
1880s	Chinese exclusion laws passed in United States, Canada, and Australia
1881	American Federation of Labor organized
1890–1920	Progressive movement enlarges role of U.S state and national governments

1900	Sales and office workers surpass manufacturing workforce in United States
1900–1914	High point of immigration to United States
1901	U.S. Steel becomes world's largest corporation
1906	British Labor Party organized
1912	American Socialist Party receives 6 percent of presidential vote
1913	Henry Ford introduces assembly-line production for automobiles
1913–1919	Women gain the right to vote in Canada and 20 European nations
1917–1918	United States participates in World War I
1917	Bolshevik Revolution declares Russia a communist state
1919–1920	Red Scare cripples American Socialist Party
1920	Nineteenth Amendment gives U.S. women right to vote
1920s	"Scientific management" and "Fordism" revolutionize U.S. mass production
1924	U.S. national origins quota law restricts immigration
1933–1940	Franklin Roosevelt's New Deal builds federal welfare state

AN AMERICAN INDUSTRIAL REVOLUTION

The British were in the best position to track America's ascent. Having industrialized first, they watched with admiration and anxiety as the United States pursued them at breakneck speed. James Bryce, who had first visited the United States in the 1870s, toured America in 1905 and was astonished at how swiftly industrial growth had advanced. Business activities "have more and more come to overshadow and dwarf all other interests," he noted. Huge industrial corporations now "covered a larger proportion of the whole field of industry and commerce in America than in Europe" and "wealth, gathered into a small number of hands, domi-nate[d] even the enormous market of America." According to Bryce's fellow countryman William T. Stead, American producers were taking over the European market, too. Following the average Englishman around as he rose from bed, Stead chronicled his use of American soap, razor blades, clothing, watches, newsprint, and breakfast cereals before he left the house for work. Stead published this catalog of imports in 1901 in a book revealingly titled *The Americanization of the World.*

In little more than half a century the United States was transformed from a sprawling agricultural nation into an industrial giant. From modest beginnings in the iron foundries and textile mills of the northeastern states before the Civil War, machine production spread rapidly to other industries and grew enormously in scale. By the time Bryce and Stead wrote, the United States had become the world's leading industrial power, with a manufacturing output exceeding the combined total of Great Britain, France, and Germany. Growing economic clout moved the United States from the margins to the center of the world economy, promoted it from Europe's debtor to its creditor, and provided the impetus for American imperial ventures abroad.

IMPORTING A REVOLUTION: AMERICA'S INDUSTRIAL SURGE

STAGES OF INDUSTRIAL ADVANCE.   How did it happen? Like so much of American history, the story of the nation's industrial transformation begins elsewhere. What scholars call "the Industrial Revolution" was actually a series of technological changes that restructured economic activity, first in Great Britain, then in the rest of western Europe, the United States, and Japan, and later elsewhere in the world. As pioneered by Britain, this transformation involved four overlapping stages of technological advance. First, mechanical and other improvements in agriculture made possible a surplus food supply and pushed farm workers from the countryside to cities, where they formed a reservoir of cheap labor. Second, waterwheels and windmills drove newly invented machinery that produced cloth and other products. By the 1790s in Britain, this system had moved manufacturing from cottages and workshops to factories, where production became systematized in steps and labor was subjected to strict rules and discipline. At this stage goods were transported from factory to market by roads, rivers, and man-made canals, which stitched together a rudimentary distribution network.

In the third phase, which began in the early nineteenth century, coal replaced wood, wind, and water as the dominant fuel. It was used to boil water into steam and to heat iron to high temperatures where it could be poured into a mold or bent into shape. Coal-fired steam engines brought factories into huge cities where labor abounded and new uses were found for machine production. They also powered riverboats, oceangoing ships, and—most importantly—railroads, whose development completed the transportation network that distributed goods faster and farther than ever before. In the fourth stage, begun in the late nineteenth century in western Europe and the United States, power output was multiplied by electricity, which was produced by turbine engines, and by oil, which when refined into gasoline, fueled the internal combustion engine. New chemicals transformed manufacturing, and stronger metals like steel built urban skyscrapers. In the early twentieth century, automobiles and airplanes accelerated transportation yet again, and electricity revolutionized consumer habits and leisure activities through household appliances, radio, and motion pictures.

In its outline and initial stages, this was the path blazed by Britain as the world's first industrialized nation, then followed by its former colony across the Atlantic. In the early decades of mechanization, the United States lagged behind British achievements by as much as 30 years, but in the age of electricity and oil it caught and then surpassed the leader. America's industrial revolution occurred through a combination of imitation and innovation. Some of the basic ingredients of industrial change were already present in the United States, such as abundant natural resources like coal, oil, and minerals, and a large domestic market to sustain demand for manufactured goods. Others, such as capital, technology, and labor, which were in short supply, could be imported and modified to fit American needs. Americans today, accustomed to their nation's status as an economic superpower, are often surprised to find out how much of their nation's industrial ascent rested upon borrowing or learning from abroad.

FOREIGN INVESTMENT. Capital for America's economic development, largely unavailable at home because agricultural expansion soaked it up, was borrowed from Europe. Throughout the nineteenth century the United States was a debtor nation, or to put it more positively, an attractive investment opportunity for foreign capital. Profits from Britain's industrial revolution were reinvested in the Americas in a process that ironically ended up subsidizing its competitors. British demand for raw cotton had earlier built the South's "cotton kingdom"; now its industrial profits helped build new factories in the United States. American railroads were also financed in part by British, Dutch, and German investments in state securities or company stock. Unlike Mexico, Argentina, and other Latin American countries, the United States had sufficient economic leverage and enough trained personnel to exploit European capital without having to cede control of its enterprises to foreign directors or absentee investors. All told, investment capital from Europe underwrote more than a third of American manufacturing.

TECHNOLOGY TRANSFER. Europe provided much of the technology as well. Whereas inventions like the McCormick reaper helped give the United States an agricultural edge, it was Britain's steam-engine technology that powered Mississippi riverboats and westward-chugging locomotives. The design of British textile machinery was memorized by Old World mechanics like Samuel Slater and duplicated when they migrated to the United States. Merchants and engineers from Baltimore who had been sent to inspect early British railways returned to build America's first line in 1830, the B&O (Baltimore and Ohio) Railroad of later board-game renown. In 1856, Britain's Henry Bessemer invented a furnace that quickly refined molten iron into steel. Adopted by Andrew Carnegie for his massive mill outside Pittsburgh, the "Bessemer converter" made possible Carnegie's steel empire. In later decades Americans imported chemical dyes from Germany, gas and diesel engines from Germany and France, and other significant technological inventions from abroad.

Railroads proved especially important in coordinating the American industrial revolution. America's natural resources and its population were spread over a vast area, requiring a huge transportation infrastructure to link the nation in a single market. Railroads transported crops, raw materials, manufactured goods, and passengers. They promoted the development of new industries, such as the Sears and Montgomery Ward's mail-order catalog businesses, and they encouraged centralization of others that had previously been local, such as meatpacking. Sears, Ward's, Armour, Swift, and other corporate giants located their headquarters at the railroads' midcontinent hub, Chicago. Construction of railways consumed much of the nation's steel output in the late 1800s, and by the century's end the United States boasted 40 percent of the world's railroad mileage.

Spurred by a consumer market that stretched across the continent, Americans did not simply copy European machines; they tailored production to the masses. Instead of crafting expensive, carefully finished products, American factories stressed quantity over quality. Railroad builders cut corners and costs to build rapidly and keep fares affordable. The sewing machine, invented but initially ignored in Europe because of a surplus of seamstresses, allowed American ready-made clothing to copy Parisian fashions for the expanding middle class. Perhaps the most dramatic example was the automobile, developed largely by French and German engineers but embraced by American entrepreneurs like Henry Ford. "I am going to democratize the automobile," Ford declared, and in 1908 he began mass-producing identical stripped-down Model Ts that made cars affordable to millions of working families. The strategy of borrowing European technology and adapting it to mass markets and new applications was repeated throughout America's industrialization. Outcompeting its teacher, the United States did to Great Britain in the 1800s and early 1900s what Japan and Korea would do with American technology after World War II. Each successful national entrant into the industrial arena served first as a customer, then a pupil, then a rival to its predecessors.

IMMIGRANT LABOR.   Immigrant workers made this ascent possible in the United States. Unlike Britain and other European nations undergoing industrialization, America could not fill its labor needs from its own population. When farms in the newly opened west attracted homesteaders, waves of immigrants arrived to end the urban labor shortage east of the Mississippi. Irish and French Canadian immigrants operated New England's textile mills, Chinese and Irish immigrants laid railroad tracks across the continent, Welsh and Poles mined Appalachian coal, and Slavs and Italians worked the Pennsylvania steel mills. Industrial America was built on the sweat of millions of immigrants. Big business owners found them a cheap and plentiful source of labor for operating machinery or performing backbreaking manual work. Most endured harsh conditions and low pay as temporary or desperate measures for escaping poverty in the Old World or the New.

GOVERNMENT AID.   Finally, through a process of economic "self-strengthening" common to many nations that were faced with the invasion of British manufactures, substantial support from government bolstered American industry. As latecomers to industrialization compared to Britain, businesses in the United States, Germany, and Japan relied on government assistance to jump-start economic growth. Government's role took different forms in each case. Germany's rapid industrial growth after 1870 resulted from top-down policies in which the national government developed and regulated business by controlling prices, allocating markets to particular firms, slapping tariffs on foreign imports, and granting legal monopolies in key industries. In Japan, after 1868, when the shogun, or military ruler, ceded power to the young emperor Meiji after agitation demanding stronger resistance to foreign economic influence, officials began an intense modernization campaign. Under Meiji rule the Japanese national government created a central bank, built the first railroads, and established and subsidized the shipping industry.

Americans avoided the German and Japanese "new mercantilist" strategy in which the state directed or owned banks and industrial enterprises, yet their governments eagerly assisted private businesses. Many Americans think of their economy as a "free enterprise" system that separates business and government, but from the 1830s onward, the national and state governments committed substantial resources to promoting business. American governments gave businesses tax breaks and subsidies, raised tariffs on imported goods to protect domestic industries, and offered virtually free grazing and mining on public acreage. The enormous land grants given to American railroads, if combined, would have equaled the area of the German Empire. While federal troops helped break strikes by labor unions, powerful corporate interests dominated Congress, and pro-business court rulings weakened antitrust and other regulatory laws.

GIVING INDUSTRIALIZATION AN AMERICAN FLAVOR

GIANT CORPORATIONS.   Each of the major powers, including the United States, differed in the strategies and emphases of its industrial revolution. Several American variations on international patterns deserve being called important innovations. Among them were general incorporation laws and giant "trusts." Shareholding companies were an old European invention that dated back to colonial trade monopolies and settlement charters. But laws enacted in United States from the 1830s onward enabled businesses to form corporations without obtaining special charters from rulers or legislators. These laws also reduced risk by limiting shareholders' liability in case of losses or lawsuits. Provisions for general incorporation stimulated competition, made it easier to raise capital through stocks and bonds, and sped the pace of industrialization. They were so successful that they were adopted by Great Britain in 1862 and Japan in 1893.

The less restrictive American environment encouraged the rise of big business. Unhampered by old distribution networks, aggressive antitrust prosecution, or gentlemanly restraint, American companies waged price wars on competitors or gobbled them up by buying their stock (which they held as trustees rather than as legal owners—hence the name "trusts") on the way to building near-monopolies. Family businesses continued to be the norm in Britain and Japan, but by the end of the nineteenth century, the U.S. economy was dominated by huge impersonal corporations. Some companies integrated "vertically" by controlling every phase of production from extracting raw materials to marketing finished goods; others integrated "horizontally" by acquiring or merging with competitors. Applying these methods ruthlessly, a few dozen companies controlled their industries nationwide and pulled strings in government to augment their advantages. The nation's largest business, J.P. Morgan's U.S. Steel, was capitalized at $1.4 billion in 1901, an amount three times bigger than the federal budget.

RAGS TO RICHES.   Americans were also the most eager to turn big businessmen into cultural heroes. Despised by labor activists for their cutthroat business practices, men like Andrew Carnegie and John D. Rockefeller were nevertheless admired and envied by many Americans. Popular magazines praised their philanthropic activities and upheld them as examples of the "rags-to-riches" journey that others might follow by working hard in the land of opportunity. In Britain, industrialists were sometimes exhibited as models of "self-help," and England's Samuel Smiles was nearly as popular a purveyor of success stories as America's Horatio Alger. Still, British entrepreneurs were snubbed as uncouth upstarts by the university graduates and landed elites who controlled the nation's political and cultural institutions. So it was especially ironic that Carnegie and other American business tycoons turned to England to find intellectual justification for their fabulous wealth. Charles Darwin had shown how natural selection caused evolutionary progress in the biological world. As formulated by the British philosopher Herbert Spencer and his followers, a version of "Social Darwinism" assured Americans that the advance of civilization depended upon the "survival of the fittest," the natural accumulation of power by those most adept at competition. Conservative Social Darwinists gave prestigious European scientific endorsement to Americans' faith in unregulated economic enterprise.

MASS PRODUCTION.   Because Americans were committed to producing goods for wide use rather than specialty markets, they took the lead in developing mass production techniques. The concept of interchangeable parts, first envisioned by inventor Eli Whitney, was adopted in gun manufacturing in the 1820s and soon was used to produce everything from nails to clocks. This innovation, which Europeans called the "American system" of manufacturing, sped production, cut labor costs, and lowered prices. When combined with the continuous production line that was pioneered by the meatpacking industry in the 1860s, it culminated in Henry Ford's automobile assembly line, where conveyor belts moved cars along steadily as stationary workers added the same part to each model. From this point it was only a short step to turn workers themselves into machines. This feat was accomplished in the 1920s by Frederick W. Taylor, whose theory of "scientific management" became influential worldwide. Taylor systematically reduced physical work to small steps that could be optimized for speed and efficiency and controlled by trained supervisors. Not surprisingly, Taylor's dehumanizing system was resisted by many workers then and now, but its widespread adoption shows how far American capitalists have been committed to mass production.

ADVERTISING.   All those goods required buyers. Consumer spending was necessary to keep mass production humming, and American manufacturers excelled at turning out practical conveniences like canned foods and household appliances. To entice Americans away from traditional thrifty ways, advertisers developed crafty appeals that aroused consumers' desires for products they did not need or had not encountered before. Throughout the industrialized West, advertising became prominent in tandem with mass-circulation newspapers and magazines. By 1900, large-print, pictorial advertisements began to take over tabloid pages, and American cities became plastered with signs and billboards. Advertising agencies—an American first—were established a few years earlier to advise corporate clients on strategies for making their brands household names. Foreign visitors noted how Americans seemed to turn everything, from park benches to streetcars, into advertisements and hoped, usually in vain, that the blight would not reach their shores.

OFFICE AND SERVICE WORK. Americans' emphasis on sales and service, together with their reliance on lawyers and the elaborate bureaucracies of giant corporations, made the nation the first to develop a large "tertiary" sector of the economy devoted to office work. (Agriculture was primary, manufacturing secondary.) By 1900, more Americans were employed in clerical work, sales, and service than in manufacturing, a position England did not reach until the 1930s and Germany until the 1960s. As will be discussed later, this had important implications for working-class organizing. It also prefigured the "postindustrial" economy dominated by the service, technology, and entertainment industries that the United States would be the first to reach in the late twentieth century.

MIDDLE-CLASS CULTURE AND CONSUMERISM

Americans' phenomenal success at mass production pioneered the development of a new middle-class culture. Industrialization made comfortable living possible for more people at the same time it created a standardized middle-class life. Thanks to economic expansion and the rise of the office and sales sectors, in the second half of the nineteenth century opportunities to achieve middle-class status widened for literate city dwellers, especially white Protestants. The older middle class of small business owners, doctors, and educators was supplemented by a growing number of office workers. Meanwhile, the increased complexity of modern work called for specialization. Banks, insurance companies, and government hired armies of salaried clerks, accountants, and managers and sorted them into a bureaucracy of functions and ranks. Office work became regularized much like factory life.

THE RISE OF SUBURBS. Especially in large cities, industrialization transformed middle-class life at home as well as at work. From the 1880s onward, as immigrants poured into neighborhoods near the central business district, streetcars stretched the city limits outward and middle-class families moved to detached suburban houses. Unlike European cities that set firm boundaries between city and country, American cities extended indefinitely along transportation lines, creating a new environment that was neither urban nor rural. As they expanded, cities became sorted into districts ringed around the "downtown" (a new American word) in concentric circles that reflected dwellers' income levels, with the wealthiest families living farthest out. Bourgeois Europeans lived in spacious apartments near the center city, but the American middle class's preference for private homes and lawns turned the European urban pattern inside out. Removed from city noise, pollution, and danger, middle-class families could enjoy domestic life in Victorian homes whose exteriors faintly resembled European temples or castles, encasing family privacy in architectural displays of status and refinement.

MIDDLE-CLASS "DOMESTICITY."   The rise of streetcar and railroad commuting separated work and home, making the household middle-class women's place. In America and western Europe, the shift to industrial society was accompanied by an ideal of "domesticity" that assigned women the tasks of housekeeping, childrearing, and churchgoing and praised them for making the home a refuge from the competitive world. Electric laborsaving devices like vacuum cleaners and washing machines lightened household drudgery. By 1900, perhaps a third of U.S. middle-class households hired live-in servants, a trend that drew heavily on female ex-slaves in the South and on female Irish immigrants in the North. Thanks to hired help, middle-class women's role shifted from doing the laundry and cooking toward supervision of household tasks, freeing time for involvement with church, clubs, or children.

THE CULTURE OF CONSUMPTION.   Middle-class women also shopped. Mass production made available an enormous array of household furniture, appliances, and decorations to choose from. Elegant boutiques imported the latest Parisian fashions, but American factories produced simpler versions in ready-made sizes. Lured by these goods and anxious to show their success, middle-class families shed traditional thrifty ways and shifted to a new emphasis upon consumption. In Paris and New York, department stores evolved simultaneously in the 1860s when dry goods stores selling fabrics and women's accessories mushroomed into multi-storied emporiums offering a dazzling variety of goods arranged in departments. The Parisian stores catered to a wealthy clientele and spread slowly, but Americans democratized department stores just as they democratized industrial production. By 1900, every major American city featured "people's palaces" of merchandise. Their elegant décor and lavish displays of goods attracted middle-class browsers and buyers. Department stores served as "lands of desire," featuring furniture sets, appliances, and innovations like electric lighting and central heating that soon appeared in homes. For Americans far from big cities, Sears and Wards catalogs functioned as surrogate department stores. Their annual Christmas "wish books" enticed families with several hundred pages of illustrated displays that promised the latest urban fashions and promoted everything from cosmetics to prefabricated houses. Purchasing became easier when retailers offered customers lines of credit or the option to pay in installments.

The flood of consumer goods burst traditional restraints on spending. It also increasingly supplanted the older emphasis on moral improvement with self-fulfillment through consumption. Advertisers preached that appearance and possessions were badges of self-worth, "new" was always "improved," and comfort and convenience were natural rights. Whether the American public swallowed this message whole or simply looked for practical benefits from their purchases, millions fell in line at the cashier. By the early twentieth century, Americans were leading the way to a culture of mass consumption that became a national trademark and a challenge for other industrialized nations to resist or imitate.

WORKING-CLASS ASPIRATIONS.   Not all Americans could afford to live like urban middle-class families. Many native-born and immigrant workers crowded into dark, unhealthy apartments near the city center, while black and white Southern sharecroppers survived in rickety shacks set on rented land. Poor families relied on child labor, and immigrant and black women formed the majority of females in the paid labor force. Still, many working-class families aspired to middle-class status. Mothers stayed home when they could afford to, or else took in laundry or boarders to bring in income. Working-class families bought mass-produced reproductions of paintings to hang on their walls and worn-out pianos to entertain guests. Pooling their family income, a surprising number purchased their own homes, aided by lower prices in outlying areas and the economy of Americans' lightly studded "balloon-frame" houses. On average, about one-quarter of American working-class families owned or were paying for homes around 1910—a much higher percentage than in industrialized Europe. The opportunity to own homes and enjoy consumer goods spurred dreams that workers could eventually achieve middle-class status, or at least harbor such hopes for their children. Small personal gains or examples of success among friends or relatives were often enough to sustain workers' faith in this "American dream."

CONTRASTS OF WEALTH AND POVERTY

Despite the comparatively large and open American middle class, the industrial revolution widened the gap between the rich and poor in the United States, as it did elsewhere in the industrialized West. Atop the income hierarchy, industrialists and financiers accumulated vast fortunes and lived lavishly. "Robber Barons" like J.P. Morgan and the Vanderbilts pocketed millions of dollars annually, stocked their urban palaces with Renaissance art, and built enormous summer "cottages" at fashionable resorts. At the bottom of the class ladder, industrial workers were brutally exploited. Men and women worked twelve-hour days at rock-bottom pay and were subjected to a frightening rate of workplace injuries. In the 1890s, unskilled workers at Andrew Carnegie's steel mills earned less than 20 cents an hour. Children began work in textile factories at age 10 and were paid 40 cents a day. Nationwide during the 1910s, industrial accidents caused a million injuries a year and took 25,000 workers' lives.

As the reach of national and international markets expanded, farmers and workers became subject to a capitalist boom-and-bust business cycle that produced periodic bouts of joblessness, bank failures, and foreclosures on farms and houses. The absence of a "safety net" of health or unemployment insurance made illness, injury, or layoffs devastating events. In large part, workers lacked protections because individuals and corporations that accrued unprecedented fortunes were able to bend public policies to their own benefit. Whether governments established and oversaw businesses, as in Germany and Japan, or whether they allowed private businesses great latitude, as in the United States, the two forces developed a close relationship that violated democratic ideals and distributed benefits disproportionately to the rich.

Class disparities in wealth and power were mirrored by heightened regional differences between agriculturally "backward" and more developed areas. In the United States, as in Italy and Europe overall, an invisible line divided the industrialized North from an agricultural South, which remained a "peripheral" economy, controlled by outside capital and confined largely to growing one or two crops for the national or world market. Sectional relations produced an "internal colonialism" that mimicked imperial practices abroad.

THE UNITED STATES BECOMES A WORLD ECONOMIC POWER. On the international scene, industrialization produced dramatic winners and losers, too. Great Britain and its major-power rivals belonged in the first category; their colonies, which fed them raw materials and were prevented from industrializing, fell into the second. America's rapid industrial transformation completed its rise from the second to the first category, its final push from "semi-peripheral" to "core" status in the world economy. No longer an economic colony of Europe, the nation had passed through an intermediary stage whereby eastern merchants brokered the export of raw materials. In the late nineteenth century, East Coast cities continued to exploit their western hinterlands, taking in their crops and raw materials, which were often transferred to Europe. Mechanization of farming produced huge surpluses of corn, wheat, and beef, which together made up three-quarters of U.S. exports in 1900. By then, however, a new stage was reached. Profits from transportation and agricultural trade underwrote the nation's economic development so that it became not simply less dependent upon foreign manufactures, but an industrial power in its own right. The sheer size of the U.S. domestic market encouraged the growth of businesses whose capacity and efficiency enabled them to penetrate the world market. Increasingly, American food exports were supplemented with industrial products, from sewing machines and household supplies to petroleum and steel. And the search for markets for these goods led Americans into the race for overseas colonies.

By diversifying into manufacturing and retaining ownership of its businesses, the United States avoided the dependence upon European (especially British) control that plagued farm and mine export industries in Latin American nations like Argentina and Mexico. More than that, it became a rival industrial power that soon outperformed Europe itself. By World War I, the United States enjoyed vast trade surpluses with Europe. Inexpensive American grain helped to eliminate famines in Europe and lengthened peoples' lives. As a result, Europe's rising population and the decline of local food production forced its peasants to migrate to cities or sail overseas in search of work. When these immigrants became a cheap source of labor for American industry, the circle was completed. Workers moving from Europe, where they were plentiful, to the United States, where they were in short supply, helped build a new industrial colossus.

A Nation of Immigrants in a World of Migrants

Sometime between 1901 and 1904, two cousins, Ida and Oreste Sola, left their northern Italian village of Valdengo. Ida, 21 years old and desperate to escape an overbearing stepmother, worked as a servant and saved enough money to buy a ticket to New York City, where she found a job in a restaurant. Meanwhile, Oreste, 17 years old and recently graduated from technical school, headed for Buenos Aires, Argentina to join relatives who had set up a construction business. The Solas' divergent paths were not unusual. Transatlantic steamships took German families to U.S and

Canadian homesteads or colonies in southern Brazil, Spanish laborers to construction sites in Argentina or plantations in Cuba, and Portuguese boatmen to New England fishing villages or Brazilian sugar ports. To European migrants, "America" did not mean simply the United States, but destinations on both continents in the Western Hemisphere.

The United States has a long history of attracting people from all over the world, and Americans pride themselves on belonging to a nation of immigrants. Approximately three-quarters of today's Americans trace their ancestry to migrants who arrived after the Revolution, and the number is increasing daily as immigration levels rise again in an age of instant communications and jet travel. The story of coming to the United States and the process of "becoming American" are central to Americans' family histories and their national mythology. Because of this, it is easy to forget that the flow of people to the United States was only one stream of a vast movement of European and Asian peoples across the oceans. To portray this migration as simply a facet of U.S. history is to misjudge its size and character. To interpret it solely as "immigration" (entry into the United States to settle there) is to ignore the migrants' varied agendas and destinations, and their link to common patterns of global migration.

PUSHES AND PULLS: THE LARGER CONTEXT OF MIGRATION

The century between 1830 and 1930 was the busiest era of migration in human history. During that time more than 50 million Europeans relocated overseas. Most went to British settler colonies such as Canada, Australia, and New Zealand, or to independent nations that Europeans originally established as colonies in North and South America. Europe's share of the world's population increased rapidly, but so did the dispersal of its people. In 1800, fewer than one in every 100 persons in the world were overseas Europeans and their descendants; by 1930 the figure was one in 11.

In the same span of years, perhaps 40 million Asians left for destinations around the Indian and Pacific Oceans. Chinese laborers moved into east Africa and southeast Asia, joined gold rushes in Australia, Peru, and the United States, and worked on sugar plantations in Hawaii. Indian migrants became indentured workers in South African mines and on island plantations of the Indian Ocean, the South Pacific, and the Caribbean.

Why did so many people leave their homelands? Scholars studying migrants explain their actions by discussing three factors: "push," "pull," and "means." During the nineteenth century, a chain reaction set off by rapid population growth, commercialized agriculture, and industrialization uprooted millions of people around the world. Several forces "pushed" Europeans to abandon their birthplace. As nutrition improved—thanks largely to new foods provided by the Columbian Exchange—people lived longer and the population of Europe exploded. From 1800 to 1900 it more than doubled, from 180 million to 400 million. Consolidation of farms and competition on the world market forced peasants off the land, while factory production displaced cottage industries and craftsmen. More people rushed to European cities than their labor markets could absorb. In general, this process coursed southward and eastward through Europe as the century progressed. Thus the British Isles sent most of their migrants overseas before 1880, whereas most Russian, Italian, and eastern European migrants left after that.

Although overall population growth in nineteenth-century Asia was apparently less steep than in Europe, in certain areas, such as the Guangdong province of southeastern China, it exceeded European rates, quadrupling during the century. Surging population put pressure on local agriculture, making periodic harvest failures catastrophic and pushing migrants elsewhere in search of survival. Many Chinese migrants also sought refuge from wars related to imperial intrusions, such as the British Opium Wars (1839–1842, 1856–1860) or local struggles between peasants and landlords or hostile ethnic groups.

Political and religious developments also forced some European migrants from their homes. For Polish and Russian Jews, who faced persecution and restrictions on mobility, emigration promised an escape. Exiles from various European political revolutions chose deportation rather than prison or death. Yet the overwhelming majority of immigrants were not refugees but jobseekers, hoping to improve their economic condition by finding work elsewhere.

JOBS AS MAGNETS.   There was a huge demand for labor overseas. Across North and South America and in Australia, new nations built transportation networks and expanded production of minerals and cash crops in order to provide tin, rubber, coffee, wool, wheat, beef, and other commodities for a world market dominated by European investors and consumers. By the late nineteenth century, the United States was industrializing rapidly and its giant coal, oil, and steel businesses rivaled, then surpassed, Europe's in their output. Settler-society and colonial enterprises required millions of cheap, unskilled agricultural and factory workers. The availability of jobs and (in some cases) inexpensive land exerted an enormous "pull" on millions of transoceanic migrants. Religious freedom, lack of military service, and a congenial climate were secondary attractions.

FROM REGIONAL TO TRANSOCEANIC MIGRATION. Overseas migration extended an old pattern. For centuries workers had been moving temporarily *within* Europe to harvest crops, work in mines, or find jobs in cities. In the late nineteenth century, this habit continued, but the number of continental European migrants was being equaled and even surpassed by those going overseas. Between 1876 and 1926, for example, 7 million Italians went to other parts of Europe and North Africa, and another million or so migrated within Italy, but 9 million migrated to the Americas. Improved transportation made longer trips viable. With the switch from sailing ships to steam vessels, ocean crossings were reduced from five weeks to eight days and were begun on regular schedules. Railroad companies from the Americas recruited immigrants overseas with advertising and sped them to inland destinations after their arrival. Enabled by these modernized "means," a vast and complex system of westward human migration developed that paralleled and quickened the transfer of commodities eastward across the Atlantic.

A similar widening of horizons occurred among Asian migrants. Many Chinese initially took overland routes to find farms in Manchuria or jobs at plantations, mines, and ports in southeast Asia. But as overseas trade with the Americas escalated and the Chinese government legalized the emigration of laborers in 1868, North America and Australia became preferred destinations.

MIGRATION AND EMPIRE. Some migrants were attracted to imperial lands, while others went elsewhere. Generally speaking, separate European and Asian streams of migration reflected the racial division of labor that European imperial powers had established earlier between temperate settler societies and tropical colonies. Some British and Dutch men took posts in their nation's imperial army or colonial bureaucracy in Africa and Asia. But the vast majority of European migrants chose destinations with moderate climates, such as the United States, Canada, or Argentina, where fellow Europeans—often from the same homeland—formed the primary labor force, diversified economies offered greater opportunity, and citizenship was possible.

In contrast, most Asian migrants came to tropical or subtropical lands. Some of these were island possessions of European powers and others were expanding new nations. Chinese and Indian migration escalated in tandem with the decline of slavery as Asian workers were imported to replace recently freed African slaves. Many migrated as semifree "coolie" laborers, bound by labor contracts or, in the worst case, indenture certificates approved by their home governments. Indenture provided free passage and basic maintenance in return for five to seven years of specific

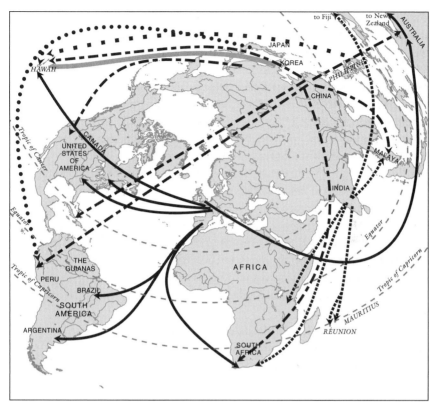

FIGURE 4-1   MIGRATION FROM EUROPE AND ASIA, 1850S TO 1920S
Source: Used with permission from Traditions and Encounters (2nd ed.), by Jerry H. Bentley and
Herbert F. Ziegler. Copyright 2002 by McGraw-Hill.

heavy labor, such as tending plantation crops, digging for minerals, or
building large-scale construction projects like railroads. Although most of
the 200,000 Chinese who came to California after the gold rush entered
freely, Indian workers on Caribbean sugar plantations, Japanese laborers
who mined guano (bird dung) in Peru, and Chinese, Japanese, Korean,
and Filipino workers who harvested sugar cane in Hawaii were often
contracted or indentured.

IMMIGRANT NATIONS.   Overseas migrants landed in many places besides
the United States. Between the early nineteenth century and World War II,
Canada, Argentina, and Brazil together took in nearly 30 percent of
European New World arrivals. Brazil, which received nearly 4 million
Europeans, boasted more Italian immigrants than the United States before
1900, and Canada opened its doors to more newcomers than the United
States in the 1920s and 30s. During the great wave of migration between
1870 and 1930, as many English and Scottish migrants went to Canada,

Australia, and New Zealand as to the United States. The overseas migrant flow from Asia, somewhat smaller than Europe's until World War II, was much less concentrated toward the United States. Ships crossing the Pacific brought Chinese, Japanese, and Indian workers to Australia, Fiji, Peru, and Cuba, as well as California. In the 1880s Chinese immigrants accounted for 1 in 50 Australians but fewer than 1 in 500 residents of the United States, including Hawaii. Of the approximately 20 million Chinese who left their country from 1820 to 1930, about 450,000, or less than 3 percent, came to the United States and its territories.

Because of this wide distribution of peoples, other New World nations besides the United States could justly claim to be nations of immigrants. In the hundred years before 1930, 5.5 million foreigners went to Argentina and 6.5 million to Canada. Because both nations had much smaller populations than the United States, the newcomers' impact was proportionally greater. By 1914, around the peak of the immigrant flow, one out of every three persons in Argentina was foreign born and one in four in Canada, compared to one in six in the United States.

GENERAL PATTERNS OF MIGRATION

"Laws of Migration."   Wherever they departed or landed, immigrants moved in similar patterns that one late-nineteenth-century scholar ambitiously labeled the "laws of migration." Waves of migrant jobseekers crested during boom times in destination countries and crashed during economic depressions (the 1870s, 1890s and 1930s) or the disruptions of world war. Most migrants were young, between 20 and 35 years old, and were drawn from the poorer but not the most destitute classes, for the latter often lacked the means to relocate. Their movements occurred in stages. For many Europeans and Asians, a trip to a nearby city or neighboring country in search of work proved the first step toward a journey across the ocean. Villagers migrated in "chains," following relatives or neighbors who had found employment and often lodging with them before gaining an independent foothold.

Temporary Migration and Ethnic Diasporas.   Other aspects of migration, such as sex ratios and return flows, varied by ethnic group. Because Irish famine emigrants and Jewish refugees fled impossible conditions, they intended to settle permanently. Theirs was a migration of families and (in the Irish case) single women. On the other hand, the majority of job-seeking migrants were male, and many of these were short-term workers. As many as 40 percent of European migrants shortly returned to the Old World, either because they found no satisfactory work or else to bring earnings home to sustain families or purchase land. Observers noticed that some migrant laborers, labeled "birds of passage" in the United States or *golondrinas* ("swallows") in Latin America, plotted annual steamship voyages so they worked on harvests in North or South America before heading back to Europe for the spring planting.

Asian migrants, who were overwhelmingly male, especially saw themselves as "sojourners" intent on a short-term stay to bring home wages from menial labor or treasure from mine diggings. More than half of the Japanese and Chinese workers in Hawaii returned to their homelands. Most of the Chinese men who remained there and in the American West lived bachelor lives, whereas Japanese families became common because Japan's government encouraged women's emigration and the U.S. government allowed Japanese wives to join their husbands.

The rise of temporary and repeat migration and the increased ease of contact with the homeland permitted by steamships and mail created what scholars call ethnic "diasporas," dispersed communities that maintain contact and solidarity across great distances. This term was initially applied to migrants who were forced from their homeland and retained an identification with it, such as Jews and African slaves. The expanding global economy and its rapid communication networks gave the voluntary dispersals of Chinese and Italian migrants a similar cast. Remittances to relatives back home, frequent back-and-forth movements, sustained engagement in homeland politics, and retention of the ancestral language— all demonstrated the existence of a dual national identity among these "birds of passage" and forecast a growing trend toward transnational lives among late-twentieth-century migrants.

ADJUSTMENT AND ASSIMILATION.   Whether working on farms or in mines and factories, most permanent immigrants settled in ethnic enclaves that reproduced their familiar customs of church, family, and leisure in an unfamiliar setting. Clusters of German farmers in Chile, southern Brazil, and the North American Great Plains maintained their language and folkways, while Italians and Slavs gathered in ethnic neighborhoods in industrial cities. Immigrants experienced a period of adjustment that was broadly similar from place to place, although local conditions affected the occupational avenues open to them and the pace of their economic mobility. Those who intended to stay were more likely to join worker organizations and to become citizens, moves prompted by hopes for better wages or government jobs. Generally speaking, among permanent immigrants a gradual economic advancement through the generations increased intermarriage rates with other groups and heightened the tendency to adopt the language and cultural patterns of the host society, a process scholars call "assimilation."

PATTERNS OF DISCRIMINATION.   In many cases, European migrants encountered hostility from local residents, often second- or third-generation
immigrants themselves, who feared that the newcomers would depress
wages or bring radical doctrines like anarchism with them. Ethnic and
religious animosities, such as Protestant prejudices against Irish Catholics
in the United States or negative stereotypes about Jews in all New World
receiver nations, crossed the Atlantic before immigrants arrived and poi-
soned their reception. Similarity to their hosts in language, faith, and skin
color smoothed the path to acceptance for some groups, such as British
migrants to the United States and Canada, or Italian and Iberian migrants
to Argentina and Brazil. In the latter case, South American leaders encouraged migration by southern Europeans as a counterweight to native
and *mestizo* peoples and a way to "civilize" (i.e., Europeanize) their
nations' population.

From the outset, Asian migrants faced unequal treatment compared
to European newcomers. In the United States and other New World
settler societies, anti-Asian discrimination ranged from restrictions on
property owning and citizenship to outright exclusion. Asian sojourners
attracted by gold rushes, imported as contract laborers, or seeking
work on their own were stigmatized as racially unassimilable and
blamed for decreasing wages. Opposition came not only from local elites
but also from white workers, many recently arrived from Europe. Dennis
Kearney, who led the Workingmen's Party of California in the 1870s
with the slogan "The Chinese Must Go," was an Irish-born teamster.
During the 1880s, Chinese immigration was restricted through harsh
quotas and head taxes in New Zealand (1881), Australia (1881), and
Canada (1885), and in 1901 Australia effectively banned Chinese entry.
The U.S. Congress passed an Exclusion Act in 1882 prohibiting the entry
of Chinese laborers. After Chinese sojourners were replaced by Japanese
job seekers, public opposition shifted to the newcomers. In 1907, the
United States negotiated a "Gentlemen's Agreement" in which Japan
agreed to cease issuing passports to laborers headed for America. Canada
negotiated a similar agreement the following year.

AMERICAN VARIATIONS

Overseas migration to the United States shared these features with the
movement to other New World nations. In relation to other immigrant-
receiving societies, however, five aspects of American immigration and
ethnic relations stand out, although only a few are unique enough to be
called exceptional.

AN ENORMOUS INFLUX.   One was the huge number of newcomers entering
the country. Between 1820 and 1930, more than 30 million foreigners came

to the United States, more than half of all European overseas migrants and five times the number who went to the second-place receiver, Canada. Each year in the early twentieth century almost a million individuals sought haven in what Jewish immigrants called "the New Golden Land." Not all succeeded: for example, the Solas and many of their Italian compatriots found the prospects brighter and cultural adjustments less jarring in Latin America. Yet millions of European newcomers—perhaps the majority—eventually found jobs that enabled them to begin their family's long climb toward middle-class status. Rates of economic mobility varied among immigrant groups. Studies of New York and Boston, for example, found that newcomers with peasant roots like the Irish and southern Italians clustered in manual-labor jobs, whereas European town dwellers such as Germans and Jews moved more quickly into shopkeeping or skilled labor. In both cases, however, a gradual upward trend in occupations and income testified to the growth of the U.S. economy and its vast absorptive capacity.

AVAILABILITY OF LAND.   Second, the United States differed from most New World receivers by offering millions of acres of affordable land to European migrants who reached the frontier. In Brazil and Argentina, men who had been given plantations or cattle estates by the government kept tight control of immigrants as tenants or wage laborers, and prospects for independent landownership were poor. By contrast, the United States provided lands virtually free for western settlers through the Homestead Act (1862). Hundreds of thousands of immigrants from Germany and Scandinavia moved westward along the Ohio River and across the Mississippi to claim their 160-acre farms or to purchase them at modest prices from railroad companies. The United States was not entirely unique in this regard. As the American frontier began to fill in, Canada became the preferred destination for land-seeking migrants. Canada's Dominion Lands Policy (1872–1930), modeled on the Homestead Act, drew over a million settlers to its western prairies after 1900.

INDUSTRIAL JOBS.   Third, despite opportunities on the frontier, the overwhelming majority of immigrants to the United States found industrial rather than agricultural work. Many European migrants to Latin America worked on plantations or large estates raising cattle or growing export crops such as coffee, sometimes displacing ex-slaves. In the United States, immigrants avoided the agricultural South, which had a staple-crop economy that was in decline by the 1870s, and where ex-slaves remained an exploited labor force. Instead, the most easily available jobs lay in the booming industrial economy of the northeastern states, where European newcomers started as unskilled or semiskilled workers. (Thus in one way or another, immigration proved detrimental to blacks in the Americas, either replacing them as farm workers or closing off industrial opportunities that might otherwise have been opened to them.) European immigrants built canals and railroads, descended into mines, and worked in textile and steel mills, making the American industrial revolution both possible and profitable.

ETHNIC VARIETY. A fourth distinctive feature of immigration to the United States was its astonishing variety of ethnic groups. Several New World receiver nations took in Asian workers, but before World War II their numbers were too small to alter these countries' overall ethnic mix. More decisive differences occurred in the massive European immigration prior to the 1930s. Whereas Canada attracted settlers mainly from Britain and Ireland, and migrants to South America were overwhelmingly Iberian and Italian, immigrants to the United States came from all over Europe. The largest group over time, from Germany, constituted only 15 percent of the total. This diffusion of immigrants' origin was the basis of the "melting pot" concept, for without one European group dominating the immigrant ranks, newcomers were more likely to mix with other groups and with the native-born white population and to contribute to a common American culture. In the long run, ethnic variety helped to ease the absorption of immigrants into American society at the same time it created new ideas of what it meant to be American.

DEBATING IMMIGRATION. Not everyone agreed with these ideas. A continuous debate over immigration and its relation to national identity represents a fifth defining—but hardly unique—feature of the U.S. experience. All immigrant-receiving settler societies faced the problem of creating a viable multiethnic nation, but each addressed it in ways that reflected its specific conditions, customs, and institutions. In the United States, as in the British settler colonies of Australia and New Zealand, ethnic questions arising before World War II were framed by the struggle between exclusion and inclusion, first relating to Asian migrants, then to various European groups. On one side of the U.S. debate stood "Anglo-conformists," proponents of defining the nation as a preserve of white Anglo-Protestants and their cultural ways. Opposed to them, advocates of the melting-pot ideal asserted that the United States should be the "asylum of all nations" and its ethnic cultures should fuse into a unique, composite people. The battle between the two ideas was the American version of the contest between "ethnic" and "civic" nationalism that has been waged in many immigrant-receiving societies, from settler colonies like Canada and new nations like Malaysia to recent European destinations such as Germany and France. Ethnic nationalism permits one ethnic group to dominate the nation's culture and to enforce its views by law;

civic nationalism defines nationality by common participation in political life and guarantees citizenship and equal rights to all ethnic groups.

THE "MELTING POT" AND AMERICAN ETHNIC RELATIONS

For most of the nineteenth century, America's open harbors indicated that the melting-pot ideal predominated, as the Statue of Liberty's welcoming beacon implied. The notion of Americans as a new kind of people, forged by the union of displaced ethnic groups in an adopted land, appeared as early as the 1780s. It flowered into a national myth as the influx of northern Europeans surged, and in the 1890s it gained popularity by merging with another potent legend, the saga of the western pioneers that novelists and historians celebrated as the essence of American uniqueness. "In the crucible of the frontier," Frederick Jackson Turner declared, "the immigrants were Americanized, liberated and fused into a mixed race, English in neither nationality nor characteristics."[1] The United States was hardly unique among the settler societies in receiving millions of immigrants, but it was exceptional in turning their story into a powerful myth central to its national identity: the nation as a great melting pot.

OPPOSITION TO IMMIGRATION. Nevertheless, when immigration to the United States soared in the late nineteenth century, the fears of Anglo-Protestant exclusionists and their allies—some only a generation removed from Europe themselves—escalated. Alarmed that non-English-speaking immigrants would never assimilate, and blaming them for crime, labor strife, and other urban-industrial problems, exclusionists built a powerful anti-immigrant movement. As in the British settler colonies, Asian immigrants were the first to be restricted. As noted earlier, federal laws banned Chinese immigrant laborers in 1882 and the Gentlemen's Agreement stopped the entry of Japanese workers in 1907. By the early twentieth century, U.S. social scientists routinely distinguished between desirable older European immigrant groups such as the British and Germans, and the darker Mediterranean and Slavic immigrants of recent years, who allegedly carried un-American customs and creeds. In 1924, after the Bolshevik Revolution in Russia heated American nativism to fever pitch, the Johnson-Reed Act set up a national origins quota system that virtually excluded Asian immigrants and allowed only token numbers of southern and eastern Europeans to enter the United States. (Somewhat milder laws restricting European immigration were adopted by other western settler nations in the 1920s and during the Great Depression.) The stream of European newcomers to the United States slowed to a trickle.

[1]Frederick Jackson Turner, "The Significance of the Frontier in American History [1893]," in *Frontier and Section: Selected Essays* (Englewood Cliffs, NJ: Prentice-Hall, 1961), 51.

Ironically, the hiatus in immigration imposed by Anglo-conformists accelerated the ethnic fusion that melting-pot advocates preached. In the 1920s and 1930s, second-generation immigrants intermarried and gained influence in national political parties. Foreign words and phrases entered American English, and American popular music and movies were enlivened by immigrant contributions. Yet the ingredients in the melting pot never completely melted. Why not?

AN INCOMPLETELY MELTED POT.   First of all, it had not included race. Anglo-conformists and melting-pot advocates drew competing portraits of their ideal America, but both envisioned it as an extension of Europe. Both excluded Africans and Asians from the picture. Racial intermarriage was outlawed in many states, and only during the two world wars were southern blacks recruited by northern industries to fill the void created by the absence of immigrants and the departure of soldiers. Asian immigrants were prevented from owning property in some states, and most remained ineligible for U.S. citizenship up to the 1940s. Not until after World War II would Americans seriously confront—or confront *again*, following the failure of Reconstruction in the 1870s—their problems of racial injustice and inequality.

Secondly, many European immigrants and their children retained distinctive ethnic and religious ways, especially in their private lives. Seeing no contradiction between professing allegiance to American institutions and honoring their Old World heritage, most identified themselves as "hyphenated Americans": Irish-Americans, Polish-Americans, and so on. This concept had been ridiculed by Theodore Roosevelt and others who advocated "100 percent Americanism" during the crisis of World War I, but it came to be accepted informally as the American norm. "Hyphenated" Americanism proved to be dynamic and flexible, allowing for individuals to stress either side of the hyphen depending on preference or occasion, or even to adopt additional ethnic affiliations as they intermarried. An incompletely melted pot offered American newcomers and their children a range of options, from active preservation of traditional ways to virtual assimilation, at the same time that ethnic groups inflected mainstream American culture with their distinctive cultural practices and beliefs.

As crystallized by the mid-twentieth century, American ethnic relations combined informal recognition—and even celebration—of ethnic groups with public policy that aimed to treat all individuals equally without discrimination. Broadly speaking, this approach set the United States on a middle course among New World settler societies that became major immigrant receivers. At one end of the spectrum stood Brazil, where the prevailing ideal of "racial democracy" attempted to subordinate ethnic affiliations, incorporated a high degree of intermarriage, and encouraged all residents to identify simply as Brazilians. At the other end was Canada, where recognized ethnic groups such as French Canadians and First Nations were accorded separate territories, bilingual rights, and a degree of self-government.

THE DEBATE OVER SOCIALISM IN THE UNITED STATES

Viewing the United States in comparative perspective helps explain why immigration is a central theme in American history. In the case of socialism, international comparisons reveal an apparent *lack of importance* that requires explanation. "Why is there no socialism in the United States?" the frustrated German sociologist (and socialist) Werner Sombart asked bluntly in 1905. The question stemmed from Americans' failure to develop a powerful socialist movement similar to those in many Western industrial societies. A generation before Sombart, the founders of modern communism, Karl Marx and Friedrich Engels, puzzled over why, contrary to their doctrine, the most advanced capitalist society had not generated a strong socialist opposition. Engels theorized that American workers lacked class resentments because their country had no hereditary aristocracy to attack. Ironically, his Marxist version of exceptionalism echoed procapitalist claims that the absence of feudalism in the United States made socialism unnecessary.

DEFINING THE ISSUES

Sombart's question, with its shorthand label "socialism" and its all-or-nothing cast, was poorly framed. It suggested that socialism was the norm against which all industrialized societies should be measured. It left little room for understanding the radical movements that *have* arisen in American history. And it dismissed by implication the gradualist, nonrevolutionary form of social politics that became most influential in western nations.

VARIETIES OF SOCIALISM.   If we recognize that socialists favor a variety of goals and methods, we can get a better grip on the issues Sombart raised. We can also see how particular measures advocated by socialists could be adopted without overturning Western capitalist economies. Because socialism is a general term for the commitment to collective ownership of the means of production (land, labor, and capital) and the equitable distribution of wealth, it covers a wide spectrum of beliefs about methods of transition to a more communal society and the role of government in that society. Toward the spectrum's left, the communism of Marx and Engels advocated class struggle and a violent revolution led by workers to over-throw capitalism and install a classless order. Marx's Bolshevik followers turned communism into a state-run "dictatorship of the proletariat" in the Soviet Union. Taking a more moderate position, many "social democrats" in western Europe foresaw socialist society arriving through nonviolent worker actions such as strikes and through electoral victories that gradu-ally extended government's responsibilities without displacing democ-racy. It was this form of socialism that made inroads into European, and to a lesser extent, American society.

THE COURSE OF SOCIALISM IN THE UNITED STATES AND EUROPE.   During the age of industrial expansion there was more militancy in the American labor movement and more of a socialist presence than many people real-ize. Between 1890 and World War II, America was as much torn by labor-management conflicts as Great Britain and other industrializing European nations. Disputes over wages and working conditions produced dozens of standoffs between American laborers and bosses. Several became bloody, such as the Homestead strike of 1892, when workers at Andrew Carnegie's steel mill protesting a lockout fought a pitched battle with company police. Ideologies such as socialism and anarchism, which had developed in the more advanced industrial conditions of Europe, were brought over by immigrant workers and influenced American labor leaders. The Socialist Party of America (SPA), founded in 1900, was led by Eugene V. Debs, a charismatic union leader and the son of Alsatian immigrants. The party grew to 118,000 members by 1912 and elected dozens of local officials in important states like California, Wisconsin, and New York. Debs ran for President in 1912 and received 6 percent of the popular vote.

After this high point, however, socialist electoral prospects waned, shattered by the party's opposition to World War I and tarred by the emer-gence of the Soviet Union as a nation committed to a communist brand of socialism. Communists provoked an internal schism among American socialists in 1919 and in general damaged the prospects of a home-grown American socialism. With the Russian Revolution, socialism shifted in the public mind from a varied program to a doctrine identified largely with the Soviet experiment. The American Communist Party failed to garner support comparable to the earlier SPA. Not even the Great Depression of the 1930s, which hit the United States especially hard, produced a mass-based socialist political movement of either the communist or the milder social-democratic kind.

Meanwhile, European unions and workers' parties, although not as successful as Sombart's question implies, became influential in several nations. The Social Democratic Party of Germany was founded in 1875. By 1912 it held more seats in the Reichstag (the lower house of the German Parliament) than any other party. France's Socialist Party became a permanent fixture in that country's political life, and during the Great Depression it briefly headed a Popular Front coalition government. Britain's Labor Party was organized by intellectuals but attracted support from England's well-established trade unions. After 1906 it played an influential role in Parliament, and its leaders became prime ministers twice in the 1920s and again after World War II. As these parties pursued electoral success, they became more reformist and less radical, abandoning the idea of violent revolution and winning gradual gains for workers through social welfare legislation, concessions to unions, and nationalization (government ownership) of key industries. Hard-line Marxists of the International Working Men's Association condemned this evolutionary form of socialism. Still, European Labor and Social Democratic parties advanced socialist programs, won support from millions of workers, and became important players in their nations' political life. They had no successful counterparts in the United States.

THE KEY QUESTIONS.   What needs to be explained, then, is not why there was no socialist movement in the United States—there certainly was—but two more carefully focused questions. First, why did American workers' protests and programs not result, as they did in Europe, in powerful political parties backed by unions and devoted to labor's class interests? Second, why did socialist agitation, which was on the rise throughout the industrialized West before World War I, evolve after that almost everywhere into reformist programs of selective nationalization and social welfare legislation? Addressing the first question means examining some distinctive features of American capitalism and politics. Addressing the second involves chronicling the rise of the modern "welfare state."

LABOR, CLASS, AND AMERICAN CAPITALISM

THE LABOR MOVEMENT.   One set of explanations for the weakness of American socialism centers upon the history of American labor organizations. In spite of dramatic strikes and periodic militant protests, a conservative, procapitalist version of unionism became the dominant thrust of American labor activism. Three major labor organizations vied for worker support during the prime era of industrial growth. The Knights of Labor, founded in 1869, sought to build a broad workers' alliance committed to replacing capitalist-run businesses with cooperative workshops. Much more militant was the Industrial Workers of the World (IWW), a union affiliate of the Socialist Party set up in 1905. Its rhetoric of class conflict and its goal of a worker takeover of industries—by force, if necessary—appealed mainly to those trapped in isolated mining towns, lumberjack camps, and migrant-worker farms. Both organizations confronted a government determined to oppose them. More than in most European nations, American courts and legislatures were fiercely committed to unregulated capitalism and hostile to labor organizing. Whereas British workers' right to strike was officially recognized in 1871 and French labor unions were legalized in 1884, American unions were not exempt from prosecution under antitrust laws and freed from lawsuits over strikes until 1914.

THE AFL AND CONSERVATIVE UNIONISM.   In contrast to the sweeping anticapitalist aims of these organizations, the American Federation of Labor (AFL) adopted limited goals and means. Led by Samuel Gompers, an immigrant cigarmaker who had learned trade-union tactics in England, the AFL rose to prominence in the 1880s. Gompers accepted the framework of wage-labor capitalism but sought to gain better conditions within it, such as higher wages, shorter hours, and the right to collective bargaining. The AFL advocated strikes and boycotts when necessary, but presented itself as a legitimate partner to corporate enterprise. Its position was ruthlessly pragmatic in two other ways. First, its membership was highly exclusionary: it organized skilled craftsmen rather than unskilled workers, and many of its local unions rejected black and female members. Second, it avoided alliances with political parties, rejecting the notion of a labor party and lobbying only for specific laws that it urged Democrats and Republicans to endorse.

UNIONS AND POLITICS.   The separation of union organizations from political parties was a distinctive feature of American industrialism. The AFL was the only union federation in Western industrial societies that did not align itself with a political party devoted to labor's interests. Meanwhile, the American Socialist Party, having failed to convert the majority of AFL members to socialist views, refused to endorse Gompers' mainstream program as a first step toward building a left-labor coalition. Both these decisions meant that the American labor movement's on-the-job militancy failed to translate into effective political protest.

By 1917, the AFL boasted 2.5 million members, far more than any other American union. Yet success came at a high price. The AFL's focus on skilled craftsmen meant that a small percentage of the American labor force became unionized: only 9 percent in 1914, compared with much higher numbers in Britain and western Europe. Not until the 1930s did the American labor movement attempt to organize the vast pool of unskilled and semiskilled industrial workers. By then, Gompers' conservative labor philosophy had become the model. From its example, immigrants and other workers learned, as the Belgian-born scholar Aristide Zolberg has written, "that to be an American worker was to be a trade unionist and a Democrat or a Republican, but *not* a Socialist."[2]

DIVISIONS AMONG WORKERS.   A second line of argument suggests that the composition of America's working class discouraged its allegiance to socialism. The majority of American industrial workers were immigrants who had not been exposed to industrial conditions or modern social ideologies. Socialism attracted literate, urban German and Jewish immigrants but held little appeal for millions of rural Irish, Italians, or Poles confronting factory life. Migrants intending only a temporary stay in America were apt to endure harsh conditions and were less likely to risk their job by joining a union. Add to these problems the language differences and ethnic divisions among immigrants, and it becomes apparent how immigration often inhibited worker solidarity. In all advanced capitalist societies, a working class segmented by ethnicity—and gender—made it difficult for labor to present a united front, but the extraordinary diversity of American immigrants made union organizing especially problematic.

Integrating divisions of skill into this picture stratifies the working class even more. Marx identified the formation of a "labor aristocracy" in England, where skilled and semiskilled jobs were manned by trusted English workers and unskilled labor was reserved for Irish immigrants. The United States, like other New World settler societies, drew upon its history of slavery and immigration to take this "split labor" system a step further. Native-born workers or second-generation immigrants dominated the skilled ranks, European immigrants formed a vast reservoir of cheap labor for unskilled industrial jobs, and racial minorities (African Americans, Asians, and Mexicans) were relegated mostly to menial tasks as maids, construction workers, or agricultural laborers. Instead of uniting unskilled and menial laborers, unions like the AFL tried to sustain skilled workers' wages by restricting membership and agitating for curbs on Asian and contract-labor immigrants.

CAPITALISM AND AMERICAN PROSPERITY.   A third cluster of explanations centers around distinctive features of the U.S. economy that made socialism unnecessary. One way or another, these arguments claim that socialism was doomed by American capitalism's success. The relatively rapid

---

[2]Aristide R. Zolberg, "The Roots of American Exceptionalism," in *Pourquoi n'y a-t-il pas de socialisme aux Etats-Unis?/Why Is There No Socialism in the United States?* ed. Jean Heffer and Jeanine Rovet (Paris: Editions EHESS, 1987), 105.

pace of American industrialization produced, on average, a higher standard of living for workers than in Europe, and, according to some scholars, a rate of upward occupational mobility that was better than in Europe. Sombart himself grudgingly admired America's ability to put "roast beef and apple pie" on working-class tables. Some historians emphasize the frontier's effect in providing an outlet for discontented eastern workers. Careful research has refuted this claim by showing that relatively few factory workers moved west or settled on homesteads. Nevertheless, as was noted previously, the cost of land was lower in the United States than in Europe, and the rate of home ownership much higher among workers of comparable status. Property ownership tended to make American workers more cautious and loyal to the economic system.

OFFICES REPLACE FACTORIES.   Other aspects of American industrial capitalism reinforce this picture of "embourgeoisement," or workers joining the middle-class mainstream. The proportion of workers employed in the manufacturing sector never exceeded one-third in the United States, whereas in Britain, Germany, and Belgium it reached more than one-half. Forming less of a critical mass, American industrial workers never became the proletarian majority that Marx foresaw. Meanwhile, America took the lead in two trends that mitigated worker discontent. As discussed earlier, the United States was the first nation to develop a large "white-collar" sector of sales, service, and office workers. In status, aspirations, and interests, these employees tended to identify with their managers more than with "blue-collar" workers, and by 1910 they outnumbered factory hands.

"FORDISM" AND THE CULTURE OF CONSUMPTION.   America also extended the integration of consumption and leisure into working-class life that had begun in England in the nineteenth century. A half-day of work on Saturday—the first "weekend"—was allotted to British industrial workers by law in 1874. Its American counterpart did not arrive until the 1910s, but within a decade Americans leapfrogged to a full two-day weekend. In heavily unionized industries and in Henry Ford's automobile factories, a five-day work week became standard by 1926, and it spread during the Depression years. Ford foresaw that good pay would appease workers—and forestall unionization—while long weekends encouraged consumer spending on items like automobiles. Mass production and consumption were thus harmonized, and even joined in the same individuals. European observers labeled this arrangement "Fordism" and called it an American alternative to socialism. Such trends diffused class consciousness in America and encouraged workers to pledge allegiance to capitalist realities rather than socialist dreams.

Skeptics rightly point out that the "success-of-capitalism" formula can hardly explain why the Great Depression failed to produce a mass-based socialist movement. The experience of the 1930s challenges other explanations for socialist weakness, too. During that decade the Congress of Industrial Organizations (CIO) rejected the AFL's model when it organized unskilled and semiskilled workers in the steel and auto industries, and the American working class was far less weakened by ethnic divisions than at the height of immigration in the 1910s. Why, then, did the Socialist Party fail to revive during the nation's greatest economic crisis?

THE IMPACT OF POLITICS AND WORLD WAR

POLITICAL OBSTACLES TO SOCIALISM.   Perhaps there is a political dimension to organized socialism's failure in the United States. A fourth contribution to the debate suggests how distinctive features of the American political system helped prevent an enduring socialist party. In the United States, unlike Britain and Germany, democratic politics and the right to vote were established prior to industrialization and working-class formation. Universal white male suffrage was achieved in the 1830s in America, but not until 1871 in Germany and 1885 in Britain. By the time American unions voiced their demands, the major political parties were well-entrenched transclass coalitions that vied for workers' votes. Third parties like the Populists of the 1890s, the Socialists of the 1910s, and the Communists of the 1930s had little chance to break the two-party monopoly.

The American electoral system posed additional obstacles. It required that third-party candidates win a plurality of the voters to gain seats in Congress, and it discouraged workers from voting for socialist presidential candidates because it might split anticonservative forces and help elect Republicans. In both cases Americans feared "throwing away their votes." By contrast, democracies with presidential runoffs (two-stage elections) encouraged first-round socialist voting, and in those with proportional representation such as Israel or France, parties winning a minority of the votes could still expect to seat representatives in the national legislature or cabinet of ministers.

REFORMERS CO-OPT SOCIALIST VOTERS.   America's two-party system proved flexible enough to lure support from socialists. During the Progressive Era (1890–1920) the Democratic Party adopted some of the socialists' milder proposals to temper capitalist excesses. In his first term as president, Woodrow Wilson established a Department of Labor and approved an anti-child-labor bill. His party pushed constitutional amendments creating a progressive income tax and direct election of senators (the Sixteenth and Seventeenth Amendments). These reforms had been on the Socialist Party's agenda for years, and their passage meant that much of the labor vote that had gone to Debs in 1912 shifted to Wilson four years later.

The process was repeated during Franklin Roosevelt's administration two decades later. Under Roosevelt's New Deal program, which will be discussed in greater detail later in this chapter, the federal government passed minimum wage and maximum hour laws, protected labor unions' right to organize, and instituted unemployment insurance and pension programs. Roosevelt's adoption of such mildly "socialistic" measures goes a long way toward explaining why Communists and Socialists made little headway at the polls during the Great Depression.

Even when mainstream American parties adopted pro-worker reforms, they were defended as antidotes to socialism rather than moderate expressions of it. Americans' avoidance of the term "socialism," or their frequent resort to it as a pejorative, suggests that many do not consider it a legitimate ideology. The entire compass of politics in the United States is set further to the right than in Britain or Europe. Socialists' emphasis upon government planning or ownership and income redistribution conflicts with traditional "antistatist" and individualist attitudes in America. To many Americans, socialism carries unwelcome and even unpatriotic overtones of "class warfare" and "big government." For these reasons as well as its overseas origins, socialists have found it nearly impossible to overcome their creed's stigma as an alien presence in American life, an "un-American" form of allegiance.

IMPACT OF WORLD WAR I AND COMMUNIST RUSSIA. World War I was an important turning point in this regard, for it had opposite effects on socialists in America and Europe. Most European socialist leaders supported their governments after war broke out in 1914. By proving themselves loyal nationalists, they gained votes for labor parties and won key concessions for workers. The American Socialist Party, on the other hand, opposed U.S. involvement in a conflict it labeled an imperialist quarrel, and after the nation entered the war prominent socialist leaders, including Eugene Debs, were jailed for criticizing the move. During a postwar "Red Scare" (1919–1920) the U.S. Attorney General arrested and deported many radical leaders, crippling the Socialist Party and the IWW.

By that time, the Bolshevik Revolution had redirected socialists from a varied menu of proposals to a single program embodied in communist Russia. This not only split the American socialist movement, it also linked socialist ideas in Americans' minds with a nation that became America's enemy and global rival. During the 1940s leftist parties in the United States—but not in Britain, France or Italy—were caught in a torrent of Cold War anticommunism from which they never recovered.

AN ASSESSMENT.   Why, then, has there been no powerful socialist movement in the United States? Each of the answers proposed to Sombart's question has merit, although none appears entirely satisfactory. Some, such as those that describe American capitalism as universally successful and those that stress class divisions among American workers, seem incompatible. The debate over American socialism may never be resolved. In fact, with the worldwide collapse of socialism at the end of the twentieth century, it lost much of its urgency. Nevertheless, this scholarly controversy has been a useful spur to comparative study and has brought to light important distinctive features of American society and politics.

Yet for all its usefulness, the two broadest implications of Sombart's question have proved misleading. As we have seen, Sombart's claim that socialism had no impact at all in the United States is mistaken. At various times, socialists formed an important segment of the American labor movement and influenced mainstream political parties. More fundamentally, Sombart's premise that all other industrialized nations besides the United States were inevitably headed *toward* socialism proved wrong.

In the twentieth century no advanced capitalist society underwent a socialist transformation. Among European nations, communism triumphed—unexpectedly—only in the economically backward society of Russia. After World War II, European leftist parties continued to exist, but they avoided revolutionary rhetoric and moved further along the path of social-democratic reform. Meanwhile, by establishing government protections for workers, the poor, and the elderly, the United States followed Europe's lead in building a "welfare state" that adopted some socialistic features. In the long history of Western industrialism, what stands out is not America's "exception" to some socialist norm, but a common process whereby governments in Europe and the New World adjusted to the transformations wrought by modern capitalism and enlarged their part in curbing its worst abuses. This process took different forms in each country, but it transcended national boundaries, and it dashed the revolutionary hopes of socialists everywhere. Western industrial capitalism proved more open to reform than either Karl Marx or Werner Sombart had envisioned.

THE RISE OF THE WELFARE STATE

Between 1880 and 1940, virtually every western industrialized nation, as well as self-described "follower nations" like Japan, developed variants of the welfare state, a national government that takes responsibility for the basic health and economic maintenance of its citizens. The conditions of modern urban and industrial life demanded that policymakers depart from nineteenth-century liberals' faith in laissez-faire individualism and rethink the traditional separation of politics from economics. What emerged was less a unified new ideology than a practical commitment to a new social politics. Faced with potentially explosive inequalities brought by urban and industrial development, social scientists and concerned citizens debated ways to protect families from capitalism's excesses and to provide public assistance to those most endangered by them. Many political leaders responded by extending the power of government into new economic and social arenas.

The welfare state embodied a compromise position that cushioned the ill effects of capitalism and endorsed socialism's ideal of collective responsibility without abolishing private property or imposing government ownership. It aimed for "Social Justice without Socialism," the title of a 1914 pamphlet by the American economist John Bates Clark. Its champions could be found all along the political spectrum and they ranged from democratic to authoritarian. In Germany of the 1880s, conservative industrialists provided the impetus, encouraged by Chancellor Otto von Bismarck, who was eager to weaken labor organizations and to co-opt workers' support for his autocratic regime. Fifty years later, socialist-led governments in Norway and Sweden levied high taxes to cover a full menu of employment, maternity, housing, and pension benefits. In most nations, however, the welfare state was put in place by new political coalitions that wedged themselves between socialists on the left and barons of land and industry on the right. Calling themselves "new liberals" in Britain, "radicals" in France, "social liberals" in Chile, or "progressives" in the United States, they tried to steer government on a stable middle course that would avoid revolts by the poor or rule by the rich.

"THE MOST BELATED OF NATIONS"

Europeans and several of their settler societies led the way in developing specific measures of reform. Inspired initially by factory laws in Great Britain and the program of Germany's Association for Social Policy (founded in 1872), reformers and government officials in western Europe, South America, and various imperial outposts began sharing ideas and exchanging visits. Municipal experiments in France's colonies in North Africa and pioneering labor laws in the British colony of New Zealand were promoted as showcases of reform. Germany's celebrated "social insurance" program of 1883, which covered illness, accidents, and invalidism for wage earners by pooling worker and employer funds, became the model for public health and accident insurance in many other countries. Old-age pension systems pioneered in Denmark and New Zealand in the 1890s were soon imitated in Germany and Great Britain. Australia's minimum-wage statutes of 1900 served as precedents for similar laws in Britain and, eventually, the United States. Influence flowed back to the welfare-state leaders when American consumer organizations and educational innovations were emulated elsewhere. As welfare-state reforms spread, it became clear that they did not radiate from a single place—a model that scholars call "diffusionist"—but instead collectively contributed to a global fund of information and experiment. From this clearinghouse of practical reforms, policymakers from Japan to Argentina and Italy borrowed programs initiated elsewhere and adjusted them to local conditions.

In most respects, Americans came relatively late to this movement toward what journalist Walter Weyl called "a more socialized democracy." "Today the tables are turned," Weyl complained in 1912. "America no longer teaches democracy to an expectant world, but herself goes to school in Europe and Australia." Americans lagged behind most industrialized nations in adopting unemployment insurance and similar social protections, and they were among the last to recognize workers' right to unionize, which was guaranteed by the Treaty of Versailles that ended World War I but which the United States did not sign. "Why has the tortoise Europe outdistanced the hare?" Weyl asked.

There were several reasons why the United States lagged behind the welfare-state pioneers. Americans' dominant traditions of respect for private property, free capitalist enterprise, and limited government put serious obstacles in the way of reform. Big business controlled the major political parties and generally resisted regulation as well as pension plans and unemployment insurance. Conservative judges used narrow contract law rather than concepts of public welfare to rule against striking workers, restrictions on child labor, and awards to injured workers. Unlike most European nations, which had developed from centralized monarchies, Americans lacked a strong central government ready to tackle industrial problems. In Germany and France, government agencies exerted top-down control over educational systems and used their authority to impose welfare regulations and family assistance. According to some scholars, such "strong states" were the first to initiate protectionist measures, while reformers in nations with weaker central governments had to work doggedly through private associations to press the government for change.

Without remnants of feudal society and the obligations attached to nobility, Americans also lacked powerful traditional elites committed to reform. In Great Britain, conservative landed aristocrats appalled by the effects of industrialization were among the first to call for factory legislation and other worker protections. In the United States, New York patrician Theodore Roosevelt was one of the few men of old money who embodied this paternalistic position, and for his outspoken views he was lambasted as a class traitor by fellow "bluebloods."

Finally, the relative weakness of the American Left also took its toll. Faced with less of a socialist threat, there was less urgent need for the government to build a welfare state. Social-Democratic and Labor parties in European countries led the push for worker legislation and social assistance, but the United States lacked strong leftist parties. American unions supported political parties selectively, and they also were aggressively antistatist in outlook. Prior to the Great Depression, most American unions, from the mainstream AFL to the radical Industrial Workers of the World, opposed welfare-state legislation as a potentially dangerous "big-government" intrusion into workplace issues better negotiated (or fought out) between unions and bosses.

WOMEN'S ACTIVISM AND THE PROGRESSIVE MOVEMENT.   Who, then, agitated for the American welfare state? More than socialists, unions, or bureaucrats, it was organized pressure from middle-class professionals that initially expanded the American government's role. These groups included male journalists, ministers, and academics, but also many women activists. In western European countries, women's movements helped shape government policy in the areas of maternal and child welfare. Because pro-government forces were weaker in the United States, women's advocacy was even more important. Working through such organizations as settlement houses (where middle-class volunteers lived in immigrant ghettoes), the National Consumers League, and the General Federation of Women's Clubs, educated middle-class women like Jane Addams and Florence Kelley mobilized support for consumer protections, mother's pensions, anti-child-labor laws, and a shorter work week for women.

The Progressive movement, the reform impulse that swept through the United States between 1890 and 1920, resulted from an alliance between such women's associations, professional men, and male politicians. In large part, Progressivism represented the breakthrough of traditional "women's issues" like consumerism, health care, children, and care for the aged into the mainstream of political debates. It also reflected women's more positive view of government. Whereas the predominant perspective among American men saw the state as the potential enemy of human liberty, women often welcomed expanded government activity as the protector of social rights. The welfare state became their distinctive contribution to American politics.

WOMAN SUFFRAGE. Because they were denied suffrage, however, women had to press such views indirectly through church, university, and reform associations and build alliances with liberal-minded politicians. Before 1907, female suffrage was promoted mainly on settler-society frontiers where women were scarce; only Australia, New Zealand, Finland, and a few western U.S. states allowed women to vote. With the rise of social liberalism, suffrage and reform became allied causes. Throughout the industrialized West, women's agitation for voting rights took place simultaneously with their promotion of welfare legislation and became entwined with it in mutually supportive ways. Women demanded the vote to improve "municipal housekeeping" and, more generally, to inject a new ethic of social responsibility into politics. Meanwhile, male politicians were interested in gaining women's support for the nation's involvement in World War I and other extensions of state power. During the years bracketing World War I (that is, between 1913 and 1919), women won the right to vote in Canada and 20 European nations stretching from Ireland and Norway to Poland and Russia. In the United States, state-by-state victories in the 1910s culminated in 1920 with passage of the Nineteenth Amendment granting women the right to vote in federal elections.

ACHIEVEMENTS OF PROGRESSIVISM. The Progressive Era gave birth to the American welfare state. The mandate to expand government's role began at the state and local levels, where federalism delegated significant powers, then moved to the national level to cover interstate and constitutional issues. Penetrating the Democratic and Republican parties, Progressivism achieved national prominence through the efforts of two reform-minded presidents, Theodore Roosevelt (1901–1909) and Woodrow Wilson (1913–1921). Roosevelt chided the United States as "the most belated of nations" in social insurance, and Wilson modeled his legislative agenda upon David Lloyd George's Liberal Party initiatives in Britain. In just a few years, Progressives produced a barrage of social legislation and an unprecedented expansion of government's reach. Between 1910 and 1917 all the American industrial states adopted a payroll-funded system of workers' compensation for industrial accidents. Some passed anti-child-labor laws and established publicly supported unemployment insurance. States approved zoning laws that restricted the spread of factories into residential areas and building codes that set minimum standards for workers' housing. Several states enacted laws setting maximum hours for working women and 15 passed minimum-wage statutes, although the latter were invalidated by the U.S. Supreme Court.

By European standards these were modest beginnings. Most Progressive-Era innovations were local experiments rather than national commitments. Except for consumer-protection statutes and a short-lived anti-child-labor law, social-welfare programs were not established at the federal level. These two exceptions reveal another pattern: largely due to the influence of women activists and America's dominant middle-class culture, American reforms concentrated on the home and family rather than the workplace. A case in point was the reception of Upton Sinclair's bestselling novel *The Jungle* (1906), which exposed horrific working conditions in Chicago's meatpacking plants. Sinclair, a socialist, intended his tract as a call for industrial reform, but American readers focused instead on his portrayal of contaminated meat. The novel spurred passage of an important consumer-protection law, the Pure Food and Drug Act (1906), but the larger issue of industrial capitalism's impact on workers remained unaddressed. The bias toward home and traditional gender roles explains why Progressives succeeded in enacting maximum-hours laws to protect women but not men. When the United States entered World War I in 1917, the movement's momentum ground to a halt far short of duplicating Britain's comprehensive, gender-neutral package of national old-age, unemployment, and health benefits.

THE GREAT DEPRESSION AND THE NEW DEAL

It took the trauma of the Great Depression to nationalize the American welfare state and extend its benefits to most workers. Only when economic crisis made social-welfare programs crucial to the nation's survival did the public learn to accept and even demand federal social assistance.

Despite popular historical fascination with the New York Stock Market crash of October 1929, the prolonged paralysis that seized the American economy at the end of the 1920s was part of a worldwide crisis. The pattern of plunging production, prices, and employment was similar almost everywhere, somber proof that by the early twentieth century most nations had become joined to a complex world economy where their fortunes rose and fell together. Yet the economic crash hit the United States especially hard. Unlike most Western industrialized nations, there was little or no public "safety net" of unemployment or health insurance to cushion its effects. The Depression also seemed to question Americans' cherished individualism, with its faith in personal responsibility and unlimited opportunity. Foreign commentators noticed that while the British labeled the crisis "The Slump," Americans adopted a term more indicative of their psychological state: depression. Perhaps only such a devastating blow could have pushed the United States toward a centrally administered welfare state.

FDR's Program.   Under President Franklin Roosevelt's New Deal, the national government took responsibility for providing jobs and relief to the beleaguered public. Beginning in 1933, two new agencies undertook huge public works programs, hiring as many as one-fifth of the entire labor force to build roads, airports, schools, and bridges. In 1935 the U.S. government established a national social security system, which funded old-age pensions, unemployment benefits, disability insurance, and aid to single mothers. Through the National Labor Relations Act of 1935 the federal government finally protected union organizing, and workers' pressure in turn led in 1938 to the Fair Labor Standards Act, which set the first federal minimum wage and maximum work week as well as out-lawed the labor of children under 16 years old.

A limited, distinctively American version of the welfare state had arrived. Roosevelt made it clear that his goal was to reform capitalism (which he called "the profit system") in order to save it. He rejected government ownership of industry in favor of regulating business and redistributing a portion of income toward those most in need. Roosevelt's more ambitious welfare-state plans encountered opposition. In 1944 he proposed to ensure all Americans a living wage, full employment, and universal medical care—a program he dubbed a "second bill of rights." But Roosevelt dropped the plan when business, farm, and even labor spokesmen opposed it. Ironically, it became the basis for a widely sup-ported expansion of the welfare state (the Beveridge Plan) in postwar Britain.

Roosevelt's New Deal program did not end the Great Depression— only mobilization for World War II returned the United States to full employment. But the New Deal enabled Americans, and their economic system, to survive the decade-long economic crisis virtually intact. Because of this achievement, Roosevelt was embraced by a large majority of American voters and the nation learned to look to the national govern-ment to provide for the general welfare, especially in times of crisis.

Global Patterns and Dangers.   Some commentators of the 1930s proclaimed that American politics had become "Europeanized" and that Roosevelt's Democratic Party, enjoying solid support from labor unions, began to resemble the social-democratic and labor parties of western Europe. The reality was that the Depression brought broadly similar effects throughout the Western world. To combat the crisis, most nations enacted social welfare measures and gave greater authority to central governments—the two effects went hand in hand. The left-liberal Popular

Front government in France, for example, provided paid vacations and proclaimed a 40-hour work week, while the socialist government in Sweden created a wide array of public benefits. Right-wing governments in Brazil, Germany, and Italy used similar techniques, although they were often coupled with attacks on labor unions and other democratic institutions. Around the world, the decisive question was not whether welfare-state protections would be adopted, but whether governments would employ them to bolster authoritarian rule. In Germany, Japan, and Italy during the 1930s, fascist leaders consolidated their power by adopting welfare-state measures such as jobs programs and pension plans in order to secure workers' acquiescence in dictatorship. Labor unions' gains in much of Latin America also came with the price of giving up their independence. Why the United States and the global network of British-dominated societies (including Canada, Australia, and New Zealand) avoided descent into authoritarianism had little to do with shared attitudes toward the welfare state, which Americans embraced much less readily than the others. More likely, it stemmed from their common tradition of constitutional government and individual rights.

AN EMERGING KEYNESIAN CONSENSUS.   By the end of World War II, most industrial nations began to follow the new economic theories of Britain's John Maynard Keynes, who had advocated that governments increase their spending and adjust their tax policies to stimulate economic recovery during downturns. Keynes's tolerance of deficit spending and his support for a public "safety net" gave the welfare state important economic legitimacy. Long after the crisis of the 1930s had passed, Western governments, whether liberal or conservative, pursued Keynes's goal of steady economic growth and social stability. They used Keynesian measures to stabilize the business cycle and bolstered them with tax-supported programs of social welfare and income redistribution. This combination of economic management and social protection proved to be social liberalism's most enduring legacy to governments in the industrialized West. "We are all Keynesians now," President Richard Nixon reportedly proclaimed in 1971.

The expansion of the welfare state in the decades after 1880 effectively warded off the socialist threat in Western democracies by adopting some of the socialists' milder proposals. By the late twentieth century, however, the welfare state itself was threatened by the collapse of the Communist challenge to Western capitalism, by demographic changes, and by intensified global economic competition. In this new context (as we will see in Chapter 6) the United States, formerly a receiver of welfare-state ideas, became instead an exporter of free-market ideology. American corporate and political leaders led a general shift away from welfare-state solutions as the nation's role in the world economy grew to what some critics considered imperial dimensions.

SUGGESTED READINGS

Baily, Samuel L. *Immigrants in the Land of Promise: Italians in Buenos Aires and New York City, 1879–1914.* Ithaca, N.Y.: Cornell University Press, 1999.
—Compares the background and adjustment of Italian immigrants to two key New World destinations.

Blackford, Mansel G. *The Rise of Modern Business in Great Britain, the United States, and Japan.* Chapel Hill: University of North Carolina Press, 1988.
—This comparative overview stresses America's lead in corporate size and structure, and attempts to explain it.

Bolt, Christine. *The Women's Movements in the United States and Britain from the 1790s to the 1920s.* Amherst: University of Massachusetts Press, 1993.
—Chronicles, compares, and shows the relations between the long struggles for women's rights in America and Great Britain.

Heffer, Jean, and Jeanine Rovet, eds. *Pourquoi n'y a-t-il pas de socialisme aux Etats-Unis?/ Why Is There No Socialism in the United States?* Paris: Editions EHESS, 1987.
—An excellent collection of essays on this controversial topic by a group of international scholars.

Koven, Seth, and Sonya Michel, eds. *Mothers of a New World: Maternalism and the Origins of Welfare States.* London: Routledge, 1993.
—Essays on Europe and the United States examine the role that women's interests and activism played in building welfare states.

Landes, David S. *The Wealth and Poverty of Nations.* New York: W.W. Norton, 1998.
—A sweeping history of global modernization and industrialization that aims to explain Europe's leading role, North America and Japan's later success, and others' difficulties.

Lipset, Seymour Martin, and Gary Marks. *It Didn't Happen Here: Why Socialism Failed in the United States.* New York and London: W.W. Norton, 2000.
—A systematic analysis of the "problem" of American socialism that stresses distinctive cultural attitudes and political constraints in the United States.

Manning, Patrick. *Migration in World History.* New York and London: Routledge, 2005.
—An up-to-date overview that places nineteenth-century migration in historical and global context.

Nugent, Walter. *Crossings: The Great Transatlantic Migrations, 1870–1914.* Bloomington: Indiana University Press, 1992.
—An informative survey of immigration to the United States compared to Argentina, Brazil, and Canada.

Rodgers, Daniel T. *Atlantic Crossings: Social Politics in a Progressive Age.* Cambridge, Mass.: Harvard University Press, 1998.
—Documents how Americans borrowed welfare-state measures from Europeans from the 1890s to the 1940s.

Rybczynski, Witold. *City Life: Urban Expectations in a New World.* New York: Scribner, 1995.
—An engaging informal history of American cities that offers contrasts with and connections to European developments.

Takaki, Ronald. *Strangers from a Different Shore: A History of Asian Americans.* New York: Little, Brown, 1989.
—Weaves historical analysis with oral testimony to create a vivid portrait of Asian immigrants, including the discriminatory practices they faced.

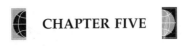

CHAPTER FIVE

ADVANCING EMPIRE

GETTING STARTED ON CHAPTER FIVE: In what ways was
U.S. overseas expansion after the 1880s a form of empire? Did it rep-
resent an extension of U.S. territorial expansion in North America,
or something new? How did American colonial rule compare to
European imperialism? What effects did World War I and World
War II have on the United States' level of global engagement?

British historian Geoffrey Perret has written that "America's wars have
been like rungs on a ladder by which it rose to greatness."[1] If "greatness"
suggests domination of North America, the Mexican War (1846–1848)
and the Civil War ensured that the nation's self-proclaimed destiny to
span the continent became manifest. If "greatness" extends beyond this to
global power and influence, the Spanish-American War of 1898 and World
Wars I and II were the crucial events. For the United States, these three
wars represented momentous steps toward global involvement. In 1898,
the United States officially graduated from continental expansion to
overseas empire; in 1917, the nation first entered a war on the European
continent; and in 1941, it joined a global military alliance aimed at defeating a coalition of powerful dictators in Europe and Asia.

Americans' participation in these wars was energized by their pride
in the nation's cultural heritage and political principles, and the desire to
spread them worldwide. Whether they fought to help liberate Cubans and
bring Anglo-Saxon civilization to the Philippines, to "make the world safe
for democracy," or to secure their way of life against fascist threats,
Americans preached a messianic nationalism that saw a universal mission
in world history for their nation. American policymakers justified the
decision to acquire an overseas empire by strategic geopolitical and

---

[1]Geoffrey Perret, *A Country Made By War: From the Revolution to Vietnam—The Story of
America's Rise to Power* (New York: Random House, 1989), 558.

economic needs that complemented their "civilizing mission." Traditionally, they had counted on publicity and trade to inspire imitation of their democratic and capitalist ways overseas; increasingly after 1898 they tried to spread them through intervention abroad. Confidence in the growing reach of American military and economic might underlay this shift. As each war left the United States stronger and weakened its rivals, the nation became poised to assume the global leadership that its prestige and prowess seemed to warrant.

DOUBTS AND DENIALS.   American empire advanced despite ambivalent attitudes and domestic opposition. In the 1890s and for a century thereafter, many Americans expressed serious misgivings about taking up an imperial mandate. As Americans opposed to overseas colonialism pointed out, to become an empire was to ignore the nation's birth in a revolt against British colonial rule and to contradict its founding principles of freedom and self-determination. Even as they flexed their muscles abroad, Americans were reluctant to call their nation an empire. To use this label meant placing the nation in a long parade of empires that began with the regional conquests of ancient Greece and Rome and continued to the modern world empires of France and Great Britain. The concept of empire implies an end to American exceptionalism, little difference from the authoritarian great powers of history, and vulnerability to a similar "decline and fall." It is not surprising that denial has been a frequent recourse. President Richard Nixon called the United States "the only great power without a history of imperialistic claims on neighboring countries." "America has never been an empire," George W. Bush declared during his campaign for president in 2000. Other interpreters of U.S. history acknowledge an imperial interlude but insist that it ended quickly and prefer to label it "expansionism" or "missionary nationalism."

VARIETIES OF EMPIRE.   In the face of imperial self-denial it is important to note that empire can take various forms. If the term "empire" is defined narrowly to mean direct control over the politics and economy of a dependent region, the United States fit this category only during its brief period of imperial rule over the Philippines and other island dependencies from the 1890s to the 1930s. But empires can take shape in less direct ways and be equally powerful. Imperial nations can control others indirectly through military intimidation, forced alliances, economic indebtedness, or pacts with local elites. Scholars frequently distinguish between "formal" and "informal" empire. Nations that practice the latter kind avoid a colonial takeover but influence another's economy, government, and foreign policy so powerfully that its independence is curtailed. This was Britain's relationship to Argentina in the nineteenth century, for example, and the United States' position toward many Caribbean basin nations in the first half of the twentieth century.

A survey of dozens of empires throughout history would find many ways that imperial power can be acquired and sustained, and a range of selfish and altruistic motives, sometimes combined in the same overseer. Imperial nations can invade (or threaten to invade) outside territories, maneuver them into dependence, or persuade them to join alliances as junior partners. Empires may aim to ensure national security; to exploit new lands for materials, markets, or manpower; to forge international blocs; or to acquire distant military bases. Empires often promise benefits to those they rule or to the international system as a whole, such as increased trade and investment, improved economic conditions, better health, education and laws, and reduced warfare. Whether they actually provide these benefits, to whom, and with what consequences are essential questions to ask. Because empires take many forms, specific combinations of motives, means, and effects determine the unique character of each dominant power—yet all can be labeled imperial.

From the early 1800s onward, episodes when the United States asserted its power beyond the nation's borders, whether in North America or overseas, can be understood in terms of empire. Recognizing this allows us to link continental to overseas expansion, to compare Americans to their imperial rivals, to chart the nation's expanding influence as it shifted from formal imperial rule to less formal control over dependent peoples, and to follow its path to global hegemony as it promoted its ideals of democracy, free-market capitalism, and moral uplift in the wake of two world wars.

TIMELINE

1803–1890	Era of U.S. continental expansion
1880–1914	Surge of Europe's "new imperialism" in the Middle East, Asia, and Africa
1898	Spanish-American War; by Treaty of Paris in 1899, Spain cedes Philippines, Guam, and Puerto Rico to the United States
	United States annexes Hawaiian Islands
1898–1902	Philippine-American War against U.S. colonization
1902–1903	United States forces Panama's independence, gains rights to Panama Canal Zone
1904	Roosevelt Corollary to Monroe Doctrine
1906–1934	U.S. military interventions and occupations in Mexico, Central America, and the Caribbean

1914	World War I breaks out in eastern Europe
1917	United States enters World War I against Germany
	Bolshevik Revolution brings communist rule to Russia
1918–1919	Paris Peace Conference drafts Treaty of Versailles; U.S. Senate rejects it
1920s	Postwar economic instability in Europe, worldwide agricultural depression
1929	U.S. stock market crash signals onset of global Great Depression
1931	Japan seizes Manchuria from China
1933	Adolf Hitler assumes power in Germany, begins German rearmament
1935–1937	Neutrality Acts aim to keep United States out of developing European conflict
1937	Japan invades and occupies coastal China
1939	World War II begins when Hitler's army invades Poland; England and France declare war on Germany
1941	Germany invades the Soviet Union
	Japan's attack on Pearl Harbor brings United States into World War II
1945	At Yalta Conference, United States, Britain, and Soviet Union plan postwar settlement
	World War II ends with surrender of Germany (May), U.S. atomic bombing of Japan (August)
1946	United States grants Philippines independence

The Course of American Empire

Three Phases. The long course of American empire can be divided into three phases: continental expansion (1803–1890), formal empire through colonial rule (1887–1920), and informal or indirect control of other nations through international alliances and economic and military power (1920–present). Of course, there is an overlap between these phases. The United States forcibly obtained imperial trade privileges in China and Japan in the 1840s and 1850s while its soldiers were invading Mexico for western territory and settlers were trekking overland to California. And despite renouncing formal colonization after World War II, the United States holds more than a dozen overseas possessions today.

Each phase of American empire matched the nation's expansionist opportunities and corresponded to reigning international rivalries and doctrines of power. The first stage, western conquest and expansion, reflected America's opportunity—common in settler societies but rare in Europe—to stretch its rule inland to adjacent territory. By the time the United States reached the Pacific and built a navy capable of overseas expansion, the race for overseas colonies begun by Europe was nearly over. America's late entry into overseas colonization during its second imperialist phase limited its acquisitions.

After World War I, European nations, no longer able to afford overseas lands or to control demands for their independence, began to lose their grip on their colonies. Increasingly, the United States, which was committed in principle to decolonization, turned against formal empire and sought its global objectives more indirectly. American policymakers recognized that it was no longer possible to build empire in the old way, and many applauded this change. Influential American writers noted that advantageous international alliances and the global penetration of American capital could build an "American Century," achieving goals like those of empire without the problems of direct rule. The United States' growing overseas economic presence after 1920 and its diplomatic and military commitments that arose after 1945 in connection with the Cold War constituted a new form of empire, more indirect and less coercive but equally powerful.

CONSOLIDATING A CONTINENTAL EMPIRE

America's first empire beckoned on the North American continent, across the Mississippi River. Extended initially by the Louisiana Purchase in 1803, the nation's landward push involved wars with Mexico and with Indian peoples as well as the Oregon Treaty with Britain (1847), the Gadsden Purchase of a small southwestern strip of land from Mexico in 1853, and purchase of Alaska from Russia in 1867. Textbooks often call this sequence of events "westward expansion" or "territorial acquisition," but its conquest of natives and replacement of existing villages with white settlements represented the evolution of British "settler colonialism" on the eastern seaboard into an interior "settler empire" after independence.

THE UNITED STATES AND RUSSIA AS LAND EMPIRES.   Conquest of natives, wars with foreign powers, and negotiated divisions of territory also characterized European imperialism. Yet America's western expansion differed from most European colonialism by being continental rather than transoceanic. By the nineteenth century, France, Germany, and Britain moved to acquire additional territories through overseas expansion because there were few lightly populated or poorly defended territories in their own hinterlands. When they did try serial conquest of neighboring nations, as in the case of Napoleon's empire, the result was a catastrophic disruption of the political equilibrium.

As was noted in Chapter 3, overland expansion made the United States comparable instead to the other great land empire of the nineteenth century: Russia. Starting earlier than Americans, the Russians constructed an empire by invading adjoining lands in Finland, Poland, the Ottoman Empire, and Muslim Central Asia—counterparts to the Americans' attempted conquest of Canada in 1814 and their thinly disguised seizure of Mexican lands in 1848. While the Americans pushed Indians westward and confined them to reservations, the Russians swept eastward across the steppes and overran the indigenous peoples of Kazakhstan and Siberia, replacing their pastures and villages with cookie-cutter industrial towns and mining camps planned and managed from afar like the railroad towns of the American West. In the mid-twentieth century, after Russia and the United States became fierce Cold War rivals, each criticized the other's "imperialist" ways. But Cold War polemics ignored how similar the two nation's earlier expansionist careers had been.

U.S. EXPANSION VS. EUROPEAN IMPERIALISM.   There were two other key differences between the American land and European overseas empires. Surveying European imperial rivalries in 1886, Theodore Roosevelt saw a crucial uniqueness in American expansionism: "European nations war for the possession of thickly settled districts which, if conquered, will for centuries remain alien and hostile. . . ; we, wiser, in our generation, have seized the waste solitudes that lay near us." Of course, the North American West was not an empty "solitude," but the home of many Native Americans and Mexicans. Yet Roosevelt's reluctance to rule "alien and hostile" peoples was revealing. The primary aim of westward expansion was to spread the domain of America's white settler society across North America. Opening the frontier for white settlement, Americans, unlike the Russians and European imperialists in Asia and Africa, were not interested in overseeing a population of alien peoples, whether Native Americans or Mexicans, using them as laborers, or negotiating authority with them. "Manifest destiny" referred to territorial ambition, not the imperial "civilizing mission" aimed at "backward" peoples that would later drive the United States overseas. Thus, American leaders pursued a policy of Indian removal and near extermination. Whereas many Americans looked upon Canada as a potential member of the Union, racist attitudes played a part in halting their annexationist ambitions at the edge of Mexico's thickly populated states.

As a consequence, American expansionism did not turn western lands into politically dependent colonies, but prepared them gradually for admission to the Union as equal states. France's African colonists were not treated as equals to native-born Frenchmen. Even Britain's settler colonies in Canada and Australia were not accepted into the United Kingdom (as Scotland had been in 1707); instead, they were ruled (as the thirteen colonies had been) by royally appointed governors. In contrast, America's western continental territories, from New Mexico north to Alaska, eventually entered the Union with full statehood rights, expanding the reach of the Republic. This was what Thomas Jefferson had in mind when he proclaimed the western lands acquired from Napoleon in 1803 an "empire for liberty."

AMERICA'S OVERSEAS EMPIRE IN COMPARATIVE PERSPECTIVE

After reaching the Pacific and consolidating domestic control, Americans looked beyond their shores to new outlets for their imperial ambitions. Between 1889 and 1904, the United States divided Samoa with the Germans; annexed Hawaii; wrested the Philippines, Guam, and Puerto Rico from Spain; and separated the Panama Canal Zone from Colombia. The acquisition of overseas colonies represented a second phase of American empire after westward expansion and a momentous decision to join the club of European nations as a rival colonizing power. How did the nation's overseas imperial move relate to its earlier career of continental expansion? What motives and rationales did American imperialists share with European contemporaries? Was U.S. colonial administration distinctive, and what impact did it have on subject peoples?

FROM LAND EMPIRE TO OVERSEAS EMPIRE. Despite the differences between land and overseas empires, the plunge into the Pacific was viewed by many Americans as an extension of frontier expansionism. President Polk wrested California from Mexico not for its gold, which had not yet been discovered, but for its Pacific harbors. Settlement of the West Coast expanded U.S. trade along the Pacific Rim of Latin America and Asia. While adventurers and traders flocked to California and Oregon, the U.S. government used force to impose trade treaties upon China (1844), Japan (1854), and Hawaii (1875). Secretary of State William Seward, who saw the Far West as the key to American influence in the Pacific, negotiated a treaty allowing Americans to cross Nicaragua to the Pacific, established regular mail service from San Francisco to Honolulu and Hong Kong, and purchased Alaska from Russia in order to establish a network of coaling stations to support American trade with Asia. Protestant missionaries justified the Gold Rush as a providential plan to people California as a staging ground for evangelizing in Asia.

Government officials were quick to make analogies between continental and overseas expansion. In suppressing the Philippine independence movement after 1898, U.S. Army generals used tactics of deception and pursuit that had been perfected during the Indian Wars in the West. American legal precedents for restricting Indians' legal rights were used to limit the political rights of peoples in newly annexed island territories. Theodore Roosevelt applauded the U.S. takeover of the Philippines by arguing that it "finished the work begun over a century before by the backwoodsman." To Roosevelt and other supporters of empire, America's inland expansion and its moves into the Pacific continued the larger westward march of enlightened modern civilization from its birthplace in Europe across the globe.

THE "NEW" EUROPEAN IMPERIALISM.   The second half of the nineteenth century saw renewed interest in colonialism among Europe's major powers. Using the technology of steamships, railroads, telegraphs, and repeating guns, Europeans overpowered indigenous rulers and imposed their control over distant lands previously immune from western takeover. Led by rapid expansion of the British Empire, the French, Dutch, Germans, and Belgians joined the scramble to divide up the Middle East, push inland from coastal regions in Asia, grab islands in Oceania, and partition almost the whole of Africa. By 1914, most of the world's trade had come under European domination, and Europe and its former settler colonies controlled more than 80 percent of the earth's land. In east Asia, Russia completed its Transiberian Railroad in 1914 and used it to penetrate Chinese Manchuria. Japan, newly emerged as a world power, wrested control of Korea from the Russian empire and Taiwan from China, and competed with Russia and the European powers in carving mainland China into spheres of influence.

Scanning these developments from the sidelines, the American public began to warm to overseas expansion. Pro-imperialists argued that overseas colonization would signal the emergence of the United States as a global power as well as Americans' acceptance of their "duty" to bring modern civilization to remaining "backward" peoples. More negatively, hesitating to take colonies would mean entering the fray after the prize territories had been gobbled up by others, leaving the United States behind in the global competition for influence. Rather than stumbling into empire, as some historians claim the British did, many Americans embraced the idea of empire before they took the leap.

AMERICAN MOTIVES AND RATIONALES.   Economic motives played a role. Although imperial rule proved costly for governments, individuals and corporations could make fortunes from it. American business leaders were eager to find new markets for American manufactured goods and surplus capital, especially in the wake of a major economic depression in the 1890s. This seemed to confirm the theory of British critic John Hobson that imperialism derived from an excess of capital seeking profitable investment overseas because it could no longer find high dividends at home. In the American case, "frontier anxiety" provided additional incentive. The government's announcement in 1890 that no large stretches of western land remained unsettled aroused fears that American society would become stagnant and "Europeanized" unless new outlets were found to promote initiative and opportunity.

Considerations of trade and national power merged in the thinking of men like Alfred Thayer Mahan and Theodore Roosevelt, who built on Seward's legacy to argue that national prowess depended on the protection of American economic and strategic interests by a large navy with bases and refueling stations around the globe. A strong American presence in Pacific and Caribbean islands would ensure favorable trade privileges in these regions and protect the nation's growing business investments abroad.

SOCIAL DARWINISM AND "SCIENTIFIC" RACISM.   Transatlantic intellectual currents helped to justify imperialist ventures. In the late nineteenth century the new social science of anthropology, reflecting Eurocentric norms, classified races, peoples, and cultures into value-laden categories ranging from savage to civilized, primitive to modern. Popularized versions of Charles Darwin's theory of natural selection merged biology with human history by claiming that the world was an arena of struggle in which only the fittest people and nations survive. "Social Darwinism" helped explain and rationalize the conquest of less "evolved" peoples as well as competition between imperialist powers. The racial prejudices that underlay "scientific" distinctions could be used to oppose imperialism as well as to support it, depending on one's view of racial possibilities. Some anti-imperialists argued that the dark-skinned peoples of Africa and Asia were incapable of productivity and self-government and that race mixture led to white degeneracy. On the other hand, imperialists could cite the British sociologist Benjamin Kidd's call for white inhabitants of temperate regions to boost the natural "inefficiency" of tropical peoples. This kinder, gentler version of racial superiority imposed a duty to "lift up" the rest of the world to the level of Western society: the "White Man's Burden," as British poet Rudyard Kipling labeled it.

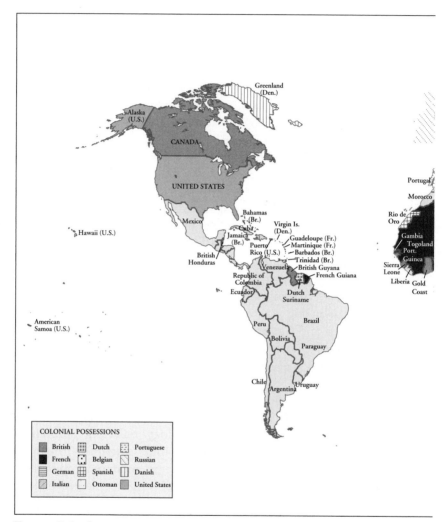

FIGURE 5-1   IMPERIALISM AT HIGH TIDE, 1900

The United States became a formal imperial power in 1898, when it acquired colonies in the aftermath of the Spanish-American War. But the United States was a decided latecomer to imperialism. During the nineteenth century, European nations dramatically expanded the reach of their empires, moving in particular in Africa and Asia. Although the British remained the world's largest imperial power by a significant margin, vast areas of the globe came under the control of other European colonizers, as this maps shows. (*Source: Used with permission from* American History *(11th ed.), by Alan Brinkley. Copyright 2003 by McGraw-Hill.*)

THE IMPERIAL MISSION. Americans' frequent invocations of Kipling underscored two important features of their imperialist move: its optimistic self-assurance and its basic similarity to European and especially British colonization. Despite rhetorical images of struggle and competition, most imperialist advocates saw colonization as a step in a grand mission of

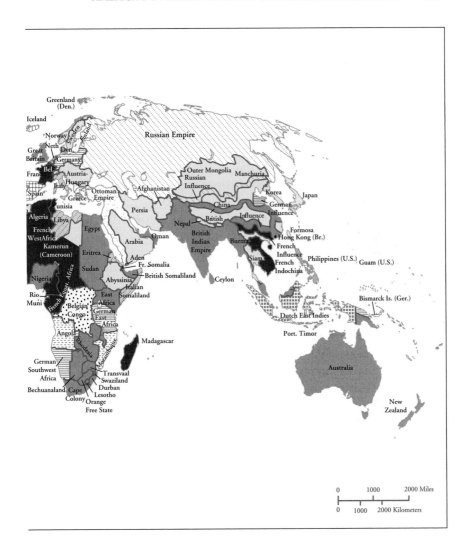

spreading the benefits of democracy, capitalism, and modern industrial life to needy peoples.

American Protestant missionaries led the way. First sent abroad by organized groups in 1810, volunteers stationed in tiny and isolated Christian missions in Burma, India, and Hawaii simply preached the gospel. By the 1870s, however, their mushrooming numbers and financial backing combined with the growing presence of American officials and businessmen in Asia and the Middle East to forge an informal alliance between Christianity and commerce. Missionaries merged Protestant responsibility to evangelize the world with promotion of American models of education, hygiene, and republican government, paving the way for trade relations. Shortly after 1900, American foreign missionaries outnumbered their British counterparts, and by 1920 they constituted 40 percent of the 30,000 Protestant missionaries stationed worldwide.

Like American missionaries, many imperial enthusiasts saw their economic and moral goals as synergistic and equally progressive. National ambitions to spread republican institutions and capitalists' interest in outfitting colonial peoples in western clothes accorded with educators' desire to promote literacy and Protestant morality. Few colonizers doubted the morality and appropriateness of this cluster of practices, and rarely were native peoples' views taken into consideration. This confident missionary impulse persisted in American foreign policy long after formal colonialism was abandoned.

FOLLOWING EUROPE'S FOOTSTEPS.   Yet it was not uniquely American. From the ancient Romans onward, most imperialisms have been rooted in a sense of mission that sees the enterprise as benevolent and progressive. Apologists for American imperialism recognized this when they aligned U.S. expansion with history's "westward course of empire." Late-nineteenth-century French imperialists waxed eloquently about their "civilizing mission" aimed at assimilating colonial peoples to the nation's language, values, and institutions. Not surprisingly, given U.S. origins as a British colony, American imperial rhetoric most closely resembled the British in its blend of modernization with a sure sense of ethnic and cultural superiority. From the British, the Americans inherited the mantle of "Anglo-Saxon" pride and the "white man's burden." "God has not been preparing the English-speaking and Teutonic peoples for a thousand years for nothing," declared Republican Senator Albert J. Beveridge in 1900. "He has made us the master organizers of the world to establish system where chaos reigns." Like the British "liberal empire" in the decades after 1858, American imperialists aimed to spread representative government, the rule of law, the capitalist market, and Protestant Christianity to subject peoples. Pro-imperialist Americans praised their British predecessors even while proclaiming that the United States would outdo them. Indeed, some American policymakers saw imperialism less in terms of competition with Europe than cooperation in the grand project of globalizing Western civilization.

EXCEPTIONALISM AND IMPERIALISM.   Exceptionalist arguments were sometimes aired by opponents of American imperialism, who feared that taking colonies would fatally compromise the nation's separation from the world's ills and its special destiny as a refuge of freedom. But as we have seen, many Americans easily translated their belief in national uniqueness into a call for all peoples to adopt their model. The debate between imperialists and anti-imperialists was not over American exceptionalism but about its genealogy—was America the heir of Anglo-Saxon Europe or a unique New World offspring? And how best to spread the American model—by action or example?

HAWAII AS A CASE STUDY.   The American annexation of Hawaii illustrated the blend of commercial, missionary, and strategic factors that brought American imperialism to distant tropical islands. In broad outlines it was a familiar story, comparable to the imposition of French rule in Réunion or British colonialism in Fiji. In each case, ship layovers and trade contacts led to missionary settlements and to foreign companies that penetrated the society by buying or leasing plantations, importing contract laborers from Asia or Africa, and financing roads and irrigation projects. Wealthy foreign planters and financiers put pressure on local government to gain concessions and on their parent country to protect their interests. When thwarted by native resistance or spurred by imperial rivalries, these elites moved toward a takeover with the help of their home government's armed forces.

Hawaiian annexation differed only in details from this typical scenario. Initially visited by Americans as a whaling stopover, Hawaii became economically important to Americans after 1810, when Yankee merchants negotiated a monopoly with King Kamahameha I on sandalwood, valuable for the China trade. Protestant missionaries soon followed, and after them came American sugar planters who forced the sale of vast lands for plantations, imported Asian laborers to replace native Hawaiians (many of whom had succumbed to western diseases), and tied the islands' economy to the ups and downs of the export market. When the tariff of 1890 eliminated the free export of Hawaiian sugar to the United States, the American island elite conspired to overthrow the nationalist Hawaiian ruler, Princess Lili`uokalani, install a provisional regime headed by an American attorney (the son of missionaries), and press for annexation to the United States. This would eliminate the defiant Hawaiian monarchy as well as the tariff. For a few years the American president, Grover Cleveland, sided with the Hawaiians in resisting annexation—an episode that demonstrated lingering doubts about American imperialism. But after the Spanish-American War opened in 1898, Hawaii gained additional prominence as an important naval stop to the Philippines and commercial way station to China, and Congress approved the islands' annexation.

COLONIAL ADMINISTRATION.   In basic features of colonial administration, too, American officials followed their European predecessors, especially the British, whose government and scientific reports were studied carefully. American policies encouraged colonies to export raw materials and plantation crops through a duty-free trade system while the parent country dominated transoceanic shipping and sought outlets for American manufactures. Like the British in Africa and Asia, the Americans built a colonial infrastructure of roads, bridges, railroads, and irrigation systems, established a standardized educational system that spread the English language to colonial elites, and passed public health measures to control tropical diseases. Both nations established racially segregated compounds for white businesses and government officials. In the American case, racism abroad clearly echoed and reinforced racism at home. Racial barriers in the American colonies were consistent with segregationist "Jim Crow" practices in the U.S. South, and subject colonial peoples were often depicted in verbal and visual terms similar to negative stereotypes of African Americans.

LIMITS OF U.S. FORMAL IMPERIALISM.   Still, there were significant differences between Americans' imperial practices and those of their British cousins. If not enough to justify American declarations of exceptionalism, they were nevertheless important. In comparative terms, the formal phase of American imperialism was late, limited, and brief.

As a late entrant to the imperial race, the United States was a second-stage colonizer in a double sense. By the time the nation entered the imperial race, most lands within its geographic range and economic interest were already taken as European colonies or captured as trade zones. In calling for an "Open Door" policy of equal Western trade privileges in China in 1899, the United States was playing catch-up, just as the scramble to annex the Philippines was meant to cut off threatened Japanese and British moves. Except for Hawaii, all the colonial possessions acquired by the United States had previously belonged to another European nation. Cuba, Puerto Rico, the Philippines, and Guam had been under Spanish control, the Virgin Islands under Danish, Samoa under German and British, and the Canal Zone under Colombian. Wresting such lands from previous colonizers through threats and diplomacy was generally easier than subduing indigenous peoples. Yet it also held the prospect of starting costly wars against European powers—a deterrent to aggressive U.S. actions outside areas held by the declining Spanish monarchy or weak New World nations.

Hence the relatively small scale of America's overseas empire. Most American colonies were islands, valuable as strategic way stations for naval or trading ships. Unlike the Europeans, Americans took no territories on the Asian and African mainland. In the Western Hemisphere, only Alaska and the Panama Canal Zone—both viewed as strategic borderlands—became U.S. mainland territories. Even with the huge territory of Alaska included, the United States added about 700,000 square miles to its empire between 1865 and 1900, whereas Great Britain, France, and Germany appropriated 4.7, 3.5, and 1 million square miles, respectively. America's colonial territories equaled less than 1 percent of the world's land surface, whereas the British Empire covered 23 percent in the 1920s and ruled nearly a quarter of the world's people.

The American empire was also peopled by few white officials or settlers. Unlike the British, Americans felt little need to settle colonies with migrants from the U.S. mainland or to administer them with a large contingent of officials. New to empire and slow to think through its implications, Americans, unlike the British, had no Colonial Office, no permanent overseas civil service, no domestic schools meant to instill imperial dogma or train its leaders. Whereas Britain stationed more than two-thirds of its armed forces overseas, the United States sent only a minuscule percentage abroad. The most dramatic contrast occurred in migration patterns. Between 1900 and 1914, about 2.6 million people left Great Britain for its imperial destinations. Most went to temperate settler societies such as Canada and Australia, but at least 100,000 worked in India as soldiers, officials, businessmen, missionaries, teachers, and doctors. Except for Hawaii, few Americans relocated to the nation's overseas colonies. Booming industrially and facing a chronic labor shortage, the United States was instead an importer of millions of migrants from around the world, many coming from British colonies such as Canada and Ireland. The lack of white settlers distinguished America's overseas colonialism not only from British imperialism but also from the earlier continental phase of American empire.

ANTI-IMPERIALISM. These features reflect a less-than-complete American commitment to formal imperialism. As people who had emerged from colonial origins, Americans proved more reluctant than Europeans to take on colonies. Domestic opponents of empire, who included Andrew Carnegie, Mark Twain, and the AFL's Samuel Gompers, pointed out that an "imperial republic" was a contradiction in terms. By ruling other peoples Americans were repudiating their principles of equal citizenship and self-determination and poisoning their unique experiment with dreams of empire. Whether it threatened to compromise the nation's republican ideology or, on the other hand, portended increased immigration and racial mixing, imperialism carried for many Americans the odor of disrepute. Small wonder that the U.S. Senate approved annexation of the Philippines, Guam, and Puerto Rico in 1899 by only a one-vote margin.

In response to this hesitation, American policymakers sought to keep imperial rule brief and to cast it as an apprenticeship in American democracy and capitalism. The dominant idea was to make over the colonial societies in the American model as quickly as possible so that they could qualify for self-government (as in the Philippines) or for admission to the Union (in the case of Hawaii and Alaska, whose absorption was made easier by the migration of white settlers). Colonial officials promoted rapid Americanization and modernization programs—the two went hand in hand—whose economic, educational, and political improvements were meant to prepare most colonies simultaneously for independence and integration into the capitalist world economy.

AMERICAN RULE IN THE PHILIPPINES

The workings of this American brand of formal imperialism were visible in the Philippines. On that tropical cluster of Pacific islands, American officials, initially confronted by a militant native independence movement, pushed the colony quickly toward self-government, with mixed results.

The Philippine colony was an unexpected byproduct of the Spanish-American War of 1898. Although the main arena of the war was the Caribbean, across the Pacific an American naval squadron destroyed the Spanish fleet in Manila Bay and the American army soon captured Manila itself. The American president, William McKinley, promised to support Cuban independence—the issue that triggered the war—but had different ideas about the Philippines. Hoping to acquire a valuable naval base and stopover for the China trade, and promising to "uplift, and civilize, and Christianize" the Filipinos, McKinley favored annexation. The American public, however, was sharply divided over taking this decisive step toward formal empire, and (as noted earlier) the U.S. Senate barely ratified the Treaty of Paris (1899), by which Spain ceded the Philippines, along with Guam and Puerto Rico, to the United States for $20 million.

PHILIPPINE-AMERICAN WAR. The Filipinos themselves put up fierce resistance. A popular movement led by Emilio Aguinaldo had fought the Spanish for independence; its members felt betrayed by the U.S. takeover and waged guerrilla war on American forces. The Philippine-American War was a far longer and more brutal conflict than the Spanish-American War that preceded it. American troops responded to the rebels' ambushes and executions by torturing captives and herding villagers into "concentration camps" to isolate combatants—tactics that the U.S. had condemned when the Spanish used them against Cuban rebels a few years earlier. By the time the main body of independence fighters was subdued in 1902, more than 4,000 Americans had been killed and 200,000 Filipinos died from battle wounds, disease, and famine—a much higher toll than the war of 1898.

THE COLONIAL PROGRAM. Despite this bloody beginning, and partly because of it, American administrators in the Philippines pursued an accommodating course. A series of pragmatic governors-general, starting with future president William Howard Taft, courted the support of the islands' wealthy and middle classes. Under an orderly "Filipinization" policy begun in 1901, Americans granted the colony increasing measures of self-rule. (Statehood was out of the question, according to U.S. secretary of war Elihu Root, because it "would add another serious race problem to the one we have already.") Municipal governments were taken over by native-born civil servants, and law enforcement was gradually turned over to a trained Filipino "constabulary." Political parties were formed and an elective legislature was created in 1907. The Jones Act of 1916 promised eventual independence. Meanwhile, U.S. colonial policy restricted American ownership of plantations and established an American-style public school system that spanned the islands and reached from kindergarten to the university level. American plans for universal education departed from other European colonial systems, which neglected basic literacy for common people and aimed instead to form a loyal, educated elite who would identify with the imperial project.

IMPACT OF COLONIAL RULE. With its economic restraint and near-term goal of self-government, the U.S. program in the Philippines compared favorably to other imperialist ventures in the region, such as the British in Burma, the Dutch in Indonesia, the French in Indochina, and especially the brutal Japanese occupation of Taiwan. Still, American colonial rule fell short of its promises. From the outset, reliance upon existing urban and landowning colonial elites compromised the Americans' democratizing program. Schools expanded literacy and the professional class, but education and free elections did not shake the patronage system that ran Philippine politics. Nor did they dislodge large landowners from power. Planters' profits soared from exporting sugar, coconut, and hemp to the world market, while American plans to distribute Spanish lands through homestead-style laws were subverted by the Filipino legislature. Share-cropping and other forms of farm tenancy doubled during the U.S. colonial era. Although the Americans' promise of eventual self-rule generally weakened local opposition to imperial control, lack of progress on land reform spurred the failed Sakdal uprising of 1935 and fed another peasant revolt a decade later. In sum, American colonial administration strengthened the power of large landowners, discouraged local industrialization, and widened the gap between rich and poor.

Nor did Americans reap the economic or strategic bonanza that imperialist proponents expected. Filipino planters provided Americans with cheap tropical crops, but the Philippine market for American consumer goods proved small and the migration of Filipino laborers to the United States threatened American wages. Rather than serving as a base for Asian trade or American naval operations, the Philippines sat beyond the effective radius of U.S. forces and proved vulnerable to the powerful Japanese navy.

The Philippine experience showed the difficulty of sustaining Americans' commitment to formal imperialism after their initial enthusiasm waned. Democratizing and modernizing colonies demanded more time and money than Americans were willing to invest, and concern for social stability compromised true colonial reconstruction. Americans tended to overestimate the beneficial effects of public education and political constitutions without buttressing them with fundamental social and economic changes. Like the Philippines, most colonies brought few economic rewards to American businesses and consumers that could not be won through less direct forms of control. These realities reinforced Americans' traditional misgivings about adopting European-style imperialism and their inclination to move colonies quickly toward self-rule. Whereas no European nation ceded independence willingly to a colony before the end of World War II, the United States granted the Philippines autonomy in 1934 and independence in 1946. Hawaii and Alaska, given territorial status in 1900 and 1912, respectively, entered the Union as states in 1959. Of America's major overseas possessions, only Puerto Rico occupied a free "commonwealth" status situated between independence and statehood.

THE AMERICAN EMPIRE IN THE CARIBBEAN

There was one great exception to this pattern of relative restraint: American domination of the Caribbean basin, which ardent expansionists sought to convert into "an American lake." Unlike islands in the Pacific, the Caribbean islands and Central America lay near U.S. borders, within the nation's economic orbit, and in a hemisphere the United States had declared in 1823 off limits to further European colonization and intervention. American interest in Caribbean islands was more like the ancient Greeks' preoccupation with nearby islands in the Aegean Sea than nineteenth-century Europe's overseas empires. Among the United States' contemporaries, the emergent world power Japan provided the closest parallel.

Nearby east Asian islands were in Japan's strategic "front yard" and were taken to forestall Russian expansion. Meanwhile, the desire to protect economic investments in Korea led Japan to occupy that peninsula. A key difference, however, is that Japan's regional thrusts were vigorously countered by Russia and western European powers, whereas after Spain was ousted from the Caribbean in the War of 1898, the United States faced competing economic claims from European nations that were reluctant to press them toward war. When American economic interests expanded in Latin America—by 1914, U.S. investment there surpassed investments in Canada or Europe—and the Panama Canal (begun in 1906) made secure shipping lanes crucial, American power was asserted in the region without apology. Mexico, Central America, and the Caribbean islands composed the first major overseas region that the United States was able to wrest from Europe's economic pull.

VARIETIES OF IMPERIAL CONTROL.   American domination of the Caribbean and Central America ran the full spectrum from formal imperialism to indirect control. Puerto Rico was purchased as the spoils of the War of 1898 and the Virgin Islands were bought from Denmark in 1917; both were annexed as territories. Elsewhere the United States stopped short of outright possession. The Canal Zone was leased from Panama. Cuba and Nicaragua were designated "protectorates" whose domestic policies and foreign relations were controlled by the United States for decades. Haiti, Nicaragua, the Dominican Republic, and Mexico were subject to periodic American military intervention and occupation. Where the United States did not intervene militarily, powerful American corporations manipulated local governments to ensure that they remained friendly to U.S. interests.

CUBA.   Cuba and Panama connected America's earlier continental expansionism with the new overseas imperialism. Lured by sugar and tobacco plantations and frustrated by exclusion of slavery from western territories, proslavery politicians had attempted to purchase Cuba from Spain in the 1850s. The Civil War cut short such initiatives, but calls to annex Cuba resurfaced in the American press after the islanders' unsuccessful 10-year rebellion against Spanish rule (1868–1878). After supporting the Cuban rebels against Spain in 1898, however, the United States pledged not to annex it. Racial concerns ruled out statehood because many Cubans shared African descent, but Cuban independence threatened instability or European intervention. Therefore, after a brief but intense period of military occupation and rebuilding, the United States controlled Cuba indirectly under the Platt Amendment (in force from 1903 to 1934), which put Cuban foreign relations in American hands, gave the United States the right to intervene to preserve order, and forced Cuba to lease a naval base

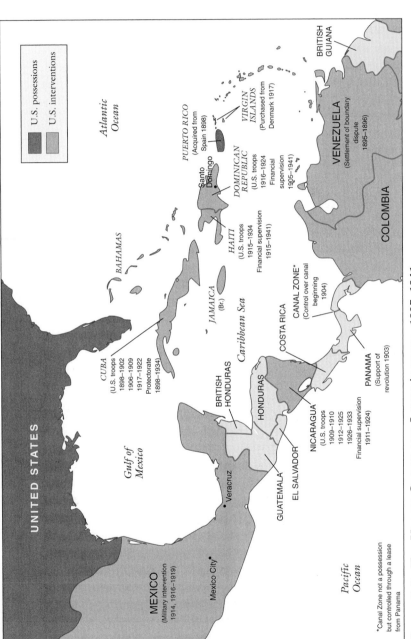

FIGURE 5-2 THE UNITED STATES AND LATIN AMERICA, 1895–1941

Except for Puerto Rico, the Virgin Islands, and the Canal Zone, the United States had no formal possessions in Latin America and the Caribbean in the late nineteenth century and the first half of the twentieth century. But as this map reveals, the United States exercised considerable influence in these regions throughout this period—political and economic influence, augmented at times by military intervention. Note the particularly intrusive presence of the United States in the affairs of Cuba, Haiti, and the Dominican Republic—as well as the canal-related interventions in Colombia and Panama. (*Source: Used with permission from American History (11th ed.) by Alan Brinkley. Copyright 2003 by McGraw-Hill.*)

at Guantanamo Bay to Americans. American investment in Cuban agricultural and mining industries soared, protected by periodic interventions of U.S. troops and the election of America-friendly but corrupt local leaders.

THE PANAMA CANAL.   Panama, too, had long been a target of American expansionists. The California Gold Rush demonstrated the need for a direct sea route connecting the East and West Coasts of the United States across the narrow strip of land (or isthmus) of Panama, a province of Colombia. The United States periodically landed troops to protect the railroad across Panama, and in 1850 signed a treaty with Great Britain providing for joint control of a canal. Four decades later, the Spanish-American War and the acquisition of Hawaii cemented Americans' resolve to deploy naval power from ocean to ocean. The British gave up their canal rights in 1901 and U.S. President Theodore Roosevelt negotiated a favorable lease with Colombia, but the Colombian Senate held out for better terms. Enraged, Roosevelt conspired with Panamanian rebels to detach the province from Colombia and protected them with American warships. In 1903 the United States was granted long-term rights to a Canal Zone by the friendly new Panama government. Accused of Colombia's "rape" by his own secretary of war, Roosevelt insisted that an American canal was "a mandate from civilization." In 1922, eight years after the canal opened, the United States quietly paid Colombia $25 million in reparations.

THE ROOSEVELT COROLLARY AND MILITARY INTERVENTION.   Roosevelt realized that the "effect of our building the Canal must be to require us to police the surrounding premises." As Britain had shown when control of the Suez Canal led it to occupy Egypt, one imperialist venture spawned others nearby. Concerned that European nations might intervene militarily in Venezuela to collect debts, Roosevelt declared in 1904 that the United States had the right to patrol the Caribbean to preserve order, protect its interests, and prevent European meddling. This "Roosevelt Corollary" transformed the earlier Monroe Doctrine from the defensive stance of a young republic to the aggressive thrust of a regional imperial power.

Between 1906 and 1934, when global events began to divert American policymakers' attention from Central America, the United States intervened repeatedly in and around the Caribbean basin. In Nicaragua, Haiti, and the Dominican Republic (as in Cuba), these interventions resulted in extended military occupations that began crash modernization programs modeled on the Philippines. Elsewhere they were brief and less ambitious, embodying a range of objectives beyond securing approaches to the Panama Canal. In Haiti, American troops were landed to suppress disruptive civil wars, and in the Dominican Republic, to collect tariff duties and forestall potential intervention by European creditor nations—a strategy dubbed "pre-emptive imperialism" by supporters. Expeditions were sent to Mexico in 1914 and 1916 to prevent potentially hostile governments from coming to power or nationalizing American investment, for by 1910 American businesses controlled more than 40 percent of Mexico's property, including railroads and mines, and produced half of its oil. In most cases the United States acted to preserve an environment favorable to American financial and trade interests.

BANANA REPUBLICS. Given overwhelming American power in the region, it is perhaps surprising that the United States actually took few colonies. This reluctance testified to Americans' distaste for imperial rule and the limited progress of long-term occupations in Nicaragua and Haiti. It also reflected the success of indirect, behind-the-scenes manipulation of Central American politics by powerful American corporations. A case in point is the United Fruit Company. Formed by the merger of two American banana importers in 1899, United Fruit not only dominated banana shipping but also acquired more than a million acres in Central America by the 1920s, on which it established plantations worked by imported Jamaican laborers and run by rigid company rules. Building roads, railroads, telephone lines, and irrigation canals, the firm modernized these regions and stemmed infectious diseases, but at a formidable price. Tropical rain forests were cleared and replaced by a monocrop system that ruined the land and directed all local production to the export market. In Honduras, Guatemala, and Panama, United Fruit became a powerful economic and political force. Allying with large landlords and local political strongmen, the company pressured governments in these "banana republics" to suppress labor and land reform uprisings and induced American military intervention to collect debts, prevent unwanted taxes, or overthrow officials who threatened to nationalize plantations and railroads.

TOWARD ECONOMIC DOMINATION. This kind of economic imperialism, sometimes called "corporate imperialism" by its critics, was not unique to the Latin American tropics. It was practiced by American sugar barons in Hawaii and by the Firestone Rubber Company in Liberia. In a sense it represented the American extension of Europe's four-century exploitation of tropical New World lands. Yet by relying upon private banks and companies, imposing free trade, and renouncing direct political rule, it also typified a new informal imperialism of indirect economic control that could also be extended to nontropical lands (as Great Britain did in Argentina) or even to new markets in industrialized countries. The transformation from debtor to creditor nation gave Americans indirect power over borrowing nations and intensified U.S. involvement in their domestic affairs. As the twentieth century proceeded, the growing world-wide reach of multinational corporations redirected attention from traditional imperial rule, which declined after World War I, to the indirect economic domination of poorer nations by a few industrialized giants, including the United States.

TOWARD AN AMERICAN CENTURY: WORLD WARS AND GLOBAL ENGAGEMENT

In February 1941, as Americans debated whether to enter a second world war raging in Europe, *Life* magazine editor Henry Luce penned a celebrated essay called "The American Century," a phrase that soon became part of the nation's public language. Begun as a call for Americans to join Britain in the war against Germany, Luce's essay evolved into a plea for Americans to take action to build a better world in the war's aftermath. Just as the preceding century was England's, the next century would be America's, Luce predicted. Freedom, equality, and economic growth were American ideals, and "it now becomes our time to be the powerhouse from which the[se] ideals spread throughout the world and do their mysterious work of lifting the life of mankind." Throwing off its isolationist tendencies, the United States should use its preeminent power and prestige to redeem the world by cooperating with other nations, if possible, and acting alone if necessary.

The notion of an "American Century" did not originate with Luce. In writing the essay, Luce, the child of American missionaries in China, gave voice to crusading impulses and missionary ideals that had infused American imperialism in the 1890s and justified America's entry into World War I in 1917. Whether makers of U.S. foreign policy preferred influence by example, unilateral action, or international cooperation, they had long blended concern for U.S. national interests with a strong dose of faith in the nation's political principles and economic practices, and the desirability of spreading them. The critical ingredient that was added by World War II was Americans' determination to use the nation's enhanced power to spread its model around the world.

COMPARING WORLD WARS.   The two world wars were related and eerily similar. Both began over territorial disputes in eastern Europe in which Europe's great powers were similarly aligned on opposite sides. In both cases the United States was initially neutral but gradually drawn into the conflict, helping Britain and France to defeat Germany and its allies. The harsh settlement of World War I made the second war almost inevitable.

Both wars sparked decolonization movements by dismembering the losers' empires and bankrupting the victors. And in both cases the United States emerged from war comparatively unscathed and economically paramount. Yet only after World War II did the United States self-consciously assume the role of global political and economic leader that its ideology and power seemed to justify. By 1945 the U.S. appeared poised to dominate "the American Century" that Henry Luce prophesied.

THE FAILED CRUSADE: AMERICA IN WORLD WAR I

American imperialism of the late 1800s had broken with the policy of limited entanglement in political affairs outside the Western Hemisphere counseled by George Washington and encoded in the Monroe Doctrine. Agreements with European powers on trade with China, war with Spain in the Pacific, the acquisition of colonies, and President Roosevelt's mediation of the Russo-Japanese War (1904–05) went far beyond traditional bilateral treaties and trade arrangements. Involvement in World War I took the United States a crucial step further toward global engagement by abandoning traditional neutrality and directly involving the United States in a European conflict. Not since the Napoleonic Wars a century earlier was there a similar crisis. Back then, the weak new American nation struggled to retain its neutral status toward England and France but drifted into a dangerous war with England. This time, England and France were allied and the United States had become an industrial giant whose arms, money, and men they desperately needed to stave off defeat at the hands of Germany. The nation had come a long way.

THE WAR'S IMPERIAL ORIGINS.   The roots of World War I lay in national and international conflicts that had been brewing for generations in Europe. Two kinds of empire were involved: first, the old landed empires of Russia, Austria-Hungary, and the Ottoman (Turkish) domains, which had gradually expanded to nearby lands and then become vulnerable to the nationalist claims of ethnic minorities; and second, the rulers of overseas colonial realms, such as Britain, France, Holland, and Germany, who vied with one another to enlarge these possessions. The internal crises of the first group joined with the rivalries of the second to create a brittle alliance system that balanced the power of England, France, and Russia against Germany, Austria-Hungary, and Italy. At Europe's center, a rising Germany mounted a growing challenge to Britain's naval and economic supremacy. But war broke out instead on Europe's eastern periphery. Both the Ottoman and Austro-Hungarian empires were declining powers threatened with the secession of ethnic nationalities and partition by major powers. When a Serbian nationalist hoping to detach Bosnia from the Austro-Hungarian Empire assassinated the heir to the throne in 1914, Austria-Hungary sought help from its ally Germany, which then declared war on Russia and France. The chain reaction continued, eventually involving not only the six nations enmeshed in the alliance system but also the Ottoman Empire, which inclined toward Germany, and Japan, which joined Britain, France, and Russia. Involvement of each nation's colonies made this "Great War" truly global.

WILSON'S INTERNATIONALISM. Following traditional American policy toward Europe, President Woodrow Wilson initially declared the United States neutral and sought to mediate the European crisis. Eventually, however, the Americans, although divided in their ethnic loyalties, joined the Allied cause. Wilson and his advisers admired British institutions and believed that German victory would spread dictatorship and militarism through Europe. U.S. trade with England and France, always strong, tripled after the war's outbreak as America became the Allies' arsenal and bank. German submarine attacks disrupted that trade in ways that were more dramatic and damaging than Britain's harassment of American shipping to Germany. With so much money from American banks underwriting the Allied war effort, American leaders became committed to an Allied victory even if it required direct American entry into the war.

America's commitment to Britain became official when German opposition escalated. In February 1917, Germany announced a policy of unrestricted submarine warfare against ships trading with its enemies. Later that month, Wilson learned that a German telegram that was intercepted by the British proposed an alliance with Mexico by which Mexico could regain southwestern lands lost to the U.S. in 1848. This "Zimmermann Note," sent just days after U.S. troops returned from chasing revolutionary leader Pancho Villa in Mexico, set German and American imperial designs on a collision course. In April 1917, Congress declared war on Germany, agreeing with Wilson that the Germans must be defeated to assure a world safe for American interests and principles.

What principles were involved? Always eager to invoke moral aims, Wilson believed that British victory over Germany (with an American assist) would promote his Progressive "internationalist" ideology, which proclaimed that the United States should lead the world toward a peaceful era of open-door trade, reduced armaments, free-market capitalism, democratic government, and transparent diplomacy. Unlike imperialists, Wilson preferred international cooperation (or "collective security") over reliance on a military balance of power among competing nations. Still, his "internationalist" views shared several characteristics with advocates of American imperialism: partiality to Britain, belief in America's messianic

role, and the goal of extending American trade, representative government, and civilization worldwide. And when persuasion failed, Wilson
was not above acting unilaterally in imperialist fashion, as his military
interventions in Latin America showed. "Unilateralist" and "internationalist" threads in American foreign policy, the latter sometimes called
"multilateralist" or "Wilsonian," vied for influence among policymakers
throughout the twentieth century. They disagreed on means but featured a
similar blend of messianic ideals and national self-interest.

THE FOURTEEN POINTS.   Under the spell of Progressive-Era reform, the
United States went to war not just to stop Germany but to further a global
agenda that universalized America's ideals and interests. Wilson believed
that with America's guidance the bloody conflict could be transformed
into a war to end all wars and "make the world safe for democracy." In
January 1918, before the war's outcome was clear, Wilson unveiled his
visionary formula for peace: the Fourteen Points. The first five embodied
the principles of free-market democracy: open diplomatic agreements,
freedom of the seas, free trade, arms reduction, and self-determination
of peoples. The next eight points outlined specific territorial changes to
recognize nationalist groups in eastern Europe. The fourteenth point,
which Wilson considered most essential, called for a "concert of nations,"
a new international body that would adjudicate conflicts peacefully
between nations, outlawing revolution and war forever.

The fresh infusion of American reinforcements broke the futile stalemate of trench warfare. After the Allies turned the tide against Germany in
eastern France in the summer of 1918, the Germans sought an armistice.
Wilson steamed across the Atlantic to the Paris Peace Conference, the first
American president to visit Europe while in office. Exhausted by the war,
many of the world's peoples longed for a "peace without victory" that
would banish imperialism and war. For the United States, too, it was a
pivotal moment. Wilson, identified with America's new global prominence
and esteemed for his prophecy of universal freedom and peace, became the
first American to be recognized during his lifetime as a world figure.

FAILURE AT VERSAILLES.   At the Versailles peace negotiations, Wilson's
messianic crusade ended in colossal disappointment. It crumbled from its
own contradictions, especially Wilson's acceptance of Allied imperialism
in Asia and Africa, and crashed against the hard reality of the Allies' reactionary fears and national self-interest. Determined to punish Germany,
expand their borders, and retain their colonies, Allied leaders imposed
huge "reparations" payments upon Germany and seized its colonial
lands, then (with Wilson's approval and U.S. participation) sent troops to
Russia to defeat the Bolsheviks, who had come to power during the war.

Wilson negotiated tirelessly, but besides a few territorial provisions of the Versailles Treaty, only its "covenant" of a league of nations reflected the influence of his beloved Fourteen Points. Wilson convinced himself that this international peacekeeping body would right the settlement's wrongs.

In a final irony, the U.S. Senate, wary of further European commitments and fearing sanctions against American intervention abroad, rejected the Versailles Treaty and with it U.S. membership in the League of Nations. Weakened by its members' war weariness and the absence of American military and economic support, the League failed to block the resurgence of German and Japanese expansionism and thus to prevent a second world war.

Effects of the War.   Besides imposing a harsh peace that set the stage for another global war, World War I had important consequences for the world and for America's place in it. Its damage to European economies shifted power away from western Europe and directed it toward the United States. The Allied victory caused the demise of three dynasties and their lands—the German, Austro-Hungarian, and Ottoman empires—and raised hopes for national autonomy among colonists and ethnic nationalities everywhere. A fourth dynasty, the Russian empire, was smashed by the Bolshevik Revolution of 1917, which opened a long ideological struggle between capitalism and communism in which the United States was to play a pivotal role. Finally, the Great War destroyed the old imperial alliance system without creating an effective international peacekeeping body or arrangement to replace it.

AMERICA'S WORLD ROLE BETWEEN THE WARS

Between Isolationism and Globalism.   Rejection of the League reflected Americans' preference for unilateral action and a free hand over Wilson's commitment to binding international commitments. This did not mean that American leaders retreated to isolationism in the 1920s, as popular histories often imply. The United States pursued an active but independent foreign policy that promoted arms control, foreign trade, and limited assistance to war-torn Europe. America emerged from the Great War as a major player in the international political and economic system. Yet Americans held back from the degree of world leadership that their increased power seemed to warrant. They kept their distance from Europe's renewed territorial disputes and the resurgence of dictatorship in Germany and Japan, and they balked at inheriting Britain's role as the main international economic stabilizer. Many nations were responsible for the economic devastation of the interwar years and the drift toward a second World War. Certainly German and Japanese expansionism were prime causes of the latter. But the limits of America's international commitments contributed to the downward spiral of the world economic and political order by the 1930s.

The United States had suffered little war damage and profited by supplying Europeans with money and arms, and it emerged from World War I with its global economic power enhanced. In 1913 it produced one-third of the world's industrial output. By 1929 the proportion rose to 42 percent, compared to 28 percent for the combined economies of Britain, Germany, and France. American policymakers believed that economic expansion overseas would benefit the nation and help stabilize world politics, but the postwar trade environment proved volatile. The annual volume of American imports and exports fluctuated erratically in the interwar years and declined overall after 1920, reflective of a general crisis in world trade.

GLOBALIZATION YIELDS TO ECONOMIC NATIONALISM.   World War I and the two decades that followed disrupted the pattern of increasing global economic interconnection that had been accelerating since the 1700s. The Industrial Revolution, imperialism, and the migrations they fostered had created a dense network of flows and exchanges that effectively globalized the world economy by 1914. Some historians label this "long nineteenth century" of 1780–1914 the "second globalization" that extended the links of the "first globalization" in the age of European exploration and colonialism. But after reaching its apex in 1914, global economic integration stagnated in the interwar years. The ravages of war, restrictive immigration laws of the 1920s in the New World, and economic depression in the 1930s slowed migration streams worldwide. The volume of world trade climbed slowly after World War I only to fall again during the Great Depression, so that its real value was virtually the same in 1939 as it had been in 1913. Faced with economic hard times, leaders of major countries (including the United States in 1930) passed high tariffs and import quotas to protect national industries and currencies. In 1931 Britain abandoned its historic commitment to free trade and the gold standard, and it was followed by the United States. These actions closed off the exchange of goods and materials that might stimulate economic recovery, and they provoked retaliatory measures from other nations. One by one, nations looked to their own resources for recovery, and trade policy became a tool of national interests.

AMERICA'S PARADOXICAL POSITION.   In one sense, this seemed less of a problem for the United States than for others. Beneath the shift to economic nationalism lay a structural change in economic relations between the United States and Europe. America's emergence as an industrial giant made obsolete the complementary nineteenth-century arrangement by which American crops and foods were exchanged for European manufactures. The new territorial division of labor left the United States less reliant than before on Europe for its trade, and less dependent on foreign trade more generally.

At the same time, however, a second structural change tied the United States closer to Europe. America entered World War I as a debtor nation and ended it as the main international creditor. During the war, American banks lent millions to U.S. Allies; afterward, they sent loans and investment money to Germany and Austria to help them rebuild. Thus, postwar Europe's economic recovery hinged precariously on the circular flow of U.S. funds to and from Europe. American loans and investments financed Germany's and Austria's reparations payments to France and England, which the French and British then passed along to the United States to repay war loans. If the Americans should stop the flow, the whole system would collapse.

THE UNITED STATES AS RELUCTANT WORLD BANKER.   That is exactly what happened. The combination of Europe's dependence upon American capital and America's relative independence of European trade proved fatal. Without a compelling political or economic stake in Europe, American leaders refused to prop up Europe's economy indefinitely. And unlike Britain, whose prosperity had relied upon a massive influx of raw materials, the United States had little need to buy the products its foreign loans and investments helped to create. As economic conditions deteriorated, there was no incentive for Americans to keep their money in Europe or to become a committed long-term stabilizer of the global economy, as the British had before 1914. In 1928, American banks and investors began withdrawing capital from Europe to pursue more favorable opportunities during the nation's speculative boom. Germany plunged into virtual bankruptcy and its economy stood on the verge of collapse. The following year, when America's speculative frenzy culminated in the October stock market crash, American banks called in their European loans and Europe's financial institutions fell like dominoes.

CAUSES OF THE GREAT DEPRESSION.   The Great Depression that devastated the capitalist world economy in the 1930s and transformed its politics had deeper roots than the Wall Street crash or the withdrawal of American capital from Europe. Historians and economists still debate its causes. Some explanations are basically enlarged descriptions of the capitalist business cycle, the recurring up-and-down pattern by which prosperous times inevitably lead to overproduction, which is then "corrected" by deflation and unemployment, until inventories are spent and investors and consumers begin the next expansion. In the 1920s, the Russian economist

N. D. Kondratiev, using prices as an indicator of growth, graphed Western economic development since the late 1700s as a series of long waves with 50- to 60-year periods, with secondary slumps every 20 to 30 years. Kondratiev's waves roughly fit the oscillating course of the modern Atlantic economy in the century after its first "panic" and depression in the 1840s. Yet the factors that caused this pattern remain controversial.

In the case of 1929, scholars point to a variety of culprits, including Europe's crippling war debt, the unreasonably high reparations payments exacted from Germany, a decade of worldwide agricultural overproduction and low prices, and the dangerous overexpansion of credit during the consumption boom of the 1920s. Some scholars see the 1929 Crash as a brief cyclical "correction" that was turned into a prolonged slump by wrongheaded national policies such as high tariffs and curbs on spending. Others argue instead that government jobs programs and other "market interference" prevented the economy from righting itself in the long run— a position discredited by John Maynard Keynes's pointed reminder that "in the long run we are all dead" and help was needed immediately.

DESTABILIZING EFFECTS.   Whatever the Depression's causes, its traumatic effects were obvious. In the United States, national output was cut in half between 1929 and 1933, and 13 million people—one-fourth of the labor force—were thrown out of work. The misery spread as nations that relied on exporting goods to the United States found that market shriveled. Throughout the industrialized world, unemployment ranged between 15 and 35 percent in the early 1930s, and through trade connections the industrialized nations transmitted the crisis to dependent lands in Latin America and southeast Asia.

The Depression's political effects were also momentous. As Chapter 4 showed, many Western governments attacked the crisis with a series of measures, including public works programs, unemployment assistance, and old-age pensions, that expanded the development of the welfare state. From Japan and New Zealand to Argentina and Egypt, the economic catastrophe destabilized existing regimes. In most cases it promoted stronger governments as desperate citizens anxious to restore order and prosperity ceded authority to powerful regimes led by charismatic leaders. The new governments sometimes leaned leftward, like Franklin Roosevelt's New Deal in the United States or Lazaro Cardenas's administration in Mexico. More often, however, they proved to be menacing dictatorships of the Right. Economic depression prepared the ground for dangerous fascist regimes in Germany and Italy, virulent racist and nationalist ideologies such as Nazism, and aggressive expansion by countries such as Japan that were eager to seize markets and raw materials abroad.

WORLD WAR II: AMERICA'S TURNING POINT

THE PATH TO WAR IN EUROPE.   In addition to the impact of economic depression, the road to World War II was paved by the punitive Versailles Treaty. In 1933 the Nazi leader Adolf Hitler assumed power with promises to reverse the humiliations of Versailles, to get the economy moving, and to rearm Germany and extend the dominion of its "Aryan" empire. As "führer" or supreme leader, Hitler persecuted German Jews and turned the economy and government into a war machine. He took Germany out of the League of Nations, formed an alliance with Italy's fascist dictator, Benito Mussolini, and began a series of territorial seizures in Eastern Europe. These included Austria, which was annexed in 1938, and western Czechoslovakia, which Britain and France ceded to Hitler (without asking the Czechs) in the infamous Munich Pact later that year. When Hitler violated his promise to end Germany's territorial grabs by invading Poland in August 1939, Britain and France declared war.

Throughout these events, America's political leaders stood on the sidelines, preoccupied by the Depression, clinging to the myth of America's isolation from Europe, and hoping to avoid a replay of Wilson's debacle. Generals, the saying goes, are always fighting the last war. A peacetime variant held true for the United States in the 1930s, when a series of Neutrality Acts (1935–37) based on lingering regrets over World War I restricted American passenger trips, loans, and arms sales to nations at war. When war broke out, President Franklin Roosevelt proclaimed the United States neutral and insisted that shipments to belligerent nations be on a "cash and carry" basis to avoid attacks on U.S. ships. All these moves were designed to prevent America's entry into an overseas conflict that seemed to share many similarities with the Great War, including a nearly identical lineup of opposing nations.

There was one key difference, however. Unlike World War I, the second world war was not a futile stalemate bogged down in the trenches and forests of eastern France. Hitler's German military machine was conquering Europe rapidly, almost at will. After France fell to the German onslaught in June 1940, Roosevelt resolved to support England at all costs as the last line of defense against German control of Europe and the Atlantic. Under the Lend-Lease Act, the United States provided billions of dollars of military aid to Britain and the Soviet Union, which Hitler invaded in June 1941. That summer, American destroyers began escorting British convoys virtually across the Atlantic. Roosevelt and Britain's embattled Prime Minister Winston Churchill expected a showdown with German submarines that would bring the United States into the war.

PEARL HARBOR AND JAPAN.   Instead, it was Japan's pre-emptive attack on Pearl Harbor, Hawaii, in December 1941 that brought the United States into World War II. American relations with Japan had been deteriorating for two decades as the Japanese sought to oust Western imperialists from Asia and dominate Korea and China. The United States, in turn, continued its insistence on an "open door" in China and drew closer to the government of its anticommunist leader Chiang Kai-shek.

During the economic downturn of the 1930s, Japan stepped up its quest for raw materials, export markets, and outlets for its population. Japan's army seized Manchuria in 1931 and invaded the Chinese coast in 1937, occupying its cities. As against German expansionist moves, the Western response was weak and uncoordinated. Japan's actions violated existing treaties, closed the "open door" in China, and threatened British and American trade with southeast Asia. But the United States, unable to counter Japanese military and naval strength, protested verbally while the League of Nations simply reprimanded Japan, which responded by withdrawing from the League. Gradually, President Roosevelt stiffened American resolve. He refused to invoke the Neutrality Acts so that the United States could give loans and military equipment to China. In 1939 the United States began trade sanctions against Japan that escalated, after Japanese troops occupied French Indochina in July 1941, into a freeze on Japanese assets in America and a cutoff of trade, including oil.

Roosevelt hoped to avoid or postpone war with Japan to focus on defeat of Germany. Even after negotiations with Japan broke down, Americans expected the Japanese to retaliate by invading British Malaya or Dutch Indonesia in search of rubber and oil. Because of American negligence and naïveté, the Japanese attack on Pearl Harbor was unforeseen and thus frighteningly effective, killing 2,400 servicemen and sinking or damaging eight battleships, nearly disabling America's Pacific fleet.

Now, however, the United States was fully committed to World War II. At stake was a clear clash of interests and systems. Japanese insistence on a free hand in its "Greater East Asia Co-Prosperity Sphere"—the name Tokyo gave to its expanding empire—clashed with U.S. demands for a sovereign China open to western trade. By 1940, when Japan joined a formal alliance with Germany and Italy, Roosevelt and American policymakers saw Japanese expansion in global terms as the Pacific wing of an offensive designed to divide the world into spheres of linked Asian and European dictatorships. This specter came alive as Germany and Italy joined Japan in war against America a few days after Pearl Harbor.

FROM THE ATLANTIC CHARTER TO YALTA. Japan's attack ended the American debate over military intervention in World War II. Its secrecy and the evil of Hitler's regime invested the war with a clear moral edge missing in World War I. Because popular enthusiasm did not have to be whipped up, America's entry into World War II lacked the shrill crusading of the Great War. Still, Roosevelt framed the war in "internationalist" terms that Woodrow Wilson would have approved. After a joint U.S.-British summit in August 1941, Roosevelt and Churchill outlined Allied war aims in an "Atlantic Charter." Like the Fourteen Points, the charter called for freedom of the seas, collective security, disarmament, economic cooperation, and the right of peoples to self-government. Victory for the United States and its allies would mean the successful defense of democracy and human rights against authoritarian, militarist regimes. A world order securing free trade, capitalist economic opportunity, and political democracy would allow people around the globe to "live out their lives in freedom from fear and want."

Except for the homage to capitalism, similar sentiments were echoed in the statement drafted at the Yalta Conference in February 1945, where Roosevelt, Churchill, and Soviet leader Josef Stalin met as their long but victorious war against Germany and Japan wound down. At Yalta the "Big Three" affirmed their hope that Allied wartime cooperation could translate into a secure and lasting postwar peace. In this spirit Roosevelt and Churchill assured Stalin that Russia would never again be invaded from Europe, Stalin guaranteed free elections and representative governments in occupied Poland, and all parties planned a founding conference for the United Nations to be held later that year.

Yet, even as Allied leaders met at Yalta, ideological differences and national interests were driving them into opposing camps. Fearing economic control by western capitalists and anxious to create a buffer zone of satellite states around the Soviet Union, Stalin had already asserted Russian dominance north of Greece. Only weeks after Yalta, he cancelled elections and installed a puppet government in Poland. For their part, the Americans and British had already excluded the Russians from shaping the peace in Italy when that nation surrendered to the Allies in 1943. After Yalta, the Americans accelerated their attack on Japan. The U.S. Air Force dropped atomic bombs on Hiroshima and Nagasaki in August 1945, in part to compel Japan's surrender before the Soviets—who had pledged to enter the war against Japan that month—could join the postwar occupation of Japan. As the victorious nations divided the territories they occupied in Europe and Asia into competing "spheres of influence," their wartime vision of international cooperation disintegrated.

EFFECTS OF THE WAR.   World War II proved to be a major turning point for the United States and for the world's economic and political system. Allied battlefield victories, with their ghastly toll of casualties, saved the

West (but not 6 million Jews and several million other "undesirables" such as gypsies, homosexuals, and political dissenters) from Nazi dreams of racial cleansing, reversed Germany's territorial gains, and prevented Japan from building an Asian empire. Wartime mobilization ended the Great Depression among industrialized powers, but most emerged from the war exhausted and bankrupt. Britain, whose debt equaled its entire annual output, was unable to keep its empire. Instead, the United States, which again emerged from world war uninvaded (except for Pearl Harbor) and more productive than other major combatants, assumed its place as the world's preeminent economic power.

Most important for America's role in world history, the global scale of the conflict banished for good the dream of American isolationism. The collapse of overseas Western empires decisively ended one world political system—the alignment of Europe's great powers in a precarious balance-of-power equilibrium. In its place came not the reign of international cooperation that American leaders like Wilson and FDR had envisioned. Nor was it exactly the American Century of unopposed influence and prestige that Henry Luce prophesied. Instead, an ideological clash emerged between the United States and another new "superpower," the Soviet Union, and with it a dangerous global "balance of terror" in which the United States was fully embedded: the Cold War between communist and noncommunist empires.

SUGGESTED READINGS

Dawley, Alan. *Changing the World: American Progressives in War and Revolution.* Princeton: Princeton University Press, 2003.
—Places Woodrow Wilson's World War I crusade in a global context that includes Bolshevism, imperialism, and anti-imperialist social movements.

Dower, John W. *War Without Mercy: Race and Power in the Pacific War.* New York: Pantheon, 1986.
—Insightfully compares American and Japanese propaganda during World War II, demonstrating their blend of nationalist and racist themes.

Garraty, John A. *The Great Depression.* New York: Anchor Books, 1987.
—Enlarges discussion of the causes, course, and consequences of the Depression to include connections and comparisons between the United States, Europe, and Latin America.

Go, Julian, and Anne L. Foster, eds. *The American Colonial State in the Philippines: Global Perspectives.* Durham: Duke University Press, 2003.
—Includes stimulating comparative essays on U.S. imperial administration.

Hobsbawm, Eric. *The Age of Empire, 1875–1914*. New York: Vintage Books, 1989.
—A sweeping history of European and American imperialism in historical context, including its global implications then and now.

Jacobson, Matthew Frye. *Barbarian Virtues: The United States Encounters Foreign Peoples at Home and Abroad, 1876–1917*. New York: Hill and Wang, 2000.
—Links American rhetoric and policies about immigration and empire, showing how stereotypes of foreigners pervaded and influenced both.

Macmillan, Margaret. *Paris 1919: Six Months That Changed the World*. New York: Random House, 2002.
—A dramatic history of the negotiations at Versailles that concentrates on the "Big Four"—Lloyd George of Britain, Clemenceau of France, Wilson of the United States, and Orlando of Italy—and details the Treaty's compromises and consequences.

Maier, Charles S. *Among Empires: American Ascendancy and Its Predecessors*. Cambridge, Mass.: Harvard University Press, 2006.
—This thoughtful essay examines the many forms of empire throughout history and suggests how the United States is both like and unlike them.

Ninkovitch, Frank. *The United States and Imperialism*. Oxford: Blackwell, 2001.
—Relates America's imperial expansion from the 1890s to World War II to crises of American identity, missionary nationalist ideals, and broad geopolitical aims.

Rosenberg, Emily S. *Spreading the American Dream: American Economic and Cultural Expansion, 1890–1945*. New York: Hill and Wang, 1982.
—Shows how the U.S. government promoted American business interests and mass culture abroad through colonialism and "liberal internationalism."

Tucker, Richard P. *Insatiable Appetite: The United States and the Ecological Degradation of the Tropical World*. Berkeley: University of California Press, 2000.
—Analyzes the workings and effects of American "corporate imperialism" in Latin American "banana republics" and elsewhere.

Weinberg, Gerhard L. *A World at Arms: A Global History of World War II*. Cambridge, Eng.: Cambridge University Press, 1994.
—The best one-volume account of the war.

Williams, William Appleman. *Empire as a Way of Life*. New York: Oxford University Press, 1980.
—This hard-hitting book was one of the first to trace U.S. imperial designs to the early 1800s and to link American continental and overseas expansion.

CHALLENGES OF EMPIRE

> **GETTING STARTED ON CHAPTER SIX:** How did the Cold War's causes, episodes, and effects reflect the United States' expanded international commitments after 1945? What ideologies and interests were at stake in the global rivalry between the United States and the Soviet Union? What "new world order," if any, replaced the polarized alliance system of the Cold War? How were American social movements of the postwar era shaped by international ideas and trends? What was novel about late twentieth-century economic globalization? To what extent was it an expression of American empire?

The United States emerged from World War II as the world's largest military and economic power. Boosted by wartime prosperity and its exemption from a mainland invasion, the nation produced almost half of the world's products in 1945. America's consumer economy and its democratic government enjoyed tremendous prestige abroad, which was enhanced by the nation's global military presence. Yet despite its economic and military might, the "American Colossus" was unable to shape the postwar global order into an unopposed "American Century." Instead, a long and dangerous standoff developed between the United States and the Soviet Union. Emerging dramatically in the rivalry of capitalist and communist empires for control of Eastern Europe, the Cold War became a worldwide struggle as communism in various forms appeared in Latin America, China, and elsewhere in east Asia. American efforts to "contain" communism and to promote democracy and capitalism led to tense showdowns with the Soviets over Eastern Europe and Cuba, and to controversial and costly wars in Korea (1950–1953) and Vietnam (1965–1975).

The Cold War had mixed effects on Americans' global ambitions. For the most part, it fueled American missionary nationalism by defining the nation as the exemplar of the Free World and the leader of an international

244

alliance against communism. Opposing the Soviets entailed not only armed resistance, but also the construction of stable capitalist democracies abroad and a trade network that assured continued American economic supremacy. At some junctures, however, the Cold War's strain on American resources and continued opposition abroad produced scaled-down visions of "peaceful coexistence" between communist and capitalist rivals. As Cold War tensions eased in the 1970s, many analysts forecast a "New World Order" that would replace its bipolar politics with a "multipolar" diplomatic system in which Europe, Asia, the United States, and others competed as equals and shared political power. Some argued that the United States was losing its clear economic and military lead. A devastating embargo by oil-producing nations in 1973–74, America's failed war in Vietnam, and the rapid resurgence of Germany and Japan led to claims that the United States was becoming simply another of the world's industrial nations rather than its dominant power.

What happened instead was quite different. From the late 1980s into the twenty-first century, America's global prospects brightened. Its economy rebounded due to gains in productivity, the emergence of the computer industry, and booms in banking and real estate, while rivals such as Japan and Germany stagnated. A surge of globalization, encouraged by aggressive American free-trade policies, opened overseas markets to American consumer and entertainment products. Critics abroad complained that globalization was a new form of American imperialism that replaced colonial rule with "Coca-colonization." In response, American leaders broadcast an updated version of missionary nationalism. Urging other western nations to cut back on worker benefits and welfare-state commitments to compete effectively on the world market, the United States championed its free-market economy and limited national government as the model for the "fittest" global competitors.

When the Berlin Wall came down in 1989 and the Soviet Union disintegrated two years later, the United States became the world's only superpower. Gradually, the significance of this "unipolar moment," as one newspaper called it, sank in and talk of a multipolar world subsided. Officials in the George H.W. Bush and Bill Clinton administrations reaffirmed America's "world responsibilities" to spread democracy and free-market economics abroad. U.S. presidents shed the post-Vietnam reluctance to deploy U.S. troops on missions to restore order or retaliate against attacks on Americans abroad. President George W. Bush expanded this mission to include "regime change." Bush responded to the terrorist attacks of September 11, 2001 by invading Afghanistan and declaring an unofficial "war on terrorism," then used the crisis as an opportunity to send troops to

Iraq to depose dictator Saddam Hussein. Post-Cold-War talk of "multilateralism" was superseded by the unilateral assertion of American power. Some critics saw economic globalization and America's new go-it-alone foreign policy as twin features of an "American empire" that was comparable to Britain's control over much of the world a century earlier.

TIMELINE

1945–1955	Decolonization spreads through southern Asia and the Middle East
1947	Truman Doctrine declares U.S. Cold War containment policy
1949	North Atlantic Treaty Organization (NATO) formed
	Soviet Union develops atomic bomb
	Communist victory in China led by Mao Zedong
1950–1953	Korean War
1952–1960	Defiance Campaign against South African apartheid
1953–1954	U.S. CIA sponsors coups in Iran and Guatemala
1954	French imperial forces defeated in Vietnam
	Brown v. Board of Education of Topeka attacks segregation in United States
1955–1965	American Civil Rights movement
1960s	Most African colonies gain independence
	International political protests and "counterculture" led by Western youth
1962	Cuban Missile Crisis
1965	Race riots in U.S. North; rise of Black Power movement
	Immigration Act spurs Latin American and Asian migration to United States
1965–1975	American war in Vietnam
1968	Soviets invade Czechoslovakia to restore communist regime
	Student and worker revolt in France topples government
	Martin Luther King, Jr., assassinated
1969–1982	U.S. and European environmental movements evolve into Green political parties

1970s	Era of détente in U.S.-Soviet relations
1973–1974	Arab nations' oil embargo triggers global economic recession
1975	U.S. government permits Indian tribal self-government
	First International Women's Conference held in Mexico City
1979	Soviets invade Afghanistan in attempt to restore communist rule
1980s	Anglo-American politics takes a conservative, free-market turn with Reagan-Thatcher alliance
	AIDS epidemic spreads through Africa, Europe, and the Americas
1989	East German communist regime falls and Berlin Wall is torn down
1991	Breakup of Soviet Union officially ends the Cold War
1995	World Trade Organization formed, sparking debates over globalization
2001	Terrorist attacks destroy NYC World Trade Center and damage U.S. Pentagon
	United States invades Afghanistan to find Al Qaeda terrorists and end Taliban regime
2003	United States invades and occupies Iraq, deposes Saddam Hussein

THE COLD WAR AS IMPERIAL RIVALRY

"Not since Rome and Carthage," declared U.S. Secretary of State Dean Acheson, "has there been such a polarization of power on this earth." In the decade after World War II, the United States and the Soviet Union constructed a bipolar Cold War system that would endure until 1991. On one side stood an American-led cluster of capitalist nations that included western Europe, Japan, and the British Commonwealth; on the other, a Soviet-dominated bloc of communist nations that stretched from East Germany through Russia into China and North Korea. On their periphery, scores of developing nations in Latin America, Africa, the Middle East, and Asia, many of them recently declared independent, beckoned as potential additions to either bloc or as arenas in which they vied for influence. Because it assumed global dimensions and because the contending superpowers possessed nuclear weapons, the Cold War threatened not just world peace but human survival.

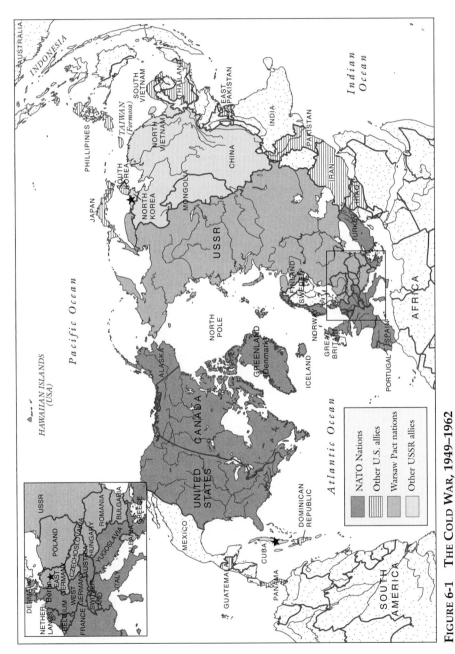

FIGURE 6-1 THE COLD WAR, 1949–1962

Source: Used with permission from Traditions and Encounters (2nd ed.), by Jerry H. Bentley and Herbert F. Ziegler. Copyright 2002 by McGraw-Hill.

THE COLD WAR'S ORIGINS AND EARLY YEARS

UNEASY ALLIES.   The American and Soviet governments had never been friends, beginning with U.S. participation in the 1918 Allied expedition against the Bolshevik regime and continuing through Americans' sluggish response to Soviet pleas for a united stand against German expansion in the 1930s. Although American observers marveled at the rapid pace of Russia's industrialization and Soviet success during the Great Depression, many were appalled when they learned the price: the lives of millions of peasants starved by forced famines and dissenters executed by the Stalinist regime.

Thrust into each other's arms by Germany's declaration of war against both, the United States and Russia were uneasy allies during World War II. Soviet leader Josef Stalin especially resented America's and Britain's delay in invading German-held territory in western Europe. Twenty million Russian soldiers and civilians died repelling Hitler's advance before the western allies launched their invasion of France in June 1944. Mutual mistrust, submerged as the Allies concentrated on defeating Germany and Japan during wartime, resurfaced—despite the pieties voiced at Yalta—as the Allies determined the fate of the postwar world.

SOVIET AND AMERICAN AIMS.   What were Soviet and Western policymakers' aims in the immediate postwar years? Stalin's motives and the ideas of his inner circle were rarely documented and must be deduced from actions. At the core were traditional aims of the Russian empire, which Stalin supplemented with the goals of communist ideology. First, Stalin operated under the imperial concept of spheres of influence. Control of European nations at the Soviets' western border would provide a buffer to protect Russia from another German invasion or other attacks, and— reflecting communist fears—would insulate the Soviets from capitalist influence. Second, like the Russian czars of old, Stalin hoped to exploit Eastern Europe's economic resources and its strategic ports. Finally, although the Soviets were in no position to wage war shortly after World War II, in keeping with Marxist-Leninist doctrine, Stalin expressed interest in spreading communist ideology as far as possible outside Soviet borders and sought to test the West's resolve to stop him.

American motives are less difficult to detect because many documents are available to historians. As the leaders of the Western coalition, the Americans emerged from World War II more convinced than ever that their nation's democratic, capitalist way of life was superior but anxious that it might not prevail. Determined not to repeat the mistake the United States made when it shunned global leadership after World War I, American policymakers sought a decisive role in world affairs. Their agenda had economic, political, and military components that added up to a vision of

American empire. First, through institutions like the International Monetary Fund (established in 1944) and the World Bank (1945), they wanted to knit the world economy into a U.S.-dominated capitalist system that revived prosperity in war-torn Europe and Japan, assured access to markets and raw materials in developing countries, and avoided a replay of the disastrous global depression of the 1930s. Second, they sought to prevent territorial gains for communism in Europe and Asia by supporting anticommunist leaders and initiatives. Finally, they planned to set up a system of military bases around the globe to defend American political and economic interests and deter attacks on the United States and its allies.

Such ambitious and opposed agendas were bound to collide. The two powers' competing designs in Europe were the immediate occasion. As the war ended, the American and British armies occupied France, Italy, and western Germany and remained to supervise postwar reconstruction and the establishment of democratic governments friendly to the West. The Soviets, meanwhile, occupied most of Eastern Europe and were determined to set up new governments that would follow their lead. Between 1945 and 1948, one-party Communist regimes entrenched themselves with Soviet help in East Germany, Bulgaria, Romania, Poland, Hungary, and Czechoslovakia, the last in a blatant coup against an elected government.

THE TRUMAN DOCTRINE AND CONTAINMENT. Although President Roosevelt publicly voiced internationalist ideals, privately he proved flexible, assuring Stalin in 1943 that Russia could be the "policeman" for postwar Eastern Europe. His successor, Harry Truman, took a firmer anti-Soviet stance, due in part to his moralistic temperament, but also as a reaction to the escalating postwar territorial struggle. In 1946 Truman stood by Winston Churchill when the British prime minister declared that an "Iron Curtain" had fallen in Europe, dividing the continent into hostile free and unfree zones. The following year Truman, confronted with a civil war in Greece between the pro-Western government and communist guerrilla forces supported by Yugoslavia's communist regime, declared that the United States would provide aid to any countries threatened by communist takeover through "armed minorities or outside pressures." This Truman Doctrine, an enormous escalation of America's military engagement outside the Western Hemisphere, globalized the American commitment to stop communist expansion. Stalin immediately tested it with an attempt to blockade the Western-occupied sector of Berlin in 1948, which was foiled by a massive Allied airlift.

Truman's "containment" policy also offered economic incentives to allies in the struggle against communism. The European Recovery Program, better known as the Marshall Plan, provided $13 billion for postwar

Europe's reconstruction, which would bolster American markets and ward off the economic instability that bred communist insurgency. The Soviets, interpreting the Marshall Plan as economic imperialism, forbade their Eastern European satellite states from participating and instead formed with them a Council for Mutual Economic Assistance (COME-CON). The same pattern of matched responses held for military alliances. In 1949, the United States and 10 European nations formed the North Atlantic Treaty Organization (NATO), agreeing to merge commands of their armed forces on the continent and to respond together if any member was attacked. This was America's first peacetime military alliance. In short order, the Soviets matched NATO with their own mutual defense agreement with the Eastern European satellites, the Warsaw Pact (1955). In a way that recalled the recent world wars, Europe was again dangerously polarized into hostile alliance systems.

COMMUNIST CHINA.   By 1949 the Cold War had spread to Asia. The civil war in China between Chiang Kai-shek's Nationalists and Mao Zedong's Communists, put on hold during the fight against Japanese occupiers, resumed after World War II. Under Truman, the United States offered limited military assistance to Chiang's regime but refused to make the enormous commitment of troops and aid that might win its survival. Instead, Truman encouraged formation of a coalition government sharing power between the Communists and Nationalists. Pressured by the advancing communist armies, in 1949 Chiang's government fled offshore to Taiwan and Mao proclaimed mainland China a "People's Republic." Truman, stung by charges that the United States had "lost" China to communism, rightly pointed out that the outcome of China's civil war was due to "internal Chinese forces," not the Soviets, who provided little assistance to Mao, or the United States, which had minimal leverage over Chinese events. Nevertheless, Truman emerged from the crisis determined to stop further expansion of communism in Asia.

THE KOREAN WAR.   The President's main opportunity came the next year, when war broke out on the Korean peninsula. The Soviets and Americans had divided it after World War II into separate occupation zones, the North housing a communist regime and the South an anticommunist government. Tensions along the border erupted into combat when North Korean troops, with Stalin's reluctant approval, invaded the south in June 1950. Truman sent American forces to repel the invasion and enlisted support and additional troops from the United Nations. Within months, these combined forces pushed northward across the old border, planning to unify Korea under non-Communist rule. At that point China, fearing the presence of U.S. troops so close to its frontier, intervened on the side of

North Korea to drive the UN troops southward. Eventually both sides bogged down and the United States settled for a literal version of "containment," agreeing in 1953 to a truce that restored the old boundary between North and South Korea. China-U.S. relations deteriorated so badly that the Americans cut off Mao's government from economic assistance and pledged military support to Taiwan if the People's Republic invaded.

AMERICA'S WAR IN VIETNAM.   One Cold War conflict led to another. Alarmed by the Communist takeover in China and hostilities in Korea, Truman decided in 1950 to support France's struggle against an anticolonial movement in southeast Asia, thus opening the long and tragic chapter of America's war in Vietnam. Previously, the United States had pledged to end colonialism in southeast Asia, but when a nationalist coalition led by the communist Ho Chi Minh fought the French to liberate Vietnam, American policymakers changed their minds. The multifaceted Vietnamese revolution, simplified by the polarizing lens of the Cold War, seemed to offer a decisive opportunity for the United States to contain worldwide communism in its Asian sphere. By 1954 the Eisenhower administration was paying most of France's military bills in Vietnam, and after the French withdrew in defeat, the Americans helped install a pro-Western government in the southern half of this divided nation. As civil war continued in Vietnam, Eisenhower's successors, Presidents Kennedy, Johnson, and Nixon, escalated the conflict into a major test of anticommunist resolve. By the end of 1965, 150,000 American troops were fighting South Vietnamese guerrillas and their North Vietnamese allies, who received some support from China and the Soviet Union. After 1969, when Nixon took office, despite an influx of additional troops and a massive bombing campaign, the Americans lost further ground in their effort to achieve victory for unpopular South Vietnamese military regimes. As U.S. military deaths neared 50,000, the American public turned decisively against the war. Gradually, Nixon withdrew American troops, and in 1975 the South Vietnamese army was overpowered by insurgent and North Vietnamese forces, which established a united Vietnam under the North's communist government. In Vietnam, American Cold War policy ran aground in the nation's longest and least successful war.

THE COLD WAR AS WORLD HISTORY:
DIMENSIONS AND CONSEQUENCES

Who or what was responsible for starting the Cold War and escalating it into a worldwide confrontation? As the conflict continued, Western historians took sides in the Cold War as if they were fighting it. Scholars who accepted the defensive rationale of U.S. policy described containment as a moral and appropriately scaled response to Soviet aggression against free societies in Europe and Asia. On the other hand, "revisionist" critics portrayed the United States as an aggressor whose leaders exaggerated or even provoked the Soviet threat and used their economic and military power to dominate the postwar world. The end of the Cold War with the breakup of the Soviet Union in 1991 made possible interpretations that are less intent on assigning blame, more attentive to both sides of the superpower rivalry (and even to third parties), and more attuned to its larger contexts.

A GREAT-POWER CONFLICT. In retrospect, we can see that the Cold War involved four dimensions of conflict between the Americans and Soviets that reinforced one another and raised the stakes for both parties. First, there was traditional great-power competition. The United States and the Soviet Union operated in a political framework inherited from Europe, which viewed the world as an arena where each nation sought to protect or extend its sway. Both also attempted to fill the power vacuum left by the war's course of destruction through Europe and Asia. As the only great power left standing in Eurasia, Russia seized the opportunity to extend its dominance at its western and eastern borders. Meanwhile, the United States, indisputably the world's premier economic and military force, sought to build a global order that would assure its continued prosperity and security. This included checking Soviet power in Europe and Asia, in part by using traditional balance-of-power tactics. At bottom, the American-Soviet rivalry was a great power conflict that stemmed from their respective geopolitical situations.

AN IMPERIAL RIVALRY. Because this rivalry moved outward to absorb other nations and regions, it involved elements of empire. The Americans and Soviets accused each other of being "imperialist," and in a sense both were right. Each superpower sought to control its regional "front yard" as a sphere of influence: the Americans in the Caribbean and the Soviets in Eastern Europe. Both sought to extend their way of life to lands in Latin America, Asia, and Africa and to develop them as markets and sources of raw materials. The Americans and Soviets established trading systems with subordinate countries, used "carrot and stick" (persuasive and coercive) tactics to extend their alliance systems, and applied pressure on neutral nations to join them. Like previous European imperial powers, they built overseas bases that stationed troops and ships in distant corners of the world. The imperial dimension of the Cold War gave it its global reach.

AN IDEOLOGICAL STRUGGLE. Third, this imperial rivalry was lent heightened intensity because leading figures on both sides defined the clash as a climactic struggle between competing ideological and social systems. Invoking the heritage of exceptionalism, American leaders believed that their way of life was superior and universally applicable, while Soviet leaders confidently preached the universal message of communist revolution. Each nation's spokesmen gave it a messianic role as the standard bearer for capitalist democracy or communism, and both declared that the forces of history and righteousness were on their side.

NUCLEAR CONFRONTATION.   Not since the medieval wars between European Christendom and the Muslim world had there been such an emotionally and ideologically charged clash of empires. While armor, horses, and gunpowder increased the carnage of the Crusades, the invention of nuclear weapons, the fourth and most original dimension of the U.S.-Soviet confrontation, lent the Cold War genuinely apocalyptic possibilities. Before 1949, when the Soviets developed their own atomic bomb, the Americans' nuclear dominance fed their determination to stop the Soviets. After that, the two sides feverishly built missiles and warheads to maintain parity in the arms race, and a precarious "balance of terror" replaced the balance of power that traditionally held empires in check. Outnumbered by Soviet soldiers, NATO forces relied on nuclear missles to deter Soviet invasion of Europe. At other Cold War crisis spots, the Americans and Soviets engaged in "brinksmanship," a tactic favored by President Eisenhower's administration, in which nuclear threats forced the other side to back down. Nuclear weapons threatened to turn each superpower confrontation into a global catastrophe.

Seeing the Cold War as an intense and unstable blend of great power struggle, imperial rivalry, ideological war, and nuclear confrontation helps us to understand several of its features shared by the United States and the Soviet Union, including its inconsistencies.

OVERHEATED RHETORIC.   First, ideological extremism overheated Cold War rhetoric. Leading spokesmen for both sides proclaimed the Cold War a life-and-death struggle between a virtuous and an evil society. Describing the Soviet Union as a "totalitarian" state like Nazi Germany, American policymakers viewed Stalin as another Hitler intent on world conquest. Invoking an analogy with the discredited Munich Pact of 1938, they were determined not to "appease" Stalin by negotiation or compromise. The Soviets, for their part, broadcast the virtues of their system and the evils of decadent capitalism. Holding to the doctrine of implacable hostility between capitalist and communist societies and Lenin's view that capitalist imperialism inevitably produced war, Stalin and his successors insisted that the United States and its allies were preparing to attack the Soviet Union. Such exaggerations raised the stakes of the Cold War rivalry, while dehumanized images of the other side made it possible to consider using nuclear weapons against them.

SIMPLIFYING SIDES.   Second, the ideological polarization of the Cold War distorted the definition of enemies. From the Truman Doctrine onward, American leaders interpreted communism as a monolithic international movement directed by the Soviets. Cold War polemics encouraged crude, broad categorization in which civil wars, leftist electoral victories, nationalist uprisings, and anti-imperialist movements around the world became indistinguishable, and every regional disturbance part of worldwide communist conspiracy. Literally colored by this view, American maps of the world featured growing areas of red, feeding fears that the Soviets sought world conquest or that one communist victory inevitably led to another nearby—the so-called domino theory. The Soviets, too, saw dreaded "capitalist imperialism" lurking everywhere, even after the notoriously paranoid Stalin died in 1953, from efforts of the American Peace Corps in Ethiopia to the household appliances President Nixon and Soviet Premier Nikita Khrushchev argued over during their famous "Kitchen debate" of 1959. The habit of fitting every situation into Cold War polarities led to dangerous American-Soviet confrontations in distant lands not directly related to their ideologies or national interests.

UNWELCOME ALLIES.   Third, although adept at finding enemies, each side found it difficult to establish credible allies. Instead of constructing alliances solely through ideological kinship, American and the Soviet leaders were governed by the old great-power notion that "the enemy of my enemy is my friend." Out of Cold War concerns, the United States supported repressive regimes in Latin America and elsewhere that were anticommunist, only to face popular resentment or lose an ally when such regimes were overthrown. In South Vietnam, American leaders sent 500,000 soldiers to solve the essentially political problem of establishing a friendly regime that the Vietnamese people would support. The Soviets faced a similar problem in Afghanistan when they intervened unsuccessfully in 1979 attempting to protect an unpopular Marxist government faced with an Islamic insurrection.

Unable to rely on ideological attraction, both the Americans and Soviets resorted to force to maintain their imperial blocs. U.S. actions were often secret, but not always: in Iran (1953), Guatemala (1954), and Chile (1973), the U.S government covertly engineered military coups; in Nicaragua (1979–1987) it supplied military aid to antigovernment guerrillas, and in Grenada (1983) it sent troops to restore an anticommunist government. The Soviets were more direct when the Eastern European satellite nations proved unwilling allies. Popular uprisings in Hungary (1956) and Czechoslovakia (1968) were suppressed by Soviet invasions, but those of the late 1980s culminated in a massive Eastern European defection from the Soviet bloc. Much like European imperialist powers in postwar Asia and Africa, the American and Soviet Cold War empires faced rebellions by dependent peoples against their control.

CRACKS IN COLD WAR ALLIANCES. Fourth, the bilateral focus of the Cold War acted as a blinder that prevented the superpowers from addressing their allies' concerns, keeping important nations neutral, or exploiting their enemy's divisions. When France's president Charles de Gaulle chafed under U.S. domination and sought to establish French-led Europe as an independent force in Cold War politics, the Americans lost a NATO ally rather than make concessions. The Soviets faced a similar challenge from Yugoslavia's Marshal Tito, whom Stalin expelled from the Soviet bloc in 1948. Other splits occurred with nonaligned nations. Like the infant United States of 1800 caught in the crossfire between France and England, third world countries faced strong pressures to abandon neutrality during the Cold War. America's insistence that neutral nations such as Egypt and India take clear sides in the Cold War soured relations and helped to drive them toward the Soviet camp.

In the case of China, because American leaders considered it firmly in the Soviet fold and even more committed than Russia to spreading communism internationally, they underestimated the rift between the Soviets and the Chinese that emerged in the early 1960s. They failed to exploit it for more than a decade. Chinese-Soviet territorial disputes and China's discontent with Russia's meager economic aid eventually led its leaders to consider resuming trade and diplomatic relations with the West.

WOOING THE "THIRD WORLD." A fifth source of Cold War tension was the two superpowers' stance toward new nations emerging from the wave of decolonization that followed World War II. In the immediate postwar period, financial bankruptcy and nationalist rebellions forced European imperial nations to set their colonies free. Within five years following the war, Britain relinquished control of India, Pakistan, Burma, and Ceylon (Sri Lanka), and the Dutch gave up Indonesia. In the Middle East, Egypt, Lebanon, Syria, Israel and Jordan gained full independence in the postwar decade, and most of Africa broke free from colonial rule in the 1960s.

The breakup of Europe's colonial empires occurred simultaneously with the Cold War and became entwined with it. Ideologically, the two superpowers were dedicated to overthrowing empires, the United States through its principles of national self-determination and the U.S.S.R. through Marxist-Leninist opposition to imperialism. Yet both nations tended to view nationalist movements through the prism of the Cold War. Dozens of new nations provided opportunities to gain new allies who could provide military bases, resources, or votes in the United Nations.

Confronted with demands that they choose sides, some emerging nations did, others remained nonaligned or played the Americans and Soviets off against one another, and still others became unwilling "hot spots" where local forces or movements armed and financed by the superpowers contended for control.

The Soviets quickly gained influence among Asian, African, and Latin American new nations and liberation movements. Marxist-Leninist ideology encouraged third-world peoples to blame their economic woes on capitalist exploitation, while the Soviets' command economy offered a way to control rapid modernization. Cuba, led by Fidel Castro after a socialist revolution overthrew a U.S.-backed dictatorship in 1959, became an economic dependent and firm ally of the Soviet Union. But Cold War geopolitics forced the Soviets to withhold their support for third world revolutions when they threatened Soviet interests in Asia or Africa or led to direct confrontation with the United States. Forced to choose between protection of Cuba and nuclear war with the United States, Soviet Premier Nikita Khrushchev sought accommodation with U.S. President John F. Kennedy in the Cuban Missile Crisis of 1962.

The United States had a harder time than the Soviets in the third world. The Americans channeled propaganda, foreign aid, and development projects toward emergent nations, but their government's hostility toward revolution hindered its quest for influence. From its revolutionary origins the United States had developed into an established great power intent on preserving stability and protecting its investments and military bases. When the Soviets promoted national liberation movements abroad, Cold War considerations impelled the Americans to oppose them. America's war in Vietnam forcefully demonstrated its willingness to subordinate its traditional anticolonial stance to the polarized great-power politics of the Cold War.

IMPERIAL OVERREACH.   Finally, as the Cold War dragged on, its protagonists confronted the classic problem of imperial "overreach." Like ancient Rome or late nineteenth-century Britain, the American and Soviet empires approached the point where global military commitments outran economic resources. The nuclear arms race, escalated as a way to maintain "mutually assured destruction," drained funds from their domestic economies, straining their ability to provide jobs and social welfare at home. In Vietnam and Afghanistan, the U.S. and U.S.S.R. proved unable to win protracted, unconventional wars against third-world nationalist movements. Meanwhile, both superpowers saw their economic standing threatened by the resurgence of postwar Japan and Germany, national economies that were less geared to military production and able to profit from U.S. Cold War aid.

EVALUATING THE COLD WAR

A NEEDLESS WAR?   Where, then, does a world-history approach that aims to be more objective and balanced than nationalistic accounts leave us in evaluating the Cold War? Do both sides' inflated rhetoric and ideological distortions mean that the Cold War was irrational, avoidable, or somehow unreal? By no means. The United States and the Soviet Union were separated by sharply contrasting political and economic systems with conflicting agendas. In the context of a postwar power vacuum in Europe and the end of European empires elsewhere, these differences made some kind of superpower confrontation inevitable. Although mistakes and misunderstandings exacerbated tensions, the Cold War's conflicts were real and resistant to compromise. Of course, both sides could have done much more to defuse tensions, to work out solutions to specific problems, and to use diplomatic rather than military approaches. The fact that negotiated coexistence, not deadly wars or costly military buildups, eventually demonstrated which side's way of life was more viable suggests that it should have been tried sooner.

EMPIRE BY IMPOSITION OR INVITATION?   Do the Americans' and Soviets' parallel moves mean that there was no moral difference between superpower empires? Ultimately, readers must judge for themselves the moral dimension of American and Soviet policies. Focusing on superpower actions abroad, historian John Lewis Gaddis has contrasted the American and Soviet Cold War empires in moral terms. Gaddis contends that American dominance in Europe arose not from coercion, but because western Europeans wanted the United States to provide a military shield against the Soviets and a postwar economic boost. Although Americans expected predominant influence in the postwar world, they sought to establish independent, democratic governments capable of full membership in the capitalist world economy, not colonies or puppet states. By contrast, says Gaddis, the Soviets promoted a blatant, formal, and violent imperial expansion. In Eastern Europe, as in the ethnic Soviet republics, Stalin and his successors set up satellite states under absolute Soviet control that abolished representative government, disregarded human rights, and allowed no deviation from Soviet dictates. In short, Gaddis writes, the American empire was limited in scope and undertaken "by invitation," the Soviet empire unlimited and run "by imposition."[1]

   This interpretation, which is rooted in the contrast between containment and expansion and between democracy and dictatorship, fits best

---

[1]John Lewis Gaddis, *We Now Know: Rethinking Cold War History* (New York: Oxford University Press, 1997), 52.

with America's Cold War practices in Europe. It applies also to Japan, where American occupation gave way to an independent government, but less so to South Korea, whose regime took much longer to democratize and where the United States held to its containment policy only when forced to by Chinese military intervention.

In Latin America and southeast Asia, the contrast between an American "empire by invitation" and a Soviet "empire by imposition" is less clear. Although the United States took no colonies in Latin America after World War II, American policing of the region bears resemblance to Soviet domination of its empire. Through official government embargoes and covert CIA operations, the United States intervened during the Cold War to topple governments in Guatemala, Chile, Nicaragua, and Grenada, and it sponsored assassination plots against Castro in Cuba. None of these actions was invited, and none of these countries was under Soviet coercion. In 1955 the United States encouraged the South Vietnamese government to cancel free elections that had been arranged by international treaty because the result would have been a communist victory under Ho Chi Minh. Instead, American leaders backed an unrepresentative regime by force, only to withdraw in defeat two decades later and watch Vietnam become unified under Ho's communist party. In Africa and elsewhere in the third world, the United States sometimes advocated peaceful negotiations in response to anticolonial wars or leftist uprisings. More typically, American support bolstered anticommunist dictators such as Joseph Mobutu in Zaire or the racist apartheid regime in South Africa, ignoring the principles of democracy and national self-determination. In sum, although America's Cold War policies in Europe were decidedly less aggressive and undemocratic than the Soviets', outside of Europe the superpower rivalry led American policymakers to compromise and even contradict their ideals.

THE COLD WAR ENDS

By the mid-1960s it seemed that the most dangerous phase of Cold War polarization had passed. The Cuban missile scare led the Americans and Soviets to negotiate a nuclear test ban in 1963. The growing rift between the Chinese and Soviets dissolved the specter of monolithic world communism and opened possibilities for diplomatic maneuvering. America's war in Vietnam paradoxically spurred U.S. policymakers to improve relations with the Soviet Union and China to avoid escalating or prolonging hostilities. In the early 1970s, an easing of tensions between the two superpowers—labeled détente—resulted in increased U.S.-Soviet trade and a new arms-limitation agreement.

Yet for another decade and a half, the Cold War continued its roller-coaster course, egged on by several factors: new crises in the Middle East and the third world, the Soviet invasion of Afghanistan in 1979, and the heightened anti-Soviet rhetoric of President Jimmy Carter, who condemned Russia's human rights abuses, and of President Ronald Reagan, who called the Soviet Union an "evil empire."

Then, quite suddenly and unexpectedly, the Cold War ended in the late 1980s, beginning with nonviolent popular uprisings against Eastern European regimes in the Soviet bloc, then culminating in the disintegration of the Soviet Union itself in 1991. Why did a half-century of imperial rivalry end so abruptly?

SOVIET WEAKNESS.   The main answer could be found in the economic weakness and inner turmoil of the Soviet Union. Obsolete factories and unproductive state farms led to chronic shortages of food and consumer goods, while the arms race and the war in Afghanistan drained resources and fueled discontent. Images from Western television, increasingly accessible behind the Iron Curtain, showed a free and prosperous West whose computer technology and global penetration were leaving the Soviets far behind. Mikhail Gorbachev, the new Soviet leader in 1985, believed that its system required drastic reform to be saved. His policies of *glasnost* (political openness) and *perestroika* (economic restructuring) began a shift away from dictatorial communist rule and central state planning. They also signaled the Soviets' unilateral withdrawal from the Cold War.

Events quickly moved beyond Gorbachev's control. After it became clear that the Soviets no longer had the will or the means to intervene in Eastern Europe, popular uprisings in Poland, Bulgaria, Hungary, and Czechoslovakia swept communist regimes out of office. In the most dramatic of these nonviolent revolutions, East German crowds forced open the Berlin Wall that divided them from the West and proceeded in the final weeks of 1989 to tear it down. Inspired by events in Eastern Europe, the Baltic republics of Lithuania, Latvia, and Estonia seceded from the Soviet Union in 1990 and were followed by Ukraine, Belarus, and several central Asian republics the following year. When Gorbachev ceded leadership to anti-Communist Party leader Boris Yeltsin in 1991, the Soviet Union was replaced by a smaller, weaker, and noncommunist Russian Federation. Not only had the Cold War ended, the Soviet Union itself no longer existed.

AMERICAN RESPONSIBILITY?   The issue of American responsibility for the Soviet collapse is likely to remain controversial among historians. Some believe that Reagan's hard line, especially his resumption of the arms race, exhausted the Soviets' resources. Others claim that Reagan's more conciliatory second-term gestures encouraged Gorbachev's reforms. If it is true that the persistent pressure of the arms race and the Americans' containment policy wore down the Soviets, then nine American Cold War presidents, from Truman through George H.W. Bush, share the credit. In the final analysis, however, military standoffs and arms races proved marginal to the Cold War's outcome. Despite both sides' imperial ambitions and military quagmires, the Cold War boiled down to the issue of how well capitalist and communist systems performed *inside* the superpower nations and their closest allies. In the end, the Soviet system proved unable to keep up with the capitalist West and unable to cope with its own citizens' demands for political freedom and a better quality of life.

THE PRICE OF VICTORY.   Americans could be thankful that their nation survived the Cold War rivalry and that it ended without destroying the world. Although some pundits celebrated an unequivocal U.S. victory, many Americans realized that the prolonged conflict had exacted a heavy toll in resources and lives. At home, Cold War paranoia gave rise to a second Red Scare that reached wider and lasted longer than its predecessor following World War I. Under federal and state loyalty programs and during congressional investigations headed by Senator Joseph McCarthy and others, thousands of people lost their jobs on the basis of flimsy accusations that they had once been communists or communist sympathizers. No other ally of the United States suffered such corrosive "witch hunts," censorship, and suppression of dissent. Meanwhile, the Cold War's enormous costs sapped funds from welfare-state programs and diverted government support for research and development into military applications. As a result, America's global economic preeminence was challenged by rapid technological advances in Japan and Germany—nations with only a small percentage of their income spent on military operations—and by China's entry into the capitalist world market.

Beyond U.S. borders, the Cold War damaged American relations with several Latin American countries, India, and much of Africa and the Middle East. Misguided alliances with anticommunist dictators blocked economic and political reforms in the developing world. The collapse of the communist alternative did not mean that history had "ended" with the triumph of democratic and capitalist values, as some pundits declared. More realistic observers pointed to surviving authoritarian governments, rising anti-Western sentiments, and growing economic inequality between rich and poor nations as potential challenges to those values. Others worried that the Cold War habit of posing simplistic contrasts between good and evil and its militarization of international disputes would persist into the post-Cold War world.

Dangerous and costly as it was, the Cold War had ordered international relations for almost half a century and shaped Americans' views of themselves and their place in the world. What "new world order" would replace it, and what role the United States would play in that order, became central questions for Americans facing the globalized environment of the twenty-first century.

POSTWAR AMERICAN MOVEMENTS IN A GLOBAL SETTING

As the Cold War began to thaw, its chilling atmosphere of political and social conformity dissipated, opening space in the West for dissenting ideas and more relaxed social norms. In the 1960s, several trends that had been building in Western nations exploded into protest and social movements that changed the face of America. The postwar economic boom spurred "revolutions of rising expectations" among groups previously left on society's margins. Black Americans renewed their agitation for legal equality with a movement that provided the model for other groups. Throughout the West, married women entered the paid workforce at record rates. Their growing purchasing power, despite workplace discrimination, laid the groundwork for a resurgence of equal-rights feminism after a hiatus that had followed winning the vote in the interwar years. Among the restless "children of prosperity," a youthful rebellion arose simultaneously in Western nations and offered new music, dress, drugs, and codes of sexual behavior. Finally, surging economies in Europe and the United States attracted new waves of immigrants from around the world who were eager to fill the need for cheap, unskilled labor in fields and factories. As African Americans, women, and the new global immigrants asserted their rights and fought for recognition of their distinctive identities, they transformed the makeup and definition of America's melting-pot society.

INTERNATIONAL IDEOLOGIES.   International events also contributed to the social revolutions of the 1960s. In Europe and the United States, the Cold War's turn toward "peaceful coexistence" opened the way for young people to question their parents' rigid anticommunism. The American war in Vietnam bred protests around the world that became incubators for Marxist organizations and national liberationist causes. Decolonization movements in postwar Asia and Africa adopted revolutionary ideologies that inspired groups who experienced oppression or "internal colonization" in Western nations. In the United States, the civil rights and women's movements went through phases that reflected progressive radicalization, culminating in ideologies of autonomy or revolution that challenged basic cultural and political norms. This "international turn" in movement ideologies brought important new ideas to America but also limited these movements' domestic appeal and elicited opposition from the cultural mainstream.

NEW TRANSNATIONAL IDENTITIES.   These social movements, especially the new migration and the youthful counterculture, were spread by stepped-up global trade and communication. Globalization—the worldwide exchange of peoples, goods, and ideas—revived dramatically in the postwar years after the interruptions of the Depression and World War II. The United States was a major hub. New streams of migrants sought jobs in the United States at the same time that America's cultural trends followed its products into Western markets. American social movements also traveled on a two-way street. Black Power activists, discovering similarities between their oppression and European colonialism in Africa, drew inspiration from third-world liberation movements, while European feminists and rebellious students took their cues from American counterparts. Movements based on transnational solidarities of race and gender or internationalist ideologies like Marxism addressed local conditions and problems even as their members retained wider allegiances or followed events elsewhere. As a result, many Americans developed dual identities that balanced their membership in transnational groups, from the African diaspora to global feminist or environmentalist organizations, with citizenship in the United States. As globalization proceeded, more and more people around the world coped with the enlarged scale of their existence by adopting a similar strategy.

BLACK ACTIVISM IN AN INTERNATIONAL CONTEXT

Post-emancipation struggles for racial quality in the United States, as in other New World nations, continued well into the twentieth century. Rights movements sustained by the descendents of slaves in their adopted lands, together with African peoples' own resistance to European control of their homelands, provided the international context for American black activism in the twentieth century. Both struggles underlay the claim by the American black intellectual W.E.B. DuBois that the fight against American racism was only "a local phase of a world problem."

PAN-AFRICANISM.   The roots of the American struggle derived from two branches of protest—one separatist, the other integrationist. Pan-Africanism, preached by Jamaican-born Marcus Garvey in the 1920s and DuBois after World War II, linked black liberation to anticolonial struggles. Both men saw New World blacks as part of an African diaspora, begun by the slave trade, that scattered Africans along the shores of the

Atlantic and Indian Oceans. Pan-Africanism asserted the unity of blacks inside and outside Africa. Its spokesmen instilled pride in African origins, urged followers to help restore Africa to native rule, and promoted programs of black self-help worldwide. In the postwar years, DuBois joined the cause of third-world liberation and eventually relocated to Africa, while Garvey's vision of economic self-sufficiency and racial pride inspired militant African American spokesmen such as Malcolm X.

ORIGINS OF THE CIVIL RIGHTS MOVEMENT.   Pan-Africanism was a minority voice among America's black minority. In the immediate aftermath of World War II, the dominant form of black activism was integrationist, built upon prewar struggles against the South's segregationist regime. A surge of black migration to the North and West during the war brought economic gains that raised the expectations of American blacks. Membership in the National Association for the Advancement of Colored People (NAACP) increased tenfold, setting the stage for lawsuits challenging Jim Crow laws. In 1954 the NAACP scored a spectacular triumph when the Supreme Court ruled in *Brown v. Board of Education of Topeka* that racial segregation in public schools was unconstitutional.

THE COLD WAR AND CIVIL RIGHTS.   Supporting the *Brown* decision, the U.S. attorney general placed racial discrimination "in the context of the present world struggle between freedom and tyranny." Although civil rights activism was sometimes smeared as a communist conspiracy, the cause gained ground in part because America's "race problem" was a major embarrassment to the nation in its Cold War rivalry with the Soviet Union. Racial segregation damaged diplomatic relations with India and several African nations, and it thwarted U.S. efforts to win allies in the third world. Although some American politicians feared that advocating racial equality would divide white supporters, Cold War considerations pushed American presidents and policymakers to live up to their advertising as exemplars of the Free World.

KING AND GANDHI.   The Brown decision energized black college students and church members to press for desegregated facilities everywhere. In 1955 a successful boycott of segregated buses in Montgomery, Alabama, brought the charismatic black minister Martin Luther King, Jr., to prominence. International influences helped to shape King's views. In divinity school, King had absorbed the strategy of militant nonviolence from the Indian nationalist Mahatma Gandhi, who had successfully advocated passive resistance against British colonial rule on the subcontinent. Working through Southern black churches in local desegregation struggles, King fused Gandhi's philosophy with traditional African American promises of Christian deliverance to inspire a powerful mass movement. In the decade after the Montgomery boycott, King and other civil rights leaders organized a series of protests, marches, and boycotts that culminated in a massive voting rights march on Selma, Alabama.

COMBATING APARTHEID IN SOUTH AFRICA.   Another international influence on King came from protests against the racially separatist apartheid regime in South Africa. Gandhi had begun his career by mobilizing South Africa's Indian minority in a nonviolent campaign for citizenship rights prior to World War I. Black leaders of the Defiance Campaign of 1952–1960, which protested the apartheid government's racially segregated townships and pass system, learned Gandhian techniques from veterans of earlier Indian struggles. King kept informed about the South African freedom struggle and sought to align the American movement with it. In 1964 he called for international economic sanctions as a peaceful tactic to weaken the South African government. Twenty-five years later, long after King's death, the combination of massive nonviolent protests—inspired by King's success in Alabama—and international pressure brought democracy to South Africa. Historian George Fredrickson has described the successful anti-apartheid movement as "Birmingham and Selma on a world scale."[2]

CIVIL RIGHTS AND AMERICAN IDEALS.   For all these foreign connections, the most powerful strategy of King and civil rights activists in the campaigns of 1955–65 was their invocation of America's national ideals. Black and white protesters cited the legacy of Reconstruction, praised American principles of equal treatment, and demanded that the government live up to them. King's speech before 250,000 supporters at the Lincoln Memorial in August 1963 prophesied a time when the emancipation proclaimed by Lincoln would be fully realized. Among peoples of the African diaspora, American blacks stood out for their strong identification with national values and their enduring faith in inclusion.

FROM CIVIL RIGHTS TO BLACK POWER.   The Civil Rights movement culminated in a federal law of 1964 outlawing discrimination in employment and another of 1965 guaranteeing the right to vote. Even as blacks celebrated these victories, many younger African Americans were turning against nonviolence and integrationist reform. Provisions for legal equality did not adequately address enduring social and economic inequalities.

[2]George M. Fredrickson, "Non-violent Resistance to White Supremacy: A Comparison of the American Civil Rights Movement and the South African Defiance Campaigns of the 1950s," in *The Making of Martin Luther King and the Civil Rights Movement*, eds. Brian Ward and Tony Badger (New York: NYU Press, 1996), 226.

Frustrated by the lack of jobs in urban ghettoes, young protesters lashed out in dozens of riots between 1965 and 1970. A new generation of leaders emerged to dispute King's moderate program and to assert "Black Power" by rejecting alliances with white liberals and taking control of their own institutions. Malcolm X became the chief spokesman for the Black Muslims (officially called the Nation of Islam), a group that tolerated violence in self-defense but emphasized black self-discipline and self-sufficiency. Young blacks' interest in African religions and international ideologies escalated as their impatience mounted with the civil rights agenda. The Black Panthers, formed in Oakland, California in 1966, merged black separatism with a program inspired by third-world revolutionaries. Their manifestoes expressed solidarity with anticolonial movements world-wide and called for reparations and territorial autonomy for American blacks. Their local legacy, however, like Marcus Garvey's, emphasized black self-help through community organizing and assistance.

Black Power political movements were plagued by violence inside and out. Malcolm X, who had moved toward multiracial tolerance after a trip to Mecca, was assassinated by rival Black Muslims in 1965, and several Black Panther leaders were killed in police raids. Hundreds of blacks died in street battles with police during summer riots in the mid-1960s. Martin Luther King, Jr., who had evolved toward stronger anticapitalist and anticolonial positions, was murdered by a white racist in 1968, touching off riots in several cities. Terrified by violence, wary of radical programs, and fearing economic recession in the 1970s, the American public turned against militant blacks, and their movement declined.

In the following years, the NAACP and other mainstream advocacy organizations continued to press for black economic and legal gains. Without rejecting this approach, many African Americans evolved Black Power into a cultural movement focused on racial pride and preservation of a distinctive group identity. Proclaiming that "black is beautiful," young people grew "Afros" instead of adopting white styles. Black Studies professors offered courses on African American society and emphasized Africa's rich history and its contribution to other civilizations. Rejecting the universalist claims of human sameness that underlay the Civil Rights movement, African Americans forged an "identity politics" and a program of cultural nationalism that became the model for other racial and ethnic minority groups.

AMERICAN BLACKS' "INTERNAL COLONIALISM." Many proponents of black cultural identity expressed solidarity with African people world-wide, based on the theory that American blacks (like others in the African diaspora) experienced a form of colonialism inside the imperial nation that is substantially similar to the position of African peoples who were conquered and ruled by Europeans. The "internal colonialism" analogy is useful in several ways. It spotlights historical differences between descendants of slaves—forced migrants—and voluntary immigrants to America. It brings forward the distinctive pattern of discrimination and exclusion from civic rights that racial groups have experienced in America. It reminds us that white racial domination in the United States is part of a world historical pattern that emerged wherever Europeans asserted control over non-Western people of color. For African Americans, cultural nationalism may also offer a transnational identity that fosters pride in African ancestry, continuing involvement with Africa, and interchanges with groups throughout the black diaspora.

Still, although American blacks did not fit the immigrant model, they were not a conquered indigenous people. Like others in the African diaspora, American blacks have been shaped by long experience in a society far from their ancestral land. As was noted in Chapter 2, as early as the 1700s a distinctive African American culture emerged as a blend of American and African heritages that includes Christianity, black English, and African folkways. After three centuries, American blacks' daily lives and aspirations are oriented to the United States even as they look and travel elsewhere. For all but a few, self-determination does not mean going "back to Africa" (as Marcus Garvey advocated) or a nationalist program of territorial rights inside U.S. borders. Instead, African Americans have sought equal treatment and open access to economic advancement while preserving their distinctive culture.

At the opening of the twenty-first century, many American blacks take pride simultaneously in their identity with an African diaspora *and* in American citizenship. The label "African American" asserts this dual identity, whose emphasis varies depending on which word one emphasizes. African American history may provide a model for the coexistence of dual national and transnational identities among American minorities in a global era.

THE CHICANO MOVEMENT AND NATIVE AMERICAN ACTIVISM AS ANTICOLONIALISM

MEXICAN AMERICANS AND COLONIALISM. Like African Americans, Mexican Americans fit partially into a colonial model, but in a different way. Their ancestors in the U.S. Southwest were indeed a conquered people whose lands were acquired in the Mexican-American War of 1846–48. Yet the vast majority of Mexican Americans came afterward to the United States as immigrants. Two other factors complicate their history, placing their experience somewhere between that of black ex-slaves and European immigrants. First, Americans traditionally relied upon Mexican peasants as cheap, temporary laborers, a relationship that was embodied formally in government-sponsored "guest worker" programs during the two world wars. Second, American racial categories placed "brown" Mexicans between blacks and whites, an indistinct location that often encouraged discriminatory racial treatment like that given blacks and Asians, but in other situations did not. Mexican Americans had to forge their identities and lives amid the ambiguities of their own brand of "internal colonialism."

THE CHICANO MOVEMENT. Not surprisingly, the course of Mexican American activism in the 1960s built upon the black civil rights movement and reflected its split into integrationist and separatist elements. Like the NAACP, the Mexican-American Political Association worked to remove legal discrimination and to elect Latino public officials. Rural migrant workers were organized by Cesar Chavez into the United Farm Workers, a union that affiliated with the mainstream AFL-CIO. At the same time, younger Mexican Americans began to pursue more radical goals. A rural alliance in New Mexico called for the return of lands taken from *hispano* villagers by the United States in violation of the 1848 treaty. From *barrios* (urban ghettoes) in Los Angeles and elsewhere came Brown Berets, militant young men who modeled themselves on the Black Panthers. Converging upon Denver in 1969, student activists adopted a new term, "Chicano," to replace the assimilationist "Mexican American." They called for the independence of "La Raza" (from "La Raza de Bronze," the brown people), pursued a cultural nationalist agenda that included bilingual education and Chicano studies programs, and organized an ethnically based political party, La Raza Unida, that won several local elections in southwestern states.

Many older and middle-class Mexican Americans shied away from the label "Chicano" and the cultural nationalism it implied. The Chicano movement, like the Black Power movement that inspired it, swung the pendulum from assimilation toward a separatism that ignored the hybrid culture and ambivalent position of most American minorities. Still, the movement brought benefits. It instilled pride among Mexican Americans and drew respect from Anglos for their culture and language. It challenged discrimination in several locales and began a political mobilization that broadened over the next decades as the Mexican American population grew and allied with millions of newcomers from Central America and the Caribbean under the "Latino" label.

NATIVE AMERICAN ANTICOLONIALISM. The one domestic people who were indisputably American colonial subjects were Native Americans, whom the national government had confined to reservations in the second half of the nineteenth century. While tribal communities were segregated from American society, government programs aimed to detribalize them and assimilate them individually to the ways of white society. The allotment of 160 acres to individual families beginning in 1887, the use of boarding schools to promote Christianity and the English language, and twentieth-century urban relocation programs for young Indians stripped many Indians of their land and cultural heritage without substituting a satisfying new identity or offering economic survival.

In the late 1960s, young Native American activists inspired by black and Chicano cultural nationalism challenged accommodationist tribal leaders and renewed the struggle against national authorities for land and autonomy. Their movement was perhaps the most direct analogue to decolonization movements abroad, although there were few direct ties. In 1969 young urban Indians representing 50 tribes occupied Alcatraz Island in San Francisco Bay for a year and a half, demanding that the land be returned to natives for an Indian cultural center. Although they did not achieve their goal, they sparked a pan-Indian protest struggle called the American Indian Movement, whose members proceeded to occupy other symbolic sites: a Bureau of Indian Affairs office in Washington, D.C., in 1972, and the next year a trading post at Wounded Knee, South Dakota, the site of an infamous massacre of Sioux families by U.S. soldiers in 1890.

While radical activists publicized "Red Power," individual tribes sued state and national authorities for the return of lost lands and won ownership of millions of acres of land in Maine, New Mexico, South Dakota, and Washington State. Meanwhile, moderate activists working through pan-Indian lobbying groups pressured Congress for expanded resources and rights of self-government. A landmark congressional report on Indian education issued in 1969 finally repudiated the government's policy of detribalizing and assimilating Indians, and in 1975, the Indian Self-Determination and Education Assistance Act allowed tribes to govern themselves and control their own schools. Despite these gains, conditions among tribal communities remained difficult, with high rates of disease, alcoholism, suicide, and joblessness. Patterns of dependence and corruption inherited from a century of government control over reservations retarded progress toward Indian autonomy, while arid Indian lands offered few viable ways to make a living. In desperation, many tribes attempted to exploit mineral rights or to open gambling casinos. These ventures conflicted with traditional Native American practices but promised, according to proponents, to create jobs and raise funds for improved housing and schools. At the outset of the twenty-first century, the rapid proliferation of Indian casinos formed a sadly ironic sequel to a century of "internal colonialism" and two decades of anti-colonial protests.

THE COUNTERCULTURE AND INTERNATIONAL STUDENT ACTIVISM

THE COUNTERCULTURE AND NEW LEFT. The Civil Rights and Black/Chicano/Indian Power movements signaled that American society was undergoing a profound upheaval in the 1960s. Fast on their heels came a general revolt of young Americans against the constricted politics and conformist lifestyles that had dominated Cold War American culture. Evidence of an emerging "counterculture" could be found in the fashion trend of blue jeans and long hair, the omnipresence of rock music, the loosening of sexual mores, and the spread of drugs like marijuana and LSD. Young "hippies" alienated from their parents' culture "dropped out" to live in enclaves like New York's East Village and San Francisco's Haight-Ashbury or to join one of more than 3,000 communes calling the disaffected "back to the land." Even before the counterculture flourished, a more political brand of radicalism took root on college campuses. Students inspired by the crusade for civil rights formed a mass political movement called the "New Left" that criticized control of government by the "military-industrial complex" and protested undemocratic conditions on campus. Over the course of the decade, the New Left's most prominent organization, the SDS (Students for a Democratic Society) was radicalized by the example of Black Power advocates and third-world revolutionaries, and especially by the escalating and unpopular war in Vietnam.

INTERNATIONAL PROTESTS. The youth culture and student protests of the 1960s were not just American phenomena. As children of the post-World War II "baby boom" came of age in the industrialized West, they formed an age cohort that sought higher education in unprecedented numbers, dominated the dress and music industries, and broke away from parental strictures. Young people throughout Europe (and in Japan and Latin America) played rock music, experimented with drugs, protested imperialist wars, and talked of revolution. In the early and mid-1960s, Japanese students opposed to nuclear weapons toppled the ruling government, French students demanded a voice in university affairs and marched against the Algerian War, English protesters campaigned for nuclear disarmament, and German and Italian students marched for educational reforms.

On both sides of the Atlantic, 1968 was a climactic year for the New Left. Young protesters took demands for revolutionary change to the streets and were often met with violence. Czech students defended the liberal regime of President Alexander Dubcek when the Soviet army invaded to suppress democracy. Mexican and Italian students staged strikes and battled police. German student leader Rudi Dutschke was shot by a would-be assassin, touching off violent demonstrations there and abroad. The most important European outbreak was the French student-worker revolt of May 1968, which brought the country to a standstill and eventually deposed the aging president, Charles de Gaulle. In the United States, at the end of a strife-torn presidential primary season that had featured victories by antiwar Democrats Eugene McCarthy and Robert Kennedy, hundreds of young protesters clashed with police outside the Democratic National Convention in Chicago. Despite the angry and often violent confrontations, students won enough victories to keep alive the dream of global change, including lowering of the voting age to 18 in the United States and several Western nations.

DECLINE AND LEGACY.   By the 1970s, however, the transatlantic student movement had run its course, dwindling, in many cases, to small revolutionary sects whose advocacy of Marxist doctrines and violence alienated liberals and social democrats. In a larger sense, the New Left was defused by the winding down of the Vietnam War and the onset of worldwide recession, which caused students to scramble for jobs and voters to turn to the Right. But the New Left, and the youth culture that gave rise to it, left indelible marks on society in the United States and abroad. Student activists gained important victories for the Civil Rights movement through Freedom Rides and local protests. Their demonstrations aroused public opposition to the Vietnam War and probably hastened its end. And among the New Left's most influential—and unanticipated—descendants were feminist and environmentalist movements that became powerful forces in the West long after the hopes and fears of 1968 had become history.

THE REVIVAL OF TRANSATLANTIC FEMINISM

Feminism, like youth and race, was a form of identity that transcended national borders even as its primary struggles took place within them. Earlier generations of American women's activists, who agitated for the vote and other reforms in the 1850s and 1910s, inspired their European and especially British counterparts and adopted ideas and tactics from them. Their parallel trajectories became clear when both groups used women's participation in World War I to goad their governments into granting women the right to vote.

Similar parallel trends and influences were at work in the 1960s. As heightened economic expectations led American and European families to have fewer children following the brief post-World War II baby boom, married women increasingly entered the paid workforce. Women's economic and educational gains underlay a new transatlantic feminist surge. Meanwhile, the development of oral contraceptives in the 1960s offered dependable birth control. Middle-class and activist women had been limiting family size in various ways for decades, but with "the pill" sexual intercourse was decisively separated from reproduction. After family planning became reliable, childbearing became a choice and childrearing no longer a lifelong endeavor for women. Careers beckoned, and freer attitudes toward sexual expression were encouraged.

ANGLO-AMERICAN PARALLELS.   In the United States, Betty Friedan's bestselling book, *The Feminine Mystique* (1963) indicted post–World War II American culture for reviving the Victorian cult of female "domesticity" that preached fulfillment through marriage, children, and consumerism. Friedan's book brought to the surface resentment that had been simmering as educated middle-class women felt trapped in suburban homes and others who entered the paid workforce encountered prejudice. The Civil Rights Act of 1964 opened the way for women to file federal complaints against discriminatory practices. The next year, young female activists in the Civil Rights and New Left movements broke with male colleagues and gathered in "consciousness-raising" sessions where they shared stories of oppression and discussed how women's actions could transform sex roles and stereotypes. The groundwork was laid for a movement that would challenge sexual injustice in every arena of public and private life.

Similar changes were at work in Great Britain. Renewed pressure from women within trade unions and the Labor Party led to a law in 1961 decreeing equal pay for men and women in the public service. (Two years later, the U.S. Congress approved a similar law.) By the late 1960s, British feminists, inspired by the American Civil Rights and women's movements, adopted a broad antidiscrimination platform. In 1975 Parliament passed the Sex Discrimination Act, which outlawed unequal treatment in education, advertising, and public facilities. Like the Americans a decade earlier, the British set up an Equal Opportunities Commission to investigate complaints and implement changes.

VARIETIES OF FEMINISM.   As these movements developed in tandem, two branches of feminism evolved. At first, "equal-rights" feminism, a traditional version of women's activism that targeted legal and economic barriers to equality, waged a struggle for equal pay and nondiscrimination. Later, emerging from the New Left, a new radical feminism (sometimes called "women's liberation") preached revolution rather than reform, critiquing conventional notions of womanhood, sexuality, and family life and envisioning wholesale changes.

The transatlantic parallels were striking, despite differences in the two nations' social contexts. British feminists had stronger ties to socialists and labor unions, while American feminists were more apt to indict male "patriarchy" rather than capitalism as the enemy. But both national feminist movements took off in the 1960s and both split into equal-rights and radical factions. Both movements ended up concentrating on legal battles over economic discrimination and abortion rights, the latter granted by a British law in 1967 and an American Supreme Court decision (*Roe v. Wade*) in 1973. In both places, radical feminists' emphasis upon autonomy and their frank acceptance of lesbianism challenged basic cultural and political conventions—a stance that popularized concepts like "sexism" and validated the trend toward looser sexual norms, but also elicited greater opposition from the mainstream.

In the late 1970s, the feminist movement's momentum seemed to wane as the equal rights campaign peaked, anti-abortion movements gained strength, and sexual experimentation alienated moderates. When the world economy slid into recession and the Anglo-American public retreated to conservative views, popular politicians declared that the liberal social changes of the 1960s had gone too far. By the 1990s, some commentators saw a dangerous "backlash" against feminism in court decisions that narrowed abortion rights, television shows that portrayed women as sexual objects, and religious groups that promoted traditional "family values." Nevertheless, in a generation's time the Anglo-American feminist movement had registered impressive gains in women's economic and social status and redefined debates over womanhood, equality, and sexuality.

Western feminism also made global inroads. To be sure, women from developing countries in Asia, Africa, and Latin America concentrated their struggles on combating hunger and disease, gaining access to education, and winning basic legal equalities rather than achieving the second-stage political and professional advances promoted by Western feminists. Yet Western and non-Western feminists have shared common ground when they link women's advancement to international agreements on human rights. A series of International Women's Conferences sponsored by the United Nations beginning in Mexico City in 1975 and continuing in Beijing in 1995 indicated that both the universalizing rhetoric of human rights and specific Western feminist aspirations were reaching women around the world and were mobilizing them to protest oppressive local laws and practices.

GLOBAL IMMIGRATION AND MULTICULTURAL AMERICA

As the 1960s progressed, newcomers to the United States joined the protests by native-born "outsiders." Calls by American blacks and women to end discrimination were followed by demands among Latinos and Asian immigrants for legal and cultural recognition. A stunning rise in immigration to the United States after World War II and a transformation of its sources prompted this new group assertiveness.

RENEWED INTERNATIONAL MIGRATION.   Both were part of worldwide trends. Although birth rates declined in industrialized nations after the 1950s, they remained high in third-world countries, and death rates dropped dramatically due to improved nutrition and medicine, causing a remarkable population explosion. Latin American, Asian, and African societies experienced the same "demographic transition" that had pushed Europeans overseas a century earlier. This population change shifted migration flows. In the nineteenth century, white settlers left the European core for colonial or postcolonial lands on the periphery of the West's economy. After World War II, migrants flowed instead from peripheral developing nations to the core economies of Western capitalism. In both cases the United States was a prime destination, but not the only one.

Thriving "first-world" economies exerted a magnetic pull on third-world peoples. Western Europe and the United States attracted immigrants to fill work needs left unmet by their own aging populations. After 1960, more than 13 million "guest workers" moved to Germany, France, Switzerland, and other western European nations from Italy, the Balkans, Turkey, and North Africa. About the same number of migrants from Mexico, Central America, and the Caribbean entered the United States. Somewhat smaller streams of Asian immigrants flowed from China, India, and southeast Asia to Australia, Canada, and the United States. As in the nineteenth century, a revolution in transportation and communications quickened these movements. Televisions broadcast alluring pictures of the prosperous West, airplane travel made migration faster than ever, and telephones transmitted instant reports from newcomers to relatives back home.

REOPENING THE DOOR.   Liberalized immigration laws reopened America's doors after the harsh restrictions of the 1920s and the bleak job market of the Great Depression. Cold War policies played a part. Special legislation allowed thousands of refugees from communist Cuba and Eastern Europe to enter the United States in the 1950s, and even more who fled the communist takeover in Vietnam in 1975. The 1980 Refugee Act removed refugees from competing for visas with other immigrants. Meanwhile, the

Civil Rights movement directed lawmakers' attention to persisting racial discrimination in immigration policies. In response, the Immigration Act of 1965 abolished the national origins quota system that had been in place (with modifications) since 1924 and replaced it with an individual preference system favoring family reunification and work skills. Later laws steadily raised the 1965 act's numerical ceilings.

THE NEW GLOBAL MIGRANTS.   The result was a dramatic transformation in the scale and sources of immigration to the United States. The annual flow of legal immigrants climbed from less than 100,000 in the 1940s to more than a million in 2000, rivaling the peak years of the 1910s. Perhaps 300,000 migrants also entered the United States illegally each year, the majority from Mexico. The new immigration reversed the earlier pattern of European predominance and replaced it with a global array of provider nations that were overwhelmingly non-European. More than 90 percent of newcomers in 1910 had come from Europe; in 2000, 90 percent came from outside Europe, about two-thirds from Latin America and one-third from Asia.

Global migration made the United States a more diverse nation in appearance, languages, and customs. For Mexican and Caribbean migrants, the movement of peoples was not an overseas journey but a "border migration," in which frequent back-and-forth travel enabled migrants to retain their language and cultural ways. For Asians, jet travel and telephone linkages promoted cultural continuities and ties with the homeland that mimicked the features of border migration and prompted scholars to extend the term "diaspora" to overseas Chinese and Koreans. Like earlier immigrants, these newcomers formed ethnic communities in cities, suburbs, and some rural areas, to which they transplanted their customs and languages. Regional concentration, foreign-language TV broadcasts, and multilingual election booklets made their differences more visible to Euro-Americans than the immigrant ghettoes of a century earlier.

AMERICAN RESPONSES.   Partly for this reason, but also due to the newcomers' non-European origins, their growing numbers, and the rising influx of illegal migrants, the new global immigration revived fears that newcomers would transform American society rather than assimilate into it and that their numbers imposed an economic burden on American citizens. Opposition to immigration surged when the national or regional economy sagged, then ebbed when it recovered, much like a century earlier. Yet the general prevalence of more tolerant attitudes, the enormous cost of border control, and the economic convenience of foreign low-wage labor prevented Americans of the early twenty-first century from enacting restrictive laws like those of the 1920s.

Global immigration challenged the earlier version of the American "melting pot," which was based on confidence in the ultimate fusion of European groups into a new (but still Anglo-dominated) American people. The new groups' racial (Asian) or quasi-racial (Latino) status and their reluctance to sever their cultural roots challenged the host society to expand its inclusiveness. The response was mixed. Asian Americans experienced a dramatic turnaround from decades of exclusion and discrimination. Legislation during World War II had lifted the ban on Chinese American citizenship, and Japanese Americans' wartime loyalty won acceptance from many whites. Postwar Asian migrants were more skilled and educated on average than other newcomers, and the removal of discriminatory barriers quickened their entry into colleges and professions, raising the median incomes of Asian American families higher than those of whites. Immigrants from Latin America were less fortunate. Escaping desperate poverty or political violence, many were unskilled manual laborers who found work in the United States as low-paid urban service workers or migrant agricultural laborers. In the 1970s and 1980s, and again in the early 2000s, Latinos became the main targets of campaigns to close the border against cheap labor, to restrict immigrant access to welfare services, or to curtail bilingual education.

MULTICULTURALISM.   Seeking to extend recent civil rights gains to immigrant and ethnic minorities, liberal activists urged the government to recognize ethnic group identities, to help maintain traditional cultures, and to take "affirmative action" to foster group achievement. By the 1980s this position was called "multiculturalism," a term imported from Canada, where government policies officially recognized group rights for indigenous peoples, British descendants, French Canadians, and later immigrants, guaranteeing their separation. In the United States, however, multiculturalism had limited legal sway. No territorial autonomy, legislative positions, or language rights were accorded ethnic minorities, and while the national government began monitoring the progress of racial and ethnic groups, it largely maintained its historic course of treating citizens individually. The most prevalent form of multiculturalism was a widespread celebration of America's "diversity." It was premised on the confidence that ethnic pluralism would be balanced by the recognition of common American ideals and values.

A GLOBAL MELTING POT.   Scholarly studies of the new global immigrants showed that they followed similar patterns of adjustment and assimilation to those of newcomers a century earlier. Gradually the majority of their children and grandchildren adopted the English language, furthered their education, and moved up the occupational ladder. Immigrant families lowered their fertility rates and intermarried with other ethnic groups the longer they remained in the United States. As had happened with European newcomers, intermarriage, social mobility, and the adoption of English made the melting pot possible.

Yet the melting pot itself was changing. As Asians, Africans, and Latinos entered American society, they diversified the melting pot's ingredients. Popular culture provided an important example. For decades, America's mass entertainment industry had drawn upon the theatrical traditions of white ethnic minorities and the jazz and blues of black musicians, the latter often filtered through white "Big Bands." After World War II this process of cultural absorption broadened to include Asians, Latinos, and increased numbers of African Americans. Latin dancing styles entered the nation's nightclubs, and Latina singers and movie stars "crossed over" to attract national audiences. West Indian and Japanese baseball players rose to stardom in the American major leagues. Black urban ghettoes incubated rhythm and blues, rap, and hip-hop music that were promoted nationwide and captivated white suburban teens. The terms of cultural absorption shifted to give greater influence to nonwhites. Whereas prewar entertainment diluted ethnic cultures to make them bland and broadly acceptable, new forms of mass culture achieved popularity because they were assertively ethnic.

The music industry's crossing of racial and ethnic boundaries symbolized the changed terms of the American melting pot. Thanks to the new global immigration, new words, foods, and religions appeared and became available for other Americans to adopt. As ethnic intermarriage increased, group affiliations became more fluid and hybrid identities were asserted as a point of pride. In 2000, a "multiracial" category was added to existing categories in the U.S. Census, a historic departure from absolute terms of racial categorizing. Behind the rise of multiculturalism was the rejection of the old idea that ethnic groups should eventually disappear. Equally striking, however, was the growing evidence that the new "global melting pot" widened the spectrum of who Americans could be. The postwar global immigrants were changing America at the same time it changed them.

EXPANSION AND DECLINE OF THE WELFARE STATE

The fact that minority, youth, and feminist movements all lost momentum in the 1970s points to an important shift in American public opinion that had counterparts elsewhere. The mounting costs of war in Vietnam, an oil embargo imposed in 1973 by Arab nations in retaliation for U.S. military support for Israel, and lagging American competitiveness led to an economic recession that sent ripple effects abroad. In the United States, Europe, and Latin America, the climate of political opinion swung rightward against the loosened mores and expanded government programs of the 1960s. One threatened casualty of this conservative turn was the welfare state that, as Chapter 4 showed, Western societies had gradually constructed during decades of political debate over the effects of urban industrialism.

POSTWAR TRENDS. The prosperous post-World War II years encouraged welfare-state expansion in Europe. To prevent communist electoral gains and to sustain postwar reconstruction, western Europeans and many of their settler nations extended social-welfare provisions. Leaders in Great Britain, for example, nationalized public transportation and utilities, established a system of national health insurance that affiliated doctors with government hospitals, and started a huge public housing program. The British example was followed in Canada and elsewhere in Europe, where governments took over important industries and set up powerful planning offices.

By contrast, the United States, which had been slower to build a welfare state, took a conservative course. Postwar prosperity eroded support for reform and revived confidence in American business methods. Under the Truman administration progressive Democrats lost control of Congress. Inflamed by the Red Scare, rabid anticommunists targeted social welfare legislation and championed free enterprise as its antidote. Republican President Dwight Eisenhower, who was elected in 1952, grudgingly maintained New Deal protections, but he rejected calls to establish federal housing and medical-care programs or to enact antidiscriminatory civil rights laws.

THE "GREAT SOCIETY" AND ENVIRONMENTALISM. During the upheavals of the 1960s a burst of government activism revived social legislating. This brief but crucial third stage in the development of the American welfare state (after Progressivism and the New Deal) began when the Civil Rights Act of 1964 extended federal protections in employment to blacks and women and mandated government oversight of federal contractors. The momentum continued with President Lyndon Johnson's "Great Society" programs, which created modest housing and food subsidy programs and set up basic medical assistance packages for the elderly (Medicare) and the poor (Medicaid). By the end of the 1960s, a vocal environmental movement emerged from student protests, backed by studies of scientists like Rachel Carson and local conflicts over nuclear power plants and toxic wastes. Citizen pressure led the federal government to create an Environmental Protection Agency in 1970, to establish standards for clean air and water, and to protect endangered species from extinction due to pollution and development. These U.S. achievements helped to spur the Green political movement in Europe, where antinuclear protests of the late 1960s gradually developed into the first Green Party in Germany in 1979. For the first time, American reformers injected a major new item into the modern welfare-state agenda rather than simply borrowing and adapting European ideas. On environmental issues, the United States seemed poised to take the international initiative.

A CONSERVATIVE SHIFT. Just as American social protections reached historic levels, economic and political forces combined to reverse the hundred-year development of welfare states in the West. In the decade after 1973, the Western world confronted its deepest economic recession since World War II, a downturn exacerbated by rising energy costs and continuing Cold War expenditures. This time, unlike the late 1930s, economic woes induced governments to cut expenses rather than incur deficits, partly because Cold War polemics had discredited government-run economies, but also because the dramatic rise of South Korea, Hong Kong, and other surging Asian economies appeared to bolster free-market capitalism as a successful alternative.

A TRANSATLANTIC "REAGAN REVOLUTION."   The public mood in America and Great Britain turned conservative. Republican U.S. electoral victories during the 1980s and 1990s showed that voters welcomed politicians who promised to dismantle "big government" and unfetter regulated capitalism. The "Reagan Revolution," initiated by President Ronald Reagan and continued by the first Bush administration, checked the expanding welfare state and cut expenditures on job programs. At the same time, Britain's Conservatives returned to power under Prime Minister Margaret Thatcher, who led a campaign to reduce government bureaucracy, limit social welfare, and break the power of labor unions. Seeing eye to eye, Reagan and Thatcher formed an alliance that recalled the David Lloyd George-Woodrow Wilson connection of the 1910s, but reversed its direction. The United States, formerly England's pupil in welfare-state measures, now became its mentor in free-market practices.

Led by the United States, there has been a general shift away from the welfare state toward market-oriented approaches since 1980. Intensified global economic competition took manufacturing jobs away from advanced Western industrial societies while their aging populations strained government health and pension systems. Caught in an economic squeeze, western nations reconsidered welfare state expenditures and many slashed them. America's resurgent conservatives considered this a boon. They deregulated sectors of the banking, transportation, and utilities industries, privatized some government services, cut taxes, reduced welfare programs, and pressured America's trading partners through such agencies as the World Bank and International Monetary Fund to take similar measures. European and South American governments followed suit, often reluctantly. Economic integration under the European Union or other regional trade groups, as well as pressures from international financial markets, forced them to reduce worker benefits.

THE SHRINKING WELFARE STATE.   Virtually everywhere, liberals and leftists retreated. Western European and Australian socialist and labor parties renounced nationalization and privatized utilities and telecommunications. The British Labor Party under Prime Minister Tony Blair and the American Democratic Party under President Bill Clinton came to power in the 1990s by advocating a leaner welfare state that concentrated on economic growth rather than social protections. Clinton moved family assistance programs from federal to state control in 1995, replacing welfare with stringent "workfare" requirements. His Republican successor, George W. Bush, preached a "compassionate conservatism" that shifted responsibility for social assistance to private individuals and churches. Conservative electoral victories and liberal and socialist backtracking on the welfare state suggested that Western nations were converging toward the American limited-government model. Some commentators, citing the collapse of communist regimes in the Soviet Union and Eastern Europe, proclaimed the worldwide victory of free-market capitalism.

Although there has been some convergence, in the early twenty-first century the welfare state is hardly dead. Most nations have merely slowed its growth. There remain substantial differences between American and European positions. European welfare states reflect deep-seated public attitudes. Many voters in France, Italy, Holland, and Scandinavia resist the American model of privatization and minimum public assistance. By contrast, Americans' commitment to the welfare state is compromised by their longstanding individualist and antistatist beliefs. Compared to western Europe, Australia, and New Zealand, the United States continues to have a lower overall rate of taxation and social spending as well as greater economic inequality. It remains the only developed western nation without government-supported comprehensive health care and child support. "Welfare" in American usage refers to one program—minimum maintenance for poor families—rather than other social protections, and it carries connotations of cheating or personal failure. Public opinion surveys show that after decades of expanded government services, Americans remain much less supportive of efforts to redistribute income or guarantee basic maintenance than Canadians and Europeans. In 1990, half as many Americans as western Europeans favored government action to reduce economic inequality (38% to 70%) and only 23 percent of Americans with high incomes thought the government should provide a decent standard of living for the unemployed, compared with 58 percent of wealthy Europeans.

LINGERING QUESTIONS.   The postwar career of the western welfare state raises critical questions. Do the ups and downs of the welfare state's history simply follow the fluctuations of national economies? Can the welfare state survive international economic competition, or is it a luxury that was possible for Europeans and their settler societies only when they dominated the world economy? Is the trend toward free-market approaches, reduced social spending, and greater economic inequality an inevitable part of globalized capitalism? Will international regulatory bodies adopt global regulations to temper the excesses of capitalist competition? Only time will tell whether the welfare state's recent decline will continue and whether this reversal will make the U.S. system of limited government, for better or worse, the global leader instead of the laggard.

GLOBALIZATION AND AMERICAN EMPIRE

As Americans travel around the world early in the twenty-first century, they encounter a discordant mixture of the familiar and unfriendly, each a different reflection of U.S. power. On one hand, there is the unavoidable presence of American mass culture abroad, visible in fast food chains and cybercafes and audible in broadcast music and spoken English. Economic globalization, promoted by aggressive U.S. free-trade policies, has spread American products and trends almost everywhere, creating a transnational consumer culture. English has increasingly supplanted native speech, making it the undisputed international language and the dominant medium on the Internet, the U.S.-invented computer network that quickened global exchange and came to symbolize it.

On the other hand, Americans overseas face an unprecedented level of hostility, based on opposition to U.S. foreign policy as well as cultural grounds. A White House task force reported "shocking" levels of anti-Americanism abroad in 2003. American tourists were warned to avoid dozens of unfriendly countries, and U.S. soldiers based overseas were met with popular protests and even violent attacks. Public opinion polls suggest that much of the world resents America's predominance. The nation's European allies and Latin American friends feel bullied by U.S. foreign policy and trade practices, developing nations complain that the U.S.-dominated World Bank and International Monetary Fund chain them to economic colonialism; and fundamentalist Muslims alienated by secular culture denounce the United States as "The Great Satan."

After the Cold War officially ended in 1991, American leaders moved from the habit of pursuing multilateral international alliances and agreements toward unilateral economic decision making and military intervention. The terrorist attacks of September 11, 2001 on the Pentagon and New York's World Trade Center gave a huge push to this move. President George W. Bush declared a global "war on terrorism" and pressured other nations to follow. The United States invaded Afghanistan to remove a regime that hid terrorists. Then, disregarding world opinion and a lack of evidence linking Iraq to 9/11 or the stockpiling of chemical or nuclear weapons, American armed forces invaded that nation in 2003 to depose its ruler, Saddam Hussein, and install a new government.

Critics abroad interpreted the nation's inescapable economic presence and its aggressively unilateral foreign policy as dual aspects of an "American empire." More surprising, this phrase, formerly a "dirty word" used only by America's enemies, was now invoked with approval by those who argued that the nation must take greater control of the new, hyperconnected world where local crises have immediate global repercussions and terrorism threatens the rule of law.

Is the United States today following the imperial model of Great Britain, whose economic and military power controlled half the globe by the time of World War I? Is globalization simply another name for American empire? Looking forward, will globalization undermine American power and influence by spreading economic competition and by generating intense opposition to the industrialized West? Will the United States move toward greater unilateral action to create global order, or will some form of shared governance emerge to deal with threatening transnational problems like terrorism, pollution, global inequality, and nuclear proliferation?

DEBATING AMERICAN "EMPIRE"

America's aggressive unilateral turn after 9/11 opened a public debate over the prospect of an "American empire," a regime not built on colonies and conquest but based on enforcing global order, promoting American values and interests, and exempting the United States from existing international agreements. As political commentators pitched in, this escalating dispute between anti-imperialists and "neo-imperialists" echoed the controversies of a century earlier, when Americans argued over annexing the Philippines.

COMPARING BRITISH AND AMERICAN EMPIRES. British historian Niall Ferguson injected a comparative dimension into this debate by recalling the successes of the British Empire and by reflecting on their "lessons" for the United States. Britain's powerful navy and its skillful manipulation of the international balance-of-power system kept European rivals from waging all-out war for a century (1815–1914)—the so-called "Pax Britannica," or British peace. Concentrating upon the less-harsh imperial regime that Britain promoted after the Irish potato famine (1845–49) and the Indian Mutiny (1857), Ferguson described how British domination spread free markets, the rule of law, and the English language, initiating a round of international trade and economic development that he dubbed "Anglobalization." Perhaps most important, according to Ferguson, Britain's planting of parliamentary institutions and a free press in its colonies prepared them for self-rule. Echoing the hopes of Britain's "liberal imperialists"—and the idealism of their American counterparts like Woodrow Wilson—Ferguson called the British Empire "self-liquidating."[3]

Ferguson and others acknowledged differences between today's American empire and its British predecessor. The United States possesses far less territory than Britain did at the height of its empire—less than 7 percent of the world's land (including the mainland United States), compared to 23 percent ruled by tiny Britain in 1913. Its control over other lands is exerted through military and economic pressure, not direct colonial rule. Americans have been more reluctant than the British to invest in overseas territories or to relocate there. In fact, Americans have attempted to extricate themselves as quickly as possible from episodes of intervention that threatened to develop into long-term rule. Ferguson brands the United States an "empire in denial" not just because its political leaders avoid the "e-word," but also because they appear reluctant to assume the full responsibility of global police.[4]

On the other hand, America's military and economic power today is more dominant than Britain's ever was, providing an ample support structure for empire. The U.S. share of total world output was more than 21 percent in 2000, compared with 8 percent for Britain in 1913. The United States operates an unequaled string of military and naval bases around the world and wields more firepower compared to its rivals than Britain did. Most important, according to neo-imperialists like Ferguson, there is a strong similarity between the two nations' ideals. When American presidents announce that they are intervening to support democracy, free trade, and human rights around the world, they are promoting a modern version of the British Empire's most praiseworthy aims. Believing that some form of empire is necessary to produce international order and protect global security, the neo-imperialists have urged Americans to take on Britain's "burden" of unilateral intervention and overseas rule.

[3]Niall Ferguson, *Empire: The Rise and Demise of the British World Order and the Lessons for Global Power* (New York: Basic Books, 2003), xxvi, xxii.

[4]Ferguson, *Empire*, 370.

DISPUTING EMPIRE.   Critics of the neo-imperialists dispute their historical analogy and its implications. They assert that the British Empire was hardly benign in its operations and effects, which included the slave trade, economic exploitation, ruthless suppression of native peoples, and destruction of local institutions and industries. They claim that promotion of free trade reflected Britain's economic interest in flooding foreign markets with British manufactured goods. They point out that those who praise the "Pax Britannica" ignore Britain's colonial wars in Africa and Asia, which culminated in massive slaughters in Sudan and South Africa in the 1890s. In the end, Britain's empire spawned a great power rivalry that led directly to World War I.

If Great Britain failed to create an "empire to end all empires," how could the United States expect to do it? Critics of America's neo-imperial turn remind readers that the Cold War's "Pax Americana" involved real wars in Korea and Vietnam, and its confrontations with the Soviets risked destroying the planet. America's economic dominance and trade policies, the anti-imperialists say, have generated resentment, and its unilateral foreign moves have failed to stem the tide against terrorism. Finally, as in the Cold War, there is the problem of imperial "overreach." The United States, critics charge, is not powerful enough to rule or police the world and will only exhaust its resources and undermine its democratic values at home and abroad if it tries.

EMPIRE OR HEGEMONY?   Whatever the merits of the analogy with Great Britain, it has stimulated debate over what role the United States should play in the post-Cold-War world. The discussion has also revived "empire" as an analytical term to describe America's global role, especially when defined broadly to include informal and indirect domination of other nations.

Some scholars argue that the term "hegemony," which implies domination through prestige, persuasion, or consent, best captures America's world position. The word was originally coined to describe the Athenians' leading role in the league of ancient Greek city-states against Persia, a usage that is analogous to U.S. leadership of the anti-Soviet alliance. In more recent usage, especially in world-system theory, hegemony describes the ability of an economic giant like the United States to impose an international commercial and financial system that promotes trade and brings the most benefit to Americans. Persuasion enters the picture through the attraction that dependent peoples have for the civilization, laws, or goods of the hegemonic nation. "A country may obtain the outcomes it wants in world politics," political scientist Joseph Nye writes, "because other countries want to follow it, admiring its values, emulating its example, aspiring to its level of prosperity and openness." Nye calls this attraction "soft power," as opposed to the "hard power" of military or economic coercion. His favorite example is America's ability to enthrall the world's people with its pop culture and ideology of freedom.[5]

Other scholars respond that hegemony is not distinct from empire but merely one of its tools. "Soft power" is the imperial nation's carrot, "hard power" its stick. From ancient Rome to modern Britain, many empires lured colonies and dependent peoples by promising prosperity and superior education, religion, and laws. An "empire by consent," such as the American Cold War alliance in Europe, remains an empire as long as one power dominates and others have correspondingly less control over their fortunes.

There is one difference, however, between empire and hegemony that may prove crucial for understanding today's world and the place of the United States in it. Empire is an all-or-nothing status—a nation is or it isn't one—and it is usually reserved for long-term domination; but hegemony can be partial and temporary. There are degrees of control over other nations and limits to its duration. Among the three realms of military, economic, and cultural power, there may be one where a nation dominates and others where it cannot. In today's intensely competitive and highly networked international economy, one where global forces sometimes appear to control nations instead of the opposite, empire may be an inappropriate analogy or an outmoded concept. This is the situation that globalization has created.

AMERICAN POWER AND GLOBALIZATION

"Globalization" is today's buzzword used to describe the intense acceleration of the movement of capital, goods, people, and information around the world during the past generation. Its most obvious symptoms are the instant communication of computers, the creation of a worldwide entertainment industry, and the ever-widening shock waves of regional economic crises. Others include the ominous rise of nuclear proliferation and global terrorism.

As we have seen, globalization is an old story. Its seeds were planted regionally when separate human societies first made contact through war, trade, and disease. It reached worldwide scope during the so-called "first globalization," when the expansion of Europe's trade and influence in the 1500s, including its colonization of the Americas, joined most of the world's people into an economic system that became dominated by western

[5]Joseph Nye, *The Paradox of American Power: Why the World's Only Superpower Can't Go It Alone* (New York: Oxford University Press, 2002), 8.

Europe. During the "second globalization" of the long nineteenth century, the British Empire played a potent role in imposing global uniformity, from the spread of the English language and legal institutions to free trade and the gold standard. The decades between the world wars saw a slackening of international connections, but after World War II, dramatic new developments were at work to quicken globalization and multiply its effects. Television advertised consumer goods everywhere and alerted viewers to humanitarian disasters far away. Jet travel sped up immigration, the expansion of multinational corporations, and the spread of diseases. Computers permitted instant transfers of capital around the world and gave isolated villages sudden access to global information. The size and speed of transnational connections had paradoxical effects, in some cases uniting people, in others making them more aware of their differences.

The United States took the lead in this third stage of globalization. In 1945 America emerged from the rubble of global war as the world's lone military superpower and its preeminent economic power. In the postwar years the United States, eager to dominate global markets, oversaw the expansion of free trade through financial institutions like the World Bank and the General Agreement on Tariffs and Trade (1947), an international pact to reduce tariffs that was replaced by the World Trade Organization in 1995. The United States pioneered advances in computer technology and the "information revolution" that replaced industrial manufacturing as the driver of economic growth. America's "soft power," broadcast to the world by American movies and television, made its way of life a model for much of the world's people. In one way or another, decisions made in Washington, Wall Street, Silicon Valley, and Hollywood have affected much of the globe in recent decades.

GLOBALIZATION AND EMPIRE.   Is globalization, then, just another name for American empire? Political Scientist Alexander Motyl envisions empire as "a hierarchically organized political system with a hublike structure—a rimless wheel—within which a core elite and state dominate peripheral elites and societies by serving as intermediaries for their significant interactions and by channeling resource flows" to and from the core.[6] Extending this metaphor, both critics and defenders of American power portray globalization as a network with a hub located in the United States and spokes reaching out to the rest of the world. This image contains much truth, but as Joseph Nye and others have pointed out, it has crucial shortcomings.

---

[6]Alexander J. Motyl, *Imperial Ends: The Decay, Collapse, and Revival of Empires* (New York: Columbia University Press, 2001), 4.

For one thing, there are several dimensions of globalization beyond the political, and in most, the United States wields strong but not controlling power. In military matters America remains dominant, as the only country whose army and navy have a global reach. Yet even here there are limits. The Vietnam War showed that American might does not easily apply to unconventional conflicts, and two wars in Iraq have demonstrated that Americans are impatient with extended military occupations abroad. International coalitions become necessary because the U.S. Army is not large enough to fight simultaneous regional wars.

Until recently, the United States has controlled economic globalization, but increasingly it has become one player among several. Some economists warn that the emergence of China and the European Union as competitors, America's mushrooming trade deficit, and the decline of the dollar relative to major world currencies are harbingers of reduced U.S. economic power. Culturally, the United States remains powerful as an exporter of movies and music, but here, too, there is increasing competition (more on this later). On the level of politics, the picture is mixed. The United States led a Western coalition that prevailed in the Cold War, but cracks developed in the alliance soon after, widened by differences in trade and Middle Eastern policy. Beyond its traditional allies, the United States faces political opposition in the Islamic world and developing nations in Asia, Latin America, and Africa.

On the level of transnational organizations that are beyond the purview of national governments, from multinational corporations to crime and terrorist networks, the U.S. government exerts relatively little control. In fact, instead of a highway radiating from an American "core," globalization often functions as a two-way street that leaves the United States vulnerable to global economic competition, to backlash against increasing economic inequality, to fluctuations in foreign oil supplies, or to damage from planetary problems like pollution. The same airplanes that bring immigrants and imported goods to the America can carry terrorists, drugs, and infectious diseases.

The hub-and-spokes image of empire overplays America's centrality as globalization develops and spreads. Contemporary trade relationships continue to reflect regional exchanges in Europe and Asia as well as older flows between European imperial capitals like London and Paris and former colonies. Recent global immigration has created Asian, Arab, and Latin American diasporas that have established their own trading networks internally and with their homelands. China, Japan, Brazil, and the European Union have built global trade webs independent of the United States. Although Americans invented the Internet, there are already more users outside the United States than inside it. As the spread of computer, missile, and nuclear technology to new nations has shown, the United States is no longer an essential link. Power is being dispersed by alternative connections between the spokes. All roads no longer lead to or through America, as it once appeared.

Instead of an American empire, it may be more accurate to view the new global order as a complex and increasingly decentralized web of relationships, much like the Internet itself. The United States promoted post–World War II globalization and was its prime beneficiary, but its hegemony was never complete and its power over the process appears to be declining. As globalization proceeds, it spreads technological capabilities and increases competition. This reduces the extent of America's dominance. As a closer look at mass culture indicates, it also changes the nature of what critics have called "Americanization" or "cultural imperialism."

GLOBAL MASS CULTURE AND AMERICAN "CULTURAL IMPERIALISM"

Evidence of American mass culture's worldwide presence is unmistakable. Brand-name products like Coca-Cola, Levi's, Nike, Kodak, McDonald's, and Kentucky Fried Chicken appear globally. American slang is used in advertisements and by young people on the street instead of their native tongue. MTV (Music Television), which began in the United States, has stations on every continent. The United States leads the world in the export of movies, music, videos, and TV programs. A Coca-Cola Company executive recently proclaimed triumphantly that "American culture broadly defined—music, film, fashion, and food—has become the culture worldwide."

AMERICANIZATION ABROAD.   How did this domination occur, and what does it mean for the world's peoples? In the late nineteenth century, the spread of American cultural influence overseas paralleled the nation's rising international prestige and its industrial exports. In the early 1900s, American-made telephones, typewriters, sewing machines, elevators, cameras, phonographs, and packaged foods became popular items in Europe and Latin America. Along with these new products, American popular culture traveled abroad in the form of western novels, Buffalo Bill's Wild West Show, and—after phonographs and film were invented—jazz and the movies. When Europe's film industry was badly damaged in World War I, Hollywood emerged as the leading producer for audiences worldwide. In the 1920s European intellectuals sounded the first general alarm that "Americanization" was smothering local culture, and overseas governments imposed quotas on American movies.

World War II gave the United States its decisive push as a dominant exporter of popular culture. The United States Information Agency, established in 1948 to launch a cultural Cold War offensive, sponsored concert tours abroad and broadcast American programs on radio. The Armed Forces Radio Network acquainted local people with American popular music wherever U.S. troops were stationed. Private initiative proved far more potent than government actions. When the Western world returned to economic health, American companies flooded overseas markets (wherever they were open—the Communist bloc was closed until the 1980s) with movies, newspapers, magazines, jazz, rock and roll, comic strips, cartoons, and television programs. It was a culture with sounds and images so beguiling that they drowned out competing voices. "Our cartoons were Donald Duck, Little Orphan Annie, Dick Tracy, and Superman," Danish literary critic Jan Gretlund recalled about growing up in the 1950s and 60s. "Our favorite boys' games were cowboys and Indians, and the movies were westerns or Walt Disney productions. . . . During our teen years we idolized James Dean and Marilyn Monroe, and we listened to Elvis Presley, Brenda Lee, and Jerry Lee Lewis. . . . Our food was Kentucky Fried Chicken, burgers, fries and Cokes, and our clothes were T-shirts, sweatshirts and jeans. . . . [O]ur language became full of American slang like 'groovy,' 'crazy,' and 'cool.'"[7] Young people in Canada, Japan, and Argentina could say much the same thing.

U.S. ADVANTAGES.   The United States was well situated to bring mass culture to the world. Its huge domestic market perfected its mass production and distribution network. The spread of English—first by the British Empire, then by American soldiers in overseas bases—made it the *lingua franca* of pop culture worldwide. Meanwhile, postwar prosperity in the industrialized West brought an enormous demand for entertainment. Standards of living rose, advertising became big business, the "baby boom" created a teenage market for music and clothes, and the custom of a two-day weekend, popularized in the United States and western Europe as a way to share employment during the Depression, became transformed into a mini-holiday of consumption and leisure as it spread globally.

There was also an important cultural ingredient in U.S. overseas success. America's ethnic diversity made its domestic market a microcosm of the world, and Americans' openness to innovation ensured a stream of new products and styles. American popular culture had arisen from the need to develop entertainment that transcended regional and cultural

---

[7]Quoted in Richard Pells, *Not Like Us: How Europeans Have Loved, Hated, and Transformed American Culture Since World War II* (New York: Basic Books, 1997), 205.

differences in a multiethnic society. Finding a simple and strong language that struck common chords in a mass audience prepared it to become a common denominator on the global market.

COMPLEXITIES OF "CULTURAL IMPERIALISM."   As American movies, music, and fashion spread internationally, fears arose that they were making everyone everywhere the same. Critics of "Americanization" noted how the onslaught of American mass culture seemed to erode traditional, distinctive national forms of expression. By the 1980s, "cultural imperialism" became a popular concept among intellectuals in Latin America, Asia, Africa, and Europe. Pursuing an analogy with political and economic imperialism, it implied the absorption or destruction of native ways by a foreign, invading culture.

Scholars studying the impact of popular culture call these fears exaggerated. The relationship between performance and audience is not simple and one-way, but complex and interactive. Watching American movies or listening to American music does not make everyone American, or even the same. American mass culture means different things in different national, ethnic, class, gender, and generational contexts, and popular culture's audiences often select or reinterpret its messages to fit their own social, political, or personal circumstances.

In communist Eastern Europe or other politically repressive societies, for example, the spread of American rock music and blue jeans was subversive and liberating. The counterculture of the 1960s promoted a generational conflict in which adolescents throughout the West defied the norms and expectations of parents by adopting anticonformist behavior. Far from enforcing American hegemony, this transnational youth culture helped to generate the vocabulary and tactics for young people around the world to criticize American foreign policy, such as the war in Vietnam, or to champion the cause of third-world revolutions. Here was a remarkable example of the transformative potential of popular culture.

Instead of homogenizing its recipients, imported popular culture can also stimulate the assertion of local or ethnic identity. For example, African American rap music has spread rapidly around the world among young people, immigrants, and ethnic minorities as a way to assert a common cultural identity or to articulate dissent in different national contexts. Strong local traditions of rap have evolved among Japanese youth and Muslim immigrants to France. Like jazz, blues, and rock and roll before it, American rap has taken complex routes from its original home to far-flung destinations.

A TWO-WAY STREET.   In fact, Americanization travels on a two-way street. British television programs built strong niches in the American domestic market, while the Beatles and Rolling Stones refashioned rock music and re-exported it to America. More recently, immigrants from Latin America have brought to the United States a rich repertoire of music and dance that can be experienced on dozens of Spanish-language radio and television stations and increasingly on the mainstream English-speaking media. "Whenever I hear about North American penetration in Latin America," the writer Gabriel García Márquez quips, "I laugh into my coat lapels because the real cultural penetration is that of Latin America into the United States."[8]

Just as economic globalization has resulted in competing centers of power, the mass culture industry has spawned powerful national players outside America. In the majority of countries, the most popular television programs are not American series but local soap operas and talk shows. Popular taste in books also continues to be regional, reflecting national politics, celebrities, and self-improvement formulas. Meanwhile, Jamaican reggae, Argentine tango, and Portuguese *fado* (love songs) are played in concert globally. India's "Bollywood" has become the world's largest film industry, and Japanese animated films dominate the global market. Soccer, not American baseball or basketball, is the world's most popular spectator sport, and England's Manchester United is its favorite team.

These examples of two-way traffic, mutual influence, and thriving national entertainment industries suggest that today's global mass culture is less and less a distinctively American-flavored or even a U.S.-controlled phenomenon. Just as the production of manufactured items like clothing and cars has been distributed in pieces among nations, so too world music, TV programs, and movie companies reflect the international context of cultural production. British, French, German, and Japanese corporations own a substantial piece of the American print and visual media industry. Every year the world's culture industry is becoming more transnational in its makeup, more multinational in its mergers, more international in its job allocations, and more global in its consumer marketing strategies.

LOCATING OURSELVES IN McWORLD. The global spread of Western popular culture is too complex and multifaceted to be subsumed under the rubric of "Americanization" or cultural imperialism. Whatever we call it, it is likely to have contradictory effects. It may bring a numbing sameness to the surface appearance of social life around the world. Political scientist Benjamin Barber calls this homogenized environment "McWorld." "Sit in a movie theater, sports arena, mall, or fast-food restaurant in any

---

[8]Interview with García Márquez by Enrique Fernández, *Village Voice*, July 3, 1984.

city around the world," Barber complains. "You are nowhere. You are everywhere."[9] At the same time, the new global culture will generate new forms of identity and stimulate people to articulate their national and ethnic differences. In an increasingly interconnected world, people may have to maintain a dual set of allegiances—one to their local or national traditions and institutions, the other to the global economy and the transnational identities it inspires—not just the youth culture and consumerism, but also identities forged by religion, feminism, and environmentalism. For Americans and other peoples, the problem will be how to live in these different worlds, trying to harmonize or reconcile them.

THE UNITED STATES AND GLOBAL GOVERNANCE

Under the complex and ever-changing regime of globalization, nations will face a similar negotiation. Because the United States cannot control the process or effects of globalization by itself, its leaders will confront calls to temper their missionary drive to make the world over in America's image. Increasingly, globalization puts a premium on balancing national interests with cooperation in the global commons.

THE LIMITS OF CONVERGENCE.   As the Cold War wound down, some influential Western scholars adopted the theory that the world's nations were converging toward the American model of free-market capitalism, democratic politics, and secular values. The most confident proclaimed that the collapse of the Soviet bloc heralded "The End of History," making representative government and the freewheeling capitalism of globalization the only game left on the planet. History quickly proved these commentators wrong. Just as there are constraints on American control over the post-Cold-War world, there are also limits to the "convergence" of modernization. Globalization has produced diverse responses among those it has touched. Western European nations hold onto their welfare states and resist the American ideal of laissez-faire capitalism. Japan, which modernized after opening to the West in 1868 and then rebuilt rapidly with U.S. assistance after World War II, has retained its cultural distinctiveness. Chinese leaders continue their search for a path that combines economic competition with authoritarian rule. Globalization has produced neither monolithic global capitalism nor uniform governments and cultures. Nations have responded to economic challenges with resources drawn from their own traditions and cultures.

[9]Benjamin R. Barber, *Jihad vs. McWorld* (New York: Random House, 1995), 99.

A "CLASH OF CIVILIZATIONS"?   Some nations have witnessed strong, even violent resistance to globalization out of contempt for the commercial, secular, and egalitarian values it appears to promote. The diffusion of Western mass media, together with the collapse of the Soviet state, helped to stimulate Islamic fundamentalism in Iran, Afghanistan, and elsewhere in the Middle East. The Al Qaeda terrorist organization has used instruments of globalization such as cell phones and international banks to construct a worldwide network of radicals pledged to wage a "holy war" against the West. Alarmed by the rise of such movements, political scientist Samuel Huntington forecast that after the ideological division of the Cold War subsided, the world would be increasingly split into national blocs representing hostile religious civilizations.

Religious backlash against global secularization is not limited to non-Christians. The "clash of civilizations" has found a faint echo in clashes within the United States between conservative Protestant fundamentalists and liberal pluralists over such issues as abortion, school prayer, the death penalty, and gay rights. There is little chance that the American "culture wars" will turn into a civil war. Whether the radical Islamic insurgency will provoke violent international conflicts seems less clear. Leaders of most Islamic nations maintain a course of peaceful coexistence and trade with the West, but they, like the United States, exert limited control over terrorist networks.

GLOBAL INEQUALITY.   Globalization has not only heightened perceptions of ethnic and religious differences, it has also widened the gap between winners and losers in the world economic system. As China opened to the West, it began to tap the potential of its enormous labor market. Some national economies, such as South Korea, Malaysia, and Ireland, were poised to take advantage of international investment; others, such as the Middle East's oil-producing states, grew rich from Western demand. Most developing nations were left behind, however. Since 1960, the income gap between people in the richest and poorest nations has doubled. The reasons are complex, but key agents of globalization bear partial responsibility. As the world becomes a single "free trade zone," American farm exports overwhelm small producers in developing lands, and multinational corporations migrate from nation to nation in search of minimal labor costs, earning huge profits for shareholders and leaving third-world laborers in the lurch. At the same time, the World Bank and International Monetary Fund have been blamed for perpetuating neocolonial economic arrangements whereby the third world is forced to provide raw materials and staple crops for the first. In the 1990s these agencies required debtor nations to privatize industries and deregulate their economies, policies that created a small class of rich beneficiaries but increased poverty and unemployment. The growing gap between rich and poor nations has fueled protests against the World Bank and World Trade Organization and brought demands that developed nations forgive third-world debt and increase the tiny proportion of national output that they currently devote to nonmilitary foreign aid.

ENVIRONMENTAL DEGRADATION. Three other issues deserve special mention as problems that grew in scale with the increased linkages of recent decades. Until the 1980s, most human-triggered environmental crises were contained within regions, sparked by episodes such as oil spills or accidents at nuclear power plants. Recent events have made people and governments aware of the alarming global scope of environmental problems. Unregulated overfishing of the Grand Banks off the North American coast destroyed habitats and virtually closed down the international codfish industry, creating a chain reaction that led to overfishing of other species in the world's oceans. On land, meanwhile, destruction of tropical rainforests and grassy plains has threatened animals and plants with massive extinction, reducing the biodiversity that preserves the earth's ecosystems and fosters human health. Most devastating of all, scientists have warned that greenhouse-gas emissions from automobiles, farms, and factories have caused an increase in the earth's atmospheric temperature that is melting glaciers and raising sea levels, with the potential to inundate many of the earth's coastal regions and cities.

GLOBAL DISEASES. Transmission of human disease across continents is as old as the bubonic plague of the 1300s and the devastating Columbian Exchange. The most serious epidemic of modern times, AIDS (acquired immune deficiency syndrome) indicated how quickly airplane travel spreads human health disasters. Whereas smallpox took more than 300 years after crossing the Atlantic to reach the Pacific Coast of North America and then Australia, AIDS took just over 30 years to travel around the globe from its place of origin in west-central Africa. By 2005, nearly 40 million people were living with AIDS, including 1 million in the United States and 26 million in Sub-Saharan Africa. More than 23 million AIDS deaths had occurred since the epidemic's outbreak.

NUCLEAR PROLIFERATION. Following the Cold War, thousands of nuclear weapons remained in the hands of governments, including the republics of the former Soviet Union. Despite the supervised destruction of many weapons and safeguards against theft, it is possible that terrorists or irresponsible states could get hold of them. Meanwhile, global trade networks have created a free market that took lethal nuclear technology to Pakistan and North Korea and threatens to spread it elsewhere, heightening fears that regional conflicts could escalate into global catastrophes.

INTERNATIONAL RESPONSES. Transnational problems require international solutions. Globalization diffuses economic and environmental consequences in addition to creating new networks of power. It makes every nation a neighbor whose nuclear tests, overfishing, environmental problems, emigrants, labor policies, or trade regulations affect all. It highlights the growing role in transnational affairs of powerful new players, especially multinational corporations. Interconnectedness creates new channels of communication, not just for humanitarian organizations but also for drug traffickers, computer hackers, and terrorists. All this suggests why the United States may not be able to continue its economic domination and why politically it cannot maintain a unilateral course. Managing the problems of globalization will require some international system of order and cooperation.

AMERICA'S ROLE. History suggests that an American empire, whether formal or informal, will not be the answer. The drive to make the world uniform and shape it to the dominant power's national interests is ultimately self-defeating. The tale of past empires shows that they fall as well as rise, doomed by military overreach, economic decline, or the resistance of subject peoples. In any case, Americans, as we have seen, have little taste for the costly overseas commitments of empire, and many fear the consequences at home. As we begin the twenty-first century, America's might, as British journalist Sebastian Mallaby has noted, is "too great to be challenged by any other state, yet not great enough to solve problems such as global terrorism and nuclear proliferation."[10] Faced with this situation of qualified and perhaps temporary hegemony, American leaders will be pressured to engage in international negotiation and compromise, or even to join new forums of shared international governance.

GLOBAL COOPERATION. What form a new system of multilateral cooperation may take is unclear. Advocates of a global "civil society" see non-governmental organizations (NGOs) such as churches, environmental groups, and humanitarian and human rights societies as key pressure groups that can monitor private and government activities globally and conduct publicity campaigns to create international standards and sanctions against violators. In fact, campaigns against unethical practices of drug companies, sweatshops, and regimes that abuse human rights have brought limited gains. NGOs can help to form a civil society that

---

[10]Quoted in Nye, *Paradox of American Power*, 40.

organizes public opinion and puts pressure on governments. Yet they cannot pass laws or create binding international agreements.

Other global activists envision government by a world federation of nations, perhaps modeled on the United Nations, that addresses pressing international issues. Pursuing an analogy with the American federal government's power over states or the European Union's authority over member governments, they urge that nations likewise delegate power to a global "federal government" to attack environmental problems, to police terrorism, or to enforce social-welfare provisions that temper capitalism's excesses just as national welfare-state legislation did previously. Critics respond that the record of the United Nations in resolving international disputes or regulating capitalism has been mixed at best, and that in any case nations will not slow their economic engines for a "world government" or cede their sovereignty to it.

At present, nations remain the most powerful political forces and the key institutions for global governance. Thus far the United States has sought international cooperation largely on its own terms, pressing for trade concessions, antiterrorist coordination, and nuclear nonproliferation agreements from other countries while refusing to reduce its export subsidies, endorse international environmental protocols, or subject its citizens to an international criminal court. At the same time, the United States has found that one-sided agreements are difficult to impose and that unilateral actions alienate allies and inflame enemies. In an interdependent world, the effects of one country's actions return in a rapid "feedback loop." As globalization continues, nations will face incentives to exchange some freedom of action for assurances of others' good will and the ultimate goal of survival. Nations, like individuals, will have to balance national with global citizenship for humankind to thrive on this earth.

Americans began their national existence by proclaiming their nation's special uniqueness and celebrating its separation from the rest of the world. The course of their nation's history has qualified these claims at nearly every turn. The challenge for Americans during their current "imperial moment" is to recall the tainted records of all empires, including their own, and to remember that their nation's future and that of the world are inextricably entwined.

SUGGESTED READINGS

Banks, Olive. *The Faces of Feminism: A Study of Feminism as a Social Movement.* London: Blackwell, 1986.
    —Juxtaposes the histories of American and British feminism, finding many parallels and mutual influences.

Barber, Benjamin R. *Jihad vs. McWorld.* New York: Random House, 1995.
—Suggests how the opposed but intertwined forces of global consumer capitalism and religious/ethnic fundamentalism are threatening democracy and reshaping today's world.

de Grazia, Victoria. *Irresistible Empire: America's Advance Through 20th-Century Europe.* Cambridge, Mass.: Harvard University Press, 2005.
—Tells how American-style advertising, chain stores, supermarkets, and consumer culture transformed traditional European ways and thwarted Nazi and Soviet alternatives.

Dudziak, Mary L. *Cold War Civil Rights: Race and the Image of American Democracy.* Princeton: Princeton University Press, 2000.
—Shows how the Civil Rights movement and the Cold War interacted, prompting U.S. policymakers to support racial equality to enhance America's image abroad.

Ferguson, Niall. *Colossus: The Price of America's Empire.* New York: Penguin, 2004.
—A British historian provocatively compares the nineteenth-century British and twentieth-century U.S. empires, blaming Americans' lack of will, not prowess, for their shortcomings.

Fraser, Ronald. *1968: A Student Generation in Revolt.* New York: Pantheon, 1988.
—A colorful chronicle that treats the 1960s youth culture and student activism as a transatlantic movement and draws upon interviews with participants.

Fredrickson, George M. *Black Liberation: A Comparative History of Black Ideologies in the United States and South Africa.* New York: Oxford University Press, 1995.
—Traces parallel developments and mutual influences between African American leaders and South African blacks as they struggled against racial subjugation.

Gaddis, John Lewis. *We Now Know: Rethinking Cold War History.* New York: Oxford University Press, 1997.
—Contrasts the pro-American and pro-Soviet Cold War blocs in Europe as empires of invitation and imposition, respectively.

Levering, Ralph B. *The Cold War: A Post-Cold War History.* Arlington Heights, Ill.: Harlan Davidson, 2005.
—This clear and concise account of the long Cold War rivalry attempts a balanced assessment of American successes and failures.

Nye, Joseph. *The Paradox of American Power: Why the World's Only Superpower Can't Go It Alone.* New York: Oxford University Press, 2002.
—A political scientist offers a succinct and historically informed assessment of globalization and its relation to American power.

Pells, Richard. *Not Like Us: How Europeans Have Loved, Hated, and Transformed American Culture Since World War II.* New York: Basic Books, 1997.

—Surveys the export and reception of American mass culture in Europe, arguing that Europeans have not become truly "Americanized."

Smith, Bonnie, ed. *Global Feminisms Since 1945.* London: Routledge, 2000.

—This collection of essays includes perspectives from South America, Africa, Asia, and the Middle East as well as Europe and the United States.

Ueda, Reed. *Postwar Immigrant America: A Social History.* New York: St. Martin's, 2004.

—Situates recent migration to the United States within global trends and documents new immigrant groups' contributions to a "world melting pot" in America.

⟮ INDEX ⟯